AF831521

The Changing Role of National Development Banks in Africa

Joshua Yindenaba Abor

The Changing Role of National Development Banks in Africa

Business Models, Governance and Sustainability

palgrave
macmillan

Joshua Yindenaba Abor
University of Ghana Business School
Accra, Ghana

ISBN 978-3-031-38638-1 ISBN 978-3-031-38639-8 (eBook)
https://doi.org/10.1007/978-3-031-38639-8

© The Editor(s) (if applicable) and The Author(s), under exclusive license to Springer Nature Switzerland AG 2023

This work is subject to copyright. All rights are solely and exclusively licensed by the Publisher, whether the whole or part of the material is concerned, specifically the rights of translation, reprinting, reuse of illustrations, recitation, broadcasting, reproduction on microfilms or in any other physical way, and transmission or information storage and retrieval, electronic adaptation, computer software, or by similar or dissimilar methodology now known or hereafter developed.
The use of general descriptive names, registered names, trademarks, service marks, etc. in this publication does not imply, even in the absence of a specific statement, that such names are exempt from the relevant protective laws and regulations and therefore free for general use.
The publisher, the authors, and the editors are safe to assume that the advice and information in this book are believed to be true and accurate at the date of publication. Neither the publisher nor the authors or the editors give a warranty, expressed or implied, with respect to the material contained herein or for any errors or omissions that may have been made. The publisher remains neutral with regard to jurisdictional claims in published maps and institutional affiliations.

This Palgrave Macmillan imprint is published by the registered company Springer Nature Switzerland AG
The registered company address is: Gewerbestrasse 11, 6330 Cham, Switzerland

To my parents, Mr. Abor Ndobire and Madam Amina Tobga, for their inspiration and commitment throughout my education. And to my wonderful wife, Prof. Patience Aseweh Abor, and our lovely children, Ivana, Bastien and Venka, for their love, support and encouragement.

Foreword

The role of national development banks (NDBs) is changing, and their value proposition has gone up in more recent years. They had largely collapsed in the wake of strong global push for radical adjustments of emerging and low-income economies in 1980s into 1990s, along with market liberalization and the advent of private banks. Political interference and loss of competitiveness in the more liberalized environment were hard to swallow for these banks. There has been a turn-around, and the changing role of NDBs is an important subject of investigation. The timely book by Joshua Yindenaba Abor just does that with a focus on Africa. Joshua is uniquely positioned to undertake this vital task. He is an accomplished development financial economist with considerable research and policy experience with the African financial landscape.

In what ways is the role of NDBs changing? Answering this requires interrogation of the evolution of NDBs. The evolution spans the unwarranted view of NDBs as panacea in the earlier days for much needed development capital, the promise of market liberalization but its inability to bridge huge financing gaps for development, and distorted political economy incentives. This book systematically catalogues such an evolution while presenting factors leading to the demise of NDBs in the earlier days, and now factors for their resurrection in the African context. Let me state, though, that the book should not be viewed as contrarian to a market-based economy. In fact, through their changing role, NDBs can leverage their deep financial and technical capacity to crowd-in private investments (e.g., derisking, identification of bankable green projects).

The financing gaps for development projects in infrastructure, agriculture, health, education and now climate, are staggering in Africa. There have been substantial investments in these areas, which have also contributed significantly to the African growth renaissance that we witnessed, which got curtailed by the advent of COVID-19. In fact, in the wake of the growth syndrome, many African countries were able to access external debt markets (e.g., Eurobonds) at arm's length. This was the bright side. Now, they are stuck with the dark side resulting from heavy borrowing at exorbitant rates, which are unlikely to be justified by the fundamentals, leading to debt unsustainability. Debt resolution has become exceedingly challenging. The gaps for financing development have also widened. What should be the role of NDBs in this regard?

The book makes a strong case that this is an opportune time to fully integrate NDBs in the national development agenda. We should grab and amplify the changing role of NDBs from those which had been government subsidized and captured politically into those which conduct efficient financial intermediation, achieve financial viability and sustainability, help build capacity and provide technical assistance, complement, but not supplant, private banks. The book systematically unpacks the genuine developmental functions of NDBs in an African context, facing the imperative of financing large-scale projects in key sectors of development, including infrastructure and agriculture. In addition, the book provides useful case studies in Africa—both national and sectoral. Moreover, the book advances key factors and ingredients for sustainability and viability of NDBs for an inclusive and green economy. For instance, the governance and regulatory framework should conform to best global practices, including NDB regulation by the same financial regulatory agency that has oversight over domestic commercial banks.

Professor Lemma Senbet
The William E. Mayer Chair
Professor of Finance & Former
Director (Founding)
Center for Financial Policy
Robert H Smith School
of Business
University of Maryland
Maryland, USA

Former Executive Director/CEO
African Economic Research
Consortium (AERC)
Pan-African Economic Research
and Training Network
Nairobi, Kenya

Preface

National Development Banks (NDBs) are usually established to address market imperfections and the financing gap between the supply and demand for finance. In Africa and other developing economies, the financial systems are mostly unable to provide sufficient long-term finance for investment by firms and to support infrastructure and other development-oriented projects, a situation which has worsened in the aftermath of the COVID-19 crisis. The global crisis has prompted many countries to establish new NDBs, with several others expanding the scope of their existing NDBs. NDBs working together with multilateral development banks (MDBs) will have a crucial role to play in mobilizing long-term funds from the public and private sectors to finance new investments. Sustaining NDBs and ensuring their success will be critical to achieving more sustainable economic growth in the future.

This book is developed out of the major areas of interest in current teaching and research in development banking. Its main aim is to provide literature on the changing role of NDBs in contemporary times. There has been a significant change in NDBs' role from simply providing credit at subsidized rates to addressing other critical issues. Therefore, it becomes imperative to improve our understanding of their changing role. Promoting successful NDBs entails a paradigm shift in approach. It involves an entirely new focus that takes into consideration the following: (1) ensuring financial viability of NDBs and their lending programmes,

(2) creating an environment that fosters financial intermediation in traditionally marginalized sectors, (3) providing non-financial support to critical sectors of the economy and (4) providing support in combating climate change and driving sustainability.

Notwithstanding their catalytic role in the growth and development of many economies, NDBs have received less attention in the literature. They are said to be an under-researched type of financial institutions in the global economy. There has not been a systematic discussion and appreciation of NDBs within the academic, research, policy and banking communities. This book provides a comprehensive presentation of NDBs by carefully and rigorously discussing their important roles and contributions in Africa. It will contribute to the evolving literature in the field by providing a comprehensive understanding of development banking for students, scholars, researchers, development bankers, policymakers and regulators. The various chapters, with specific cases on NDBs in Africa, will prepare students and practitioners for advanced research and practice in the area. It will also be useful for policy analysis and implementation. The book should have a strong appeal in emerging and developing countries and among students and scholars in Europe, America and Asia, studying African economies and financial systems.

The book is made up of sixteen (16) chapters. The first chapter provides an introduction to NDBs by examining their nature, main characteristics, also highlighting the landscape of NDBs in Africa. The subsequent chapters include: Overview of Development Finance Institutions; Theoretical Perspectives and Rationale for NDBs; Contemporary Roles, Contributions and Challenges of NDBs; the Role of NDBs in Agricultural Financing; the Role of NDBs in Financing Infrastructure Development; NDBs and Sustainable Development; NDBs and Climate Finance; Business Models of NDBs; Monitoring and Evaluation, and Impact Evaluation; Corporate Governance of NDBs; Risk Management of NDBs; and Regulation and Supervision of NDBs. Also included are chapters providing specific case studies on the operations and activities of NDBs in selected African countries (Ghana, Uganda and South Africa) with the view of bridging the gap between theory and practice.

Accra, Ghana Joshua Yindenaba Abor

Acknowledgements

I am very thankful to the Almighty God for the strength and wisdom to complete this book. I am also grateful to Professor Nicholas Biekpe (University of Cape Town, South Africa) and Professor Victor Murinde (SOAS University of London) for introducing me to research in development finance. The book has benefited from useful comments from colleague academics, students and development finance experts. I am particularly grateful to Professor Joe Nellis (School of Management, Cranfield University, UK), Professor Michael Graham (University of Stellenbosch Business School, South Africa), Professor Fanta Ashenafi (University of Stellenbosch Business School, South Africa), Professor Patience Aseweh Abor (University of Ghana Business School), Dr. Anthony Kyereboah-Coleman (Senior Manager/Development Research Economist, African Export and Import Bank, Egypt), Mrs. Elsie Addo Awadzi (Second Deputy Governor, Bank of Ghana), Dr. Lordina Amoah (University of Ghana Business School) and Dr. Daniel Ofori-Sasu (University of Ghana Business School), for reviewing the manuscript. I appreciate Nana Akyaa Obeng Adiyia (Deputy CEO, Ghana Export-Import Bank), Dr. Kofi Osei Adu (Assistant Manager, Research Department, Ghana Export-Import Bank), Solomon Nii Amon Kotey Dsane (Assistant General Manager, Internal Audit Department, Ghana Export-Import Bank), Joyce Kporvie (Assistant Manager, Research Department, Ghana Export-Import Bank), Patricia Ojangole (CEO, Uganda Development Bank Limited), Francis Abibi (Head, Monitoring and Evaluation,

Uganda Development Bank Limited), Patrick Dlamini (CEO, Development Bank of Southern Africa) and Zeph Nhloko (Chief Economist, Development Bank of Southern Africa), for providing insights on NDBs in Africa from the perspectives of their respective banks. I also appreciate the excellent research support provided by Dr. Daniel Ofori-Sasu, Dr. Angela Azumah Alu, James Atambilla Abugre, Benjamin Agyeman, Khadijah Iddrisu, Isaac Kofi Bekoe, Jephthah Owusu Osei, Dennis Hehetror, Emmanuel Acheampong-Bonsu, Annie Florida and Bright Oduro. I wish to thank Dr. Charles Asante, Language Centre, University of Ghana, for the excellent work in proofreading and language editing. I also appreciate Abigail Lardi Akolmolga for providing editorial assistance. I am, however, responsible for all missed or overlooked errors in this book.

I am grateful to African Center for Economic Transformation (ACET) for the opportunity to serve as Lead Consultant on the project 'Challenges and Changes: The Political Economy of National Development Banks in Africa', which urged me further to complete this book.

I am incredibly grateful for the financial support the Bank of Ghana and the Ghana Export-Import Bank provided to complete this book project.

Contents

About the Author

Joshua Yindenaba Abor is a Financial Economist, qualified Accountant and Professor of Finance with numerous years of expertise, mainly in development finance and economics research, as well as in senior-level practitioner, policy and consulting roles. He holds a Ph.D. in Finance from the University of Stellenbosch Business School, South Africa, after completing the Ph.D. course work in Financial Economics in the Department of Economics, Harvard University, US. He is also a Fellow of the Association of Chartered Certified Accountants (FCCA), UK. He is the former Dean of one of the largest Business Schools in Africa, the University of Ghana Business School. He is an External Fellow at the Centre for Global Finance, SOAS University of London, and a Researcher with the African Economic Research Consortium. He is also an Adjunct Professor of Development Finance at the Stellenbosch Business School and an Adjunct Professor in both the Department of Economics and the Department of Banking and Finance of the University of Business and Integrated Development Studies, Wa, Ghana. He was a Visiting Professor of Finance at University of Cape Town, South Africa (2022–2016). He has also held a Visiting Scholar positions at the International Monetary Fund (IMF) in Washington, US, and is an Afreximbank Research Fellow at the African Export–Import Bank, Egypt. He is a member of the American Economic Association, the Canadian Economic Association, the Economic Society of South Africa, and a Fellow of the Ghana Academy of Arts and Sciences.

He has contributed to the financial economics literature, mainly in the areas of banking and finance, monetary policy, development finance, financial market development, FinTech innovation and financial inclusion, corporate finance and governance, international trade finance and international financial flows and growth. His papers have appeared in reputable international journals. His books and edited books include '*Entrepreneurial Finance for MSMEs*' published by Palgrave Macmillan, *Financial Markets and Institutions by Digibooks*, '*Money and Banking in Africa*' by Springer, '*Contemporary Issues in Development Finance*' by Routledge, '*The Economics of Banking and Finance in Africa*' by Palgrave Macmillan, '*Sustainable and Responsible Investment in Developing Markets*' by Edward Elgar Publishing, '*The Economics of the Oil and Gas Industry*' by Routledge, and '*Sustainability Management in the Oil and Gas Industry*' by Routledge.

He has been involved in projects sponsored by the World Bank, the International Finance Corporation (IFC), the Africa Economic Research Consortium, the International Growth Centre, the WK Kellogg Foundation, the African Center for Economic Transformation (ACET), French Development Agency, the UK Department for International Development (DFID), the Economic and Social Research Council (ESRC) and Ghana Oil and Gas for Inclusive Growth (GOGIG). He has consulted extensively for a number of international and local institutions, including the World Bank, International Development Cooperation, African Development Bank, Bank of Ghana, SNV Netherlands Development Organisation, Italian Development Cooperation, ECOWAS Bank for Investment and Development (EBID), Development Bank of Southern Africa (DBSA), Industrial Development Cooperation of South Africa, Uganda Development Bank Ltd., Ghana's Ministry of Finance, Ghana's Ministry of Health, South Africa's Ministry of Trade and Industry, British Council and ActionAid. He is a Director and Senior Consultant with the Corporate Support Group (a management, financial and economic consulting firm). He also serves on the boards of SAS Investment Management Ltd. and the Ghana Investment and Securities Institute (GISI). He chairs the boards of Allianz Life Insurance Ghana Ltd., Best Western Premier Hotel, Macro Shipping Ltd., and Oasis Capital Ghana Ltd., and has served as chairman of the board of SIC Life Company Ltd. He is a member of the Monetary Policy Committee of the Central Bank (Bank of Ghana).

List of Figures

List of Tables

PART I

Overview of Development Finance Institutions and National Development Banks

CHAPTER 1

Introduction to National Development Banks

1.1 Introduction

The world economy needs development assistance and various sources of finance from different geographical regions to bridge the widening development gap, especially in developing countries. Development banks are financial institutions that usually provide long-term subsidized financing for industrial development. They are important players in many countries, both developed and developing. Development banks are regarded as an important intervention for addressing market imperfections that would leave profitable projects or ventures that generate positive externalities without funding (Bruck, 1998; Yeyati et al., 2004). They are useful in mitigating capital shortages and supporting businesses by promoting new or existing industries in economies with significant capital constraints.[1] They also provide credit to businesses, which would otherwise not be able to carry out projects, due to the unavailability of long-term funding (Abor et al., 2020; Attridge et al., 2021; Griffith-Jones et al., 2018; Rodrik, 2004; Yeyati et al., 2004).

Development banks provide long-term financing for investments in capital-intensive industries. Apart from lending, they also provide equity financing themselves or help in raising capital elsewhere by facilitating

[1] D. Rodrik (2004). Rethinking growth policies in the developing world. Draft of the Luca DÃ¡ gliano Lecture in development Economics delivered on October 8.

© The Author(s), under exclusive license to Springer Nature Switzerland AG 2023

J. Yindenaba Abor, *The Changing Role of National Development Banks in Africa*, https://doi.org/10.1007/978-3-031-38639-8_1

the issuance of equity securities. Development banks have a pragmatic approach as they are not only interested in closely monitoring the projects they finance, but are also concerned about the appointment of board members of firms they lend to and in which they hold an equity stake. Furthermore, development banks usually have in-house technical expertise that enables them to participate in decisions with respect to technology options, technological innovations, size and location. In addition to offering guarantees, development banks are able to leverage resources by attracting key providers of debt finance that may not have similar technical expertise to evaluate the potential and viability of projects. They also play a very important counter-cyclical role, which helps to maintain a country's overall investment levels and protect its productive structure in times of economic downturn.

It is difficult to ascertain the number of development banks around the world because of the challenges associated with identification and data. They initially emerged and rapidly expanded in developing countries in the 1950s and 1960s to support social and economic development. However, the economic liberalization and reforms that took place in the 1980s and 1990s resulted in their numbers declining significantly. Estimates from the Inter-American Development Bank (IADB) indicate that 250 development banks were privatized during the period, 1987–2003, while a large number of them were either restructured or liquidated.

Privatization meant that there was a likely change in the goals of development banks towards profit orientation and business support. However, in spite of their privatization and liquidation during the 1980s, some other development banks have been established since then. There are several development banks operating across the globe and they operate at the international, regional, sub-regional and national levels. They are managed independently, and they ensure the financial implementation of the public mandate which has been entrusted to them. Currently, there are many multilateral development banks that focus on specific regions and countries. In fact, multilateral, regional and national development banks play very important roles in development finance in both developed and developing countries. At the national level, for instance, national development banks (NDBs) have been established in many developed and developing countries (Griffith-Jones et al., 2018) as state-owned development banks. They are controlled by a national government (distinct from multilateral development banks like the World Bank) and typically have a mandate of promoting domestic industrial development. In emerging markets and developing economies (EMDEs), NDBs have played a critical role in their response to the global financial crisis and recently to the COVID-19 pandemic (Abor et al., 2022). It is estimated that NDBs are concentrated in South and East Asia, Africa, Latin America and the Caribbean (Musacchio & Lazzarini, 2014).

It is interesting to note that organizations such as the World Bank that were previously critical of the relevance of NDBs are now supportive of these banks, following the global financial crisis (Porta et al., 2002; Griffith-Jones et al., 2018). In addition, the Addis Ababa Action Agenda (AAA 2015), which had the approval of the members of the United Nations in the 2015 'Financing for Development Conference', was also supportive of NDBs. The Agenda recognized the critical role NDBs can play in providing access to financial services and also collaborating with other private financial institutions and investors to support infrastructure financing as well as the sustainable development goals (Griffith-Jones et al., 2018).

The rest of the chapter is organized as follows: Sect. 1.2 focuses on what NDBs are; Sect. 1.3 discusses the main features of NDBs; Sect. 1.4 discusses the differences between development banks and commercial banks; and Sect. 1.5 projects the landscape of NDBs in Africa. The chapter also discusses the purpose of this book in Sect. 1.6 and also provides an outline of the book in Sect. 1.7. Section 1.8 concludes the chapter.

1.2 What Are National Development Banks?

In general terms, development banks are special financial institutions that focus on providing high-risk, medium- and long-term financing to support productive investment, often through technical assistance. Development banks include multilateral development banks (MDBs), regional development banks (RDBs) and national development banks (NDBs). The various types of development banks are discussed in detail in the next chapter. This section focuses mainly on defining NDBs.

NDBs refer to any types of financial institution that are wholly or partially owned or controlled by a national government and have the mandate of attaining socio-economic goals in a particular region, sector or market segment (World Bank, 2018). They are institutions mainly incorporated by a state legislative instrument to provide long-term finance in mostly EMDEs. NDBs have huge potential in supporting their countries' development goals considering their unique advantages of integrating well within the public sector and the fact that they tend to be very connected to the domestic private sector.

NDBs are also known as public development banks and assume very critical positions as development actors of any economy. In comparison with international or regional financial institutions, NDBs are deeply rooted in the national context, established in national policy frameworks and are linked to both public and private sector players at the country level. Therefore, they can play a very active role in the domestic economy, supporting the growth of domestic firms, performing a counter-cyclical role in dealing with economic crises, contributing to long-term economic transformation and as well sustaining low-carbon and climate-resilient economies (Griffith-Jones et al., 2020; Studart & Gallagher, 2016).

NDBs are usually established to address market imperfections and the financing gap between the supply and demand for finance. In Africa and other developing economies, the financial systems are mostly unable to provide sufficient long-term financing for investments by firms and to support infrastructure projects. The COVID-19 crisis has further worsened this situation. The aftermath of the crisis has prompted many countries to establish new NDBs with several other countries expanding the scope of their existing NDBs. Working together with MDBs, NDBs will have a crucial role to play in mobilizing long-term funds from the public and private sectors to finance new investments. Sustaining NDBs and ensuring their success will be critical to achieving more sustainable economic growth and development in the future. They provide both loans and equity investments, which means they have an obvious interest in closely monitoring the projects, hence a further interest in developing a particular form of banking relationship.

Not only do NDBs provide financing for only projects that the formal financial sector is reluctant or unable to fund, but they also contribute to the creation and development of new market niches, the development of innovative schemes to attract and direct private sector finance for supporting large infrastructure projects and the development of public sector capacity. The tools used by these banks vary, but generally include medium- to long-term credit, credit at subsidized interest rates, credit guarantees, equity and technical assistance (Lazzarini et al., 2015).

1.3 Main Features of National Development Banks

NDBs exhibit a number of features, and these could be looked at in terms of their large size, large number, legal status, policy mandate, ownership and government support, financial instrument, sources of financing and regulation (see Chandrasekhar, 2016; Studart & Gallagher, 2016). These are briefly discussed below.

- **Large size**: One feature of NDBs is that they are generally large financial institutions with a huge asset base. Many African countries tend to have about one or two NDBs and in some instances about three or four as in the cases of Tanzania, Nigeria and South Africa. Therefore, if these are established as wholesale NDBs, they tend to be large financial institutions.
- **Large number**: Another important feature of NDBs is their large number in the world economy. There are several NDBs worldwide, with the majority located in developing countries. In fact, there are far more NDBs globally than recognized MDBs. Many of these NDBs are located in Latin America, the Caribbean, Africa, Asia and the Pacific, Europe and West Asia.
- **Legal status**: NDBs are financial institutions with their own legal personality. Unlike government credit schemes/programmes or some governmental agencies, they have their own registered legal identity and prepare their own separate financial statements.
- **Policy mandate**: NDBs have a mandate that is backed by public policies, often linked to the national development plan. NDBs are typically set up with the aim of maximizing development impact as opposed to making profit, even though they also seek to make some minimal commercial returns. Some NDBs have a narrow or specific mandate that clearly makes reference to particular sectors or types of client or activities they are required to support, e.g., micro, small and medium enterprises (MSMEs), agriculture and infrastructure. Xu, Marodon, et al. (2021) identified seven specific mandates to include specific sectors or clients, including rural and agricultural development, international trade, social housing, infrastructure, international financing of private sector development, local government and MSMEs. Others also have a broad mandate or flexible development mandate, which is formulated in general terms without identifying

any specific sector, activity or client. Examples could be the promotion of socio-economic development. NDBs with a flexible mandate are usually very large (de Luna-Martinez & Vicente, 2012; Xu, Marodon, et al., 2021). According to a World Bank (2018) survey, 49% of NDBs surveyed have a narrow policy mandate because they were established specifically to provide support for MSMEs, infrastructure projects, agriculture, international trade, local government and housing. Some NDBs surveyed also serve more than one sector.

- **Ownership and government support**: NDBs tend to have government involvement and this may take different forms. Some governments create NDBs by either having part or full ownership. Government involvement may be in the form of providing financial support or having board representation. NDBs may be owned, administered and controlled by the government (state). In this case, it is responsible for the strategic direction of the development bank as well as appointing the board and management (de Luna-Martinez & Vicente, 2012). According to a World Bank (2017) survey, about three-quarters of NDBs surveyed have 100% government ownership, 21% of them have between 50 and 90% government ownership, while only 5% of the NDBs have government as minority owner. Apart from government having direct ownership of NDBs, it could also indirectly own NDBs through other state-owned DFIs or other public institutions. However, private involvement in NDBs as direct shareholders is not widespread, but this is not unusual (Xu, Marodon, et al., 2021).
- **Financial instruments**: They use revenue-generating financial instruments such as medium- to long-term loans, equity investments, credit guarantees and insurance that are designed for clients whose business model ensures that they are able to repay the loans. The lending products of NDBs are mainly in the form of long-term loans, working capital loans, syndicated loans and unsecured loans. This explains why NDBs are said to be a major source of patient capital and are suitable for financing infrastructure projects that generate returns after a long period of time. NDBs also provide credit at subsidized interest rates, typically financed from government budget transfers. They also provide loan guarantee products to partly cover the losses faced by private financial institutions when customers default (Luna-Martinez & Vicente, 2012).

- **Sources of financing or funding structure**: In addition to the grants or subsidies they receive, NDBs are expected to be self-financing, as opposed to relying on periodic budgetary support from the central government. The financing structure of NDBs is fundamentally different from other banks. They tend to rely on long-term and more stable sources of finance. While commercial banks finance their activities essentially through the mobilization of deposits, NDBs mainly raise finance from the capital markets. Since their financing is mainly long-term in nature, they are better placed to finance long-term projects without experiencing a term mismatch or maturity gap as commercial banks do (Griffith-Jones et al., 2018).
- **Regulation**: While some NDBs are self-regulating, the majority are regulated and supervised by the same regulator for commercial banks. According to the World Bank (2017), 76% of NDBs surveyed are actually regulated and supervised by the same regulatory institution (i.e., the central bank or the reserve bank) for private commercial banks in their respective countries. A majority (78%) of the NDBs also indicated that they were supposed to comply with the same prudential requirements (minimum capital, minimum capital adequacy, loan classification and provisioning, etc.) just like the private commercial banks (de Luna-Martinez & Vicente, 2012). The issue of whether NDBs should come under the same regulatory and supervisory framework as commercial banks or need to be regulated differently is an important matter to look at, and this is dealt with in detail in Chapter 13 of this book.

1.4 Differences Between Development Banks and Commercial Banks

Development banks and commercial banks differ in a number of ways and these differences are mainly based on the purpose they serve in the economy. The main difference is that while development banks are established to provide financing for infrastructural and socio-economic development, commercial banks focus on providing financial services to institutions and individuals. Development banks pursue their mandate of promoting development by providing long-term loans to finance infrastructure development, agricultural and industrial sectors, usually at concessionary rates. They also offer grants and guarantees to these sectors.

On the other hand, commercial banks accept deposits and provide loans to corporates and individuals at commercial rates.

In addition, Gottschalk et al. (2021) identified the main features that make NDBs distinct from commercial banks as follows:

a. Apart from the objective of making a profit, NDBs have a mandate of pursuing development outcomes. Commercial banks, however, are mainly interested in maximizing profit.
b. NDBs generally have state support and therefore have access to long-term funding. Only a few NDBs are deposit-taking, while commercial banks rely mainly on deposits.
c. NDBs have accumulated technical know-how, particularly, in large, complex projects and in assessing and monitoring risks that commercial banks are not involved in. For larger NDBs with a general mandate, such characteristics enable them to provide long-term financing, as well to support large-scale projects and activities. Some of these projects are infrastructure development in important sectors such as education, health, water and sanitation, logistics, urban mobility and energy. Others are activities for promoting more and better jobs, reducing regional inequalities and poverty, and preparedness for and adaptation to climate-related hazards, which are required for achieving the SDGs.

Further, NDBs tend to serve as the financing wing of national governments in pursuing strategic developmental objectives and driving sustainable development. They are also counter-cyclical in nature and seek to protect the national economy from shocks and downturns.

Beyond the main characteristics and functions of NDBs, they do not perform any major functions in national payments systems, are not involved in profit-making through excessive risk taking, leverage less, do not undertake more difficult kinds of securitization that have implications for financial and reputational risks, and do not use financial derivatives for speculating but rather for hedging. They are less pro-cyclical in nature compared to commercial banks. Table 1.1 concisely portrays the main differences between the two types of banks.

Figure 1.1 presents a typical financial system in Africa and shows how NDBs fit into the whole African financial architecture.

Table 1.1 Differences between development banks and commercial banks

Basis of comparison	*Development banks*	*Commercial banks*
Definition	Banks that operate as multi-purpose financial institutions, with a broad development agenda	Banks that provide financial services to organizations and individuals by accepting deposits and providing loans
Ownership	They are mostly owned by the government	They are mostly owned by private entities and individuals
Establishment and Regulation	They are usually established under a Special Act and are sometimes regulated by the Central Bank or Reserve Bank. They are sometimes self-regulated	They are established under the 'Companies Act' and are strictly regulated by the Central Bank or Reserve Bank
Nature and Motive	They tend to be more counter-cyclical and have a development mandate and orientation	They are more pro-cyclical in nature and have a profit motive or orientation
Source of Funds	Their sources of funds are mainly the national government, borrowing from the capital market, and through the issuance of debt securities such as bonds	Their sources of funds are mainly deposit mobilization and the offering of investment products
Lending	They concentrate on providing long-term loans for businesses and the government/public sector	They mainly focus on providing short-term loans and saving plans for corporate organizations and individuals
Purpose	They are set up to achieve socio-economic development by providing loans at concessionary rates and offering grants	They are set up to make profit by providing loans or lending at commercial (high) interest rates
Responsiveness	They tend to be more proactive as they engage in the promotion of projects and businesses	They are reactive in the sense that they respond to business opportunities based on how bankable a business idea is
Clients and Customers	Their customers include businesses and government or the public sector	Their customers include organizations and individuals

Source Author's construction

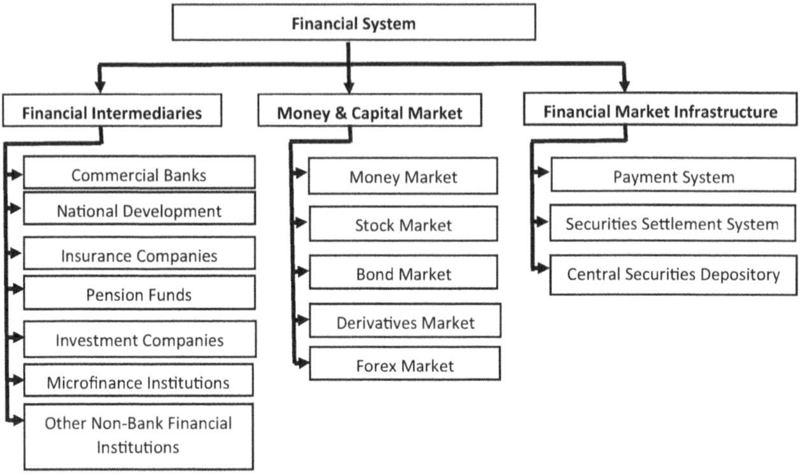

Fig. 1.1 Typical African financial system

1.5 The Landscape of National Development Banks in Africa

African NDBs seem to be pervasive with almost every country having at least one NDB, with the exception of South Sudan and Somalia. Some African countries have more than one NDB, with Nigeria having the highest number (11 NDBs), followed by South Africa (7). Available evidence suggests that the number of NDBs in a country may not really correspond to the size of its economy. Some smaller countries tend to have high concentrations of NDBs. These include Eswatini (with 5) and Botswana (with 4). Some of these banks have a very long history. The Development Bank of Ethiopia (DBE), established in 1909, seems to be one of the oldest on the continent, while many others trace their establishment to the end of the colonial era and early independence. About 30 new NDBs were founded during the period, 1950–1970. With respect to the former French colonies, many NDBs were previously 'social banks', set up during the colonial regime to address the needs in agriculture and housing and then later metamorphosed into 'development banks' when states assumed independence. During this period, banks focused on lending at subsidized interest rates to the agriculture and housing sectors of the economy. However, NDBs came under political pressure to lend to businesses or projects that were favoured by political actors, leading to bad loans in the books of the banks (Attridge et al., 2021).

In 1980, the establishment of new NDBs slowed as they were seen more and more as ineffective and as distorting the market. Furthermore, the World Bank's Structural Adjustment Programs (SAP) encouraged in the 1980s and 1990s resulted in the liberalization of financial sectors and interest rates, which prevented NDBs from providing credit at subsidized interest rates. Aside from that, the rapid population growth in many African countries appeared to indicate that new emerging commercial banks were profitable. Consequently, these new commercial banks captured the market that NDBs had previously served. These developments tended to weaken the competitive advantage of NDBs, resulting in the collapse of many of them. However, there has been a dramatic shift in the last decade, with 23 new NDBs established after 2010, and many others emerging from mergers and restructuring of previous institutions. In 2019 alone, 4 NDBs were created in West Africa, specifically in Benin, Burkina Faso, Côte d'Ivoire and Guinea (Attridge et al., 2021). A large number of NDBs were also established in the period, 2020–2022, mainly in response to the COVID-19 crisis.

The mandate of an NDB outlines its stated scope and mission. NDBs that have a broad economic development mandate tend to have more resources and flexibility, as well as the scope to determine the nature of their operations. They may have a more diversified investment portfolio compared to NDBs with a particular sector mandate such as agriculture, housing, tourism and manufacturing, which may be susceptible to sector-specific economic shocks. In spite of this, NDBs with a narrow mandate can avoid mission creep, allow governments to keep a tighter rein on them and also hold them accountable (World Bank, 2016). The majority of NDBs in Africa seem to have a broad mandate of general development, while some target MSMEs. Some NDBs with a narrow mandate or specific sectoral focus, like Ghana's Agricultural Development Bank and the Agricultural Development Bank of Zimbabwe, have over time expanded their operations (Attridge et al., 2021).

Attridge et al. (2021) found in their study that only about half of the population of African NDBs had published information, and a few others had up-to-date financial reports. They also show that transparency and reporting standards were quite high for some NDBs, but this is not the case with the majority of African NDBs. Most NDBs relied on international standards of accounting or financial reporting in the preparation of their annual statements, while only three of the NDBs they studied relied on national accounting standards. The quality of financial reporting was mostly high. Only two NDBs had qualified opinions from an external auditor accompanying their annual reports in consecutive years, indicating reporting issues, whereas five had received a qualified opinion.

While this was not a universal standard, 13 NDBs (mainly larger institutions with broad mandates) published formal social and environmental impact frameworks, and many of them indicated corporate social responsibility (CSR) activities in their annual reports. These were essentially large NDBs in South Africa, including the Industrial Development Corporation (IDC), and the Development Bank of Southern Africa (DBSA). Relatively small NDBs such as the Uganda Development Bank Limited (UDBL) have also been active in carrying out sustainability and climate-oriented activities (see Box 1.1).

Box 1.1: Sustainability and Impact—Uganda Development Bank Limited

The Uganda Development Bank Limited (UDBL) is wholly owned by the government of Uganda. Before 2020, it was regulated by a parastatal monitoring body, which was then moved to the Central Bank following compliance with international practice (The Independent Uganda, 2020). The Chief Executive Officer (CEO) is chosen by the Board of Directors. In addition, the CEO is part of national planning bodies and the President's Council, and is well connected with government's decision-making entities. The bank is therefore entrenched in national development planning. Though the bank's main focus is on the agricultural sector, in line with recent trends on sustainable investment, it has factored environmental, social and governance (ESG) concerns into its investment activities. It has therefore been trying to increase its investments in green finance projects, both in agriculture and in other sectors (Griffith-Jones et al., 2020). The bank is currently seeking accreditation for the Green Climate Fund (GCF), which would create an opportunity for it to obtain funding for green and low-carbon projects. The accreditation process for the GCF is quite burdensome and banks are expected to obtain an international credit rating as part of the process. This makes it difficult for smaller banks with limited capacity to pursue this.

Source Attridge et al (2021).

1.6 Purpose of the Book

This book was developed out of the major areas of interest in current teaching and research in development finance and development banking. The main aim is to provide literature on the changing roles of NDBs in contemporary times. There has been a significant change in NDBs' role from just the provision of credit at subsidized rates to include other critical issues. Therefore, it becomes imperative to improve our understanding of their changing role. Promoting successful NDBs entails a paradigm shift in the approach. This involves an entirely new focus in approach that takes into consideration the following: (1) ensuring the financial viability of the development banks and their lending programmes and (2) creating an environment that fosters financial intermediation in traditionally marginalized sectors, as well as providing non-financial support to sectors of the economy. NDBs have not been given much attention in the literature in spite of their vital importance to the growth and development of many economies. They are said to be an under-researched type of financial institutions in the global economy. There has not been a systematic discussion and appreciation of NDBs within the academic, research, policy and banking communities.

This book presents a comprehensive examination of NDBs by carefully and rigorously discussing their important roles and contributions in Africa. It examines various thematic issues: Overview of Development Finance Institutions; Theoretical Perspectives and Rationale for NDBs; Contemporary Roles, Contributions and Challenges of NDBs; Agricultural Financing in Africa: The Role of NDBs; Financing Infrastructure Development in Africa: The Role of NDBs; NDBs and Climate Finance; Business Models of NDBs; Monitoring and Evaluation, and Impact Evaluation; Corporate Governance of NDBs; Risk Management of NDBs; Regulation and Supervision of NDBs; and cases on the operations and activities of NDBs in selected African countries.

In addition to the thematic issues, the book looks at selected cases on NDBs from some African countries in order to provide diversity in location, history, mandate, roles, contributions, financing structure, business model, corporate governance, monitoring and evaluation, impact evaluation, risk management, regulation and supervision. Examining NDBs from different perspectives is useful for a better appreciation of the entire development banking ecosystem and provides an understanding of how NDBs can drive the growth agenda in Africa. It will contribute to the evolving literature in the field by providing a comprehensive understanding of development banking for students, scholars, researchers, development bankers, policymakers and regulators. The various chapters, with specific cases on NDBs in Africa, will prepare students and practitioners for advanced research and practice in the area. The book will also be useful for policy analysis and implementation. The book will have a strong appeal in emerging and developing countries and also among students and scholars in Europe, America and Asia who are studying African economies and financial systems.

1.7 Organization of the Book

This book, *The Changing Roles of National Development Banks in Africa*, is made up of sixteen (16) chapters. The remaining chapters are organized as follows:

Chapter 2 provides an overview of Development Finance Institutions. It covers Development Finance Institutions, Types of Development Finance Institutions, a Comparison between Multilateral Development Banks and NDBs, Traditional and New Approaches to Development Finance Institutions, and Conditions Necessary for Successful operations of Development Finance Institutions in Africa.

Chapter 3 discusses the Theoretical Perspectives and Rationale for NDBs. The chapter looks at the Historical Background of NDBs, Structural Challenges NDBs Seek to Address, Theoretical Perspectives for NDBs, and Prevailing Views, Need and Rationale for NDBs.

Chapter 4 covers the Contemporary Roles, Contributions and of NDBs, as well as the Main Challenges Confronting NDBs.

Chapter 5 looks at Agricultural Financing in Africa: The Role of NDBs. The chapter specifically provides an Overview of Agricultural Development in Africa and then discusses the Challenges and Opportunities of Agricultural Financing in Africa, Agricultural Financing Mechanisms, as well as the Role of NDBs in Financing Agricultural Development in Africa.

Chapter 6 discusses Financing Infrastructure Development in Africa: The Role of NDBs. It examines the Challenges of Infrastructure Development in Africa, Infrastructure Financing Instruments and The Role of NDBs in Infrastructure Financing.

Chapter 7 discusses NDBs and Sustainable Development. The chapter begins by providing an Overview of Sustainable Development and then discusses the COVID-19 Crisis and Sustainable Development, Challenges of Financing Sustainable Development and the Role of NDBs in Driving Sustainable Development.

Chapter 8 examines NDBs and Climate Finance. It provides an Overview of Climate Finance and then discusses the Challenges in Climate Finance and the Place of NDBs, the Role of NDBs in Scaling up Climate Finance and How NDBs Leverage Private Finance.

Chapter 9 discusses the Business Models of National Development Banks. The chapter covers the Policy Mandate of NDBs, Sectors and Clients Targeted, Funding Sources of NDBs, Lending Models of NDBs, Instruments for Providing Financing, Financial Products and Services, Pricing and Subsidies, and Risks and Costs of NDBs,

Chapter 10 focuses on Monitoring and Evaluation, and Impact Evaluation. The chapter covers the definition and concepts of Monitoring and Evaluation, Monitoring and Evaluation Framework of NDBs, Concepts and Techniques of Impact Evaluation, the Theoretical Framework of Impact Evaluation of NDBs, the Design and Implementation of Impact Evaluation Practices, the Approaches to Ex Post Impact Evaluation of NDBs, the methods for analysing impact evaluation of NDBs, the Deliverables/Outcomes of NDBs, the Challenges of Impact Evaluation Practices and Recent Developments in Impact Evaluation of NDBs.

Chapter 11 examines the Corporate Governance of NDBs through the Theoretical Perspectives of Corporate Governance, Corporate Governance Characteristics of NDBs, Political Influence and Corporate Governance of NDBs, and Corporate Governance and Performance of NDBs.

Chapter 12 examines the Risk Management of NDBs. The chapter defines Risk and discusses Risk Management, Financial Instruments Used by NDBs in Normal Times, Instruments Used by NDBs during Pandemics and How NDBs Benefit from Risk Management.

Chapter 13 looks at Regulation and Supervision of NDBs. It discusses the Justification for Regulating Financial Institutions, Evolution of the Basel Agreements, and whether NDBs should be regulated.

Chapters 14–16 provide cases on the operations and activities of NDBs in selected African countries (Ghana, Uganda and South Africa) in order to bridge the gap between theory and practice. Specifically, it provides an Overview of Development Finance Institutions in each individual country. It then focuses on a particular NDB in each country by looking at the Historical Background, the Political Economy and Institutional Context, Corporate Governance Arrangements, Risk Management, Regulation and

Supervision, Monitoring and Evaluation, and Impact Evaluation Practices, Business Models (including policy mandate, sectors served, funding sources, lending models, products and services, and pricing and subsidies), Financial Performance, Main Achievements and Contributions, as well as the Challenges Confronting the NDB.

1.8 Conclusion

This chapter provides an Introduction to National Development Banks. Development banks are seen as special financial institutions that focus on providing high-risk, medium- and long-term financing for the purpose of productive investment, often achieved by technical assistance. They include MDBs, RDBs and NDBs. In the case of NDBs, they refer to any types of financial institution that are wholly or partially owned or controlled by a national government and have a mandate to achieve socio-economic goals in a region, sector or market segment. We identified the main features on NDBs to include large size, large number, legal status, policy mandate, ownership status, financial instrument, sources of financing and regulation. We also discussed the differences between development banks and commercial banks. The chapter examines the landscape of NDBs in Africa. It also mentions the purpose of the book and provides an outline of the various chapters in the book.

References

Abor, J. Y., Agbloyor, E. K., Donkor, G. N. A., & Alu, A. A. (2022). The COVID-19 pandemic and Africa's financial systems: How do we reform post-COVID-19 financial systems? In *The economics of banking and finance in Africa: Developments in Africa's financial systems* (pp. 1013–1037). Springer.

Abor, J. Y., Adjasi, C. K. D., & Lensink, R. (2020). Introduction to contemporary issues in development finance. In J. Y. Abor, C. K. D. Adjasi, & R. Lensink (Eds.), *Contemporary issues in development finance* (pp. 1–19). Routledge.

Attridge, S., Chen, Y., & Mbate, M. (2021). *Financial performance and corporate governance: Evidence from national development banks in Africa* (ODI Report).

Bruck, N. (1998). The role of development banks in the twenty-first century. *Journal of Emerging Markets, 3*, 39–68.

Chandrasekhar, C. (2016). National development banks in a comparative perspective. In A. Calcagno, S. Dullien, A. Marquez-Velasquez, N. Maystre, &

J. Priewe (Eds.), *Rethinking development strategies after the financial crisis, Volume II—Country studies and international comparisons* (1st ed., pp. 21–30). UNCTAD.

de Luna-Martinez, J., & Vicente, C. L. (2012, February). *Global survey of development banks* (Policy Research, Working Paper; No. 5969). World Bank.

Gottschalk, R., Castro, L. B., & Xu, J. (2021). Should national development banks be subject to Basel III? *Review of Political Economy*. https://doi.org/10.1080/09538259.2021.1977541

Griffith-Jones, S., Ocampo, J. A., Rezende, F., Schclarek, A., & Brei, M. (2018). The future of national development banks. In S. Griffith-Jones & J. A. Ocampo (Eds.), *The future of national development banks*. Oxford University Press.

Griffith-Jones, S., Spiegel, S., Jiajun, X., Carreras, M., & Naqv, N. (2020). *Matching risks with instruments in development banks* (Working Paper No. 9). International Research Initiative on PDBs and DFIs Working Groups.

La Porta, R., López-de-Silanes, F., & Shleifer, A. (2002). Government ownership of banks. *Journal of Finance, 57*(2), 265–301.

Lazzarini, S. G., Musacchio, A., Bandeira-de-Mello, R., & Marcon, R. (2015). What do state-owned development banks do? Evidence from BNDES, 2002–09. *World Development, 66*, 237–253.

Musacchio, A., & Lazzarini, S. G. (2014). *Reinventing state capitalism: Leviathan in business*. Harvard University Press.

Rodrik, D. (2004). Industrial policy for the twenty-first century. *Harvard University*. https://doi.org/10.2139/ssrn.617544

Studart, R., & Gallagher, K. (2016). *Infrastructure for sustainable development: The role of national development banks*. Boston University Global Economic Governance Initiative. https://www.bu.edu/pardeeschool/files/2016/08/Infrastructure.Sustainable.Final_pdf

World Bank. (2016). *Lessons from international experience in designing the Development Bank of Nigeria*. World Bank. https://openknowledge.worldbank.org/bitstream/handle/10986/30048/126401-WP-P146319-PUBLIC-Nigeria-Development-Finance-Study.pdf?sequence=1&isAllowed=y

World Bank. (2018). *2017 Survey of national development banks*. World Bank.

World Bank Group. (2017). *Report from the Executive Directors of the International Development Association to the Board of Governors*. Retrieved on 30 October 2018 from http://documents.worldbank.org/curated/en/348661486654455091/pdf/112728-correct-file-PUBLIC-Rpt-from-EDs-Additions-to-IDA-Resources-2-9-17-For-Disclosure.pdf

Xu, J., Marodon, R., Ru, X., Ren, X., & Wu, X. (2021). What are public development banks and development financing institutions?—Qualification criteria, stylized facts and development trends. *China Economic Quarterly International, 1*, 271–294.

Xu, J., Ru, X., & Song, P. (2021). Can a new model of infrastructure financing mitigate credit rationing in poorly governed countries? *Economic Modelling, 95*, 111–120.

Yeyati, E. L., Micco, A., & Panizza, U. (2004). *Should the government be in the banking business? The role of state-owned and development banks*. Inter-American Development Bank.

CHAPTER 2

Overview of Development Finance Institutions

2.1 Introduction

The relevance of finance in ensuring economic growth and development is clear in the extant literature (see Goldsmith, 1969; McKinnon, 1973; Schumpeter, 1934; Shaw, 1973). Gurley and Shaw (1955), Gerschenkron (1962) and Goldsmith (1969) have emphasized the importance of financial intermediation and resource accumulation in the economic growth process. With the advent of the endogenous growth models, the majority of theoretical and empirical studies such as Pagano (1993), Levine (1997), Barro and Sala-i-Martin (1998), Montiel (2003), Arestis et al. (2015), Ruiz (2018) and Amoah et al. (2020) have revisited the issue and continue to emphasize the importance of the financial sector to economic growth. The financial system can actually drive economic growth in several ways. These include improving the average productivity of capital, facilitating the flow of investment funds to firms in the intermediation process, savings and reallocation of resources into productive sectors. It is important to note that both domestic resource mobilization and an optimal level of external capital inflows are necessary to finance growth and development, and this is the focus of development finance (Abor et al., 2020).

The extant literature recognizes the importance of development finance in expanding capital availability for achieving economic growth and development. Development finance focuses on the need to fill the

© The Author(s), under exclusive license to Springer Nature Switzerland AG 2023

J. Yindenaba Abor, *The Changing Role of National Development Banks in Africa*, https://doi.org/10.1007/978-3-031-38639-8_2

gaps between capital required and capital available through various interventions. The financing gap is due to the failure of financial markets to supply the necessary financing for economic activity. It becomes critical when a country's financial system is inefficient and ineffective, and the government is also unable to mobilize resources. Indeed, development finance focuses on how domestic as well as the global financial systems facilitate economic growth and the development process. It also deals with structuring and reforming the financial system in ways that promote growth and development at both the macro- and microlevels in developing and emerging economies. Development finance is important for financing private enterprises and promoting their operations as a way of complementing other forms of financing. Development finance interventions are aimed at improving the level of efficiency of financial markets by curtailing market imperfections as well as establishing alternative financial institutions or development finance institutions to engage in the direct provision of finance in the financial market (Abor et al., 2020).

Development finance institutions (DFIs) play a critical role in development policies. They serve as critical financial intermediaries for channeling the long-term finance required for promoting private investment to realize economic growth and development. DFIs mobilize resources for private sector projects, and there has been a significant increase in the amounts available, occasioned by re-investment of profits and other sources of new capital. They also leverage private sector sources of capital for investment in projects. In general terms, the field of development finance has changed significantly over the past few years as evident in the increasing levels of funds available, types of funds and institutions, and the number of developing countries involved. Resources from official development assistance (ODA) have dwindled, and since 2000, official inflows from donors have constituted a small portion of the overall development finance. The shift has been driven by growth in private capital flows, such as Foreign Direct Investment (FDI) and remittances, and the increasing reliance on domestic resources mobilization. Overall, trends in development finance suggest a development finance architecture that is no longer reliant on ODA but rather on other sources of capital, including FDI, private lending, domestic resources and DFIs (Savoy et al., 2016).

However, available records suggest that DFIs in Africa and other developing countries have not been effective in performing their role as promoters of economic growth. Moreover, efforts at reforming the overall financial system in order to increase access to finance have also resulted in disappointing outcomes and a number of factors are responsible for the failure of DFIs. Obviously, developing countries cannot do without DFIs. But the issue is that the previous approach to DFIs has been unsuccessful and it is necessary to consider a completely new approach that will make DFIs sustainable and also effective in bridging the financing gap in the market (Ndikumana, 2006). This chapter provides a review of DFIs by considering the various types of DFI, comparing multilateral development banks (MDBs) with national development banks (NDBs), examining new approaches to effective development financing and examining the conditions for successful DFIs in Africa. The chapter provides a useful foundation for discussing new strategies of DFIs for driving economic growth in Africa.

The rest of the chapter is structured as follows. Section 2.2 explains what DFIs are. Section 2.3 discusses the types of DFIs. Section 2.4 compares MDBs with NDBs. Section 2.5 examines the traditional and new approaches to DFIs. Section 2.6 discusses the conditions for successful DFIs in Africa, and finally, Sect. 2.7 concludes the chapter.

2.2 What Are Development Finance Institutions?

Development finance institutions (DFIs) are alternative financial institutions that are concerned with providing long-term finance (including, long-term loans, equity and risk guarantee instruments) to stimulate private investment with the aim of promoting economic growth and sustainable development, while ensuring that they remain financially viable. They mainly concentrate on areas that providers of conventional finance tend to avoid and they also focus on markets which have limited access to sources of domestic and external capital. DFIs are said to occupy the intermediary space between public aid and private investment by focusing on high-risk investments in sectors that have limited access to capital markets. They are capable of raising huge amounts of capital from global capital markets for providing loans or equity investment on a commercial and sometimes concessional basis (Abor, 2017; Dickson, n.d.).

DFIs are financial institutions or development agencies which are involved in providing finance for start-ups or development projects in areas where commercial banks are not interested in investing, with no guarantee of financial participation. The OECD describes DFIs as specialized financial institutions established for promoting private sector development in developing countries. They typically have majority government ownership and tend to raise their capital from national and international DFIs. They also benefit from government guarantees, which improves their creditworthiness, enabling them to access the global capital markets and provide finance on very competitive terms. They seek to provide financing for sustainable investment, provide technical services to support sustainable development and also promote responsible investment practices. They contribute significantly to the economic growth in many countries, and they have a stronger impact, especially in developing and low-income countries.

The traditional role of DFIs is to help address the failure or imperfections in financial markets. In the view of Dixit and Pindyck (1994), uncertainty significantly and negatively affects investment, which entails large sunk and irreversible costs and where there is a choice to delay the investment decision until additional information is made available. The risks associated with such long-term investments tend to discourage private sector investors. DFIs assist in correcting risk perceptions, promoting a favourable environment for private investment to thrive, as well as providing social infrastructure and other activities that have positive economic outcomes. They tend to focus on developing countries with limited access to local and external capital markets by providing long-term finance for infrastructure projects in such countries. DFIs facilitate private sector investment and provide risk guarantees that provide comfort for investors. They provide finance that is linked to the design and implementation of capacity-building programmes adopted by government (te Velde, 2011).

DFIs also play an active role in financing micro, small and medium enterprises (MSMEs), which are often perceived risky by other finance providers. In this respect, they take the first mover advantage in markets with high growth potential. They often have a double bottom line, which includes pursuing profit and development impact. On the one hand, they invest for the purpose of generating returns which enable them to undertake more investments, while on the other, they facilitate the economic development of countries they invest in (Dickinson, n.d.).

DFIs contribute by adding value to the economic development process, and Dalberg (2009) states three ways by which they do this:

- *Investing in underserved project types and settings*: The business model of DFIs is designed in such a way that they are able to invest in highly risky projects in developing countries. They have the capacity to tolerate high-risk and make long-term investments, especially in areas private investors consider too risky to commit resources.
- *Investing in undercapitalized sectors*: They specialize in investing in sectors such as agriculture, energy, the financial sector and infrastructure, which are critical to driving economic growth.
- *Mobilizing other investors*: They promote knowledge sharing, standards setting and collaboration, and this helps in attracting other investors. Their track records enable other investors to scale up their investment and they also build local capacity in fund management.

2.3 Types of Development Finance Institutions

This section discusses the various types of DFI, which include multilateral, regional and bilateral or country-specific DFIs.

2.3.1 Multilateral Development Finance Institutions

Multilateral DFIs include private sector outfits of international financial institutions (IFIs), which are founded by a number of countries and are subject to international laws. They are generally owned by national governments but sometimes with ownership participation by international or private entities. They provide financing for projects in the private sector mostly through equity, long-term loans and guarantees. They tend to have stronger financing capacity and provide the opportunity for close cooperation between governments. Multilateral DFIs or multilateral development banks (MDBs) are financial institutions established by various countries with the objective of supporting development activities through long-term loans and grants. They mostly provide lending at low or no interest and sometimes provide grants to finance projects in areas that promote development. In more specific terms, the financing provided by multilateral DFIs takes the following forms:

1. *Long-term loans*: Such loans usually have up to 20 years' maturity and interest rates are based on market rates. Multilateral DFIs

typically acquire funds from the global capital markets and in turn on-lend them to developing countries' governments.

2. *Very-long-term loans*: These loans are also termed *credits* and usually have maturity between 30 and 40 years with interest rates pegged below market interest rates. Funding for such loans is obtained from direct contributions made by governments of donor countries.
3. *Grant financing*: Some multilateral DFIs also provide grants typically for technical assistance, advisory services and project preparation.

Multilateral DFIs have memberships, which comprise both developed countries (which serve as donors) and developing countries (which are the borrowers). The European Bank for Reconstruction and Development (EBRD); Multilateral Investment Guarantee; Agency (MIGA); Asian Development Bank (ADB); African Development Bank (AfDB); Inter-American Bank Group (IDB); European Investment Bank (EIB); Development Bank of Latin America (CAF); African Export-Import Bank (Afreximbank); Islamic Development Bank (IsDB); Asian Infrastructure Investment Bank (AIIB); and International Fund for Agricultural Development (IFAD) are some examples. Details on the IFC and MIGA are provided in Boxes 2.1 and 2.2, respectively.

There are also sub-regional MDBs with membership comprising only borrowing countries. MDBs tend to raise finance from the global capital markets at lower costs and on-lend to their members. Examples include: the Central American Bank for Economic Integration (CABEI); Caribbean Development Bank (CDB); Black Sea Trade and Development Bank (BSTDB); ECOWAS Bank for Investment and Development (EBID); West African Development Bank (BOAD); East African Development Bank (EADB); Eurasian Development Bank (EDB); Economic Cooperation Organisation Trade and Development Bank (ETDB); and the New Development Bank (NDB) (formerly BRICS Development Bank).

Some multilateral DFIs tend to have more limited memberships and mostly concentrate on financing specific activities. Examples include: International Fund for Agricultural Development (IFAD), International Investment Bank (IIB), International Finance Facility for Immunisation (IFFI), European Commission (EC), OPEC Fund for International Development (OFID), Nordic Investment Bank (NIB) and Arab Bank for Economic Development in Africa (BADEA).

Box 2.1: International Finance Corporation

The IFC was established in 1956 to represent the World Bank Group's private sector arm with the objective of advancing economic development through investment in commercially viable projects and ventures in order to reduce poverty and promote development. It is aimed at creating an enabling environment for people to flee poverty, through the provision of resources for private businesses. Its headquarters is situated in Washington DC and it is considered the largest global development finance institution which focuses on providing support for the private sector in developing economies. The IFC provides three main services, including investment services, asset management services and advisory services.

The idea of establishing the IFC was proposed by Robert L. Garner when the World Bank employed him in 1947 as a senior executive. He believed that private business had a significant role to play in global development. Robert L. Garner and some of his colleagues, in 1950, mooted the idea of creating a new financial institution that will focus on promoting private sector investments in the developing countries that the World Bank served. The US government supported this idea of a new international institution to work closely with the World Bank to support investments in private enterprises without demanding government guarantees, without directly participating in the management of these enterprises and by collaborating with other investors. In 1956, the IFC was officially established and began operations with Robert L. Garner as its first leader. It made its very first investment in 1957 by advancing a loan facility of US$2 million to an affiliate of Siemens & Haiske (Siemens AG) based in Brazil. It has subsequently increased its investments in many developing and emerging countries.

The IFC has 184 member countries as its owners and is governed by a Board of Governors, comprising one governor per member country. Each member country is also expected to appoint one alternate governor in addition to the governor. The Board of Governors is vested with all corporate powers, and it has in turn delegated most of such powers to a 25-member board of directors chaired by the President of the World Bank Group. The board of directors is responsible for reviewing and making decisions on investments and providing overall strategic direction to IFC's executive leadership, made up of the CEO of the IFC, CEO of the Asset Management Company and 9 Vice-Presidents.

The IFC's core areas of operation include providing investment services (consisting of equity, investment loans, syndicated loans, trade finance, structured and securitized finance, treasury and liquidity management, and client risk management services), advisory services (supporting corporate decision-making with regard to business, environment, social impact and sustainability) and asset management, which is done through its wholly-owned subsidiary, IFC Asset Management Company. It has, since 2009, focused on some developmental projects with the aim of improving education and health, increasing sustainability in agriculture, increasing access to financing for micro and small enterprises, helping small businesses to grow revenues, investing in climate health and supporting infrastructure development.

The IFC has, however, come under criticism from the NGO community that it is unable to track its funds since the former invests through financial intermediaries. For instance, Oxfam (2015) reported that the IFC was not carrying out the necessary due diligence and was not ensuring proper risk management in the financial intermediaries it has investments in. The report indicated that the IFC has little accountability for investments worth billions of US dollars into banks, hedge funds and other financial intermediaries, and this has resulted in projects that are causing human rights abuses across the world. Another area of concern is that the IFC seems to focus mainly on large companies or wealthy individuals who are in a position to finance their own investments and may not require external funding. Therefore, investing in such large companies or wealthy individuals presupposes that IFC investments have not had a significantly positive development impact. One example frequently cited is the financing provided by the IFC to a Saudi prince for the construction of the five-star Mövenpick Hotel in Ghana (see Einhorn, 2013).

Source Abor et al. (2020)

Box 2.2: Multilateral Investment Guarantee Agency

The Multilateral Insurance Guarantee Agency (MIGA) is a multilateral development agency, which was established in 1988 as one of the institutions under the World Bank Group. Based on the convention that established MIGA, the aim of the agency is to encourage the flow of investments for development purposes among member countries, particularly to developing member countries, thereby augmenting the activities of the International Bank for Reconstruction and Development (IBRD), the International Finance Corporation (IFC) and other international development finance institutions. The MIGA encourages private sector investment by providing cover to lenders and investors against political risks. MIGA's multilateral character and joint sponsorship by developed and developing countries are viewed as significantly increasing confidence among cross-border investors.

The MIGA has 182 member countries made up of 154 developing countries and 28 industrialized countries. A Council of Governors and a Board of Directors guide MIGA's programmes and activities. Each country appoints one governor and an alternate. MIGA's corporate powers are vested in the Council of Governors, which delegates most of its powers to a Board of 25 Directors. Voting power is weighted according to the share of capital that each Director represents. MIGA's Board is situated at the World Bank Group headquarters in Washington, DC, and meets frequently to review and decide on investment guarantee projects and oversee general management policies. It is imperative to note that among the World Bank Group, and the older regional MDFIs (ADB, AfDB, IADB), only MIGA offers political-risk coverage for investments. In the past, just as with the World Bank, MIGA did not cover sub-sovereign risks but merely provided coverage under an agreement with the Host Government. However, in 2013, MIGA coverage was extended to State-Owned Enterprises (SOEs).

The guarantees that MIGA offers cover currency convertibility and transfer risks; expropriation (including creeping expropriation); war and civil disturbance; and breach of contract by governments and SOEs. It also extends credit enhancements for defaulting on payment obligations. MIGA's coverage is targeted at cross-border equity investments or loans. Other forms of investment, such as technical assistance and management contracts, asset securitizations, bond issues, leasing, services, and franchising and licensing agreements, may also be eligible for cover. MIGA's guarantee can cover up to 95% of the scheduled payments of loan principal (plus up to 1.5 times the principal to cover loss of interest) or 90% of the equity investment (plus up to 5 times the investment to cover loss of profits). In addition, up to $220 million can be insured in any one project for MIGA's own account. MIGA can normally provide coverage for 15 years and for 20 years based on the justification provided.

MIGA only supports sound investments that meet high social and environmental standards. MIGA applies a thorough set of social and environmental performance standards to all projects and provides expertise in working with investors to ensure agreement with these standards.

2.3.2 *Regional Development Finance Institutions*

The regional DFIs include the regional development banks (RDBs) and these are essentially part of multilateral DFIs, but they tend to focus on specific regions of the world. They aim at financing development activities in particular geographical areas. They are owned by governments of those regions and the shareholders of these institutions are mainly the regional countries and major donor countries. RDBs are considered 'clones' of the World Bank in terms of their structure, functions and operations, but they tend to have a more limited focus. The main regional DFIs are the Inter-American Development Bank (IDB), African Development Bank (AfDB), Asian Development Bank (ADB) and European Bank for Reconstruction and Development (EBRD).

Among the main RDBs, the Inter-American Development Bank for Latin America was the first to be established in 1959. This was followed by the African Development Bank in 1964, the Asian Development Bank in 1966 and then the European Bank for Reconstruction and Development in 1991. As mentioned, the RDBs have similar structures and functions like the World Bank, though they are different in some other respects. For instance, both the RDBs and the World Bank have 'hard' and 'soft' lending facilities, where the terms under the hard lending facility are very similar in all the institutions and the soft lending is funded directly by donors. As mentioned earlier, with respect to World Bank's soft lending, this is provided through the IDA. Soft lending programmes by IDB, AfDB and ADB, for instance, are conducted through the Fund for Special Operation (FSO), African Development Fund (ADF) and Asian Development Fund (AsDF), respectively. Hard lending takes the form of loans on market-based terms, while soft lending takes the form of grants and concessional loans, which are associated with longer repayment periods and lower interest rates. Most loans typically have a maturity of 25–40 years. In terms of their governance structure, both the World Bank and the RDBs are governed by boards of governors, on which every member country is supposed to have a representation of one governor and one alternate governor. The Boards of Governors, which are the highest authority of the institutions, in turn appoint and delegate the exercise of most of their powers to the Boards of Directors, which provide general direction to the entities.

One major challenge faced by regional development banks is that donor governments prefer to channel resources through the World Bank

Table 2.1 Overview of regional DFIs

Regional Development Banks	*Area*	*Year founded*	*Headquarters*	*Main goal*
Inter-American Development Bank (IDB)	Latin American, Caribbean	1959	Washington, DC, (US)	Promoting poverty reduction, social equity, environmentally sustainable economic growth
African Development Bank (AfDB)	Africa	1964	Abidjan (Cote D'Ivoire)	Spurring sustainable economic development and social progress in its regional member countries (RMCs), thus contributing to poverty reduction
Asian Development Bank (ADB)	Asia and Pacific region	1966	Manila (Philippines)	Fostering economic growth and cooperation in the region
European Bank for Reconstruction and Development (EBRD)	Central and Eastern Europe and Central Asia	1991	London, UK	Promoting transition to market-oriented economies in the Central and Eastern Europe and Central Asia countries

Source Abor et al. (2020)

rather than through the regional development banks. This also means that borrowing countries tend to attach more importance to their relationship with the World Bank than to their specialized RDBs.

An overview of the main regional DFIs is provided in Table 2.1.

2.3.2.1 Inter-American Development Bank

The Inter-American Development Bank (IDB), which was created in 1959, has its headquarters in Washington, DC. It is the oldest RDB and it represents the largest source of multilateral development financing for supporting socio-economic development, institutional development projects, trade and regional integration programmes in Latin America and the Caribbean. The IDB is owned by 48 countries which comprise 26 Latin American and Caribbean states, 16 European countries, the US, Canada, Israel, China, Japan and Korea. The 26 Latin American and Caribbean states are the borrowing member countries that regularly acquire loans from IDB and the others constitute non-borrowing member countries.

The idea of creating a DFI for the Latin American region was initially proposed during the earliest efforts to establish an inter-American system at the First American Conference in 1890. The IDB came to fruition under an initiative proposed by the then President of Brazil, Juscelino Kubitshek. The IDB was officially set up on 8 April 1959, with the Organisation of American States drafting the Articles of Agreement to establish the Bank.

The main goals of the IDB involve promoting poverty reduction, social equity and environmentally sustainable economic growth. It focuses on the following priority areas in the attainment of these goals:

- Foster competitiveness by supporting policies and programmes that enhance the potential of a country for development in the global marketplace;
- Modernize the state by enhancing the level of efficiency and transparency of public sector institutions;
- Invest in social programmes which are capable of expanding opportunities for the poor;
- Promote regional economic integration by fostering relation among countries in order to develop bigger markets for their commodities.

It also helps regional initiative efforts by providing information and knowledge to aid policy discourse as well as providing funding for technical cooperation in order to strengthen regional integration. It provides governments with technical assistance on issues regarding trade and regional integration and undertakes public outreach programmes and activities targeted at promoting such integration. IDB uses its Fund for Special Operations to provide concessional lending.

2.3.2.2 Central American Bank for Economic Integration

The Central American Bank for Economic Integration (CABEI) is an RDB founded in 1960 with the aim of supporting integration and development among its member countries. It currently has two headquarters located in Tegucigalpa (Honduras) and San Salvador (El Salvador) in addition to national offices in each Central American country. Its membership is as follows:

- Its five founding members, made up of Costa Rica, El Salvador, Guatemala, Honduras and Nicaragua, were the countries that signed the Founding Covenant establishing the CABEI.
- It has two non-founding regional countries—Dominican Republic and Panama.
- Its five non-regional countries comprise Argentina, Colombia, Mexico, Spain and Taiwan. They joined the CABEI in order to have a permanent regional presence, thereby enhancing their global projection by supporting development in the founding countries.
- It has beneficiary countries. In addition to regional countries, Belize joined the CABEI to acquire loans and guarantees. However, unlike the other member countries, Belize does not hold any shares in CABEI. Argentina and Colombia also benefit from loans and guarantees from CABEI.

The process of Central American regional economic integration began on 13 December 1960, with the signing of the General Treaty on Central America Economic Integration. The signing of the Treaty then resulted in the establishment of the CABEI, which has become the financial arm for the integration and development of Central America.

As a regional DFI, CABEI provides support for the public and private sectors of the economy. It focuses on acquiring funds and channeling these into promoting investments in its core areas, including energy, infrastructure, industry, agriculture and rural development, human development, urban development and services for competitiveness, and financial trading and development finance.

2.3.2.3 *African Development Bank*

The African Development Bank (AfDB) or Banque Africaine de Development (BAD) was founded in 1964 with its headquarters situated in Abidjan, Cote d'Ivoire (but in 2003, the headquarters temporarily moved to Tunis, Tunisia, because of the Ivorian war and then returned in September 2014). Its owners are made up of 81 member countries (shareholders), comprising 54 African countries and 27 non-African countries. There are two other entities under the African Development Bank Group and these are the African Development Fund and the Nigeria Trust Fund.

The growing desire for more unity within the continent, after the colonial period in Africa, resulted in the creation of two draft charters, for establishing the Organisation of African Unity (founded in 1963 and replaced later by the African Union) and an RDB. An agreement for establishing the AfDB was prepared in 1963, and this materialized on 10 September 1964. The Bank was formally established under the auspices of the Economic Commission for Africa but started its operations in 1966. Though the Bank initially had only African countries as members, a number of non-African countries have been allowed to join since 1982.

The overall objective of the AfDB Group is to spur sustainable economic development and social progress in its regional member countries (RMCs), thus contributing to poverty reduction. The AfDB Group is focused on mobilizing resources and allocating them for investments in the RMCs. It also provides policy advice and technical assistance to support development efforts of the RMCs. Its primary functions include:

- Making loans and equity investments for the economic and social advancement of the RMCs;
- Providing technical assistance for development projects and programmes of the RMCs;
- Promoting the investment of public and private capital for development;
- Assisting in organizing the development policies of RMCs.

The AfDB is also expected to pay particular attention to national and multinational projects that are required to promote and facilitate regional integration.

Its main sources of financing include subscribed capital, reserves, borrowed funds and accumulated net income. Its shareholding is structured in such a way that two-thirds of the total capital is held by the RMCs while one-third is held by non-regional members. AfDB is also a triple-A credit rated institution, allowing it to borrow from the international capital markets on favourable terms. It provides finance to the governments of African countries and to private companies that invest in the RMCs. AfDB lends on a non-concessional basis at market interest rates. It also provides development finance on concessional terms through the African Development Fund to its low-income member countries that do not qualify to obtain loans on non-concessional terms. Funds for concessionary loans are typically obtained from the 27 non-regional members, which come in the form of grant contributions.

2.3.2.4 *Asian Development Bank*

The Asian Development Bank (ADB) was founded in 1966 with its headquarters based in Manila, the capital of the Philippines. With an initial membership of 31 countries at its establishment, ADB is currently owned by 67 member countries, which are made up of 48 countries within the Asian and the Pacific regions and 19 from other parts of the world.

The idea for establishing the ADB was considered at the beginning of the 1960s. The proposal was to establish a financial institution that was Asian in nature to focus on fostering economic growth and cooperation in the region. In 1963, a resolution was subsequently passed to provide clear direction for establishing the bank. This was done at the first Ministerial Conference on Asian Economic Cooperation, which was held by the United Nations Economic Commission for Asia and the Far East. The Bank was eventually set up on 19 December 1966. The ADB served a predominantly agricultural region by providing assistance mainly in the areas of food production and rural development during the 1960s.

ADB focuses on promoting social and economic development in Asia and the Pacific through inclusive growth, environmentally sustainable growth and regional integration. It is concerned with helping its member countries, specifically the developing countries, to pursue poverty reduction and improvement in the quality of life of citizens through equity investments, loans, guarantees, grants, technical assistance and policy dialogue. Its core areas of interest include infrastructure (energy, ICT, transport, water and urban development), environment, regional cooperation and integration, financial sector development, education, health, agriculture and natural resource and public sector management.

Its main sources of finance include bond issues, recycled repayments on its loans and member countries' contributions. A significant percentage of the cumulative lending it gives is from its ordinary capital. The concessional lending it provides to its developing member countries is done through the African Development Fund. It also manages a number of trust funds and assists in channeling grants from bilateral donor partners to the recipient countries.

2.3.2.5 *European Bank for Reconstruction and Development*

The European Bank for Reconstruction and Development (EBRD) is the youngest among the main RDBs and it was established in 1991 with its headquarters situated in London. The EBRD was established with the aim of promoting the transition to market-oriented economies among countries in Central Europe, Eastern Europe and Central Asia. Its owners are made up of 65 countries and 2 intergovernmental institutions: the European Union and the European Investment Bank.

The EBRD was founded during the period of the dissolution of the Soviet Union and communism in Central and Eastern Europe and these countries needed support to develop a new private sector in an atmosphere of democracy. The Bank was set up after reaching an agreement regarding its charter, size and share of power among the shareholders.

EBRD is also a triple-A credit rated institution, which allows it to borrow from the international capital markets at favourable market rates. In spite of its public sector shareholders, EBRB directs its investments largely to private enterprises in collaboration with commercial entities. It is committed to developing democracies and building market economies in some Central European and Central Asian countries through its investments. The EBRD provides loans and equity finance, trade finance, project finance, leasing facilities, guarantees and professional development through its support programmes. The EBRD also supports publicly owned companies in their privatization efforts and is committed to promoting environmentally sound and sustainable development.

2.3.3 *Sub-Regional Development Finance Institutions*

There are other regional or sub-regional regional DFIs which include Central American Bank for Economic Integration, the European Investment Bank (EIB), Islamic Development Bank (CABEI), Islamic Development Bank (IsDB), Development Bank for Latin America (CAF), Council of Europe Development Bank (CEB), African Export-Import Bank (Afreximbank), ECOWAS Bank for Investment and Development (EBID), West African Development Bank (BOAD), East African Development Bank (EADB) and Development Bank of Central African States, etc. Boxes 2.3 and 2.4 present cases on Afreximbank and EBID.

Box 2.3: African Export-Import Bank

The African Export-Import Bank was founded in 1993 under the purview of the African Development Bank and functions as a multilateral development bank with the mission of promoting and expanding African commerce and the goal of increasing Africa's participation in world trade.

This mission is carried out via a diverse set of financial programmes that promote both trade and trade-enabling infrastructure.

Among the bank's programmes are line of credit, syndications, direct financing, special risks program, note purchase, receivables purchase/ discounting and project financing. The majority of funding comes from wholesale debt, which is supplemented by deposits from African central banks, financial institutions, and member-state corporations.

In 2020, the bank increased its lending operations in support of its member states, disbursing US$10.95 billion to entities and governments in those countries in order to combat the COVID-19 pandemic and boost African trade. The Bank successfully implemented 73 financial initiatives across Africa. These initiatives (investments) are expected to generate 71,030 new jobs, provide trade credit to 48,960 small and medium-sized businesses, and add more than $1 billion to Africa's fiscal income.

By the end of 2020, the Bank was projected to have provide 286 trade credit lines totalling US$6.5 billion to 20 African nations to address their trade financing needs. This led to 48,960 sub-loans to women and youth-owned small and medium-sized businesses.

Afreximbank Annual Report (2020)

Box 2.4: ECOWAS Bank for Investment and Development

The ECOWAS Bank for Investment and Development (EBID) is the financial arm of the Economic Community of West African States comprising fifteen (15) member states. EBID emerged as a banking group after the transformation of the erstwhile Fund for Cooperation, Compensation and Development of the Economic Community of West African States in 1999.

EBID is meant to build the groundwork for the Community's long-term development by supporting regional and national (public and commercial) initiatives. The Bank intervenes through Long, Medium, and Short-Term Loans; Equity Participation; Lines of Credit Granting and Framework Agreements for Refinancing; Loans, Debentures, Bonds, and Other Securities Issue and Guarantee; and Financial Engineering Operations and Services.

The Bank has years of experience in investment projects within and among ECOWAS member states; it has been a key partner in regional integration programmes and the implementation of public-private sector partnerships in member states. It founded the African Biofuels and Renewable Energy Fund (ABREF), which is now known as African Biofuel and Renewable Energy Company (ABREC).

After seventeen years of operation (i.e., 2004–2020), the Bank's net obligations in respect of 136 active projects have expanded 9.5 times from UA121 million in January 2004 to UA 1,153 million at the end of December 2020. From the institution's founding (the ECOWAS Fund), EBID provided net support to member states of UA1.77 billion (USD 2.54 billion) for 253 projects in various sectors.

EBID in Brief (2021)

2.3.4 Bilateral Development Finance Institutions

Bilateral DFIs are either set up as independent financial institutions (such as the International Development Corporation (IDC), South Africa and Netherlands Development Finance Company (FMO)), or they may be part of larger bilateral development banks (such as the German Investment and Development Company [DEG], which is part of the German development bank [KfW]). Bilateral DFIs include:

- Belgian Investment Company for Developing Countries (BIO), Belgium;
- Belgian Corporation for International Investment (BMI-SBI), Belgium;
- Canada's Development Finance Institution (FinDev), Canada;
- Commonwealth Development Corporation, and Colonial Development Corporation (CDC Group), UK;
- Compañía Española de Financiación del Desarrollo (COFIDES), Spain;
- Finnish fund (Finnish state fund) (Finnfund), Finland;
- French Development Agency—Agence Francaise de Developpement (AFD/Proparco, France;
- German Development Bank (KfW);
- Investment Fund for Developing Countries—Investeringsfonden for Udviklingslande (IFU), Denmark);
- Swedfund International AB, (Swedfund), Sweden;
- Swiss Investment Fund for Emerging Market (SIFEM), Switzerland;

- Netherlands Development Finance Company (FMO);
- Norwegian Investment Fund for developing countries (Norfund), Norway;
- Oesterreichische Entwicklungsbank (OeEB), Austria Cassa depositi e prestiti/Società Italiana per Le Imprese all'Estero—SIMEST Spa (CDP/SIMEST), Italy;
- Overseas Private Investment Corporation (OPIC), US;
- Sociedade para o Financiamento do Desenvolvimento (SOFID), Portugal.

The Swedfund International AB is presented in Box 2.5.

Box 2.5: Swedfund International AB

Swedfund International AB (Swedfund) is a bilateral DFI with a focus on investing in emerging markets. It is committed to eliminating poverty through the creation of sustainable businesses in developing and emerging countries. It is owned by the Swedish government and operates as a Limited Liability Company.

Swedfund provides finance that is used to invest in countries that qualify for ODA finance. Priority is mostly given to least developed countries (LDCs) and investment projects that are regarded to have high development impact. Swedfund also provides financing for investments in non-EU member countries in Eastern Europe. Swedfund's investment policy includes investing not more than 15% of its capital in a single project and not exceeding 20% where a Swedish strategic partner is involved or more than 20% in a single country. The strategic partner should be willing to absorb risk equal to or greater than the risk exposure of the Swedfund.

Its areas of investment include: infrastructure, financial institutions, industry, manufacturing and telecommunication. It prohibits investments related to alcohol/hard liquor and tobacco.

Source Dalberg (2009)

Bilateral DFIs also include country-specific DFIs operating mostly in developing and emerging countries and having the mandate of providing long-term capital to finance the private sector, with particular value-added development objectives on a sustainable commercial basis. Bilateral DFIs may also include microfinance institutions, NDBs or state development banks, community development finance institutions, microenterprise funds and revolving loan funds. Examples of bilateral DFIs in

Africa include the Development Bank of Seychelles, the Development Bank of Mauritius, the Development Bank of Ethiopia, Uganda Development Bank, Development Bank of Rwanda, Tanzania Agricultural Development Bank, the Infrastructure Development Bank of Zimbabwe, the Development Bank of Zambia, Botswana Development Corporation, the International Development Corporation, the Development Bank Ghana and the Development Bank of Nigeria. The nature, operations and activities of two bilateral DFIs in Africa—the International Development Corporation (South Africa) and the Rural Development Fund (Ghana)—are detailed in Boxes 2.6 and 2.7, respectively.

Box 2.6: Industrial Development Corporation

Industrial Development Corporation (IDC) is a national development finance institution established in 1940 with the aim of promoting economic growth and industrial development. It is owned by the South African government and has the mandate of contributing to the creation of balanced, sustainable economic growth in South Africa and the rest of the African continent.

With funding from debt, other DFIs, investment income, among others, the IDC is able to invest in 'higher-risk funding' projects and fosters national and international partnerships, thereby playing a catalytic role in South Africa's economy. The IDC has been in charge of the implementation of the national industrial policy for over 70 years, leading to the setting up of petro-chemical, agricultural, fabric and mining industries among others. The mandate of the IDC was extended in the 1990s to include investments in other African countries, thereby allowing IDC to make its first foreign investment in the Mozal aluminium smelter in Mozambique. It subsequently launched its investments in many other African countries.

During the period, 1996–2016, the IDC invested billions of South African Rands in a wide range of sectors including R46 billion (US$2.74 billion) in metal and machinery, R34 billion (US$2.02 billion) in mining, R20 billion (US$1.19 billion) in chemicals and petroleum, R16 billion (US$9.51 billion) in agro-processing and R11 billion (US$6.54 billion) in tourism and restaurants, facilitating the creation of more than 453,000 jobs through those investments. It has also invested in renewable energy and several other infrastructural developments in and outside South Africa.

Box 2.7: Rural Development Fund Ghana LBG

The Rural Development Fund (RDF) Ghana LBG is a DFI established in Ghana to provide access to funds and capacity-building services to Agriculture, Agribusiness, and Renewable Energy. RDF provides wholesale funds to a wide range of financial intermediaries for on-lending to MSMEs.

The RDF started in March 2016 as a project under the Danish International Development Agency's funded Support to Private Sector Development Programme, Phase III (SPSD III). The SPSD III is the last programmatic cycle of private sector development support by DANIDA, ending a development cooperation era between Ghana and Denmark and ushering in an era of collaboration in trade, investments and politics. RDF was incorporated as a company limited by access to provide finance, while leveraging on its funding to collaborate with other like-minded institutions.

The members of the RDF are the Government of Ghana represented by the Ministry of Finance and the Government of Denmark represented by the Danish Investment Fund for Developing Countries.

Over the years, DANIDA has supported access to finance and the capacity development of Rural & Community Banks (RCBs), including the supply of wholesale funds and provision of loan guarantees through universal banks and savings and loans companies. The seed fund for the RDF was an amalgamation of all the revolving funds from DANIDA's past engagements in the access to finance space within the private sector.

Source www.rdfghana.com

2.4 Comparison Between Multilateral Development Banks and National Development Banks

MDBs and NDBs differ in a number of respects. While NDBs have little North-South cooperation, MDBs have more North-South cooperation through providing financing to developing countries although they provide little support to developed countries, even in periods of crisis. These two types of development bank tend to have a similar financial structure, focusing more on debt as opposed to equity financing. There is sufficient information on the ideal structure and organization of a typical MDB, but little is known about how an NDB is organized. NDBs do not seem to share best practices or even engage in cross-border communication, thus limiting their potential scope and scale. NDBs, especially in developing countries, are more focused on the domestic economy with the mandate to finance development projects and achieve specific development objectives in the domestic economy.

NDBs are mostly interested in financing projects that the private sector is not willing or not able to finance. They also help in creating and developing new market niches, developing innovative schemes in attracting and channeling private sector resources to large infrastructure projects, building capacity in public and private sector institutions, conceiving and structuring new investment projects, and facilitating the execution of public-private partnerships. MDBs also tend to have a similar focus, but their scale and impact are much bigger than those of NDBs. Considering the global scope of MDBs, they mostly lack the ability and local knowledge to have orderly changes in industry in the local economy. On the other hand, NDBs are better placed to do this and they offer benefits such as: (1) a unique opportunity to design policy prescriptions that define best practices for NDBs and (2) suggest areas for improvement in their effectiveness and efficiency.

MDBs have struggled to close the significant financing gap alone with respect to infrastructure financing, climate mitigation and adaptation. This difficulty is attributed to lack of support from national governments and the relatively low capitalization of MDBs. Though MDBs have been instrumental and contributed in providing counter-cyclical financing during periods of economic crisis, the COVID-19 pandemic has placed greater demand and more urgent action, in respect of which MDBs have not been able to live up to expectation. NDBs, on the other hand, have proven more capable of providing this type of scalable financing. MDBs and other international financial institutions failed in providing the needed relief to capital markets for a COVID-19 economic recovery. NDBs across the globe were able to rise to the occasion by providing rapid response to the impacts of the COVID-19 and increasing disbursements. The ability of NDBs to respond quickly by increasing capital and disbursing funds to the sectors of the economy shows their unique importance in funding economic recovery. It is, however, important to note that both NDBs and MDBs can play complimentary roles by creating financial instruments that prioritize sustainable long-term investments.

In addition, there are significantly more NDBs across the globe than recognized MDBs. In the study by the Columbia Center on Sustainable

Investment (2021), NDB total assets are more than 3.5 times the size of MDBs. The assets of all recognized NDBs increased from US$6 trillion to about US$8.3 trillion and those of MDBs increased from US$1.7 trillion to about US$2.5 trillion. Also, the differences in annual disbursements between NDBs and MDBs show the variations in terms of their ability to provide counter-cyclical financing for a post-COVID-19 recovery. Their report showed MDB disbursements total approximately US$155 billion per annum compared to over US$1.2 trillion by NDBs. NDBs seem to be more effective in disbursing long-term capital to both developed and developing financial markets. Further, every year, NDBs disburse 20% of their total assets, while MDBs disburse less than 9%. In spite of the constant calls for MDBs to increase their capital, little change has actually taken place over the past decade. Financing by the MDB is mostly politicized, with many countries declining to provide or receive financing. On the flip side, financing from the NDB is typically provided locally, indicating a country's ability to fund its own development. This difference is critical in appreciating the significant role that NDBs play and are expected to play in economic recovery (Columbia Center on Sustainable Investment, 2021).

2.5 Traditional and New Approaches to Development Finance Institutions

The traditional approach to establishing DFIs was in line with a development philosophy that supported government-led economic development. The DFIs that were created under this view were conceived to implement subsidized credit schemes targeting specific sectors. These institutions operated just like any other government-owned or public enterprises with poor managerial expertise as well as weak financial performance and viability. This approach to DFIs led to a poor credit culture characterized by reliance on subsidies, high default rates, undiversified portfolios and mis-targeted credit allocation (Yaron et al., 1998).

Many of these DFIs tended to rely mainly on government financial support with no incentives to seek alternative sources of funding. Moreover, considering that they were focused on providing credit at subsidized rates, they could not raise funds from the capital market at the competitive rates. The financial viability based on the traditional approach to DFIs is threatened by high default rates resulting from the fact that the targeted borrowers have low levels of income and tend to engage in risky activities. The reason for the high default rates is high political influence which often undermines the lending operations of these DFIs. In most cases, provision of credit by the DFIs is based largely on political consideration as opposed to economic development objectives, thus transforming these DFIs into an avenue of wealth accumulation and rent-seeking for the political class (Ndikumana, 2006).

Promoting successful DFIs in Africa entails a paradigm shift which involves a totally new focus in approach that takes into consideration the following: (1) ensuring financial viability of the DFIs and their lending programmes and (2) creating an environment that fosters financial intermediation in traditionally marginalized sectors, especially the rural sector that focuses on agriculture and non-agricultural activities, and the informal sector, comprising small and medium enterprises (SMEs). Creating an environment that fosters financial intermediation requires establishing an environment that creates incentives for financial institutions to venture into new areas and activities. There are a number of policy initiatives that the government could undertake to promote or develop such an environment.

In the first place, the government can strengthen the legal framework in such a way as to enforce creditor rights, which reduces credit risk. Also, the government can design and enforce rules regarding ownership of assets, including land, which has direct implications for households' and firms' ability to access credit. For instance, the titling of land ownership enables households and firms to use land as a collateral to apply for loans, thus improving their creditworthiness. Secondly, the government can promote an environment that fosters financial intermediation by consolidating macroeconomic policy and establishing a regulatory environment that is investment-friendly. Sound macroeconomic policy minimizes uncertainty and encourages financial institutions and borrowers to engage in long-term lending and investment. Prudential regulation of the financial system reduces exposure to systematic risk, which protects both borrowers and depositors. It is obvious that a sound and stable banking system is necessary for developing a solid network of DFIs that become an important source of long-term financing (Ndikumana, 2006).

2.6 Conditions for Successful Development Finance Institutions in Africa

There is a need for African countries to consider adopting a number of strategies and guiding principles to improve the performance and viability of DFIs on the continent. Ndikumana (2006) identified some of the key requirements for establishing sound and effective DFIs, which include the integration of DFIs into the national development agenda; appropriate governance systems; efficient operating procedures; implementation of cost recovery policies; and creative strategies for mobilizing stable long-term funds. These are discussed below.

2.6.1 Integration into National Development Agenda

Increasing national DFIs' contributions to economic development requires the need to design the national development plan taking into consideration the specific roles of these institutions in the funding and implementation of the various components of the plan. This requires that, first, DFIs should be given specific mandates in relation to the specific sectors they should focus on and the implied distribution of resources across activities. Secondly, the government must develop a clear monitoring system to evaluate the performance of DFIs vis-à-vis their specific mandates. Thirdly, the government must design an incentive scheme that rewards high-performing DFIs and penalizes underperforming ones. This would be useful in motivating national DFIs to contribute to economic development. A well-designed incentive mechanism would be useful in motivating national DFIs to contribute to economic development. This approach prevents government or political interference in the operations and credit allocation function of national DFIs, which is not sustainable in the long run.

2.6.2 Appropriate Governance System

An appropriate and efficient governance system is necessary for the success of DFIs, which is a key condition for their sustainability. In this regard, it is important for DFIs to be given a high degree of managerial autonomy, especially political autonomy. They also need a management team with the requisite know-how and high-quality staff. National DFIs or NDBs are mostly managed in the same manner as other state-owned enterprises, and as a result, suffer from political interference in managerial and credit decisions. Appointments of management and staff are mostly not based on merit but on political considerations, thus undermining efficiency. The new approach to DFIs requires these institutions to operate under principles of efficiency, just like commercial banks or other private financial institutions. It is, however, important to note that DFIs need to balance their social and developmental objectives with profit-making objectives. DFIs are interested in pursuing the objectives of profit and development impact.

2.6.3 Efficient Operating Procedures

Adopting efficient operating procedures is a necessary condition for successful DFIs in Africa, which is critical in ensuring their financial viability. Yaron et al. (1998) outlined a number of strategies to achieve this objective, including:

- *Establishment of low-cost delivery systems*: DFIs must seek to minimize the costs of delivering financial services. Adopting modern banking techniques, including ICT and financial innovations, would be useful in achieving this objective.
- *Mobile banking services*: DFIs can improve their reach by extending their service delivery to the customer in addition to the conventional services offered at bank branches. Mobile banking services assist development banks, for instance, to reach potential customers who may ordinarily not be able to access banking services due to transportation costs and other limitations.
- *Flexible loan terms*: DFIs need to adopt flexible loan terms, considering the fact that they mainly serve low-income earners. Given their mandate, DFIs are interested in reaching many underserving sectors, but they are equally important in minimizing default rate.
- *Close monitoring of loan performance*: Loan recovery is also a critical strategy to financial viability of national DFIs. Therefore, DFIs need to establish critical mechanisms and tools for monitoring loan recovery performance in addition to the strategies for addressing the identified weaknesses.

2.6.4 *Ensuring Cost Recovery Policies*

The inability of DFIs to recover their costs is one of the causes of their failure. Considering the fact that DFIs provide credit on a concessionary basis, political influence that causes DFIs to offer credit at even much cheaper rates to politically-connected persons makes it difficult for DFIs to recover their costs and therefore post profits. The new approach requires that DFIs aim at formulating lending policies that ensure cost recovery of funds and also avoid or minimize political influence. Even if loans are provided on a concessionary basis, they should be pegged at rates that enable DFIs to recover their costs and even break even, provided that development impact is achieved. Thus, the ability of DFIs to recover their costs enables them to serve many unbanked or unserved.

2.6.5 *Mobilizing Stable Long-Term Funds*

The success of DFIs is also dependent on the contribution they make in financing long-term investment in both the private and public sectors (public investment), in addition to their contribution to enhancing access to finance for the rural and informal sector, including SMEs. In order to achieve these objectives, DFIs need to expand their sources of finance outside of the conventional sources such as governmental budgetary support and donor funding. One important way is to consider collaborating with private banks in order to mobilize idle liquidity in the banking and corporate sectors into long-term investment funds (Nzobonimpa et al., 2006). DFIs may also consider playing a lead role in establishing regional institutions to be able to attract resources at the regional level, which is in line with improving continental efforts towards regional integration.

2.7 Concluding Remarks

This chapter has given an overview of DFIs, which are financial institutions or development agencies, involved in providing finance for start-ups or development projects in areas in which traditional or commercial banks tend to reluctant to invest, with no guarantee of financial participation. They seek to provide financing for sustainable investment, provide technical services to support sustainable development and also promote responsible investment practices. They contribute significantly to the economic growth in many countries, and they have a stronger impact, especially in developing and low-income countries. The different types of DFIs include: multilateral, regional and bilateral or country-specific DFIs. Multilateral DFIs are private sector branches of international financial institutions established by more than one country. Thus, they are subject to international laws. Regional DFIs are part of multilateral DFIs, but tend to be regionally concentrated and owned by the governments of those regions. Bilateral DFIs belong to the majority of national governments that implement each governments' development policies with foreign or external cooperation. Multilateral, regional and bilateral DFIs complement the efforts of each other in providing long-term financing needs of emerging and developing economies

DFIs in Africa and other developing economies were created with a view to implementing subsidized credit schemes targeted at specific sectors of the economy. However, these institutions operated just like other government-owned enterprises with poor managerial expertise as well as weak financial performance and viability. This resulted in a poor credit culture and high default rates. Promoting successful DFIs in Africa, thus, entails a paradigm shift in the approach, which involves ensuring financial viability of the DFIs and their lending programmes, and also, creating an environment that fosters financial intermediation in traditionally marginalized sectors. A number of key prerequisites are necessary for establishing sound and effective DFIs, including their integration into the national development agenda, appropriate governance, efficient operating procedures, emphasis on cost recovery policies and creative strategies for mobilizing stable long-term finance.

References

Abor, J. Y. (2017). *Entrepreneurial finance for MSMEs*. Palgrave Macmillan.

Abor, J. Y., Adjasi, C. K. D., & Lensink, R. (2020). Introduction to contemporary issues in development finance. In *Contemporary issues in development finance* (pp. 1–19). Routledge.

Amoah, L., Adjasi, C., Soumare, I., Osei, K., Abor, J. Y., Anarfo, E., Amo-Yartey, C., & Otchere, I. (2020). Finance, economic growth, and development, In J. Y. Abor, C. K. D. Adjasi, & R. Lensink (Eds.), *Contemporary issues in development finance* (pp. 20–50). Routledge.

Arestis, P., Chortareas, G., & Magkonis, G. (2015). The financial development and growth nexus: A meta-analysis. *Journal of Economic Surveys, 29*(3), 549–565.

Barro, R. J., & Sala-i-Martin, X. (1998). *Economic growth*. Cambridge, MA: MIT Press.

Columbia Center on Sustainable Investment. (2021). *Development banking in the global economy, state of play and future direction*. ccsi.columbia.edu.

Dalberg. (2009). *The growing role of the development finance institutions in international development policy*. https://www.findevgateway.org/sites/default/files/publications/files/mfg-en-paper-the-growing-role-of-the-development-finance-institutions-in-international-development-policy-2009.pdf

Dickinson, T. (n.d.). *Development finance institutions: Profitability promoting development*. http://www.oecd.org/dev/41302068.pdf

Dixit, A. K., & Pindyck, R. S. (1994). *Investment under uncertainty*. Princeton University Press.

Einhorn, C. S. (2013). Can you fight poverty with a five-star hotel? *Foreign Policy*.

Gerschenkron, A. (1962). *Economic backwardness in historical perspective—A book of essays*. Harvard University Press.

Goldsmith, R. W. (1969). *Financial structure and development*. Yale University Press.

Gurley, J. G., & Shaw, E. S. (1955). Financial aspects of economic development. *The American Economic Review, 45*(4), 515–538.

Levine, R. (1997). Financial development and economic growth: Views and agenda. *Journal of Economic Literature, XXXV*, 688–726.

Mckinnon, R. (1973). *Money and capital in economic development* (1st ed.). Brookings Institution.

Montiel, P. (2003). *Macroeconomics in emerging markets*. Cambridge University Press.

Ndikumana, L. (2006). *Revisiting development finance institutions for the purpose of accelerating*. African Economic Development.

Nzobonimpa, O., Nkurunziza, J. D., & Ndikumana, L. (2006). *Promoting a development-oriented financial system in Burundi* (AERC Research Paper)

Oxfam. (2015). *Billions in "out of control" IFC investments into third-parties causing human rights abuses around the world*. Oxfam International. https://www.oxfam.org/en/pressroom/pressreleases/2015-04-02/billions-out-control-ifc-investments-third-parties-causing-human-rights-abuses

Pagano, M. (1993). Financial markets and growth—An overview. *European Economic Review, 37*, 613–622.

Ruiz, J. L. (2018). Financial development, institutional investors, and economic growth. *International Review of Economics & Finance, 54*, 218–224.

Savoy, C. M., Carter, P., & Lemma, A. (2016). *Development finance institutions come of age, policy engagement, impact, and new direction*. Center for Strategic and International Studies.

Schumpeter, J. A (1934). *The theory of economic development* (R. Opie, Trans.). Harvard University Press (Original work published 1921).
Shaw, E. S. (1973). *Financial deepening in economic development*. Oxford University Press.
te Velde, D. W. (2011). *The role of development finance in tackling global challenges*. Overseas Development Institute.
Yaron, J., Benjamin, M., & Charitenenko, S. (1998). Promoting efficient rural financial intermediation. *The World Bank Research Observer, 13*(2), 147–170.

CHAPTER 3

Theoretical Perspectives and Rationale for National Development Banks

3.1 Introduction

Financing is critical for the development of any economy. Countries in both the developed and developing world require large-scale counter-cyclical financing to drive economic activity and particularly to contribute to sustainable growth and create employment. One of the main mechanisms that has been used by governments and the international community to support this process and achieve growth and development outcomes is development banks. Generally, this type of financial institutions tends to leverage public and private resources to assist in curtailing economic deterioration, support recovery, as well as to finance structural transformation (Columbia Center on Sustainable Investment, 2021).

Development banks are government-sponsored financial institutions that provide long-term and short-term capital and channel long-term capital to support industrialization (de Aghion, 1999). To properly reflect the categories of its members, the broad category can be subdivided into the global, regional, national or global and local mix. The global category includes some governments creating a financial institution to channel funds internationally and may include promoting activities outside their national borders. The regional category is financial institutions set up by particular governments. These institutions are mostly concentrated in a particular region, but may be outside the borders of most of the individual governments. The national category is the vast majority of financial

© The Author(s), under exclusive license to Springer Nature Switzerland AG 2023

J. Yindenaba Abor, *The Changing Role of National Development Banks in Africa*, https://doi.org/10.1007/978-3-031-38639-8_3

institutions that extend funding in their national territories or beyond. This category is further refined to distinguish those whose operation is confined to national territories from those whose mandates allow them to offer finance abroad. The local category is not very common, and they are established by national authorities to serve the needs of their local authorities.

NDBs have great potential to support the development goals of their countries (Griffith-Jones et al., 2020) and are sometimes partners of international DFIs. NDBs have some unique advantages that integrate well within the public sector and are well connected to the national or domestic private sector. This gives them the incentive to back the execution of government development strategies (Attridge et al., 2021). The multilateral, regional and bilateral DFIs may not get involved with the activities of NDBs due to their high dependence of national governments and political interference. Thus, NDBs have political embeddedness that gives them comparative advantages over multilateral or regional development banks (Attridge et al., 2021).

This chapter examines theoretical perspectives and rationale for establishing NDBs. The remainder of the chapter is structured as follows: Sect. 3.2 provides a historical background of NDBs. Section 3.3 discusses the structural challenges NDBs seek to address. Section 3.4 examines the theoretical perspectives for NDBs. Section 3.5 discusses the prevailing policy views, need and rationale for establishing NDBs, and finally, Sect. 3.6 concludes the chapter.

3.2 Historical Background of National Development Banks

Since the end of World War I, countries across the globe and the international community have attempted to bridge the gap in long-term financing through the establishment of NDBs and multilateral development banks (MDBs). In spite of their common name and objective, MDBs and NDBs offer unique abilities in financing sustainable development (Columbia Center on Sustainable Investment, 2021). NDBs trace their historical roots to the Bretton Woods agreement in 1944, which was influenced by the work of John Keynes and Europe's reconstruction plans after World War II (Skidelsky, 2011). The objective was to establish an institution for promoting financial stability through a permanent supply of funds for the reconstruction agenda and support agricultural production, thereby preventing the damaging impact of private finance on post-World War II economic recovery. This was followed by the creation of the International Bank for Reconstruction and Development (IBRD), with the provision of its first loan in 1947 to France (World Bank, 2013b). In fact, a number of NDBs were established prior to the end of World War II, but most of them were also created at different times after World War II. About half (49%) NDBs were established during the period, 1946–1989, whereas 39% were set up during the period, 1990–2011 (Chandrasekhar, 2016). For instance, the KfW in Germany was established in 1948 with the aim of channeling funds for promoting long-term growth, infrastructure development and modern industry. In the developed world, NDBs focused on niche areas, while those in developing economies, such as the Brazil's BNDES (which was founded in 1953), initially focused on promoting a plan of catching up (Mazzucato & Penna, 2018; Torres Filho & Costa, 2012).

The 1950s marked the golden age of NDBs, when developing economies pursued a rapid industrialization drive. This continued through the 1980s, when a wave of privatizations led to the privatization of over 250 state-owned banks (Meggison, 2004). The Washington Consensus curtailed the role of NDBs in the development of domestic capital markets (Bruck, 1998). In fact, there is an aspect of the extant literature that describes NDBs as being inefficient and market-distorting (La Porta et al., 2002; World Bank, 2013a). La Porta et al. (2002), for instance, argue that any form of government ownership of banks results in slowing down financial development. In the literature, the work of Bond (2013) suggests that NDBs are associated with lack of transparency and have the tendency to favour certain economic groups, and their credits are associated with high levels of subsidy. Nonetheless, NDBs are considered necessary for addressing the failure of the financial market by providing long-term finance, and their proponents stress their relevance in driving economic development (Gutierrez et al., 2011). The China Development Bank (CDB), which was founded in 1994, was perceived as one of the active NDBs and by the year 2000, was investing in regional economic development and industrial catching up. It was focused on supporting and nurturing new ventures and innovation development and in later years, began focusing on financing green growth-related projects (Sanderson & Forsythe, 2013).

Indeed, after the 2007/2008 global financial crisis, a number of countries reconsidered NDBs as a means of smoothing the impact of the liquidity and credit squeeze caused by the crisis. Globally, NDBs supported counter-cyclical financing by scaling up their loan portfolio on average by 36 percent during the period 2007–2009, with about 10 percent of them increasing their loans by over 100 percent. NDBs are considered ubiquitous and they offer an important source of long-term finance in several countries (de Luna-Martinez & Vicente, 2012; Gutierrez et al., 2011). Most countries that have found it necessary to establish NDBs provide long-term capital at near-commercial rates and 'policy banks' to provide credit to specific sectors, including agriculture or the small-scale sector, which require long-term financing at subsidized interest rates. The emergence of NDBs has mainly been a result of failure of private financial markets to provide suitable long-term finance. The failure of financial markets has forced many governments to rely on development banks. Bruck (1998) in his study identified a number of development banks, globally, including NDBs, multilateral, regional and sub-regional development banks. These development banks were found in 185 countries, with developing countries having about three or more NDBs each. Latin America and the Caribbean are said to host the highest number of NDBs, followed by Africa, Asia and the Pacific, Europe and West Asia (Chandrasekhar, 2016).

Over time, there has been a change in the roles of NDBs, from serving as a means of achieving industrialization to focusing on more varied objectives (Torres & Zeidan, 2016). NDBs at all levels continue to be ignored even among finance experts. However, the impact of the COVID-19 crisis has caused renewed interest in the importance of NDBs in addressing economic shocks. NDBs are estimated to have a combined asset size of about US$ 8.5 trillion, which is equivalent to around 50% of the total assets of the US banking industry (Columbia Center on Sustainable Investment, 2021).

In fact, the evolution of NDBs varied across countries and regions. In Chapter 2, we provided an overview of the landscape of African NDBs. From Chapters 9–14, the specific historical backgrounds of NDBs are provided for selected countries, including Ghana, Côte d'Ivoire, Rwanda, South Africa, Zimbabwe and Tunisia.

3.3 Structural Challenges National Development Banks Seek to Address

There are three reasons why structural challenges motivate African countries to establish NDBs. The first reason is to correct the failure of the capital market. Financial markets and institutions are expanding in Africa, although their overall size remains modest. Despite the strong growth, the proportion of African economies in 2022 was lower than that of advanced economies in 1980. Growth was slow in low-income countries. More importantly, institutional investors, including pension funds, insurance companies and mutual funds, have been identified as potential investors in development projects in the region. However, the size of these investors in large African economies exceeds 40% of GDP, which is a small percentage compared to developed countries. In addition, efforts by international development finance organizations to raise private capital have so far been limited (and a good example is infrastructure financing). Many African economies are now correcting capital market failures by organizing their NDBs. For African economies, earmarking credit through NDBs is important for financing long-term projects that hitherto would not be funded because of the failure of financial markets. Many poor countries within the region have difficulties in accessing finance for long-term projects except by mobilizing from the domestic financial markets or global financial institutions (Torres & Zeidan, 2016).

In addition, the reduced role of official development assistance (ODA) and tax revenues means that the government needs to seek extra-budgetary financial resources, such as those of the NDBs, to implement development projects. The considerable volume of ODA aimed at stimulating economic development has not really been effective. The relevance of ODA in alleviating poverty and facilitating long-term growth has been largely disappointing in past years (Ocran et al., 2020). Tax revenue generation has also not been adequate in supporting governments' development agenda. This situation has often been attributed to a low level of compliance, a high level of informality, a complicated tax system and corruption in the tax administration system, especially in developing economies like Africa. The existence of NDBs becomes essential under these circumstances.

Also, NDBs have contributed to national development, serving as policy tools that enable governments to overcome legal and political constraints on financial management. In addition to this factor, fiscal redistribution is often difficult because current fiscal structures reflect past political and social struggle for priorities. In particular, governments are more likely to provoke public discontent when trying to divert large amounts of tax revenue from consumer spending to capital investment. This prospect may leave governments inactive, especially in democracies where elected officials begin to focus on the next election from their first day in power. NDBs have been used by executives to circumvent legal and political difficulties in mobilizing tax resources in countries such as France and Korea (Kim, 2018). Due to the limited role of private funds and donors, the domestic institutional difficulties in expanding tax investments, as well as the conduct of the theoretical and ideological battle for state economic activity, NDBs' interest in the developing world is expected to continue. The efficient operation of NDBs requires a certain degree of technical knowledge, market information and coordination ability. However, NDBs need to be encouraged in the face of potential challenges.

In the World Bank (2017) survey of NDBs, several challenges were identified, which include: their ability to manage risk; becoming financially independent and self-sustaining; improving their corporate governance structure and transparency; gaining more flexibility in recruiting and retaining highly qualified personnel; and reducing undue political influence (see World Bank, 2018). NDBs serve a wide range of customers that the private sector cannot reach due to high risks or operating costs. They serve small owners, start-ups, small and medium enterprises (SMEs) or firms operating in new sectors of the economy, as well as low-income families in rural or remote areas. Finding the right balance in risk management can be a challenge for them. In addition, an individual bank may have minimal access to relevant information about the market positions it serves. For example, it will have limited information on production costs, business penetration, the number of market participants, the market niche, the level of competition between companies, the historical company performance rates and the failure percentages of companies that serve this market niche. They may not have a full appreciation of the risks their customers are exposed to. Price volatility, natural disasters, insufficient infrastructure to store goods, cost and time to resolve commercial disputes between private parties can be a challenge. Accessing financial instruments (loan guarantees, insurance products and financial derivative instruments) from the NDB to mitigate credit or market risks can be difficult. Again, the individual bank faces challenges such as: the ability to adapt its financial instruments to its customers' business needs (e.g., repayment terms, payments and repayment schedules); internal guidelines and instruments that allow the bank to limit credit risk and negotiability according to the type, region or activity of the customer; effective analytical tools to monitor the performance of its loan portfolio; and effective ways to collect loans (World Bank, 2018).

3.4 Theoretical Perspectives for National Development Banks

The financial sector has performed well in both developing and developed countries over the last several decades, dating back to post-World War II. However, there were political fears regarding 'financially repressed' structures that were ineffective. In theory, the idea of 'efficient financial markets' promoted financial liberalization with little or no regulation.[1] In the context of 'efficient financial markets', the presence of public financial institutions was viewed as virtually passive development banks. As a result, development banks were considered to be almost passive and they have faced both fair and unfair criticism. In line with the criticism, some have argued that the development of the financial conditions in the community is enhanced when a company's profits grow properly, which implies that finance does not lead to economic growth, but rather it responds to the demand emerging from the real sector (Lucas, 1988; Miller, 1988; Robinson, 1952). This has been popularly referred to as the 'demand-following hypothesis'. They explained that the basis of good economic growth tends to favour the development of the financial sector. Conversely, others have argued that the financial sector is able to foster economic growth due to its accessible capital boost. The implication is that the financial sector plays a significant role in economic growth through their function of capital accumulation and through facilitating investment and savings (see Goldsmith, 1969; Gurley & Shaw, 1955; Mckinnon, 1973, 1993; Romer, 1989; Stiglitz & Greenwald, 2003; Stiglitz & Uy, 1996; Stiglitz & Weiss, 1981). This has also been popularized as the 'supply-leading hypothesis'. In the context of the demand-following hypothesis, the role of the financial sector, especially the banks, has drastically diminished in several countries. An alternative

[1] Gurley and Shaw (1955) and McKinnon (1993).

approach emphasizes credit rationing, which explains a situation in which banks may refuse to finance, even if agents are willing to offer a higher interest rate on funds to finance their investments. In this sense, the credit rationing approach substantiates the presence of development banks that deliver the required credit for investments that are not obtainable in the private financial system.

The first critical method reflects the theory of market failure.[2] Credit rationing is the result of an imbalance in financial markets, due to a lack of information or inconsistent information, which impedes the proper functioning of financial markets. When borrowers have more information than lenders about the expected performance of their business, the demand for credit will be greater than the supply, but interest rate hikes will not change. In addition, adverse selection and moral hazard exacerbate this market failure, which is likely to be endemic as these markets are mainly information-intensive (see Abor et al., 2020; Stiglitz & Weiss, 1981). This makes the information inconsistent and makes incomplete contracts in other areas of the economy. Therefore, in most financial markets, market failures outweigh government failures. Under such circumstances, government intervention is considered more desirable than in other sectors when the benefits exceed the costs. This first basis is a solid argument for public development banks and can be the bases for a strict regulation of the private financial markets.

From a complementary theoretical perspective, many commentators argue that both investors and banks prefer liquidity, which is responsible for limiting the supply of credit to the economy. Even with well-developed national and international financial systems, there may be a lack of investment credit. Hence, the importance of the development bank goes beyond 'market failure', although it may include it (Atkinson & Stiglitz, 1980; Ndikumana et al., 2021). Due to uncertainty about the future, banks often do not lend or provide sufficient (particularly, long-term) credit, even in a developed financial system. Consequently, the existence of development banks is justified by the presence of sectors or investment projects that require long-term financing for the future development of the economy but which are associated with great uncertainty about their future success. Hence, they cannot be financed by the private financial system, which favours sectors or investment projects with expected

[2] Stiglitz and Weiss (1981).

returns that are relatively certain. These sectors or projects are often very complex and expensive and require special expertise in assessing the positive effects on the economy as a whole (positive externalities) and/or those in which social returns exceed private returns (Atkinson & Stiglitz, 1980; Ndikumana et al., 2021).

A major disadvantage for the functioning of financial markets in general is the 'boom and bust' cycle. Based on the theoretical foundations of Keynes and Kindleberger, who developed an analysis that sees the financial crisis as a reaction to past excesses, it is clear that these excesses appear to be much larger in more liberal and poorly regulated banking and financial markets. The pro-cyclical nature of private funding suggests that public development banks are essential in providing counter-cyclical funding, especially in the short-term and long-term (Griffith-Jones & Ocampo, 2014).

The world has entered a new era of the sustainable development goals after 2015. This includes fighting poverty, inclusive economic growth, education for all, full employment, reducing income inequality, fighting poverty, fighting climate change and promoting the sustainable use of global ecosystems. Economic transformation is crucial to making these social, economic and ecological goals viable and sustainable. Economic change requires long-term investments to support capacity expansion, as well as building infrastructure that supports industrial activities and reduces bottlenecks. The period after World War II led to the emergence of the World Bank and regional banks. Since their inception, these banks have played significant roles in financing for the regional and global public goods, and promoting long-term financing in developing countries. Despite their size, their aggregate credit volume is limited.[3] The lack of funding is not due to a global savings deficit, but rather to the fact that most savings are held in the form of assets from developed countries offering low returns. Some of these savings can be used for long-term investments in the real economy. The bottom line is that new and existing development banks need to bridge the gap between end-user funding and development projects. Development banks must provide support at all levels—national, regional and international—in order to meet the financial needs of developing countries. Hence, NDBs play a critical role in supporting the growth of these countries.

[3] Intergovernmental Committee of Experts on Sustainable Development Financing (2014).

3.5 Policy Views, Need and Rationale for National Development Banks

NDBs serve as a means by which the government intervenes in the financial system, with the objective of dealing with market failures in the supply of finance. They provide finance to segments of the market that have limited or no access to the financial system. These market segments include projects with social benefits exceeding commercial benefits; long-term projects; new or risky ventures (including new technologies); projects situated in poor or distant regions; and MSMEs with no collateral. In essence, while public finance may be allocated to projects with no possibility of cost recovery, private finance is allocated to projects that have the objective of making profits. Development banks tend to fill the gap between these two positions. They target long-term projects with high risk that can generate limited returns. Development banks seek to lower the risks of such projects and crowd-in private sector investment. Apart from providing financing, NDBs also offer developmental services including, advocacy, technical assistance and research.

3.5.1 Prevailing Policy Views of Establishing National Development Banks

The extant literature identifies four main policy views regarding the purpose for establishing development banks, which include the industrial policy view, the social policy view, the political policy view or orthodox political view, and the dynamic view (Marois, 2022; Musacchio & Lazzarini, 2014; Yeyati et al., 2004). Each of these policy views presents a different perspective on the role that governments, through NDBs, play in addressing market failures. Also, each of these policy views provides a different set of expectations in terms of which financial instruments are suitable for achieving specific objectives.

3.5.1.1 Industrial Policy View

The industrial policy view suggests that development banks were created in response to market failures in the provision of the required financing for entrepreneurial activity and industrialization (de Aghion, 1999; Gerschenkron, 1962). The industrial policy view is based generally on the assumption that industrialization and entrepreneurial activity will drive economic growth, thus improving overall welfare. With respect to this view, capital market constraints are perceived as factors inhibiting entrepreneurship, and financing for infrastructure development to support industrialization may also be lacking. The constraint in terms of lack of long-term financing is in respect of large industrial and infrastructure projects (Gerschenkron, 1962), as well as financing of the discovery of new technologies and productive processes to support new ventures (Hausmann & Rodrik, 2003). In addition, asymmetric information and the risk associated with such projects leads to high interest rates, which serve as a deterrent for investors. High asymmetric information is more pronounced with respect to small investors looking for private sector finance. On the other hand, medium- to long-term loans address the duration constraint on financing, and government's funding for NDBs offers lower-than-market interest rates, which in essence, subsidizes the infrastructure cost of industrial projects. In addition to providing patient capital, NDBs also provide guarantees that serve to unlock private sector capital for development projects (Riding & Haines, 2001; Zecchini & Ventura, 2009).

3.5.1.2 Social Policy View

In terms of the social policy view, the government intervenes in the capital markets in order to address certain social issues such as unemployment, lack of housing and energy dependency (Shapiro & Willig, 1990; Shirley, 1999). With respect to the social policy view, development banks leverage their competitive financing to support firms to recognize their roles in contributing to social issues. As a result, as policy banks, NDBs may provide financing for negative net present value (NPV) projects with significant positive social externalities (Shapiro & Willig, 1990; Yeyati et al., 2004). NDBs tend to focus on long-term, subsidized credit, as an essential tool in promoting socially beneficial projects. NDBs may also rely on equity financing to support the establishment and growth of firms with the main aim of addressing relevant social issues, including financing a new venture in an underdeveloped region and financing the growth of businesses that have a huge potential for job creation. NDBs may be interested in new employment creation, irrespective of the productive structure of new jobs (De Negri et al., 2011). The social policy view holds that NDBs use both debt financing and equity financing to support the growth and development of firms while taking cognizance of the prioritization of different social objectives.

The social policy view is related to the ***heterodox development view*** of development banks. The heterodox development view is said to be typically advanced by Keynesian economists, and this view of NDBs or public banks is characteristically positive. The thinking here is that public banks are able and willing to facilitate economic development in ways that private banks are unwilling or not able to do, especially with respect to longer-term projects and less profitable but no less socially-significant sectors and the public good (Bennett & Sharpe, 1980; Gerschenkron, 1962; Marois, 2022). The heterodox development view holds that public banks need to be very active when there are market failures coupled with a need to intervene without competing with the private sector. They need to function where there is poor institutional development in order to support private sector financial growth. Others also argue that public banks should go beyond market failures and financial gaps to engage in other activities such as regulating competitive markets, creating new markets and effecting counter-cyclically during times of instability (Marois, 2022; Mazzucato & Penna, 2016).

3.5.1.3 Political Policy View

The political policy view also indicates that development banks are set up mainly as instruments to serve the interest of politicians or as a means of rewarding politically-connected industrialists (Ades & Di Tella, 1997; Shleifer & Vishny, 1998). The orthodox political view is usually advanced by neoclassical economists and liberal political economists, and this view of NDBs or public banks is characteristically negative. Advocates of this view suggest that governments acquire control of enterprises and banks with the aim of providing employment, subsidies and other benefits to supporters, who return the favour in other forms such as votes, political contributions and bribes (La Porta et al., 2002; Marois, 2022). NDBs or public banks are seen as political firms that are 'predestined for political uses' and so become 'subject to political interference from the political class, special pressure or interest groups' (Marcelin & Mathur, 2015). Under the political policy view, the investment criteria used by NDBs move away from addressing the financing gaps in the capital market or providing direct financing to rather fund preferred projects of political actors. In some cases, such projects tend to lack the objectives set out under the industrial policy and social policy views. This results in the misallocation of funds, leading to distortions in the financial and labour markets. There are two hypotheses that explain how the misallocation may occur and these are the soft-budget constraint hypothesis and the rent-seeking hypothesis.

The first, which is the soft-budget constraint hypothesis, suggests that NDBs are used to' 'bail out' failing firms (Kornai, 1979). In contrast to the industrial policy view that considers government subsidies for stimulating investment and development, the soft-budget constraint hypothesis involves the use of subsidy, guarantees and/or long-term credit serve to direct funds towards inefficient market players instead of efficient ones. This tends to restrict capital that could otherwise be applied more productively, thus weakening incentives for firms to achieve the industrial and/ or social objectives outlined under the industrial policy and social policy views (Shleifer & Vishny, 1998).

The second hypothesis under the political policy view is the rent-seeking hypothesis, which tends to present a slightly more nuanced form of misallocation. Unlike the industrial policy view and the social policy view, where subsidies and long-term lending enable NDBs to facilitate optimal productive investment, in the case of political policy view, these are rather subverted to projects that are not inhibited by gaps in the capital markets. Even though projects could be financed by investors through the capital markets, NDB funds are used through 'cronyism,' a behaviour that rewards political supporters with easier access to government funds. This behaviour could also enable high-powered industrialists to benefit from strategic political leveraging and thus access loans from NDBs at more competitive terms (Ades & Di Tella, 1997; Claessens et al., 2008).

3.5.1.4 An Alternative Dynamic View

A dynamic view is a theory of development based on the framework where the social or industrial forces shape and reshape the institutional functions of public banks, which in turn changes the meaning of being a public bank in a time- or place-bound context (Ho & Marois, 2019; Marois, 2021; Marois & Güngen, 2016; McDonald et al., 2020). A dynamic view interprets NDBs as institutions in the '*public spheres of states or public sector*' (i.e., the space within national states where governing authorities can (if not necessarily) exercise power, influence, control and privilege over public institutions) within '*global financialized capitalism*'. This concept provides the framework for NDBs to connect the shifting strategies or mandates of social forces (individual or collective forces that act or react in the public or private interest) to the institutional functions and the reproduction of public banks within the boundaries of capitalism. At first glance, 'NDBs are institutions that are developed and evolved within a societal whole, acted upon and acting onto larger and smaller scales of existence' (Hanieh 2018, p. 15; Ho, 2017, pp. 9–10). It is within the public sphere that governing authorities can shape or reshape what NDBs do, how they function and for whom. In the same vein, the social forces can also influence and shape NDBs through the public sphere and/or can make NDBs function as though they were private profit-seeking financial institutions or banks (i.e., corporatized) (Marois, 2012; McDonald, 2016; McDonald et al., 2021). This explains why NDBs have acquired functions seemingly unique to public banks, but are not in and of themselves derived from being publicly owned.

The public sphere is internally linked to the state and class-divided society, and the states could be more complex than the public sphere, but not independent of capitalist markets. Thus, NDBs and their functions in society evolved within capitalism (Marois, 2021). Proponents of the dynamic view explain how private investors and development partners seek to bend NDBs to ensure their own accumulation results in a strategic response to any form of crisis in financing or climate finance. The alternative dynamic view attempts to explain how the conditions of institutional existence and reproduction of NDBs can be leveraged differently through the lens of public and private interests (see Palermo, 2019). Thus, the alternative dynamic view can describe NDBs as 'dynamic and socially constructed and reconstructed institutional social relations that reflect historically specific relations of power and reproduction between banks, firms, states, and contentious individual and collective social forces' (Marois, 2010, 2021, 2022). Therefore, NDBs are development banks whose functions are subject to the pull of interests from the public and private in a class-divided society, each attempting to shape for whom the bank is mandated to function. This positions NDBs in four dimensions, including: having a binding public mandate and mission and operating under public law; performing financial intermediation and banking functions without policy orientation; functioning in both public and private interests; and functioning in the dimension that allows them to think as a credible, contested and evolving institution (Ho, 2020). By contrast, these dimensions set NDBs in a capitalist society that acquire multiple institutional functions within states under the shadow of capitalism.

3.5.2 *The Need and Rationale for National Development Banks*

The need and rationale for the establishment of NDBs have been well justified by both developed and developing countries. NDBs started in early 1946, when developing countries in many regions including Africa sought long-term financing to support industrial development. Over the period until now, the NDBs have been an important part of the development finance structure in most developing countries. NDBs play a significant role in mobilizing resources from the public and private sectors to support new investments across the globe, and their continued success will be crucial in achieving more sustainable economic growth in the future. Development banks provide financing for long-term investments, such as capital-intensive industries. In addition, these banks offer loans and equity investments, which means that they have a clear interest in following the projects closely and thus establishing a special form of banking relationship. They help counteract the pro-cyclical nature of the private financial system, which leads to higher credit demand in times of expansion and to credit rationing in times of crisis. The private sector often does not provide enough funding for innovative small businesses and infrastructure projects, a gap that NDBs tend to bridge. In addition to financing projects, NDBs also help create and develop new market niches, develop innovative programmes to attract and manage private sector resources for large infrastructure projects and the development of industrial capacity. They design and structure new investment projects as well as facilitate the establishment of public–private partnerships. They also support the numerous investments in innovative activities, loans to small producers and environmental projects that are required to make the economy more dynamic, inclusive and sustainable. While governments provide their own paid-up capital, NDBs raise capital in the domestic and international capital markets. In addition, loans from NDBs, often co-financed by the private sector, can be particularly beneficial for governments faced with budgetary constraints during and after a financial crisis. The global financial crisis and the COVID-19 pandemic have led some African, European and Asian governments to create new NDBs, while others have expanded their scope.

The development finance paradigm has shifted towards a balanced public–private mix for providing long-term finance. In a broader sense, development banks play crucial roles including counteracting the pro-cyclical behaviour of the private financial sector, promoting innovation and structural change, strengthening financial inclusion, supporting the financing of infrastructure investments and supporting the promoting the public good. It is interesting to recognize that the World Bank, which has been quite critical of NDBs in the past (see Stiglitz & Greenwald, 2003; Stiglitz & Uy, 1996; Stiglitz & Weiss, 1981), has increasingly supported development banks, especially since the 2007/2008 crisis (de Luna-Martinez & Vicente, 2012; La Porta et al., 2002). The literature provides the important role that NDBs have played in financing industrial development in both advanced and emerging countries (Epstein & Dutt, 2018). For instance, the World Bank (2018) provided evidence that NDBs stimulate domestic investment, boost output growth and employment and help cushion the negative implications of economic shocks and have helped speed up economic recovery, including that of the 2007/ 2008 Global Financial Crisis.

More recently, NDBs have helped in speeding up the recovery from economic crises occasioned by the COVID-19 pandemic (McDonald et al., 2020; Uğurlu & Epstein, 2021). The COVID-19 crisis has caused severe harm to economies and financial systems around the world, including Africa, and calls for the implementation of prompt and ambitious policy responses and reforms in the financial system, including promoting the establishment of NDBs. This will help to ensure soundness and stability to drive growth (Abor et al., 2022). NDBs have the mandate and capacity to support the financing of both the post-COVID-19 recovery and longer-term global sustainable development efforts. The national and domestic nature of NDBs suggests that they mostly operate in a domestic policy vacuum. Both developing and developed countries continue to establish them with the mandate of expanding infrastructure finance, providing financing for new types of environmentally friendly projects and mobilizing additional financing to meet developmental objectives. There is clearly a need for a concerted effort at scaling up and directing NDBs' financing in addressing both the severe impact of the COVID-19 pandemic and its structural impact (Columbia Center on Sustainable Investment, 2021). The Department of IMF Fiscal Affairs has indicated that some NDBs, mostly the public banks, if financially sound and sufficiently resourced, could be employed to complement such efforts specifically in situations where the private banks are unwilling to provide lending (IMF, 2020).

3.6 Concluding Remarks

The issue of financing has been identified as critical in driving the growth and development of any economy, while the establishment of NDBs is seen as an important mechanism for supporting this process. NDBs tend to leverage public and private resources to help curtail economic deterioration, support recovery and finance structural transformation. This chapter examined theoretical perspectives and rationale for establishing NDBs. It has provided a historical background of NDBs and has specifically discussed the structural challenges that NDBs seek to address. The chapter has also examined the theoretical perspectives that have been proposed to motivate the existence of NDBs. It has further examined the prevailing policy views, the need for and the rationale for establishing NDBs. The golden age of NDBs actually started in the 1950s, when developing countries pursued a rapid industrialization drive. This continued through the 1980s, when a wave of privatizations led to many state-owned banks being privatized. The renewed interest in the importance of NDBs in the economy is supported even by the Work Bank, which was previously opposed to the idea. The impact of the 2008 global financial crisis, coupled with the impact of the COVID-19 crisis, has brought renewed interest in the importance of NDBs in addressing the economic shocks.

The structural challenges that have motivated African countries to mobilize NDBs include the failure of the capital market, the reduced role of ODA and tax revenues, and the legal and political constraints on financial management. There are two main theoretical perspectives of NDBs: the theory of market failure and the complementary theoretical perspective. The theory of market failure suggests the limitations of the capital market in providing long-term financing, which necessitates the use of NDBs to fill the financing gap. From a complementary perspective, the presence of NDBs is justified by the existence of sectors or investment projects that require funding beyond the private financial system, but are associated with great uncertainty about their future success. The procyclical nature of private funding suggests that NDBs become necessary in providing counter-cyclical funding, as well as financing the SDGs.

The literature identifies three main policy views regarding the purpose of establishing development banks: the industrial policy view, the social policy view and the political policy view. The industrial policy view suggests that development banks were created in response to market failures in the provision of the required financing for entrepreneurial activity and industrialization. With respect to the social policy view, the government intervenes in the capital markets in order to deal with specific social issues such as unemployment, lack of housing and energy dependency. The political policy view also indicates that development banks are set up mainly as instruments to serve the interest of politicians or as a means of rewarding politically-connected industrialists. The need and rationale for the establishment of NDBs have been well justified by both developed and developing countries. NDBs are necessary in mobilizing resources from the public and private sectors to support new investments around the world. There is evidence to suggest that NDBs stimulate domestic investment and boost output growth and employment, and they help cushion the negative implications of economic shocks and have helped speed up the recovery of the 2007/2008 Global Financial Crisis. In addition, NDBs have recently helped in speeding up the recovery of economic crisis caused by the COVID-19 pandemic.

References

Abor, J. Y., Adjasi, C. K. D., & Lensink, R. (2020). Introduction to contemporary issues in development finance. In J. Y. Abor, C. K. D. Adjasi, & R. Lensink (Eds.), *Contemporary issues in development finance* (pp. 1–19). Routledge.

Abor, J. Y., Agbloyor, E. K., Donkor, G. N. A., & Alu, A. A. (2022). The COVID-19 pandemic and Africa's financial systems: How do we reform post-COVID-19 financial systems? In *The economics of banking and finance in Africa: Developments in Africa's financial systems* (pp. 1013–1037). Springer.

Ades, A., & Di Tella, R. (1997). The new economics of corruption: A survey and some new results. *Political Studies, 45*(3), 496–515.

Atkinson, A. B., & Stiglitz, J. (1980). *Lectures on public economics*. McGraw-Hill.

Attridge, S., Chen, Y., & Mbate, M. (2021). *Financial performance and corporate governance: Evidence from national development banks in Africa* (ODI Report).

Bennett, D., & Sharpe, K. (1980). The state as banker and entrepreneur: The last-resort character of the mexican state's economic intervention, 1917–76. *Comparative Politics, 12*(2), 165–189.

Bond, P. (2013). *The BRICS bank and shifts in multilateral finance: A view from South Africa*. Presented at the SouthGovNet conference panel: Institutions of South-South Cooperation. Fudan University Institute of International Relations, Shanghai, China.

Bruck, N. (1998). The role of development banks in the twenty-first century. *Journal of Emerging Markets, 3*, 39–68.

Chandrasekhar, C. (2016). National development banks in a comparative perspective. In A. Calcagno, S. Dullien, A. Marquez-Velasquez, N. Maystre, & J. Priewe (Eds.), *Rethinking development strategies after the financial crisis, Volume II—Country studies and international comparisons* (1st ed., pp. 21–30). UNCTAD.

Claessens, S., Feijen, E., & Laeven, L. (2008). Political connections and preferential access to finance: The role of campaign contributions. *Journal of Financial Economics, 88*(3), 554–580.

Columbia Center on Sustainable Investment. (2021). *Development banking in the global economy, state of play and future direction*. ccsi.columbia.edu

De Negri, J. A., Maffioli, A., Rodriguez, C. M., & Vázquez, G. (2011). *The impact of public credit programs on Brazilian firms* (No. IDB-WP-293). IDB Working Paper Series.

de Luna-Martinez, J., & Vicente, C. L. (2012, February). *Global survey of development banks* (Policy Research, Working Paper; No. 5969). World Bank.

de Aghion, B. A. (1999). Development banking. *Journal of Development Economics, 58*(1), 83–100.

Epstein, G., & Dutt, D. (2018). Public banks, public orientation and the great financial crisis of 2007–2008. In *Financial innovation and resilience* (pp. 327–343). Palgrave Macmillan.

Gerschenkron, A. (1962). *Economic backwardness in historical perspective—A book of essays*. Harvard University Press.

Goldsmith, R. W. (1969). *Financial structure and development*. Yale University Press.

Griffith-Jones, S., & Ocampo, J. A. (2014). Global governance for financial stability. In *Contributions to economic theory, policy, development and finance* (pp. 273–295). Palgrave Macmillan.

Griffith-Jones, S., Spiegel, S., Jiajun, X., Carreras, M., & Naqv, N. (2020). *Matching risks with instruments in development banks* (Working Paper No. 9). International Research Initiative on PDBs and DFIs Working Groups.

Gurley, J. G., & Shaw, E. S. (1955). Financial aspects of economic development. *The American Economic Review, 45*(4), 515–538.

Gutierrez, E., Rudolph, H., Homa, T., & Beneit, E. B. (2011). *Development banks: Role and mechanisms to increase their efficiency* (World Bank Policy Research Working Paper Series 5729).

Hanieh, A. (2018). *Money, markets, and monarchies: The Gulf Cooperation Council and the political economy of the contemporary Middle East*. Cambridge University Press.

Hausmann, R., & Rodrik, D. (2003). Economic development as self-discovery. *Journal of development Economics, 72*(2), 603–633. https://www.oecd.org/development/development-finance-institutions-private-sector-development.htm

Ho, P. (2020, April). The credibility of (in)formality: Or, the irrelevance of institutional form in judging performance. *Cities, 99*, 102609. https://doi.org/10.1016/j.cities.2020.102609

Ho, P. (2017). *Unmaking China's development: The function and credibility of institutions*. Cambridge University Press.

Ho, S., & Marois, T. (2019). China's asset management companies as state spatial-temporal strategy. *The China Quarterly, 239*, 728–751.

IMF. (2020). *Assessment, E.B., IMF Executive Board Concludes 2020 Article IV Consultation with France.*

Intergovernmental Committee of Experts on Sustainable Development Financing. (2014). *UNCTAD*. https://www.ituc-csi.org/IMG/pdf/icesdf_report.pdf

Kim, K. (2018). *Lean on me: Development financial struggles and national development banks*. Unpublished paper in Developing Economics, A Critical Perspective on Development Economics, Department of International Development at King's College, London.

Kornai, J. (1979). Resource-constrained versus demand-constrained systems. *Econometrica: Journal of the Econometric Society, 47*, 801–819.

La Porta, R., López-de-Silanes, F., & Shleifer, A. (2002). Government ownership of banks. *Journal of Finance, 57*(2), 265–301.

Lucas, R. E., Jr. (1988). On the mechanics of economic development. *Journal of Monetary Economics, 22*(1), 3–42.

Marcelin, I., & Mathur, I. (2015). Privatization, financial development, property rights and growth. *Journal of Banking & Finance, 50*, 528–546.

Marois, T. (2012). *States, banks, and crisis: Emerging finance capitalism in Mexico and Turkey*. Edward Elgar.

Marois, T. (2021). *Public banks: Decarbonisation, definancialisation, and democratisation*. Cambridge University Press.

Marois, T. (2022). A dynamic theory of public banks (and why it matters). *Review of Political Economy, 34*(2), 356–371.

Marois, T., & Güngen, A. R. (2016). Credibility and class in the evolution of public banks: The case of Turkey. *Journal of Peasant Studies, 43*(6), 1285–1309.

Mazzucato, M., & Penna, C. C. (2016). Beyond market failures: The market creating and shaping roles of state investment banks. *Journal of Economic Policy Reform, 19*(4), 305–326.

Mazzucato, M., & Penna, C. C. (2018). National development banks and mission-oriented finance for innovation. In S. Griffith-Jones & J. A. Ocampo (Eds.), *The future of national development banks*. Oxford University Press.

McDonald, D. A., Marois, T., & Barrowclough, D. V. (Eds.). (2020). *Public banks and Covid-19: Combatting the pandemic with public finance*. Municipal Services Project (Kingston), UNCTAD (Geneva), and Eurodad (Brussels). https://publicbankscovid19.org/

McDonald, D. A. (2016). To corporatize or not to corporatize (and if so how)? *Utilities Policy, 40*, 107–114.

McDonald, D. A., Marois, T., & Spronk, S. (2021). Public banks + public water = SDG 6? *Water Alternatives, 14*(1), 117–134.

McKinnon, R. I. (1973). *Money and capital in economic development*. The Brookings Institution.

McKinnon, R. I. (1993). *The order of economic liberalization: Financial control in the transition to a market economy*. JHU Press.

Meggison, W. (2004). *The financial economics of privatization*. Oxford University Press.

Miller, M. H. (1988). The Modigliani-Miller propositions after thirty years. *Journal of Economic Perspectives, 2*(4), 99–120.

Musacchio, A., & Lazzarini, S. G. (2014). *Reinventing state capitalism: Leviathan in business*. Harvard University Press.

Ndikumana, L. Naidoo, K., & Perez, F. (2021). *There a case for national development banks in Africa? Conceptual rationale and empirical evidence* (Working Paper Series). Political Economy Research Institute, University of Massachusetts Amherst.

Ocran, M. K., Senadza, B., & Osei-Assibey, E. (2020). Foreign aid and economic development. In J. Y. Abor, C. K. D. Adjasi, & R. Lensink (Eds.), *Contemporary issues in development finance*. Routledge.

Palermo, G. (2019). Power: A Marxist view: Coercion and exploitation in the capitalist mode of production. *Cambridge Journal of Economics, 43*(5), 1353–1375.

Riding, A. L., & Haines, G., Jr. (2001). Loan guarantees: Costs of default and benefits to small firms. *Journal of Business Venturing, 16*(6), 595–612.

Robinson, J. A. (1952). The generalization of the general theory. In *The rate of interest and other essays*. Macmillan.

Romer, P. M. (1989). Human capital and growth: Theory and evidence. *Carnegie-Rochester Conference Series on Public Policy, 32*, 251–286.

Sanderson, H., & Forsythe, M. (2013). *China's superbank: Debt, oil and influence—How China Development Bank is rewriting the rules of finance*. Wiley.

Shapiro, C., & Willig, R. D. (1990). On the antitrust treatment of production joint ventures. *Journal of Economic Perspectives, 4*(3), 113–133.

Shirley, M. M. (1999). Bureaucrats in business: The roles of privatization versus corporatization in state-owned enterprise reform. *World Development, 27*(1), 115–136.

Shleifer, A., & Vishny, R. W. (1998). A survey of corporate governance. *Journal of Finance, 55*(2), 737–783.

Skidelsky, R. (2011). The relevance of Keynes. *Cambridge Journal of Economics, 35*, 1–13.

Stiglitz, J. E., & Greenwald, B. (2003). *Towards a new paradigm in monetary economics*. Cambridge University Press.

Stiglitz, J. E., & Uy, M. (1996). Financial markets, public policy, and the East Asian miracle. *The World Bank Research Observer, 11*(2), 249–276.

Stiglitz, J. E., & Weiss, A. (1981). Credit rationing in markets with imperfect information. *The American Economic Review, 71*(3), 393–410.

Torres Filho, E. T., & Costa, F. N. D. (2012). BNDES e o financiamento do desenvolvimento. *economia e Sociedade, 21*, 975–1009.

Torres, E., & Zeidan, R. (2016). The life-cycle of national development banks: The experience of Brazil's BNDES. *The Quarterly Review of Economics and Finance, 62*, 97–104.

Uğurlu, E. N., & Epstein, G. (2021). *The public banking movement in the United States: Networks, Agenda, initiatives, and challenges*. Political Economy Research Institute.

World Bank. (2013a). *Rethinking the role of the State in finance* (Global Financial Development Report).

World Bank. (2013b). *History*. go.worldbank.org/65Y36GNQB0

World Bank. (2018). *2017 Survey of national development banks*. World Bank.

Yeyati, E. L., Micco, A., & Panizza, U. (2004). *Should the government be in the banking business? The role of state-owned and development banks*. Inter-American Development Bank.

Zecchini, S., & Ventura, M. (2009). The impact of public guarantees on credit to SMEs. *Small Business Economics, 32*(2), 191–206.

PART II

Contemporary Roles of National Development Banks

CHAPTER 4

Contemporary Roles, Contributions and Challenges of National Development Banks

4.1 Introduction

The public sector has become the lifeline for millions of people and companies in distress. Governments around the world require long-term counter-cyclical financing to help maintain economic activity, and they often depend on development banks to do this (Columbia Center on Sustainable Investment, 2021). Development banks are an important government tool for providing medium- to long-term financing. Aghion (1999) describes NDBs as government-sponsored financial institutions concerned mainly with the provision of long-term capital to industry. Development banks and for that matter NDBs hold a unique place in the world of public banks and specialized financial institutions, considering their emphasis on having development impact. Their contribution to financing the economy presents them as a distinct element of public policy. Development banks are highly diverse and are generally referred to as 'public development banks' (PDB). They are managed independently and ensure the financial implementation of the public mandate entrusted to them.

The literature broadly identifies the roles of development banks in the development process as: (i) provide counter-cyclical financing or counteracting the pro-cyclical nature of private financing; (ii) promote innovation and structural transformation, which are inherent to dynamic economic growth; (iii) enhance financial inclusion; (iv) support the

© The Author(s), under exclusive license to Springer Nature Switzerland AG 2023

J. Yindenaba Abor, *The Changing Role of National Development Banks in Africa*, https://doi.org/10.1007/978-3-031-38639-8_4

financing of infrastructure investment, which is also crucial for economic growth; and (v) support the provision of public goods and particularly combatting climate change and, more broadly, promoting environmental sustainability and 'green growth' (Griffith-Jones et al., 2018).

It is important to examine in detail the important roles that NDBs play in the growth and development process in both developed and developing countries. This discussion will provide useful insights for researchers, private sector investors and policymakers.

This chapter discusses the contemporary roles and contributions of NDBs. It is organized as follows: Sect. 4.2 discusses the contemporary roles of NDBs; Sect. 4.3 examines the achievements and contributions of NDBs; Sect. 4.4 identifies the main challenges confronting NDBs; and Sect. 4.5 concludes the chapter.

4.2 Contemporary Roles of National Development Banks

NDBs are recognized to play very important roles in the growth and development processes of countries. As mentioned in the introduction section to this chapter, there are at least five crucial roles of development banks in the development process, according to Griffith-Jones et al. (2018). These include: (i) providing counter-cyclical financing; (ii) promoting innovation and structural transformation; (iii) enhancing inclusive finance; (iv) supporting infrastructure investment and development; (v) financing the provision of global public goods, and particularly combatting climate change; and (vi) deepening of financial markets and intermediation. These functions are discussed below.

4.2.1 Providing Counter-Cyclical Financing

There is growing consensus that one of the most important functions of development banks is to act as a counter-cyclical force when private lending decreases drastically, particularly during and after financial crises (Griffith-Jones & Ocampo, 2008). This is especially important to help preserve long-term investment, such as infrastructure, to guarantee the continuation of existing projects while also assisting the introduction of new initiatives that are beneficial for both short-term and long-term development. Griffith-Jones and Gottschalk (2012) further argue that multilateral development banks across the globe increased their grant and lending support to emerging and developing countries by over 72% between 2007 and 2009, during the period of the global financial crisis, and slowed down in economic growth, which impeded the flow of private capital into these economies as it had in the past. This represented a major counter-cyclical response, which helped sustain investment and economic activities in those emerging and developing countries.

In emerging and developed nations, this counter-cyclical lending by multilateral and regional development banks was supplemented by NDB lending. In circumstances when private trade lines failed, a group of NDBs (including the Brazilian development bank BNDES and many Asian national development banks) helped to keep trade finance flowing within and outside their economies. Through the quick development of existing methods as well as newly formed ones, they greatly expanded their total lending to developing countries in the years when they were most hit. Their contributions during crises contribute to keeping economies afloat. Luna-Martinez and Vicente (2012) show that from 2007 to 2009, the NDBs boosted their loans from US$1.16 trillion to US$1.58 trillion. They further argue that development banks increased short- and long-term lending to existing and new customers who were having challenges refinancing or acquiring new lines of credit to run their businesses. The huge NDBs' unique counter-cyclical role is demonstrated by the fact that the average growth of their loan portfolio increased from 10% in 2005–2007 to nearly 25% in 2008, before declining (Griffith-Jones et al., 2018).

NDBs provide counter-cyclical funding, according to a growing amount of comprehensive empirical evidence. Brei and Schclarek (2013, 2018) analysed the response of the national governments and private bank lending to financial crises and discovered evidence that the average private bank's lending growth rate is larger than the average public bank's during normal times. In economic crises, however, private banks' lending growth rate slows while public banks' accelerates. This means that public banks have played a counter-cyclical role in their banking systems, while private banks behaved pro-cyclically. Three factors account for this. First, unlike their private counterparts, the goal of state-owned banks is not simply to maximize profits in the face of risks, but also to sustain and foster economic recovery. Rudolph (2010) argues that state financial institutions have less variable risk aversion and hence, provide a steadier source of financing. Second, because of the implied government guarantee, public banks may see fewer deposit withdrawals and meet the liquidity needs of customers and hence, financial assets issued by these institutions also have a preference in the market during crises. Finally, in times of crisis, authorities may be able to more readily capitalize public sector banks than private banks which may have difficulty raising the necessary additional capital (Griffith-Jones et al., 2018).

Mazzucato and Penna (2016) argue that private banks' pro-cyclical behaviour is exacerbated by the fact that they have become increasingly focused on short-term profits over the past decades, implying that they seek low-risk, short-term gains through the trading of securities and other investments, rather than financing long-term productive and innovative projects.

4.2.2 Promoting Innovation and Structural Transformation

In general, there has been a growing recognition of the need for mechanisms to implement more long-term national development policies for structural transformation and innovation, particularly national development banks. This is in line with the recognition of the value of a modern 'industrial policy' (Rodrik, 2004a) and the importance of a 'entrepreneurial and development state' (Mazzucato, 2013), which, in collaboration with the private sector, helps to provide an evolving boost for private sector research and development, innovation and structural change. Mazzucato (2013) further demonstrates that most of the important innovations in the US were driven and stimulated by public support for innovation, but executed by the private sector. This helps in industrial and sector diversification by lowering credit risk, fostering financial development and ultimately transforming the structure of national economies.

To boost productivity, the formation of a learning society and a knowledge-based economy is required for sustainable and sustained growth. NDBs are a critical institution for achieving this goal. They play this innovative role in twofolds. First, technology requires significant funding for research and development (R&D), which carries a high risk of failure due to factors such as project failures in the hunt for successful solutions and long project timelines with low transitional economic returns. Second, as technological advances become more functional and their deployment gains traction, large-scale and long-term investment financing is required. NDBs are better clothed with a variety of funding options of equity, loans and grants that can be exploited to raise the needed capital from its wide range of stakeholder through coordination to finance any technological advanced innovations to transform the structure of the economy. NDBs could, therefore, participate in the financing of major infrastructure with significant positive outcomes. This will allow full-scale implementation of sustainable projects that may be less appealing to the private sector due to their magnitude or duration, and because social benefits may overshadow the financial benefits that private sector investors are focused on (Griffith-Jones et al., 2018).

4.2.3 Enhancing Inclusive Finance

One of the important roles played by DBs is the provision of finance for SMEs and microenterprises, including household agricultural activities on a long-term credit basis. These microeconomic activities and agents are usually faced with challenges in accessing credit to finance their activities and if they do, it comes with high cost and short-term maturities which are unsustainable in enhancing financial inclusion and promoting productivity. NDBs play an important role by supporting the implementation of national development strategies aimed at improving the financial inclusion of these sectors of the economy that are traditionally excluded from the formal financial sector, especially those found in the rural periphery of nations (Griffith-Jones et al., 2018).

Financial inclusion of SMEs is a precondition for productive development, creativity and innovation, and increased production. Access to financing by sole traders and small businesses remains an important policy issue in many emerging nations as well as some advanced economies, particularly during and after financial crises or recessions. Generally, financial systems in developing nations are fragmented and they exclude large portions of the real sectors of the economy including micro, small and medium enterprises, which account for greater proportions of employment and income-earning opportunities for economic growth and innovations.

SMEs commonly face significant barriers to financing, thereby limiting their capacity to expand and grow. As a result of the financing challenges, they employ much less external financing for both working capital and fixed asset investment and to finance the latter with a very large component of short-term borrowings, which comes at a high cost of servicing in developing economies. This was further worsened after the global financial crisis and has deepened in recent times due to the impact of the COVID-19 pandemic.

Firms' industrial output and ability to develop and thrive are restrained when external finance is limited. This generates a vicious circle in which smaller industry players remain vulnerable and grow slowly resulting in significant societal effects such as poverty and inequality. The provision of funding for micro and SMEs whose operational activities are characterized by high transaction costs and risk make them unattractive to most traditional lenders with a profit motive. This is a common reason for development banks and similar organizations in both developed and developing countries to emerge and fill this gap. NDBs, or special institutions focused on lending to micro and small businesses, are supposed to address this market failure by tailoring their lending and other services to the specific needs of micro and small businesses. NDBs can collaborate with credit unions and community-based banks to provide valuable insights and channels for meeting the financial needs of micro and small businesses. As a result, these agents' access to rediscounting and direct lending from NDBs is critical (Griffith-Jones et al., 2018).

However, NDBs are always faced with the challenge of fundamental uncertainty due to their inability to ascertain the success rate or otherwise of projects they finance. NDBs should, therefore, not only be interested in the provision of venture capital but also in the provision of social capital through their networks, which offers a wide range of channels to the SMEs to trade with. NDBs can also finance various portfolios of SMEs so as to diversify the idiosyncratic risks associated with SMEs operations.

4.2.4 *Supporting Infrastructure Investment and Development*

Public funds have often been used to finance a huge amount of infrastructure development in Africa and elsewhere. Considering the dwindling nature of public finance, governments' budgets are unable to support such large-scale public infrastructure projects. Though MDBs such as the World Bank and the IMF are important in providing infrastructure financing, they are mostly unable to fully finance the large infrastructure financing requirements of developing countries. NDBs have been identified to play a significant role in providing funding for infrastructure in general, complementing governmental and private investment in infrastructure, and particularly in times of fiscal challenges.

Considering the huge volume of the initial investment requirements with respect to infrastructure expansion, NDBs are designed to provide long-term financing to support infrastructure development. Also, NDBs tend to have high credit ratings and investor confidence due to the collateral involvement of the state. This could be used as a bargaining instrument to raise long-term capital from the capital markets at a cheaper cost and to pass it on to their borrowers.

The role of NDBs in infrastructure financing is discussed in greater detail in Chapter 6.

4.2.5 *Financing the Provision of Global Public Goods*

One key threat to the efforts of achieving global sustainable development is the challenge of climate change. NDBs' function of financing the provision of global public goods involves promoting environmental sustainability by combatting climate change. The issue of climate change has become a social, economic and environmental threat to the existence of humankind, and the survival of the world economy has in recent years become the most expensive global item to finance. The global community is therefore faced with the challenge of defining a preventive and adaptive approach to climate change aimed at achieving a sustainable growth that is sensitive to environmental issues and that balances climate and economic growth.

NDBs play an essential part in the pursuit of a sustainable development agenda because they bring the benefits of varied expertise, administrative efficiencies and convening capacity. NDBs can aid in the mobilization of extra funds, the development of relevant policy frameworks and the implementation of successful projects that demonstrate the sustainability of particular green investments, such as renewable energy. Above all, they may assist in ensuring that a sustainable climate policy is fully compatible with the post-2015 global development goals and the Paris Agreement. NDBs can achieve this global good of combating climate change through the mainstreaming of climate change into their activities and operations, adaptation and financing mechanisms. This can be done through the option of financing projects that are low carbon in order to help in the global quest to reduce and end poverty and inequality in every shape or form, and the initiation of green development projects. The financing of projects by NDBs should take into account the incorporation of environmental externalities and the introduction of adaptive technologies that are sustainable, such as renewable energy, even if the short-term returns are minimal or non-existent. There are several considerations which will eventually result in measurable environmental benefits. These include, increasing the demand for investments and finance in climate-friendly projects (pre-investment phase) by addressing sector-specific and country-specific constraints; promoting appropriate and stable enabling environments for investing, creating awareness, building capacity to analyse and structure climate-related interventions and bringing projects and companies to a level of investment readiness.

The role of NDBs in climate finance is discussed in greater detail in Chapter 8.

4.2.6 Deepening of Financial Markets and Intermediation

The role of financial markets in financial intermediation and economic growth has been widely acclaimed by many scholars. It has the potential to propel the growth of the private sector, which is fundamental to job creation and economic development. However, the extent to which a country's financial market responds to the forces of demand and supply remains one key factor that determines its effectiveness in the intermediary role it plays in the allocation of funds in the economy. Thus, a well-developed and functioning financial market efficiently distributes funds to economic agents in need of capital to invest in businesses through the issuance of various securities traded in the financial market. In the same manner, a less developed financial market does not promote financial intermediation among investors and those who need capital to start or expand their firms, as is the case in the emerging and developing economies.

In the above circumstances, NDBs have become instrumental in moderating the functions of financial markets, especially in the money and stock markets in both developed and emerging economies. NDBs focus on the maximization of the social well-being and benefit of the public, and hence, they offer long-term credit maturity arrangements to their consumers. Their participation in the financial market, therefore, brings competition and a lower credit cost and access to capital. Other participating financial institutions and investors are therefore compelled by the forces of the market to be efficient in the trading activities of the financial market in order to stay afloat in the competitive financial environment.

The intermediary and collaborative role played by NDBs between governments and the private sector has been seen as a compelling factor that ensures the deepening of the financial markets. NDBs can be used by various governments to mobilize funds from the private sector to undertake investments in infrastructure and other public goods. NDBs usually act as brokers (transaction advisors) and investment advisors to both the government and the investors, respectively. The raising of these funds is usually done through the issuance of domestic and foreign bonds, which requires a functional local financial market. The reverse is true for private investors who seek debt securities to finance their operational and investment activities in order to set up or expand their firms. Governments through NDBs purchase shares floated by investors to raise capital and other long-term securities from the financial market. This directly and indirectly provides funding to the private sector through the financial market to boost economic growth. This approach has been used by many developed and emerging economies including India, China, South Africa and Japan to rapidly grow and develop their financial markets in the recent past.

NDBs usually collaborate with other private financial institutions in the mobilization of the needed resources, both financial and human, to deliver on their mandate of financing development projects critical to the growth of the economy and providing the needed expert advice to the government on policy and project implementations. The collaborative effort in project financing by the NDBs deepens the financial market, which serves as the conduit for the conduct of trading activities.

The point needs to be made that the presence of NDBs presents some advantages. Griffith-Jones (2015) suggests that NDBs are also needed to assist in financing sectors or projects with important externalities, suggesting that social returns are higher than market returns, a typical example of which is the case with environmental externalities. NDBs offer diversification benefits. First, they may encourage competition among various financial institutions, leading to enhanced efficiency. Second, a more diversified financial system may result in low systemic risk, contributing to improved financial stability. Third, if various types of financial institutions exhibit strengths, then a more diverse system increases the possibility of achieving the important functions of the financial sector (Griffith-Jones, 2015).

4.3 Contributions and Achievements of National Development Banks

NDBs have made very useful contributions to the socio-economic growth of various countries in the following respects:

i. Serving as key actors in financing central and local development projects;
ii. Serving as important levers for transforming national economies and contribute immensely to industrialization;
iii. Providing financial and technical support to promote trade development;
iv. Bridging the savings and financing needs of individuals, farmers, public firms and private firms;
v. Creating employment by absorbing age groups from the labour market;
vi. Acting as a critical tool for supporting proactive growth strategies;
vii. Mobilizing private sector finance to fill the financing gap to achieve the SDGs.

4.3.1 NDBs Serve as Key Actors in Financing Central and Local Development Projects

They have recently been recognized as key actors in financing local development projects in a variety of developing and industrialized countries. Over the past decade, the popularity of NDBs may be evident due to their growing interest in pursuing government development and industrial strategies. Several observations focused on the growing trend of government activity as a catalyst to the expansion of NDBs around the world. Therefore, NDBs are back in fashion and are here to stay. Some countries benefited from the global economic boom in the first decade of the twenty-first century, by increasing their exports and raw material revenues. The governments of these countries store part of the surpluses in the current account and in fiscal accounts and use the capital to develop the state's financial institutions. Some prominent types of institutions in Africa have grown rapidly, notably the Development Bank of Nigeria (DBN), the Southern African Development Bank (DBSA) and the Botswana National Development Banks, which often provide financial returns or performance, sustainable socio-economic development and growth incentives as their main task. Much attention has been paid to how the activities of these organizations have become a global force. For example, the Norwegian fund has invested in 73 countries, including shares in more than 9,000 companies (Kim, 2018), and China has become the world's largest source of official development finance (Gu & Carey, 2019).

4.3.2 NDBs Serve as Important Levers for Transforming National Economies

Over the years, NDBs have been important levers for transforming national economies and, in particular, have contributed immensely to industrialization (World Bank, 2017). Most development banks in sub-Saharan Africa (e.g., Uganda Development Bank, Development Bank of Rwanda, National Development Bank of Botswana, Southern African Development Bank, etc.) have stirred up the creation of new industries and offered many benefits to an inclusive development strategy.

4.3.3 NDBs Provide Financial and Technical Support to Promote Trade Development

NDBs have been instrumental in providing trade financing for promoting trade development in order to spur economic growth and development. Apart from providing financial support, NDBs also provide technical support in terms of formulation of trade promotion policy, capacity building of both public and private actors within the trade environment, providing opportunities for promoting intra- and extra-African trade, as well as the provision of finance for building the necessary trade-enabling infrastructure, among others.

4.3.4 NDBs Bridge the Savings and Financing Needs of Individuals, Farmers, Public Firms and Private Firms

They have played a vital role in bridging the savings and financing needs of individuals, farmers, public companies and private companies (World Bank, 2017). They have helped in providing long-term finance, unlike commercial financial institutions, which focus on short-term finance, projects and returns. In addition to providing long-term financing, development banks have advanced counter-cyclical lending, making economies more resilient to financial and economic shocks and downturns. In doing so, they have supported countries by securing their production capacities for their next phase of expansion. NDBs help in providing public goods and have shown significant bias towards economic stability and political freedom.

4.3.5 *NDBs Create Employment by Absorbing Age Groups from the Labour Market*

Moreover, NDBs have helped in creating employment and by absorbing age groups from the labour market. NDBs' contribution to employment generation has been done both directly and indirectly. First, NDBs are able to offer employment opportunities as they expand their scope of operation and make efforts to reach out to clients in important sectors. They also do this indirectly by financing projects and businesses that are able to create opportunities in generating employment. NDBs' financing of development projects that focus on supporting productive sectors tends to have a huge employment impact. For instance, NDBs' financing of infrastructure projects contributes to employment since the project employs local workers during the construction phase. Also, these projects impact on employment generation as well as the entire value chain given that construction materials and machinery are necessary for the projects.

4.3.6 *NDBs Act as a Critical Tool for Supporting a Proactive Growth Strategy*

NDBs have been instrumental in contributing to a proactive growth strategy. They have been useful not only in addressing market weaknesses, such as long-term funding gaps due to risk and uncertainty, but also as a critical tool in supporting a proactive growth strategy at the national level. The main argument for encouraging development banks is that they can fill the gaps left by private, often commercial financial institutions. Often, the widest gap is one of the insufficient funds for economic transformation. Initiatives for economic transformation often include large-scale projects that require long-term financing and therefore involve risks that banks are reluctant to take. In addition, there is a lack of long-term financing because financing through commercial banks is usually short-term. Long-term financing requires a change in maturity period, which carries risks that traditional banks tend to avoid. For these reasons, development banks are designed and licensed to make the required contributions.

4.3.7 *NDBs Mobilize Private Sector Finance to Fill the Financing Gap to Achieve the SDGs*

Also, NDBs have been essential in mobilizing private sector finance to fill the financing gap so as to achieve the SDGs. NDBs exist in almost every country, regardless of the level of development of the country's economic or financial sector. They have generally supported sectors such as agriculture, international trade, infrastructure, tourism, housing and small and medium-sized businesses. In recent years, new NDBs have been established to address various development challenges. They finance sectors or activities where there is significant external influence, which means that social returns are higher in these areas than those of the market. Recent developments in Africa are a good example of the relationship between information development and social goals. Due to the lack of structural change, Africa missed many of the Millennium Development Goals, in some cases by a large margin. Rapid transformative growth requires a more independent development strategy and longer-term investment by developing countries to support capacity building. Hence, the contributions of NDBs should not be seen as a threat to developed international financial institutions.

4.4 Main Challenges Confronting National Development Banks

NDBs have a completely different mandate, with a focus on softer objectives such as economic development, poverty alleviation, economic integration, promotion of a market economy, job creation, fighting climate change and gender equality. They usually assume more risk and target long-term project returns. They were often relieved of pressure in connection with economic performance and profitability. However, the present generation of NDBs are expected to achieve the dual objective of making development impact and remaining financially sustainable. As a result, NDBs are confronted with specific challenges that are not encountered by traditional commercial banks. These include lack of commercial focus, weak risk management systems, a changing competitive environment and political interference in governance and management, reaching out to small and medium enterprises (SMEs), matching foreign currency funding with local lending, difficulty in striking a balance between supporting the private and public sectors, determining the right level of capital, and attracting and retaining qualified personnel (see Joseph, n.d). These are discussed subsequently.

4.4.1 *Lack of Commercial Focus*

Since NDBs are mainly state-owned financial institutions, they have traditionally been regarded as banks for the underserved in the economy with very generous credit conditions. NDBs often lack commercial focus because their mandate goes beyond the profit motive. Over time, their objective of financing development projects is often confused with the absence of a need for profit. Loans from NDBs are mostly treated as grants, leading to high default rates. Borrowers tend to consider such funds as coming from the government and therefore are not mindful of servicing and repaying the loans. The lack of commercial focus in the name of development banking has resulted in adverse selection, with NDBs offering credit to ventures that are not viable. This lack of commercial focus creates a system of poor monitoring and control. Even with NDBs that attempt to follow a good credit management system, their development mandate has often caused them to lend to sectors that ordinarily do not qualify for credit. These developments have resulted in bad loans in the balance of NDBs. A number of NDBs that provided credit to the agricultural and other underserved sectors in Africa and other developing countries have had problems having these loans repaid. This tends to impact on the quality of NDBs' loan portfolios and in many instances necessitate a shift in focus. The Agricultural Development Bank and National Investment Bank in Ghana are examples of NDBs that had to change focus to commercial banking because of this problem.

4.4.2 *Weak Risk Management Systems*

Instituting an effective and efficient risk management system is critical for NDBs just like commercial banks. An effective and efficient risk management system ensures the sustainability of NDBs and therefore enables them to continue pursuing their mandate without having to depend on government for additional capital injections, saving government's tax revenue. However, NDBs in many developing countries tend to implement weak risk management systems. A weak credit risk management system leads to poor project selection and poor identification of non-productive assets. It also results in poor quality portfolios, caused by high default rates. NDBs have not been up to date with new trends with their credit risk management system, lending architecture and information system. They also do not exhibit strong research capabilities to identify viable sectors to support their lending activities. Though a few DFIs and other NDBs have restructured their operations to become commercially viable with support from multilateral DFIs, a number of them still have weak systems for managing risk.

4.4.3 Changing Competitive Environment

NDBs in the global economy and especially in developing economies like Africa are often confronted with the challenge of adapting to the changing environment. In terms of funding, NDBs are experiencing a reducing trend in the level of concessionary assistance they previously received from traditional sources, externally and locally. Also, developments in the international capital markets, the deregulation of national financial systems and the intense competition for funding from new deficit units have all complicated the situation as NDBs are mostly non-depository financial institutions. With respect to lending, NDBs tend to face intense competition from commercial banks and non-bank financial institutions with financial products to operate in the long-term loan market, which was previously captured by DFIs like NDBs.

4.4.4 Political Interference in Governance and Management

Governments in EMDEs have largely used NDBs as tools for driving national development objectives, mostly in sectors like agriculture, infrastructure, housing and industry. Although pursuing these objectives is in tandem with the mandate of development banking, the challenge in most developing countries is that over time, the funding and policy support required for this have decreased. Also, considering that the government tends to hold a significant stake in these financial institutions, in developing countries like Africa, a number of such institutions have experienced political interference in their governance and management structures.

Political actors have tended to influence the appointment of the board and management of these NDBs, with the aim of obtaining political gain as opposed to genuinely seeking their growth and development. Also, NDBs are expected to operate at the forefront of societal and economic change. They are expected to lead the way in areas as diverse as sustainable development, gender equality, corporate governance and environmental responsibility. They certainly require a strategy to guide them towards achieving their set objectives just like any organization. However, this is often a problem for NDBs considering the soft aspects of their mandate, the nature of their governance system and their often complex structure, making them susceptible to political interference.

4.4.5 *Reaching Out to Small and Medium Enterprises*

SMEs are recognized as major contributors to the growth and development of many economies. They contribute to employment creation, innovation, GDP growth, export earnings and market-oriented local projects, with great domestic impact. However, they mostly fail to meet their potential as a fundamental engine of growth and development due to limited access to finance. SMEs in most markets have difficulty in raising the needed financing. They are often discriminated against due to their high-risk profile and lower profitability for banks. For instance, in Africa, the lack of SMEs' access to finance is mainly attributable to the fact that the supply of finance in Africa is generally considered riskier than other regions of the world. Moreover, the provision of finance to SMEs is globally regarded riskier compared with large companies (Abor & Biekpe, 2007; Abor et al., 2014; Collier, 2009; Quartey et al., 2017). Though SMEs globally have problems raising finance, the situation is even more pronounced in developing countries, considering that the weaker legal and business environments render SMEs very fragile. Also, for political reasons, NDBs are every now and then motivated to achieve quick and visible results, leading to an emphasis on infrastructure or large corporate projects. However concentrating on larger projects that are usually few in number would betray the NDB's mandate.

4.4.6 *Matching Foreign Currency Funding with Local Lending*

NDBs' Asset-Liability Management is mostly informed by the longer-term nature of their funding, thus, reducing their liquidity risk. By accessing funding in foreign currency, NDBs can mitigate their currency and interest rate risks by also lending in hard currency. That is done by hedging currencies, which involves lending in the same currencies as their funding. However, this suggests transferring the currency risk to the poor clients, who are mostly not well equipped to manage such risks or may even be unaware of them. They may just be convinced of the opportunity to borrow at lower interest rates and longer maturities. Lending in local currency is especially important to serve MSMEs or less sophisticated clients, who do not understand the whole idea of currency risk.

4.4.7 *Striking a Balance Between Supporting Private and the Public Sectors*

Given that NDBs are public institutions, they may be tempted to concentrate their activities on large infrastructure or public projects. This may have a high impact on the country's economic conditions and enhance the lives of its citizens, while improving visibility. NDBs can also achieve local development, contributing to the emergence of market-oriented economies by promoting private and entrepreneurial initiatives. The existence of an efficient infrastructure in an economy will facilitate private sector development, but in the same vein, a vibrant private sector will provide justification for investments in infrastructure. The notion of NDBs' involvement in private sector development is thus obvious when market failures suggest the private sector cannot obtain the required level of financial support. NDBs' support may assume various forms, including corporate lending, equity investment and technical assistance. NDBs could benefit from maintaining an important private sector activity, given that they can instil discipline in investment decision-making and sustain a healthy contact with the real economy.

4.4.8 *Determining the Right Level of Capital*

NDBs and other DFIs are involved in raising equity financing, mainly from governments. They also benefit from government guarantees. These ensure their creditworthiness, which enables them to raise huge funding from the international capital markets and thus, offer credit on very competitive terms. However, considering that NDBs are not motivated by profit, the absence of a target return on equity or a market-based determination of the cost of capital can result in overcapitalizing the NDBs. This would clearly amount to waste of public resources, and poor allocation of resources, countering productive competition. The key is to allocate the capital to the mission, objectives and needs of NDBs.

4.4.9 Attracting and Retaining Qualified Personnel

Engaging personnel with the right skills set is critical for the success of NDBs. Development banking is a special area and as such, requires staff with the right training and understanding of development banking. Attracting personnel with training in development banking can be a challenge, considering that there are not many institutions offering training or programmes in development finance or development banking. Staff with a good understanding of the culture and business of development banking are essential. Typical commercial bankers have a completely different orientation and may not be suitable for a development bank, without appropriate training. NDBs are often in competition with the private sector to attract good talent. They are mostly at a disadvantage when it comes to the levels of staff remuneration, though they provide job security and a sense of purpose, which serve as motivation to work with them. Just as commercial bankers may not be suitable for development banks, employees of development banks moving to a commercial bank could be a challenge considering the fact that they might have limited experience in negotiating profitable margins, acceptable maturity periods and collateral requirements. The risk here is creating life-long employees, thus lowering efficiency, motivation and competence. A healthy staff turnover may be necessary for ensuring that fresh blood is regularly brought on board, while long-standing employees exist and consider other roles outside development banking.

4.5 Concluding Remarks

This chapter has examined the Contemporary Roles, Contributions and Challenges of NDBs. It has discussed the NDBs are an important government tool for providing medium- to long-term financing. NDBs are described as government-sponsored financial institutions, which are focused mainly on providing long-term finance to industry. NDBs occupy a unique place in the world of public banks and specialized financial institutions, considering their emphasis on having development impact. Their contribution to financing the economy makes them a distinct element of public policy. NDBs perform a number of important functions and these include: (i) providing counter-cyclical financing; (ii) promoting innovation and structural transformation; (iii) enhancing inclusive finance; (iv) supporting infrastructure investment and development; and (v) financing the provision of global public goods, and particularly combatting climate change; and (vi) deepening of financial markets and intermediation.

The chapter has also identified a number of useful contributions NDBs have made to the socio-economic growth of various countries in the following respects: serving as key actors in financing central and local development projects; serving as important levers for transforming national economies and contribute immensely to industrialization; providing financial and technical support to promote trade development; bridging the savings and financing needs of individuals, farmers, public firms and private firms; creating employment by absorbing age groups from the labour market; acting as critical tool for supporting proactive growth strategy; and mobilizing private sector finance to fill the financing gap in order to achieve the SDGs. The present generation of NDBs are expected to achieve the dual objective of making development impact and remaining financially sustainable. As a result, they are confronted with specific challenges that are not encountered by traditional commercial banks. These challenges include lack of commercial focus, weak risk management systems, a changing competitive environment, political interference in governance and management, reaching out to SMEs, matching foreign currency funding with local lending, difficulty in striking a balance between supporting the private and the public sectors, determining the right level of capital, and attracting and retaining qualified personnel.

The discussion could have policy implications. It appears that having relatively large public sector development banks is critical in order for them to play a bigger role in providing counter-cyclical finance and hence contribute significantly to economic recovery during a crisis or slowdown. A large number of NDBs may be useful for various reasons, including assisting in the provision of low-cost credit to MSMEs and others in key sectors such as sustainable infrastructure and innovation, where profitability is typically long-term, in addition to supporting structural transformation to a sustainable and inclusive development path.

References

Abor, J., & Biekpe, N. (2007). Small business reliance on bank financing in Ghana. *Emerging Market Finance & Trade, 43*(4), 93–102.

Abor, J. Y., Agbloyor, E. K., & Kuipo, R. (2014). Bank finance and export activities of small and medium enterprises. *Review of Development Finance, 4*(2), 97–103.

Brei, M., & Schclarek, A. (2013). Public bank lending in times of crisis. *Journal of Financial Stability, 9*, 820–830.

Brei, M., & Schclarek, A. (2018). The counter-cyclical behaviour of national development banks. In S. Griffith-Jones & J. A. Ocampo (Eds.), *The future of national development banks*. Oxford University Press.

Collier, P. (2009, May 1). Rethinking finance for Africa's small firms in "SME financing in SSA". *Proparco Magazine* on Private Sector and Development.

Columbia Center on Sustainable Investment. (2021). *Development banking in the global economy, state of play and future direction*. ccsi.columbia.edu

de Aghion, B. A. (1999). Development banking. *Journal of Development Economics, 58*(1), 83–100.

de Luna-Martinez, J., & Vicente, C. L. (2012, February). *Global survey of development banks* (Policy Research, Working Paper; No. 5969). World Bank.

Griffith-Jones, S. (2015, July). *The positive role of development bank, financial for development*. 3rd International Conference, Addis Ababa, Ethiopia. https://www.un.org/esa/ffd/ffd3/blog/positive-role-development-banks.html

Griffith-Jones, S., & Gottschalk, R. (2012). *Exogenous shocks—Dealing with the only certainty: Uncertainty*. Paper prepared for the Commonwealth Secretariat, London, p. 25.

Griffith-Jones, S., & Ocampo, J. A. (2008). A counter-cyclical framework for a development-friendly IFA. In J. Fanelli (Ed.), *Macroeconomic volatility, institutions and financial architectures: The developing world experience* (1st ed., pp. 25–44). Palgrave Macmillan.

Griffith-Jones, S., Ocampo, J. A., Rezende, F., Schclarek, A., & Brei, M. (2018). The future of national development banks. In S. Griffith-Jones & J. A. Ocampo (Eds.), *The future of national development banks*. Oxford University Press.

Gu, J., & Carey, R. (2019). China's development finance and African infrastructure development. In *China-Africa and an economic transformation* (pp. 147–172). Oxford University Press.

Joseph, A. (n.d.). *Development financial institutions in the Caribbean—The need for re-orientation*.

Kim, K. (2018). *Lean on me: Development financial struggles and national development banks*. Unpublished paper in Developing Economics, A Critical Perspective on Development Economics, Department of International Development at King's College, London.

Mazzucato, M. (2013). *Entreprenuerial state: Debunking public vs. private myths*. Anthem Press.

Mazzucato, M., & Penna, C. C. (2016). Beyond market failures: The market creating and shaping roles of state investment banks. *Journal of Economic Policy Reform, 19*(4), 305–326.

Quartey, P., Turkson, E., & Abor, J. Y. (2017). Financing the growth of SMEs in Africa: What are the constraints to SME financing within ECOWAS? *Review of Development Finance, 7*(1), 18–28.

Rodrik, D. (2004a). Industrial policy for the twenty-first century. *Harvard University*. https://doi.org/10.2139/ssrn.617544

Rodrik, D. (2004b, October, 8). *Rethinking growth policies in the developing world*. Draft of the Luca DÃ¡ gliano Lecture in development Economics.

Rudolph, H. (2010). *Can they be relied on to kick-start lending? (Crisis response note* (No. 12, p. 7). The World Bank Group.

World Bank Group. (2017). *Report from the Executive Directors of the International Development Association to the Board of Governors*. Retrieved on 30 October 2018 from http://documents.worldbank.org/curated/en/348661486654455091/pdf/112728-correct-file-PUBLIC-Rpt-from-EDs-Additions-to-IDA-Resources-2-9-17-For-Disclosure.pdf

CHAPTER 5

Agricultural Financing in Africa: The Role of National Development Banks

5.1 Introduction

Agriculture remains a key employer of the economically active population across the world. Globally, the sector employs an average of about 40%[1] of the labour force and is the backbone of the economy of many developing countries. It is a multifaceted industry that plays a variety of roles in different communities, particularly rural ones. Due to its degree of complexity, agriculture continues to generate unfavourable opinions surrounding the perceived riskiness of agricultural finance. Providers of financial services in Africa seemed to be poorly informed about the future of agricultural development and agricultural finance. The establishment of competitive financial markets that are supported by institutions that are both sustainable and effective in order to service the agricultural sector has been a difficult process globally, and worst of all in Africa. NDBs are without a doubt an essential component of the contemporary financial systems in both industrialized and developing nations.

The need to finance industrialization and structural transformation in developing economies is one of the primary drivers of interest in NDBs in these countries. This type of financing must be long-term and more

[1] See more details from: http://www.momagri.org/UK/agriculture-s-key-figures/With-close-to-40-%25-of-the-global-workforce-agriculture-is-the-world-s-largest-provider-of-jobs-_1066.html.

© The Author(s), under exclusive license to Springer Nature Switzerland AG 2023

J. Yindenaba Abor, *The Changing Role of National Development Banks in Africa*, https://doi.org/10.1007/978-3-031-38639-8_5

risk-tolerant than what commercial banks are willing or able to provide, thus the need for NDBs to fill this gap. In developing nations, and particularly in Africa, the issue of securing adequate funding for agricultural production continues to be one that is of national importance. The lack of support for agriculture in Africa is a substantial obstacle to the region's economic growth, particularly in the light of the continent's huge financing requirements. Therefore, it is necessary for a shift to a new model of agricultural finance in Africa in the years to come. Access to suitable amounts of financial resources is one of the many factors that contribute to the success of the agricultural industry.

Schmidhuber et al. (2011) suggest that the forecasted investment requirement for primary agriculture and its downstream companies in the developing countries towards the year 2050 is estimated to be US$9.2 trillion. This estimate is based on projections made for the period, 2010–2050. It is currently much harder for many farmers to gain access to financing than it was before the COVID-19 pandemic (Koloma & Kemeze, 2022). As a result, there is an urgent need for new and creative approaches to finance agricultural activities across the continents. This chapter examines the role NDBs play in the financing of agricultural development.

The rest of the chapter is structured as follows: Sect. 5.2 provides an overview of agricultural development in Africa; Sect. 5.3 discusses the challenges and opportunities of agricultural financing in Africa; Sect. 5.4 looks at agricultural financing mechanisms; Sect. 5.5 then examines the role of NDBs in financing agricultural development, while Sect. 5.6 concludes the chapter.

5.2 Overview of Agricultural Development in Africa

Agricultural development involves the process of lending a helping hand to farmers by utilizing a variety of agricultural resources. This is necessary for driving agricultural growth and is what generates the required circumstances for the sector to realize its full potential (Pan et al., 2021). In many African countries, the agricultural sector is expected to play a significant role in the economic growth process. Agriculture continues to be the most important source of employment, wealth and general prosperity in many African nations. The industry makes the largest contribution to total revenue and foreign exchange, and accounts for a significant portion of personal savings and corporate capital formation. Agriculture continues to play an essential role in the economies of the vast majority of African nations, and it provides a livelihood for well over half of the continent's total population.

The agricultural sector has experienced low levels of investment over the years, despite that the important role that the sector plays in economic development and the alleviation of poverty in Africa. The low and even falling budget allocations that African governments provide to the agricultural sector are more evidence of the underinvestment that occurs in the continent's agricultural sector. In spite of the fact that agriculture contributes between 20 and 50% to a nation's GDP, it receives less than 10% of the national budget in many nations. This is because there are few governments that emphasize agriculture in their policies and spending (Food & Agriculture Organization, 2021).

In the 1960s and 1970s, there was a major slowdown in the growth of agricultural output in many African countries. During this period, the overall agricultural production in Africa expanded at an annual rate of 2.2%; however, between 1971 and 1983, this pace dropped to about 2%. During this period, about two-thirds of African nations reported an annual growth rate in agricultural production that was less than 2%, and one-third of the countries recorded a growth rate that was less than 1%. The steep rise in the amount of food that many countries needed to import was one unintended effect of the low agricultural performance. Imports of grain products into African countries climbed at an average rate of roughly 8% a year from 1960 to 1970, but this rate dropped to as low as 10% a year between 1971 and 1983. Rice imports climbed at a rate that was the highest within this group. Other items such as sugar, beef, and animal and vegetable oil also saw significant rises in their growth rates over the course of the preceding decade (Osakwe & Ojo, 1986). Even though the percentage of people who are employed in agriculture as a proportion of overall employment has been on a downward trend from 2004 to 2019, it is still rather high at 42.8% in Africa and 52% in sub-Saharan Africa (International Labour Organization, 2021).

The sector employed 65% of the labour force in 2021, and 59% of the target of upgrading agriculture for greater productivity and production set forth in the African Union's Agenda 2063 was met. The continent is falling short of its zero-hunger goal because it is not making the most of the agricultural sector's potential. In 2019, the prevalence of undernourishment was 19.1%; by 2030, this number is expected to climb to

25.7% (Adzawla et al., 2022). Due to its multiplier effect on the economy, agriculture has been a primary priority in Africa for decades. Therefore, Africa's progress depends on an agricultural revolution. Financing agriculture at a level that allows it to reach its full potential is a primary motivator in Africa's development.

However, studies have shown that the increase in agricultural funding has not been sufficient to close the massive financing gap in agriculture, and that only a few of African nations devote more than 10% of their overall public expenditures to the sector (Adzawla et al., 2022; Koloma & Kemeze, 2022). Dalberg and KfW (2018) estimate that in 2017, agri-small and medium-sized enterprises (SMEs) and farmers in sub-Saharan Africa faced a credit shortfall of US$180 billion. This funding shortfall hinders the expansion of the agricultural sector, which might have negative effects on the standard of living of the continent's rural and agricultural populations as well as their income and productivity. Credit extended to the agricultural sector reached an all-time high of US$16.7 billion in 2017, up from a previous high of US$16.2 billion in 2017 (FAO, 2021). However, between 2000 and 2019, the percentage of Africa's total credit allocated to the agricultural sector rose somewhat, from 3.9% to 4.3%. By 2050, it is expected that emerging nations would need to invest US$9.2 trillion in primary agriculture and its downstream businesses (Schmidhuber et al., 2011).

Increasing capital-intensive modes of production requires huge investment in capital goods (Saidi & Wolf, 2011; Schmidhuber et al., 2011). There has been a rise in the previous two decades in the amount of money African nations put into the agricultural sector. Despite this growth, the sector still receives a smaller percentage of total government investment. In 2019, it was 3.6%, down from 5.7% in 1990 (Koloma & Kemeze, 2022). World Bank estimates put the yearly investment needed to feed Africa at US$80 billion. As a result, achieving Africa's agricultural potential depends critically on the continent's access to suitable financial services. This requires enough sector finance, accurate information, technology, resource acquisition and the proper distribution of inputs and products. Again, with global food costs on the rise, a successful agricultural sector in Africa is critical. Food consumption will increase proportionally to the predicted doubling of Africa's population by the year 2050. Agricultural progress will not only help feed Africa's growing population but boost the continent's economies.

5.3 Challenges and Opportunities of Agricultural Financing in Africa

This section discusses the challenges and opportunities of agricultural financing.

5.3.1 *Challenges to Accessing Agricultural Finance in Africa*

Agriculture provides two-thirds of the means of subsistence in Africa, while the cost of food makes up two-thirds of the budgets of the continent's most impoverished households. Despite the fact that it is a significant aspect of the lives of people in Africa, the governments of those countries appear to pay relatively little attention to it. Throughout history, finance for agriculture has been quite limited; for instance, in 2019, this sector received just around 4.3% of the overall credit to the African economy (Food & Agriculture Organization, 2021). According to the findings of Adzawla et al. (2022), only few nations in Africa devote 10% of their entire public spending to agriculture. The World Bank emphasized that restricted access to formal finance is the primary barrier to agricultural output and growth, particularly for small-scale producers (World Bank, 2013a).

A number of factors have been identified as being responsible for the financing challenges in the agricultural sector, including a high level of seasonality, excessive exposure to risk that cannot be diversified, limited availability of usable collateral, lack of records on farming, prohibitive information and transaction costs, competing priorities of banks and other financial institutions, and inadequate access to long-term finance (see International Finance Corporation, 2012; Koloma & Kemeze, 2022).

5.3.1.1 *High Level of Seasonality*

Most agricultural activities in developing countries follow a seasonal pattern and are marked by extended gestation periods. This indicates that cash flows from the industry have a tendency to be unexpected, whereas clustered or erratic cash flows make it difficult to control liquidity while also imposing an additional cost, since customized products will have to be designed in an unfamiliar territory.

5.3.1.2 *Excessive Exposure to Risk that Cannot be Diversified*

Most agricultural activities are highly exposed to undiversifiable risks such as drought, floods, fire and prices. Because most agricultural production activities face the same risks, true diversification is difficult to attain and this increases the risk of default in the sector. The fact that the majority of agricultural production activities are exposed to the same dangers makes it challenging to achieve meaningful diversification, which in turn raises the probability of default in relation to agricultural loans. This problem is even severe when the insurance market for agricultural production is not nearly as established as it should be. According to Muhammad et al. (2013), the primary factors that contribute to the unpredictability of a farmer's income source are production risk, technological risk, price risk, pest risk, government policy risk and most importantly financial risk. Frequently, financial institutions are unable to lend money because of the inherent risks of agriculture, the inability of farmers to offer adequate collateral and the fluctuation of crop prices (IFAD, 2009). The vast majority of financial institutions are hesitant to embrace the frequent dangers that the industry presents. However, governments are now intensifying efforts at attracting investment into agricultural production. Despite these efforts, however, the lack of understanding of the financial risks and opportunities in agriculture deprives the sector of funds that are desperately needed to boost production, processing and marketing.

5.3.1.3 *Limited Availability of Usable Collateral and Lack of Records on Farming*

The agricultural industry mainly operates in an unofficial capacity, which means that it lacks the documentation and registered collateral that is necessary for accessing loans. Furthermore, the majority of farmers do not possess adequate collateral, such as real estate, automobiles or other certified property. Most assets of agricultural households, such as land and houses, are not appropriately titled because of the constraints posed by both the legal and societal norms. As a result, for the lender, the potential assets that the farmer may put up as collateral provides an inadequate level of protection against the risks of default. In addition, farmers do not meet the requirements to be eligible for conventional production credit since they do not possess adequate collateral in the form of agricultural land. Moreover, even if they are approved for financing, the rate of interest that is provided is higher, in order to compensate the financier for the higher risk that the farmer offers to the business. Again, the lack of proper records and information on farming activities makes it difficult for financial institutions to ascertain whether or not financing would be appropriate. This alters the requirements necessary for accessing financial services.

5.3.1.4 *Prohibitive Information and Transaction Costs*

Agriculture is characterized by high information and transaction costs because of its weak infrastructure, dispersed population and scattered communities. In rural regions, there is frequently inadequate infrastructure, including roads, drinkable water, power and telecommunications. When taken together, these considerations make it challenging for banks and other types of financial institutions to successfully establish branches in rural communities (IFAD, 2009).

5.3.1.5 *Competing Priorities of Banks and Other Financial Institutions*

Banks have several competing priorities involving reaching out to many more firms in the metropolitan areas, establishing new branches in densely populated urban areas, investing in new technology, etc., and these areas are viewed as having a higher potential for profit. Due to such competing interests of banks and other financial institutions, the agricultural industry is not regarded as strategically vital to the profitability of banks. Investing in the agricultural sector is typically considered to be banks' lowest investment priority. This is mostly due to the widespread belief that agriculture has a poor potential for profit.

5.3.1.6 *Inadequate Access to Long-term Funding*

A very small percentage of businesses throughout the world have access to long-term funding. This problem is even more severe in developing nations, particularly with regard to agriculture, mostly due to the high cost of long-term finance and the complexity due to maturity mismatch. The decline in productivity witnessed by the industry over the course of recent years is one factor that contributes to the limited access to long-term capital. According to Koloma and Kemeze (2022), low agricultural production appears to be one of the reasons that dissuades banks from assisting the agricultural sector. Another reason is the lack of government assistance for the agricultural sector.

5.3.1.7 *Agriculture's Economic Slump*

In agricultural activities, there is typically a significant time lag between the effort put in and the return received, and this is especially true at the time when costs are being incurred. During this period, there is a possibility that the production of agricultural commodities may fluctuate, which will cause farmers' financial arrangements to be thrown off. As a direct result of this, farmers will be forced to contend with yet another layer of complexity in their daily lives. It is possible that structured finance groups may use this as an excuse to turn down financing applications for agricultural businesses.

5.3.1.8 *Inappropriate Financing Models Applied by Commercial Banks*

Banks' poor understanding of agribusiness may result in the application of inappropriate financing models to agricultural lending. When it comes to providing loans to farmers in Africa, most banks and financial institutions do not use the appropriate financing models. The primary reason for this is that the majority of these institutions have not conducted research into the nature of the agricultural sector and agribusiness on the continent. As a result, the majority of these institutions have been restrained in their efforts to channel capital into the industry.

5.3.1.9 *Low Levels of Education and Financial Literacy*

The vast majority of people involved in agriculture in rural areas tend to have a very low level of education or none at all. The high level of illiteracy tends to restrain banks and other financial institutions from providing financial services to the people involved in the sector.

5.3.1.10 *The Financial Sector May Not be Sophisticated Enough in Some Developing Countries*

It is often difficult to get sector-specific financial instruments and services, and there is little room for innovation in these areas. Additionally, despite the fact that financial services may be offered, it is possible that they are not appropriate for all forms of agricultural operations. These activities will have various requirements in terms of the schedule for disbursements, quantities and dangers, among other things. However, the client's particular requirements might not be met by the financial solutions that are being offered since they might only be accessible to large-scale agricultural businesses that have a proven track record of success.

5.3.2 *Opportunities of Agricultural Financing in Africa*

Despite these obstacles, business viability in agricultural financing is possible. The agricultural industry presents viable investment opportunities for many financial institutions. A number of factors have been identified to open more financing avenues in the agricultural sector. These factors include a growing demand for food, agricultural diversification potential, the need to handle sector-specific risk through financial innovations like index insurance, a low degree of financial inclusion in agriculture and deteriorating climate change.

5.3.2.1 *Growing Demand for Food*

The growing demand for food in Africa is driven by a growing population and changes in dietary habits. The ever-increasing human population is largely responsible for the rising cost of food. With an estimated 10 billion extra mouths to feed by 2050, global food production must keep pace with population growth (Estrada et al., 2020). Global food demand is projected to grow by 50% by 2030[2] and 70% by 2050. More than one-ninth, or 821 million, of the world's population is hungry every day (World Food Programme, 2020). However, agricultural productivity is only growing at an average yearly rate of 1.63%, which is less than the estimated 1.73% needed to double agricultural production by 2050 in a sustainable manner in the light of the expected growth in the world's population (Steensland, 2019). To meet this growing food demand, farmers in Africa will require financial assistance to pay for or invest in inputs like certified seeds, fertilizer and agrochemicals in order to increase agricultural production and supply the rising demand. As a result of this need, providers of inputs will face a higher indirect demand for funding. As consumer demand rises, businesses across the agricultural value chain will require access to capital.

5.3.2.2 *Agricultural Diversification Potential*

The agricultural sector provides an opportunity for financial institutions to broaden and diversify their portfolios. Financial institutions are able to widen and diversify their portfolios through proving credit to the agricultural sector. It is possible for financial institutions to widen their area of

[2] Read more details from: http://www.un.org/waterforlifedecade/food_security.shtml.

diversification and increase their potential for profit by joining the agricultural sector. This is helpful for financial institutions to manage risk. For instance, in the heat of the global crisis in 2008 and the COVID-19 pandemic, agricultural prices skyrocketed. A study by the International Finance Corporation in 2012 revealed that countries with a large share of agriculture in GDP had declining non-performing loans (NPLs) during the crises, while the reverse was the case for countries with a lower share of agriculture in GDP. This is because agricultural businesses seem to have very little correlation with financial markets.

5.3.2.3 The Need to Handle Sector-Specific Risk Through Financial Innovations Like Index Insurance

The risky nature of agriculture in terms of floods, droughts, fires and livestock disease outbreaks such as swine flu, though a challenge, presents an opportunity in the sector for financial institutions to develop risk-mitigation products and services specifically for the sector to meet its needs. The fact that the majority of agricultural production activities are exposed to the same dangers makes it challenging to achieve meaningful diversification, which in turn raises the probability that agricultural loans would be unpaid. The volatile nature of agriculture in terms of output, price and market creates opportunities for designing risk-mitigation derivative products such as forward and futures contracts as well as weather insurance.

5.3.2.4 Low Degree of Financial Inclusion in Agriculture

A vast majority of the rural population in Africa lives in agrarian communities, and the vast majority of these people do not have bank accounts and are therefore excluded from the financial system. The large proportion of the unbanked population, especially in the agricultural sector, provides an opportunity for financial institutions to rope in this underserving segment into the mainstream financial system.

5.3.2.5 Deteriorating Climate Change

Because climate change is getting worse, there is the need to investigate sustainable methods of production. This presents an opportunity for financial institutions to create and customize financial products and services to sustainable production systems in a manner that is consistent with strategies for climate change adaptation.

5.4 Agricultural Financing Mechanisms

Any form of agricultural development initiative that seeks to encourage agricultural finance and boost agricultural production must have a framework for agricultural financing as an essential part of the overall plan. Irrigation, agricultural mechanization and land expansion are all activities that require farmers to have access to sufficient capital in a timely manner. However, because of the challenges of accessing finance, it is imperative that financing strategies for the agricultural sector be designed to reduce the credit risk in the sector.

5.4.1 Direct Finance

Financing a specific player within the agricultural sector has often been the method of choice in African countries when it comes to financial investment. It is not only farmers who are included in this category, but also other actors including input providers, processors, merchants and exporters. Every player in the sector requires finance in order to get food from the farm to the final consumer. According to Ruete (2015), the key financial instruments that are utilized in direct finance are savings, microfinance, traditional financing, leasing and factoring, weather-based insurance and credit guarantee schemes. Community savings and other kinds of informal group finance systems are often used for financing agricultural endeavours (IFAD, 2000).

Most African nations rely heavily on microfinance, which involves a wide range of financial products such as small loans, microsavings accounts, microinsurance, money transfers and even guarantees for gaining access to larger sums of money. Commercial banks, agricultural development banks, non-governmental organizations (NGOs), cooperatives and investors are some of the potential sources of traditional funding (Ruete (2015). Factoring involves the sale of invoices by a business to an outside entity (the factor) at a discount in order to boost the business' cash flow, as opposed to leasing. In the agricultural sector, leasing is used to finance machinery, vehicles and equipment. These tools are an attempt to mitigate some of the agricultural hazards associated with conventional financing. Insuring against poor weather and providing guarantees to groups who do not have access to credit by covering a part of the default risk of the loan are two ways in which weather-based insurance helps those who would otherwise have trouble gaining access to credit. The value of the guarantee is recouped by the lender in the event of a default (OECD, 2010).

5.4.2 *Value Chain Financing*

Value chain finance is an alternative to direct financing that has been widely used across the rest of Africa. Farmers, input suppliers, processors, dealers, exporters and retailers are just some of the members of the value chain who benefit from this financing solution, which capitalizes on the trust and cooperation already present among them. It lessens the commercial bank's exposure to credit risk and hence decreases the farmer's cost of borrowing. Under this financing arrangement, instead of providing funding directly to the farmer or entrepreneur, the emphasis of the financing is on the commercial exchange between two or more linkages in the chain. In short-term financing, value chain financing is often used as a risk-mitigating strategy. It is most successful in environments with high levels of demand from final customers, high levels of trust among businesses, and frequent and substantial business dealings between those businesses.

The systematic transmission of information among actors along the value chain using mobile phones has boosted economic integration and collaboration in Africa. Communication and contactless payment enabled by mobile phones link all the financial participants in a supply chain (Ruete, 2015). The objective is to improve the flow of funds, goods and data among supply chain participants. Miller and Jones (2010) argue that value chains can be internally or externally financed, depending on the preferences of the firm. Relationship-based internal finance occurs between parties throughout the value chain, such as when a fertilizer firm supplies fertilizers and the farmer only pays the firm after the harvest has been sold. Included in this strategy are product financing, trade credits, input-supplier credits, marketing firm credits and lead firm credits. When a farmer needs funds to purchase fertilizer, for instance, an external source like a microcredit bank will step in to help. There are a number of tools available for this purpose, such as trade receivables financing, loan guaranteeing, factoring and forfaiting.

5.4.3 *Infrastructure Development Financing*

The infrastructure essential for farming can also be a primary focus of funding. Infrastructure is crucial to the success of the agricultural industry, including transportation networks in rural areas, as well as irrigation networks, water supply networks, sanitation networks, power grids, storage facilities and communication networks. These endeavours call for substantial financial resources. A well-functioning agricultural sector necessitates appropriate infrastructure, such as roads to connect rural areas to markets, irrigation technology to lessen farmers' reliance on rain, storage facilities to safeguard harvests from weather and pests, telecommunications to facilitate trade, water distribution and power generation. However, rural infrastructure is chronically underfunded worldwide (The Economist, 2014). Roads and other forms of large-scale infrastructure are especially in need of funding.

5.4.4 *Research and Development Financing*

This strategy puts a premium on providing financial backing for the sector's knowledge-development efforts. This entails the development of agricultural technology as well as new technical information regarding agricultural goods, processes and services (Anandajayasekeram, 2011). Knowledge gained via R&D is also useful for financial planning and credit evaluation by financial institutions, as well as for government planning in general, which helps producers form business plans for banks or other financial institutions. In the past, the World Bank has covered R&D expenses including running costs and capital investments in the region of sub-Saharan Africa (Lynam et al., 2012).

5.4.5 *Financing Farmers and Agricultural Entrepreneurs*

This method involves targeting those in the agricultural industry who are actively seeking funding. Farmers and small business owners like small supply firms require access to capital in order to increase output and/or diversify their offerings. Resources for inputs, manufacturing and advertising are all examples (Food and Agriculture Organization & World Bank, 2013). A budget is required for the acquisition of seeds, fertilizer, machinery, equipment, processing, packing and shipping. One of two methods, direct finance or indirect financing, can be used to accomplish this (IFC, 2012; Ruete, 2015). Direct financing allows financial institutions to learn about the needs of recipients and provide them with a range of services beyond just loans. Indirect finance involves loaning funds through a farmer-based organization, which helps to lower the default risk. There is a direct financing success story in Kenya, where a bank worked with various institutions and the Kenyan government to provide low-interest loans to farmers (Issahaku et al., 2020). Another country where indirect finance was used successfully was Zambia. There, farmers submitted their requests for the inputs they would need to a farmers' union, which then sent the request to a bank for financing.

5.4.6 Financing Agriculture by Using Capital Market Instruments

The agricultural industry requires a wide range of capital market instruments to meet its varied demands. The three main capital market instruments for financing agriculture are debt, equity and derivative instruments. The capital market is particularly important because it provides long-term finance for the sector. The financial instruments available within each of these three categories vary from country to country, depending on the sophistication of the local financial system and the risk appetite of financiers. One challenge with the African banking system is the limited access to long-term loans beyond five years. However, plantation crops typically take more than five years to harvest, creating a mismatch between farmers' investment horizon and the tenure of funds. The use of debt, equity and derivative instruments in the capital market can help farmers and agricultural businesses in Africa to access long-term capital to reduce such a mismatch between their investment horizon and the maturity of their funds (Issahaku et al., 2020).

Agricultural businesses on a massive scale and commercial operations might attract long-term financing from bond investors by offering bonds with varying maturities. Equity involvement is another way for agribusinesses to generate capital for investment. Companies in the agricultural industry can generate capital for investments in long-term projects with positive net present values by issuing shares to the investing public. Both bonds and shares can be publicly traded on an exchange or privately deposited with a small group of institutional investors. Corporate bonds, project bonds, infrastructure bonds and green bonds are only some of the types of bonds that agribusinesses might issue, and through a formal listing procedure, an agricultural firm with the aid of an underwriter can sell its shares to the general public and obtain capital. Firms in the agricultural sector can also make use of derivatives as a source of funding by hedging against certain types of the risks inherent in the industry. Spot contracts, forwards, futures, options, exchange-traded funds and swaps are only some of the derivative instruments that can be used in the agricultural industry.

5.4.7 *Financing Agriculture Using Risk Mitigating Instruments*

The agricultural sector is saddled with a great deal of risks, and these risks also present financing opportunities for financial institutions. Most agricultural activities are highly exposed to undiversifiable risk, such as drought, floods, fire and prices. Since most agricultural production activities face the same risks, true diversification is difficult to attain, and this increases the risk of loan default in the sector. An innovative approach to financing agricultural risk is to incorporate insurance into a credit scheme. Examples of innovative risk management financing instruments are insurance instruments and market-based instruments (Issahaku et al., 2020).

Since few businesses are willing to risk insuring the agricultural sector on their own, there is a pressing need for a hub that brings together many insurers so that they may collaborate on developing unique policies for the industry. Insuring the agricultural industry presents unique obstacles, but when many insurers work together, they are able to better meet the needs of their agricultural clientele by creating insurance policies that are uniquely tailored to each individual's needs. Forwards, futures, options contracts and exchange-traded swaps are all market-based price risk management tools that may be used to mitigate various types of risk in agriculture. Emerging nations such as Argentina, Brazil, China, India and South Africa have markets that help manage price risk for players in agriculture (Issahaku et al., 2020).

5.5 The Role of National Development Banks in Financing Agricultural Development

There is a critical need for national development banks (NDBs) in both emerging and industrialized nations. Many academic works, notably those published in the wake of the 2008 financial crisis, have stressed their importance (Griffith-Jones & Ocampo, 2008; World Bank, 2018a, b). Because of the COVID-19 pandemic's effect on the economy, the need for NDBs has been brought up for discussion once more (McDonald et al., 2020). The crisis has sparked new discussions on the value of national development banks and other types of public banks in providing counter-cyclical funding, inclusive finance and solutions to other economic problems that developing countries face. The need to finance industrialization and structural change is a major driver of national development bank interest in Africa and other developing nations since it demands long-term and more risk-tolerant financing than commercial banks are often willing or able to supply (Ndikumana et al., 2021).

It was under the state-led growth models of the 1960s and 1970s that Africa's NDBs became an integral element of the policy machinery. Even more, during the liberalization phase of the 1980s and 1990s, many of them collapsed or were privatized. While some failed, others are thriving, and some have even been founded in the new millennium (Ndikumana, 2009), Africa's economies would benefit greatly from a solution to their current lack of access to medium- and long-term credit if their NDBs were given greater leeway in how they lend and how they run their businesses (Ndikumana et al., 2021). NDBs have been a mainstay of Africa's banking and financial sectors for decades, facilitating growth and facilitating fundamental shifts in the continent's economy. Publicly owned financial institutions (PFIs) are often established by governments to meet the credit and financial service needs of citizens which are not being met by private financial institutions to the level desired by policymakers. The responsibilities of NDBs might range from general economic growth promotion to the completion of particular assignments. In Africa, NDBs are often entrusted with bolstering agriculture, small and medium-sized enterprises (SMEs) and international commerce.

5.5.1 NDBs Can Help Manage Risks that Come with Financing in the Agricultural Sector

NDBs have a greater need for effective risk management than other types of financial institutions because they tend to work in more high-risk industries, such as agriculture; their exposures tend to be more concentrated, and the risks they face, such as those associated with long-term or infrastructure financing, are more difficult to predict. Given the nature of their industry, they have to put a premium on risk management. Examples of BNDES taking calculated risks include their funding of promising emerging industries like biotechnology and renewable energy. Further, some nations have historically utilized their development banks to promote and support private investment in industries like Chile's tremendous growth of forestry, which created substantial exports of paper and cellulose, in addition to wood. Development banks have been at the forefront of investing in cutting-edge industries and technologies in all of these cases, setting the standard while also following national or regional objectives set by governments in conjunction with the private sector. NDBs possess extensive technical competence, particularly in large, complicated projects, as well as the ability to identify and manage risk, which commercial banks do not possess (Gottschalk et al., 2021). These characteristics enable big, general-purpose NDBs to lend at scale, offer long-term financing and support a wide range of projects and activities. Infrastructure initiatives in the areas of health, schooling, drinking water and sanitation, transportation, urban mobility and energy are a few examples that can all support the growth of agriculture. Additionally, NDBs can serve as the financial arm of national governments, making strategic decisions for the development of the agricultural industry. These decisions may include investments in innovation which, while posing risks, have the potential to produce impressive returns over the very long-term.

5.5.2 NDBs Can Help Mitigate Market Failures that Prevent Investment by Financial Institutions into the Agricultural Sector

While growth, economic development and agricultural sector development are all dependent on a well-functioning financial sector, some financial services are underprovided in a free-market context, including, most likely, the farm sector. The easiest way to fix this could be to set up NDBs. Costs of information and its uneven distribution, which may, for example, support insufficient finance for farmers, are two common examples of market failure that justify the existence of development banks and the work they do. For example, climate and energy initiatives have a hard time attracting adequate funding due to externalities, or the fact that the benefits of these endeavours are difficult to appropriate. NDBs have long been seen as an integral element of the economic policy toolset and the financial market environment, with the primary goal of filling voids in certain sectors, such as long-term financing (for projects like infrastructure) and business lending. Gottschalk et al. (2021) opined that NDBs operate significantly less pro-cyclically than other banks; they do not take huge risks based on a profit motive, use very little leverage, avoid more complicated structures of securitization that carry potential monetary and reputational risks, and use derivatives to protect their transactions rather than making a prediction. Therefore, NDBs avoid the kinds of practices that lead to numerous market failures. According to Mazzucato and Penna (2016), NDBs proceed over and above merely correcting market failure to developing and shaping the market, which is more crucial for the innovation and development of the agricultural sector. The four types of activities they use to develop and shape the market involve, counter-cyclical activities, developmental projects, venture capitalist and challenge-led activities (Mazzucato & Penna, 2016).

5.5.3 NDBs May Undertake Counter-Cyclical Lending in the Agricultural Sector

Additionally, NDBs' ability to insulate their financing sources from market fluctuations enables them to exhibit counter-cyclical behaviour by increasing agricultural sector loans when private credit declines. Although the source of financing is important, the total amount is also a factor. NDBs must be reasonably substantial and have a long-term perspective of risk assessment in order to compensate for a dramatic decline in the supply of private lending to the agricultural sector. NDBs can function counter-cyclically in the macroeconomic sphere, shielding the economy from shocks and downturns that could directly affect the agricultural sector. This helps to prevent damaging detours from the path of sustainable development and the growth of the agricultural sector (Gottschalk et al., 2021).

5.5.4 NDBs Can Also Work With the Private Sector to Leverage Private Finance and Encourage a 'Development-friendly' Financial Sector in the Agricultural Lending Environment

NDBs have the power to impact the evolution of financial sector development by increasing the proportion of private investment that is directed towards development. This improves the financial sector's capacity to service the agriculture sector and achieve key development goals. In addition to providing loans and guarantees, NDBs could also provide other services. Venture money, serving as business angels, leasing and factoring, securitization and consulting services are all potential examples of these types of investments. Some of them are also quite engaged in the field of strategic long-term investing. NDBs act as a financial credibility indicator to individuals and as an endorsement for other investors, are closer to local credit and energy markets as well as local environments in general, and have developed extensive knowledge, a solid reputation and years of experience in financing projects by acting as early adopters (Morgado et al., 2019). They have been referred to as 'the technical bank', which is technically proficient and assists in educating commercial banks about the hazards associated with investing in new sectors like the agricultural sector (Geddes et al., 2018; Zhang, 2020).

5.5.5 *National Development Banks, by Making Credit Accessible to Farmers May Help Foster Agricultural Development in the African Region*

Disbursing agricultural credit on a short-term, intermediate-term and long-term basis is crucial to meeting farmers' financial needs over the spectrum of the crop cycle, which includes a wide range of farming operations. Most short-term loans are used to finance harvesting and shipping during peak agricultural seasons. Agricultural operations, such as the purchase of agricultural machinery with irrigation equipment and the formation of Agro-based companies, are typically aided by the provision of long-term financing. Lack of access to financial services is generally seen as the primary barrier to the poor's full realization of their economic potential in many developing nations. The inability to obtain credit is a major barrier to the rural poor's ability to improve their work prospects, savings and investment strategies, consumer habits, etc. Credit, it is believed, also enables farmers to make investments in things like sophisticated agricultural techniques, market research and storage facilities (Islam, 2020). Furthermore, evidence suggests that lending by NDBs is efficient in the sense that funds are channeled into productive purposes, and that they benefit SMEs and large firms (Lazzarini et al., 2015; Oliveira, 2019).

5.5.6 *National Development Banks in Africa May Serve as Intermediaries Channeling Funds from Those Wishing to Save to Farmers Wishing to Borrow to Invest in the Business*

It is expected that greater investments will be made in the agricultural sector as a result of the process of credit extension by the banks, which will raise productivity and, as a result, contribute to an increase in the growth of the country's gross domestic product. This, in turn, has a favourable influence on both the general development of the country and the growth of the economy. Therefore, a bank may be referred to as an engine of growth in the communities in which it operates; consequently, the function of NDBs becomes crucial in the promotion of economic growth and development on a continent such as Africa. NDBs may be a useful instrument for developing nations to route and utilize foreign financial resources because of their powerful position in the local credit markets.

5.5.7 *National Development Banks Can Also Help Eliminate Financial Waste from the African Economy by Helping to Channel All Available Resources Towards Productive Sectors Like the Agricultural Sector*

NDBs not only protect the depositors' funds, but they also put those deposits to work by on-lending to those who need the loans for investment. They also contribute to the economic growth of a nation by encouraging the expansion of agricultural production. Nyikos and Kondor (2022) assert that NDBs act as financial intermediaries for a variety of financial instruments, such as investment platforms or financial instruments and actively participate in financing infrastructure projects.

Boxes 5.1, 5.2 and 5.3 provide cases of Agricultural Development Bank of Tanzania (TADB), Agricultural Development Bank, Ghana and Agricultural Bank of Egypt (ABE) in agricultural financing in Egypt.

Box 5.1: Agricultural Development Bank of Tanzania (TADB)
In September 2012, the Company Act, 2002 CAP 212 authorized the formation of Tanzania Agricultural Development Bank Limited (TADB). To aid the Government of Tanzania in formulating and implementing policies and initiatives for agricultural and rural lending, the Bank was

founded to spearhead capacity-building strategies and programmes that would fortify the agriculture finance value chain. Asset and liability management, risk management, corporate and capital planning, credit underwriting, risk-based pricing, product development and costing, as well as the enhancement and/or development of relevant strategies, procedures, gender, internal audit and procurement guidelines, to name a few, are just some of the policies and procedures that TADB has implemented over the past five years. In order to maintain currency and incorporate best practices, these policies and procedures are reviewed once each year or once every two years. TADB has maintained consistent performance over the duration of the project. With a growing loan and advance portfolio, the company's interest revenue has nearly quadrupled from TZS 5,283,189,743 (US$2.26 million) in 2015 to TZS 17,926,904,859 (US$7.7 million) as of the end of the fiscal year in September 2020.

Annual net profit margin jumped from 8.51% in 2015 to 34.98% in 2020, while the lending profitability ratio (Net Interest Margin) went from 9.1% on average in 2015 to 16.27% in 2016 and then down to 2.54% in 2017 before rebounding to 6.93% in 2020. With ADB backing, more than 198 loans have been dispersed, and over 2.4 million farmers have been touched. While loans have been disbursed all throughout Tanzania, the Lake Zone (coffee, meat) has received more than half of the entire amount (cashew nuts). Loans to TADB clients accounted for more than 90% of the total amount borrowed. Increases in both paddy output and agricultural exports can be attributed to the use of project money. Cashews, cotton, cloves and sisal are all examples. Since the same period in 2019, traditional exports have nearly quadrupled, from $567.5 million to $914.8 million (US). The export of sisal increased due to both volume and price impacts, whereas the export of cashew nuts, cotton and cloves increased due to increased output.

Source African Development Bank (2022)

Box 5.2 Agricultural Development Bank, Ghana

ADB was founded by Parliament in 1965 to profiably serve Ghana's agricultural industry. The Bank offers unique Universal Banking products and services focused on agriculture to local and international clients. The Bank recorded profit after tax of GH¢ 81,602 (US$6,799.94) (2020: GH¢ 65,403 (US$5,450.07)) and transferred GH¢ 40,801 (US$3,399.97) from retained profits to the Statutory Reserve (2020: GH¢ 32,702 (US$2,725.08)). At year-end, the Statutory Reserve Fund has GH¢ 182,015 (US$15,167.41) (2020: GH¢ 141,214 (US$11,767.44)). The Bank maintained its admirable commitment to the agriculture sector throughout the epidemic. The Bank awarded the 2021 National Best Farmer GH¢ 600,000 (US$49,998.34) and increased its financial intermediation in the agricultural sector to meet its strategic goal of increasing the percentage of agricultural loans in its loan portfolio.

Except for animal and crop producers, aggregators/stockists, agro-processors, agro-marketers and input distributors, loans to cover working capital and capital expenditure needs were prioritized. In 2021, the Bank authorized GH¢ 160.0 million (US$13.33 million) as working capital to the National Food Buffer Stock Company Limited to purchase products from farmers for supply to essential national institutions such Senior Secondary Schools and food buffer storage. The Bank supported the One District One Factory Programme (1D1F) in 2021. By year-end 2021, the Bank had sanctioned GH¢ 113.87 million (US$9.49 million) for eighteen feasible projects, including broiler production and processing, fruit processing, general manufacturing, construction, jute bag production, and fish farming and processing.

The Bank boldly financed the rehabilitation and retooling of the former Kumasi Jute Factory to create jute bags for cocoa, cashew, grain and other crop farmers and aggregators/marketers. The initiative is projected to greatly reduce imports. This great programme received GHS26.0 million (US$2.17 million). The Bank also supported local soya bean, rice and tomato value chains. Our poultry producers struggled in 2021. Avian influenza and rising feed and feed component prices hurt the chicken industry. The Bank supported our farmers by postponing payments, rearranging facilities and injecting capital to restore these firms. As one of our focuses, the poultry sector should improve in 2022.

Source Agricultural Development Bank, Ghana (2021)

Box 5.3: Agricultural Bank of Egypt

ABE was created in 1930 to boost Egypt's agricultural industry. The bank quickly became the largest Arab financial institution servicing farmers' interests. The bank is one of the largest Arab and Middle Eastern agricultural banks and Egypt's most prominent agricultural development organization. Agriculture loan underwriting dominates the bank business. Its 1200+ rural Egyptian branches offer agricultural loan kinds and services. In November 2020, the bank's loan portfolio reached EGP 44 billion, up 37.5% from 32 billion nine months earlier. The bank's latest rural development service and funding product is microfinance.

It was intended to benefit all Egyptian villages, especially the poor. The new funding initiative targets rural women, small merchants and handicraft proprietors. It finances programmes to grow birds, chickens, goats, sheep, domestic industries, handicrafts, dairy products and small businesses to empower people economically and boost production. As one of the leading banks specializing in financing agricultural projects and important industrial operations, the bank promotes investment in all agricultural sectors. The bank quadrupled agricultural loan funding to EGP 7.6 billion (US$256.3 million), helping 280,000 farmers. Compared to 2021's EGP 11.922 billion (US$401.2 million), livestock project finance reached EGP 13 billion (US$438.46 million), including EGP 4.950 billion (US$166.96 million) for the national veal revival project, which helped 18,500 recipients grow 238,000 cow heads.

The Central Bank of Egypt's (CBE) intervention to provide EGP 55bn to fund the evolution of contemporary irrigated agriculture without interest and in equal annual instalments for 10 years has led the bank to focus heavily on expanding programmes to finance this transformation in coordination with the agriculture and irrigation ministries. The bank again invested EGP 1bn in New Valley agriculture and animals. The bank gave 60% of these financing to several important agricultural projects totalling EGP 600 million (US$20,237,657.40), including new land reclamation and infrastructure. To improve the governorate (administrative division of a state), small farmers received various types of agricultural loans.

Source Agricultural Bank of Egypt (2022)

5.6 Concluding Remarks

There is a real need for NDBs in both emerging and industrialized nations. In this chapter, we focused on the challenges and opportunities of agricultural financing in Africa, agricultural financing mechanisms and the role of NDBs in agricultural financing development. NDBs can help to manage risks that come with financing in the agricultural sector, mitigate market failures that prevent investment by financial institutions into the agricultural sector, undertake counter-cyclical lending in the agricultural sector, work with the private sector to leverage private finance and encourage a 'development-friendly' financial sector in the agricultural lending environment. They also make credit accessible to farmers, foster agricultural development in the African region and channel available resources towards productive sectors like the agricultural sector.

References

Abdulghany, Y. (2022). *Agricultural Bank of Egypt*. https://egy-africa.com/en/2020/12/26/agricultural-bank-of-egypt/

Adzawla, W., Bindraban, P. S., Atakora, W. K., Camara, O., & Gouzaye, A. (2022). Economic viability of smallholder agriculture in the Savannah and transitional zones of Ghana: Implications of farm output commercialization and farm diversification. *Sustainability, 14*(18), 11548.

African Development Bank. (2022). *Tanzania—Tanzania agricultural development bank* (Project Completion Report). https://www.afdb.org/en/documents/tanzania-tanzania-agricultural-development-bank-project-completion-report-0

Agricultural Development Bank, Ghana. (2021). *Annual report and financial statements*. https://agricbank.com/wp-content/uploads/2022/08/Website_2021-ADB-Annual-Report.pdf

Anandajayasekeram, P. (2011). The role of agricultural R&D within the agricultural innovation systems framework. In *Innovation in small-farm agriculture* (pp. 75–87). CRC Press.

Dalberg and KfW. (2018). *Africa agricultural finance market landscape*.

Estrada, A., Garber, P. A., & Chaudhary, A. (2020). Current and future trends in socio-economic, demographic and governance factors affecting global primate conservation. *PeerJ, 8*, e9816.

FAO & World Bank. (2013). *Financing smallholder agricultural term investments*. http://www.ruralfinance.org/fileadmin/templates/rflc/documents/6_financing_smallholder_web.pdf

Food and Agriculture Organization. (2021). *FAOSTAT statistical database*. FAO. http://www.fao.org/faostat/en/#data/IC

Geddes, A., Schmidt, T. S., & Steffen, B. (2018). The multiple roles of state investment banks in low-carbon energy finance: An analysis of Australia, the UK and Germany. *Energy Policy, 115*, 158–170.

Griffith-Jones, S., & Ocampo, J. A. (2008). A counter-cyclical framework for a development-friendly IFA. In J. Fanelli (Ed.), *Macroeconomic volatility, institutions and financial architectures: The developing world experience* (1st ed., pp. 25–44). Palgrave Macmillan.

Gottschalk, R., Castro, L. B., & Xu, J. (2021). Should national development banks be subject to Basel III? *Review of Political Economy*. https://doi.org/10.1080/09538259.2021.1977541

International Finance Corporation. (2012). *Innovative agricultural SME finance models*. International Finance Corporation.

International Fund for Agricultural Development (IFAD). (2000). *Ghana: Rural financial services project, 2000*. http://www.ifad.org/gender/learning/sector/finance/41.htm

International Fund for Agricultural Development (IFAD). (2009). *Rural finance: Small amounts making a big difference*. http://www.ifad.org/events/microcredit/eng.pdf

International Labour Organization. (2021). *Key indicators of the labour market*. International Labour Organization.

Islam, M. M. (2020). Agricultural credit and agricultural productivity in Bangladesh: An econometric approach. *International Journal of Food and Agricultural Economics (IJFAEC), 8*(1128-2020-1530).

Issahaku, H., Asiedu, E., Nkegbe, P. K., & Osei, R. (2020). Financing agriculture for inclusive development. In J. Y. Abor, C. K. D. Adjasi, & R. Lensink (Eds.), *Contemporary issues in development finance* (pp. 287–317). Routledge.

Koloma, Y., & Kemeze, F. H. (2022). COVID-19 and perceived effects on agricultural financing in Africa: Evidence and policy implications. *African Development Review, 34*, S63–S79.

Lazzarini, S. G., Musacchio, A., Bandeira-de-Mello, R., & Marcon, R. (2015). What do state-owned development banks do? Evidence from BNDES, 2002–09. *World Development, 66*, 237–253.

Lynam, J., Beintema, N., & Annor-Frempong, I. (2012, June). *Agricultural R&D: Investing in Africa's future—Analyzing trends, challenges, and opportunities*. Reflections on the conference. http://www.ifpri.org/sites/default/files/publications/astifaraconfsynthesis.pdf

Mazzucato, M., & Penna, C. C. (2016). Beyond market failures: The market creating and shaping roles of state investment banks. *Journal of Economic Policy Reform, 19*(4), 305–326.

McDonald, D. A., Marois, T., & Barrowclough, D. V. (Eds.). (2020). *Public banks and Covid-19: Combatting the pandemic with public finance*. Municipal Services Project (Kingston), UNCTAD (Geneva), and Eurodad (Brussels). https://publicbankscovid19.org/

Miller, C., & Jones, L. (2010). *Agricultural value chain finance: Tools and lessons*. Practical Action Publishing.

Morgado, N., Taskin, O., Lasfargues, B., & Sedemund, J. (2019). *Scaling up climate-compatible infrastructure: Insights from national development banks in Brazil and South Africa*. OECD Publishing.

Muhammad, A. A., Muhammad, A., Ahmad, Z., Arif, M., Qasim, A., & Mahmood, R. (2013). Plant growth promoting rhizobacteria and sustainable agriculture: A review. *African Journal of Microbiology Research, 7*(9), 704–709.

Ndikumana, L. (2006). *Revisiting development finance institutions for the purpose of accelerating African economic development*. African Development Bank.

Ndikumana, L. Naidoo, K., & Perez, F. (2021). *There a case for national development banks in Africa? Conceptual rationale and empirical evidence* (Working Paper Series). Political Economy Research Institute, University of Massachusetts Amherst.

Nyikos, G., & Kondor, Z. (2022). The involvement of national development banks promoting sustainable finance. *The Central European Journal of Regional Development and Tourism, 14*(1), 147–163.

OECD (Organisation for Economic Co-operation and Development). (2010). *Facilitating access to finance: Discussion paper on credit guarantee schemes*. http://www.ruralfinanceandinvestment.org/sites/default/files/45324327_pdf.pdf

Oliveira, F. N. D. (2019). Investment of firms in Brazil: Do financial restrictions, unexpected monetary shocks and bndes play important roles? *Revista Brasileira de Economia, 73*, 235–251.

Osakwe, J. O., & Ojo, M. O. (1986). An appraisal of public sector financing of agricultural development in Africa with particular reference to Nigeria. *Economic and Financial Review, 24*(2), 8.

Pan, W. T., Zhuang, M. E., Zhou, Y. Y., & Yang, J. J. (2021). Research on sustainable development and efficiency of China's E-Agriculture based on a data envelopment analysis-Malmquist model. *Technological Forecasting and Social Change, 162*, 120298.

Ruete, M. (2015). *Financing for agriculture: How to boost opportunities in developing countries* (Policy Brief, 3). Investment in Agriculture.

Saidi, M. D., & Wolf, C. (2011). *Recalibrating development co-operation: How can African countries benefit from emerging partners?* (Working Papers, No. 302). OECD Development Centre.

Schmidhuber, J., Bruinsma, J., & Boedeker, G. (2011). Capital requirements for agriculture. In *Looking Ahead in World Food and Agriculture: Perspectives to 2050* (p. 317). FAO.

Steensland, A. (2019). *2019 global agricultural productivity report: Productivity growth for sustainable diets and more.*

The Economist. (2014, March 22). Infrastructure financing: A long and winding road. http://ww2.cfo.com/credit/2014/03/infrastructurefinancing-long-winding-road/

World Bank. (2013a). *Rethinking the role of the State in finance* (Global Financial Development Report).

World Bank. (2013b). *History*. go.worldbank.org/65Y36GNQB0

World Bank. (2018a). *2017 Survey of national development banks*. World Bank.

World Bank. (2018b). *Poverty and shared prosperity 2018: Piecing together the poverty puzzle*.

World Food Programme. (2020). *Risk of hunger pandemic as COVID-19 set to almost double acute hunger by end of 2020*. https://insight.wfp.org/covid-19-will-almost-double-people-in-acute-hunger-by-end-of-2020-59df0c4a8072

Zhang, F. (2020). Leaders and followers in finance mobilization for renewable energy in Germany and China. *Environmental Innovation and Societal Transitions, 37*, 203–224.

CHAPTER 6

Financing Infrastructure Development in Africa: The Role of National Development Banks

6.1 Introduction

The contributions of all factors of production are largely dependent on the accessibility of infrastructure facilities and services as well as the effectiveness of such services. Infrastructure investments in areas like energy, water, transportation and communication aid in economic development, reduce poverty and enhance living situations in emerging nations (OECD, 2013). The importance of infrastructure development to economic growth and the enhancement of the well-being of citizens cannot be overemphasized. By lowering production costs and enhancing transition efficiency, infrastructure aids in boosting returns on investment. Access to social infrastructure such as education, health, water and sanitation among others, guarantees social capital for the underprivileged and dignified human living conditions to the average citizen. It is not surprising, therefore, that SDGs 4, 8, 9 and 10 of the United Nations Sustainable Development Goals place a premium on infrastructure development to propel inclusive growth, decent work, clean cities and accessible services among others. Goals 1 and 2 of ending hunger and ensuring food security are equally hinged on transport infrastructure; otherwise, their attainment would remain a mirage. To this end, achieving the SDGs without a robust infrastructure will be difficult. Goal 11 of sustainable cities and communities cannot be achieved without clean water, adequate sanitation, a reliable and affordable electricity supply, and

© The Author(s), under exclusive license to Springer Nature Switzerland AG 2023

J. Yindenaba Abor, *The Changing Role of National Development Banks in Africa*, https://doi.org/10.1007/978-3-031-38639-8_6

mass transit systems, to make Africa's growing cities habitable (Kuttu et al., 2020).

The economic and social impact of infrastructure development can be intermediate or long-term. Infrastructure expansion, in the short-term, creates employment and boosts aggregate spending in the industrial and construction industries and ultimately boosts supply of goods and services and thus increases the productive capacity of the economy in the long run. Infrastructure has been seen as one tool that can be used to reduce poverty and inequality. Calderon & Serven (2004) posit that infrastructure development has a disproportionate positive effect on the human capital of the poor households and the vulnerable groups in society because it has the potency to increase their employment and income prospects. They further contend that infrastructure development has the tendency to reduce income inequality in developing regions such as those of Africa if the resultant effect of the infrastructure provision is tailored for improved access and quality services to the low-income group and the socially excluded.

Infrastructure can generally be classified into two main categories: economic and social infrastructures (Simpson & Zimmermann, 2012). Economic infrastructure encompasses all basic facilities that define and determine economic development. These include transport, energy, electricity and telecommunication are crucial to engender growth. Social infrastructure, on the other hand, is the combination of social amenities that are essential or crucial for human development. These social facilities include education, health, water, sanitation and housing. The combination of both social and economic infrastructure in a complementary manner ensures a holistic development of any given region that is faced with underdevelopment, such as Africa. Given the enormous relevance of infrastructure in both economic and social dimensions, it has become highly imperative for African nations to invest huge resources to drive the growth of infrastructure in order to expand the productive capacities of their economies and improve the human development dimension of the citizenry. However, infrastructure development is capital intensive and technologically driven. Thus, huge financial investments coupled with robust and advanced technology must exist before sustainable infrastructure development can be achieved. Major deficits in the rudiments of infrastructure development have been cited as some of the causes of Africa's underdevelopment in both social and economic infrastructure fronts.

Infrastructure needs are substantially larger, and a massive infrastructure effort is necessary to keep up with the continent's fast population and rising aspirations. However, a long-term foundation for environmentally and socially sustainable growth and prosperity will also require a focus on sustainable infrastructure. The available funding sources have been unable to keep up with the growing demands. In view of this, the role of NDBs has become paramount and their impact of their contribution to infrastructure development in Africa merits attention.

The rest of the chapter is structured as follows: Sect. 6.2 identifies the challenges of infrastructure development in Africa; Sect. 6.3 discusses the infrastructure financing instruments; Sect. 6.4 examines the role of NDBs in infrastructure financing; and Sect. 6.5 concludes the chapter.

6.2 Challenges of Infrastructure Development in Africa

One of the critical developmental challenges facing the African continent is limited access to sustainable infrastructure. In comparison with other regions of the world, Africa is plagued with pricey and poor infrastructure services. This limits productivity and lowers the continent's GDP (Calderon & Serven, 2004). Several factors account for the poor and inefficient state of Africa's infrastructure. These include huge capital and financial requirements, political and social risk, inadequate data and lack of strategic planning, high cost of infrastructure, low technical expertise and a high proportion of infrastructure spending.

6.2.1 Huge Capital and Financial Requirements

Infrastructure development generally involves the commitment of huge financial resources and capital from various stakeholders. Economic infrastructure such as roads, railways and energy, among others, is capital intensive and thus requires sustainable financial resources. The African Development Bank (2018) estimates that Africa requires between US$ 130 billion and US$ 170 billion annually to fund the infrastructure deficit that it faces, especially in the economic and social sectors of the continent. This is expected to balloon further given the plummeting of the global economy and the continuous rise in prices of global goods and services in recent times. Given the fact that nearly two-thirds on average of African countries' annual budgets are donor-supported and externally sourced from the international capital market (World Bank, 2018b), infrastructure financing on the continent has experienced low investment and unstable allocations. The heavy dependence on the external capital market, coupled with unfavourable conditions associated with grants and loans from bilateral partners, makes it extremely challenging to marshal the needed finances to meet the infrastructure needs of the continent.

Countries are therefore compelled to embark on small pieces of investment adventures that are either not yielding the needed dividends to attract private players into the economy due to limited production capacity or to engage in shoddy constructions that do not stand the test of time and raise sustainability challenges. Thus, infrastructure development on the African continent can be described a cyclical problem with an average life span of 15 years for roads and 35 years for port infrastructure (Calderon & Serven, 2004). It is equally important to note that budgetary allocations to infrastructure development over the years in Africa continue to witness a consistent decline in both absolute and relative terms. Policy-makers do not rely on relevant data to allocate resources to the most productive sectors of the economy; rather, in most instances, they rely on political manifesto fulfilment with the objective of retaining political power. The World Bank (2018a) indicates that capital expenditure, especially on infrastructure by African countries, reduced from 30% in 2012 to about 15%, making it the continent with the least capital expenditure. This is despite the fact that the continent has the biggest infrastructure deficit in the world with millions of its citizenry living without access to basic services like water, sanitation, primary health care, education and electricity.

6.2.2 Political and Social Risk

Political and social risks over the years have crippled investment into infrastructure development in Africa. Corruption has served as a disincentive to foreign investors coming to Africa. Financial resources have been squandered by corrupt duty bearers that could have been used for infrastructure development. Nearly 30% of the continent's GDP is lost through corrupt activities annually (see Standard & Poors, 2015), which could close the infrastructure funding gap by up to 40%. Policy uncertainty, political interference, bureaucracy, poor and unfavourable legal environment, frequent changes in governments and endemic corruption have characterized the socio-economic ecosystem of the continent, which contribute in many diverse ways to stifle and affect investment in infrastructure. Investors, donors, operators among other stakeholders in the infrastructure front are faced with clarity issues regarding government policies, regulations, contracting and procurement procedures and processes, project planning, arbitration and taxation (tariff setting). Insecurity and social unrest have engulfed the continent for far too long. The emergence of terrorism in several African countries such as Mali, Niger, Nigeria, Burkina Faso, Togo, Chad, Cameroon and Somalia, which often targets foreign nationals, has the tendency to scare away investors. The 2010–2011 uprisings in the northern African countries of Egypt and Tunisia are disincentives to foreign investment inflows. The recent political and social unrest in some countries such as Burkina Faso, Mali, Gambia, Guinea and northern Nigeria is inimical to infrastructure development. Political stability, social cohesion, transparency and accountability are fundamental to facilitating investment in an economy. Thus, the absence of these factors serves as a breeding ground for the continuous infrastructure deficit recorded on the continent year in and year out. This is expected to worsen due to the increasing insecurity of insurgency, political overthrows and social unrest in the years ahead.

6.2.3 *Inadequate Data and Lack of Strategic Planning*

The inadequacy or lack of reliable data and non-prioritization of infrastructure interventions through strategic planning present a major setback for infrastructure delivery in Africa. Continuous population growth in Africa places high demand on social and economic infrastructure by households and communities. Africa is also increasingly becoming more urbanized, thereby fuelling the demand for more infrastructure. The steady and fast growth of the population coupled with the increasing urbanization of the continent puts a lot of pressure on the limited existing infrastructure, and this reduces the lifespan and by extension the quality of services they provide. Inadequate and lack of reliable data on key sectors further exacerbate strategic interventions in the provision of infrastructure. With competing demands from other areas, governments in Africa remain disillusioned in providing the needed infrastructure through prioritized resource allocation and policy decision-making using scientific data and planning tools.

6.2.4 *High Cost of Infrastructure and Low Technical Expertise*

Project delays and variations in scope often characterize most infrastructure execution in Africa. These have the potential to lead to budgetary overruns in project management. Poor project initiation and management often ignore key stakeholder involvement, which is paramount in a successful implementation of complex and risky projects with many interconnected parts of service provision for different end-users. Social and economic factors such as political interference, absence of inputs including water, power, accommodation and ports, among others, are inimical to facilitating the process and execution of infrastructure provision in Africa. Skilled labour, equipment, machinery and materials are usually imported with huge time lags and could constitute enough grounds for delays in project implementation and increases in cost of financing.

Poor project management, capital-rationing and irregular releases of funds to contractors, legal and environmental requirements, bureaucracy, policy changes (political interference) and technical expertise are among the factors associated with project delays, resulting in overruns in infrastructure delivery in Africa. Also, macroeconomic variables such as inflation, currency swings and controls, global financial market dynamics and technical factors including monitoring and evaluation, project cost estimations, impact assessment and financial controls are critical to the success of any project implementation, and these are usually lacking in most African countries and may likely contribute to high cost and poor quality of infrastructure provision.

6.3 Infrastructure Financing Instruments

Generally, public funds have constituted the primary source that support infrastructure development. Considering the intrinsic public good nature of infrastructures and the favourable externalities frequently produced by them, governments were the main financiers of infrastructure provision through budgetary allocation. However, fiscal deficits, rising public debt-to-GDP ratios and occasionally the public sector's inability to deliver efficient capital spending have reduced the amount of public funds dedicated to infrastructure in many nations. Different financing instruments and vehicles as well as alternative capital streams can be employed to finance infrastructure development. This section discusses some of these financing instruments or mechanisms, including infrastructure project finance (project debt finance, project mezzanine finance and project equity finance), balance sheet finance (debt instrument, equity instruments and hybrid instruments) and market vehicles.

6.3.1 *Infrastructure Project Finance*

In contrast to corporate finance, project finance involves the financing of a separate, clearly-defined economic unit (Weber & Alfen, 2010). It is the structured finance of a specific economic entity—the special-purpose vehicle (SPV), also known as the project company—created by sponsors using equity or mezzanine debt and for which the lender considers cash flows as being the primary source of loan repayment, whereas assets represent only collateral (Gatti, 2013). Under this arrangement, the cash flows from the project are ring-fenced and used to repay the loan and lending agreements are based on the project's ability to generate cash flow. It involves risk sharing among the different project stakeholders. Only the provided equity capital is liable, and lenders frequently have little recourse against key stakeholders.

Project financing frequently uses Public–Private Partnerships (PPP) contracts. Although PPPs are not the only project finance structures accessible, they have become a significant legal structure to define project finance investment. The main PPP financing models include Build-Operate-Transfer (BOT) Model, Build-Transfer-Operate (BTO) Model, Buy-Build-Operate (BBO) Model, Lease-Develop-Operate (LDO) Model, Perpetual Franchise Model, Wraparound Addition, Temporary Privatisation, Speculative Development, Value Capture and the Use-Reimbursement Model. Each financing model differs in respect of the contribution, responsibilities and rewards of each partner (public or private venture) (Finnerty, 2013; Kuttu et al., 2020).

6.3.2 *Project Debt Finance*

Infrastructure projects typically have higher levels of debt than non-infrastructure investments, considering the less volatile cash flows and the willingness of project sponsors to accept higher levels of debt. Infrastructure projects are often financed by debt instruments and may range between 70 and 100% debt finance. Project finance debts are mostly denominated in the local currency to minimize currency mismatch between revenues from the project and financing flows, although hard currency issuance could be made. For countries where currency derivatives are traded, cash flows may be hedged, allowing for multi-currency financing structures. Countries that have shallow debt markets will require certain legal frameworks and the enforceability of contracts to be established, in addition to other supportive conditions such as sound fiscal and monetary policy frameworks. Infrastructure debt finance may arise through direct project loans and project bonds (OECD, 2015b). Box 6.1 shows a case of project bond issued in South Africa to finance the Touwsrivier Solar Project.

Box 6.1 Project Bond Case Study—South Africa's Touwsrivier Solar Project

In South Africa, one of the innovative ways for financing infrastructure projects is through the use of a fixed income capital markets such as the 'Touwsrivier Solar Project bond'. The financial system of South Africa has shown evidence of sustainable development with an increasing institutional investor base comprising of ZAR 3 trillion (US$ 177 billion) assets under management. This project was classified under the green fund project to support the economically poor or remote areas in the country. For instance, a green bond with a face value of ZAR 1 billion (US$ 59 million) was issued to fund the construction of a 44 MWp concentrated photovoltaic plant. The bond, which has a term of 15 years and a coupon of 11%, has a repayment structure similar to that of a home loan—a first. As already mentioned, it is difficult to adjust to the financing of a bullet structure of a representative project bonds and can pose the risk of refunding. This risk is effectively controlled through a risk management framework. A similar characteristic of such project was the returns provided by the REFIT programme of South Africa's, which allowed the country's electricity companies, with the support of the South African Department of Energy, to buy renewable sources of energy that have fixed prices. Thus, leading to an issue that increases the creditworthiness or credit rating of the capital market (i.e., rating the bond at the time of issue to Baa2 by Moody's rating criteria).

Source Deloitte report on Project Bonds: An Alternative Source of Financing Infrastructure Projects. www2.deloitte.com/za/en/pages/finance/articles/project-bonds-an-alternative-to-financinginfrastructure-projects.html

6.3.3 *Project Mezzanine Finance*

Project mezzanine finance includes a privately-placed subordinated loan or bond used in project finance or private equity investments and often includes equity participation. It is associated with higher risk and pays higher yields than senior issues. Project mezzanine finance provides further credit support for the senior debt and may be its requirement for securing the senior debt tranche of a project finance deal. Such issues would absorb credit losses before senior issues, thus helping to raise the credit quality of senior tranches. Subordinated debt can be issued by development banks, commercial banks or project SPVs through private placements or on the public market. Tranching of debt also creates different risk/return profiles for investors. The higher yields and equity participation rights in connection with mezzanine debt may be attractive to some investors such as pension funds (OECD, 2015b).

6.3.4 *Project Equity Finance*

Projects are typically initiated by project sponsors who contribute initial equity to the project's SPV, or in the case of PPP structures, participate as bidders for projects tendered by the public sector (Weber & Alfen, 2010). Project sponsors are also involved in the management of the SPV, while other equity finance providers (financial sponsors) are generally not part of running the operations of the SPV. Equity investment may range from 10 to 30% of the overall capitalization of the project. Equity investors are generally exposed to a greater level of risk associated with the project. In times of financial stress, such as the credit crisis, debt holders may demand higher levels. Equity investors often prefer keeping their stake as low as possible, thus limiting their liability and increasing their returns. Equity markets are important in financing infrastructure that seeks long-term engaged investment to sustain innovation, value creation and growth. Equity financing is mainly useful for projects with a high-risk-return profile, such as innovative and high-growth technologies and projects. Debt finance providers generally tend to shy away from financing projects with unstable or unpredictable cash flows, or where future growth is a large component of expected return (OECD, 2015b).

6.3.5 *Balance Sheet Finance*

The conventional method of non-public infrastructure financing is corporate finance. Investment and management firms sell their shares on the open market or debt finance from capital markets to finance their projects. Companies are made up of a diverse portfolio of projects with various operational and performance concerns. Shares in infrastructure companies may be bought directly by retail and institutional investors, or they may use investment managers to choose securities on their behalf.

6.3.6 *Debt Instruments*

Corporate debt instruments such as straight corporate bonds, subordinated bonds and convertible bonds can be issued in bond markets. Bond issuers can raise long-term debt finance through bond markets. However, considering the underdeveloped nature of the corporate bond market in Africa, corporates tend to fall on bank loans through the syndicated loan market, in which loans are bundled and offered to investors on the market. Banks can pool individual smaller loans through securitization and offer them as securities on the bond market. Similar to securitization, collateralized loan obligation (CLOs) increases the amount of potential liquidity available to banks by utilizing the capital markets. Corporate entities can access private market channels to raise equity and debt finance through direct or co-direct investments by institutional investors.

Governments and regulators have used taxes as a potent instrument to reshape the capital markets. Debt becomes an element of an effective capital structure for infrastructure corporate finance when interest payments are treated as a pre-tax expense, which lowers the after-tax cost of issuing debt. The weighted average cost of capital (WACC) for infrastructure projects decreases as a result of low-interest rates and the advantages of the tax shield, increasing returns to equity holders (Bitsch et al., 2010). In addition to the WACC advantages, higher debt levels lower agency costs associated with splitting ownership by limiting the amount of free cash flow that managers can use as they see fit, or the so-called discipline of debt (Helm & Tindall, 2009). Government, municipal and sub-sovereign bonds constitute significant financing instruments of infrastructure. Central and local governments, as well as sub-sovereign organizations like government agencies and multilateral development banks that have the tacit support of the sovereign body, sponsor the issuances of such bonds.

6.3.7 *Equity Instruments*

Private and public equities are the two main types of equity financing. Private equity investors invest equity capital in unlisted firms, whereas public equity investors focus on firms, funds or assets that are listed on a stock exchange. Additionally, private equity providers might be deeply involved with or support the initial shareholders/owners or managers in the development and management of the asset, whereas public equity investors are not usually active in the management of the company (and are typically minority shareholders).

6.3.8 *Hybrid Instruments*

By design, hybrid instruments have elements of both debt and equity. Due to their ability to absorb losses, convertible bonds, subordinated debt and preference shares provide credit support to senior debt instruments. However, because they carry higher credit or equity risk, they tend to have higher return potential.

6.3.9 *Market Vehicles*

The use of market vehicles involves pooling capital for financing infrastructure through a diversified portfolio of financial securities, loans or private share holdings. A wide range of investors are drawn to public market funds such mutual funds, index funds, exchange-traded funds (ETFs) and open-ended funds. Such funds provide daily liquidity and come under the regulation of the securities markets regulators, and occasionally, in the case of ETFs and listed open-ended funds, they are traded on stock exchanges. Retail and institutional investors can invest in infrastructure securities such as shares and bonds through such channels, offering a high degree of diversification and transparency. Bond and loan indices typically follow issuance in the wider market, but they may also contain infrastructure-related debt that complies with index inclusion requirements. Private market funds serve as general partnerships (GPs) and they are a unique investment channel targeted at institutional investors. The limited partners (LPs) in such funds include investors who gain access to infrastructure investments such as unlisted equity or private debt in a diversified manner and appeal to smaller pension funds or insurance firms that lack the internal ability to handle assets directly (OECD, 2015b).

6.4 The Role of National Development Banks in Infrastructure Financing

Over the recent decade, there has been a resurgence in the establishment of new NDBs, with new institutions being founded in the United Kingdom, Colombia and Nigeria among others. NDBs controlled around 6.5% of global banking assets in 2018, a figure that is expected to rise. They can be beneficial in filling market gaps and providing conservative financing to national priority projects with long-term repayment schedules. They can take risks that the private sector would not, and support projects that have enormous social benefits but low financial returns. NDBs' lending can also compensate for private credit contractions during recessions. However, they may compete unfairly with commercial banks thereby stifling private investment within the financial ecosystem.

NDBs play different key roles in the promotion of infrastructure development on the continent (including supporting infrastructure investment and financing) provision of public goods, and the deepening of financial markets and instruments among others. The roles of NDBs are discussed in this section.

6.4.1 Supporting Infrastructure Investment and Growth

According to Bhattacharya and Holt (2015), emerging and developing economies have significant unmet infrastructure needs including energy, transport, water, health and education, which will stifle growth if not addressed quickly and on a large scale. It is projected that between 2014 and 2030, the gap between present and required infrastructure investment in African nations will average between US$1 and US$1.5 trillion per year in the core infrastructure sectors. Traditionally, public funds have been used to finance a large portion of infrastructure development in both developed and developing countries. State budgets, in recent times, have dwindled and cannot meet the demand for infrastructure needs. Since the global financial crisis of 2008, budget limitations in many nations throughout the world have led to a decline in public sector investment, negatively impacting output, private investment, unemployment and growth prospects. Additionally, while existing MDBs such as the World Bank, IMF, among others, play an important role in infrastructure financing, they can only cover a portion of the large infrastructure financing needs of developing nations.

NDBs have been identified as playing a critical role in helping to fund infrastructure in general, complementing governmental and private investment in infrastructure, particularly in fiscally challenging times. Given the huge volume of the initial investment requirements associated with infrastructure expansion and the extended duration of amortization of credit facilities, NDBs are specifically designed to provide infrastructure development and financial needs. Furthermore, NDBs frequently have very high credit ratings and investor confidence due to the collateral involvement of the state. This could be used as a bargaining instrument to raise long-term finance from the capital markets at a cheaper cost and pass it on to their borrowers.

There is a bigger case for NDBs to play a significant role in infrastructure finance. Studart and Gallagher (2016) suggest that NDBs can play leading roles in reducing costs and identifying the risks of projects, leveraging global and local finance, and in governance and leadership on projects and project goals. At their best, they can ensure confidence, reduce risks, bring in relevant instruments and encourage participation of other sources of financing at both the initial phase and maturity stage of the project. As honest brokers, they can support the bringing together of governments, the private sector, investors and civil society, and help in establishing replicable and scalable models. Boxes 6.2 and 6.3 illustrate the roles of Infrastructure Development Bank of Zimbabwe and the Development Bank of Southern Africa in infrastructure financing, respectively. Studart and Gallagher (2016) also note a few challenges faced by NDBs to financing infrastructure. A major one is their size relative to countries' investment needs. This goes beyond a simple balance sheet constraint, but a small size limits the 'capacity to engage in an efficient manner with project identification, design, and beyond'.

The limited availability of private lending, coupled with huge infrastructure needs in advanced and developing economies, provides a basis for increased funding by NDBs to fill these gaps. The establishment of new MDBs such as the Asian Infrastructure Investment Bank (AIIB), which is focused on infrastructure development, demonstrates the value of infrastructure in Asia and among the BRICS.

Box 6.2 The Mandate of Infrastructure Development Bank of Zimbabwe in Infrastructure Development

The Infrastructure Development Bank of Zimbabwe (IDBZ) draws its policy mandate from the Act of Parliament (IDBZ Act, Chapter 24:14) and was established on 31 August 2005, after taking over from the Zimbabwe Development Bank (ZDB). The Bank acts primarily as an infrastructure DFI with the primary focus on providing infrastructure development support in order to stimulate the social and economic development as well as improve the living standards of Zimbabweans. Based on the IDBZ Act, Chapter 24:14, the Bank seeks to prioritize its support for development projects and programmes in sectors such as energy, transport (roads, railways, etc.), housing, dams, water and sanitation systems, sewerage, as well as information and communications technology (ICT), public facilities and services. In addition, the Bank makes significant contributions to businesses and development projects by building institutional capacity in ventures and companies that are engaged in infrastructure development in Zimbabwe including capacity building in business and development projects.

Source www.afida-africa.org

Box 6.3 The Development Bank of Southern Africa and Infrastructure Financing

The Development Bank of South Africa (DBSA) is a government DFI institution established in 1983 with the objective of promoting economic growth and regional integration of sustainable development projects and programs in South Africa including the Southern African Development Community and all of sub-Saharan Africa. The Bank aims to build Africa's prosperity by driving inclusive growth and ensuring innovative solutions that drive social and economic development in emerging economies in sub-Saharan Africa. Specifically, the Bank mobilizes funds for an influx of projects that aim at creating sustainable planning and infrastructure development across the continent. In terms of the Bank's contributions, it facilitated the implementation of projects and programs targeted at infrastructural development. For instance, in the year 2020, it provided a funding value of R196 million (US$ 11.6 million) to the Government of South Africa for the implementation of infrastructure development projects such as those in the education, health and housing sectors, as well as several community infrastructure programs. This includes assisting the government in renovating and modernizing key government infrastructure and buildings for security, arts and culture, and military operations. The Bank supports key national programs implemented by the government, such as the 'Accelerated School Infrastructure Delivery Initiative' to address underfunded school infrastructure, National Health Insurance, Ideal Clinic Programs and the National Human Settlements programmes and the Student Housing Infrastructure Programme (SHIP).

Source www.dbsa.org

6.4.2 *Financing the Provision of Public Goods*

One major threat to the efforts of achieving global sustainable development is the challenge of climate change. Climate change has become a social, economic and environmental threat to the existence of humankind and the survival of the world economy, and has in recent years become the most expensive global item to finance. The global community is therefore faced with a challenge of defining a preventive and adaptive approach to climate change aimed at achieving a sustainable growth that is sensitive to environmental issues, and balances climate and economic growth. NDBs play an essential part in this pursuit of sustainable development agenda because they bring the benefits of varied expertise, administrative efficiencies and convening capacity. NDBs can aid in the raising of extra funds, the development of relevant policy frameworks and the implementation of successful projects that demonstrate the sustainability of particular green investments, such as renewable energy. Above all, they may assist in ensuring that a sustainable climate policy is fully compatible with the post-2015 global development goals and the Paris Agreement.

NDBs can achieve this global good of combating climate change through the mainstreaming of climate change into their activities and operations, adaptation and financing mechanisms. This can be done through the option of financing projects that are low carbon in order to help in the global effort to reduce and end poverty and inequality in all forms and shape and facilitate the initiation of new green development projects. The financing of projects by NDBs should be geared to the incorporation of environmental externalities and the introduction of adaptive technologies that are sustainable, such as renewable energy, even if the short-term returns are minimal or non-existent.

The role of NDBs in climate finance is discussed in greater detail in Chapter 8.

6.4.3 Deepening Financial Markets and Instruments

The role of financial markets in the economic growth process is well established in the extant literature. Financial markets have the potential to propel the growth of the private sector, which is fundamental to job creation and economic development. However, the extent to which a country's financial market responds to the forces of demand and supply remains one key factor that determines its effectiveness in the intermediary role it plays in the allocation of funds in the economy. Thus, a well-developed and functioning financial market efficiently distributes funds to economic agents in need of capital to invest in infrastructure through the issuance of various securities in the financial market.

In the above circumstances, NDBs have become instrumental in moderating the functioning of financial markets, especially in the debt markets. NDBs focus on the maximizing the social well-being and benefit of the public, and hence, they offer long-term credit maturity arrangements to finance infrastructure. Their participation in the financial market, therefore, increases access to long-term debt finance at lower costs. Their presence also helps in attracting other participating financial institutions and investors in the financial market. Such market participants are therefore compelled by the forces of the market to improve their level of efficiency in order to stay afloat in the competitive financial environment.

The intermediary and collaborative role played by NDBs between governments and the private sector has been seen as a compelling factor that ensures the deepening of the financial markets. NDBs can be used by various governments to mobilize funds from the private sector to undertake investments in infrastructures and other public goods. NDBs usually act as brokers (transaction advisors) and investments advisors to both the government and the investors, respectively. The raising of these funds is usually done through the issuance of domestic and foreign bonds, which require a functional local financial market. The reverse is true for private investors who seek debt securities to finance their operational and investment activities in order to set up or expand their firms. Governments, through NDBs, purchase shares floated by investors to raise capital and other long-term securities from the financial market to fund their infrastructure needs. This directly and indirectly provides funding to the private sector through the financial market to boost economic growth. This approach has been used by many developed and emerging economies including India, China, South Africa and Japan to rapidly grow and develop their financial markets and expand infrastructure in recent years. NDBs usually collaborate with other private financial institutions in raising the needed resources, both financial and human to deliver on their mandate of financing development projects critical to the growth of the economy and providing the needed expert advice to the government on policy and project implementations. The collaborative effort in project financing by the NDBs deepens the financial market, which serves as the conduit for the conduct of trading activities.

Other funds and innovations may emerge through the activities of NDBs and offer long-term debt finance through the capital market to financial consumers. This strengthens the capital market and offers a wide range of instruments that meet the needs and demands of financial consumers. These innovative financial instruments can be adopted by emerging and developing economies to develop their emerging and frontier financial markets. It has been argued that this approach can equally be used to develop the local currency and make it attractive to foreign investors. Box 6.4 shows the creation of an infrastructure value chain financing in Zimbabwe.

Box 6.4 The Creation of Infrastructure Value Chain Financing in Zimbabwe

The Infrastructure Value Chain Financing (IVCF) is a financing vehicle that was launched by Infrastructure Development Bank of Zimbabwe (IDBZ) in 2018. This was purposely to promote infrastructure development through the enhancement of capacity of key stakeholders in project financing to improve their efficiency and effectiveness in infrastructure delivery through the value chain operations. The IVCF increased access to the financial market and marshalled over $18.5 million dollars in just 6 months through loans to provide infrastructure in water and sanitation sectors. Nearly $7 million was approved from the fund to finance infrastructure development in these two sectors which were considered as some of the most lacking social infrastructure in many communities of the country. The IVCF provided lines of credit to avail the much needed foreign currency required to retool the business environment and enhance the productive capacity of the economy in order create jobs and support the efforts of government in infrastructure expansion drive. Overall, the loan book, incorporating the IVCF and housing projects, grew to US$ 58 million in 2019

6.5 Concluding Remarks

The immense role played by infrastructure in the socio-economic transformation of any economy cannot be downplayed. However, the continuous widening of the infrastructure gap that Africa experiences poses a major challenge to its effort to transform itself into a developed continent. The challenges of inadequate capital, political tensions, insurgency, insecurity, social unrest and mass corruption are among the many factors that hold back the efforts of many countries in Africa to embark on aggressive infrastructure development. Various financial instruments are available that can be leveraged upon by nations in Africa to mobilize and pool resources required for the purposes of infrastructure expansion. Key among them is the setting up of NDBs with a focus on financing infrastructure development. The use of NDBs to embark on infrastructure development has been well tested and established in both literature and in practice, and it is therefore seen by many as an alternative option to solving the challenges associated with infrastructure financing in recent times. The adoption of the NDBs' model of financing infrastructure is therefore recommended. South Africa, Zimbabwe, Egypt and Tunisia are some of the nations in Africa with concrete evidence of how NDBs can serve as a vehicle in developing infrastructure projects. NDBs can support infrastructure development in Africa in their roles of supporting infrastructure investment and financing, provision of public goods and deepening of financial markets and instruments.

References

African Development Bank. (2018). *African Economic Outlook 2018*. https://www.afdb.org/fileadmin/uploads/afdb/Documents/Publications/African_Economic_Outlook_2018_-_EN.pdf

Bhattacharya, A., & Holt, R. (2015). *Assessing the changing infrastructure needs in emerging markets and developing countries* (G-24/GGGI Paper Series).

Bitsch, F., Buchner, A., & Kaserer, C. (2010). Risk, return and cash flow characteristics of infrastructure fund investments. *EIB Papers, 15*, 1.

Calderon, C., & Serven, L. (2004). *The effects of infrastructure development on growth and income distribution* (Policy Research Working Paper; No. 3400).

Finnerty, J. D. (2013). *Project financing asset-based financial engineering*. Wiley.

Gatti, S. (2013). *Project finance in theory and practice*. Elsevier.

Helm, D., & Tindall, T. (2009). The evolution of infrastructure and utility ownership and its implications. *Oxford Review of Economic Policy, 25*(3), 411–434.

Kuttu, S., Fanta, A., Graham, M., & Abor, J. Y. (2020). Infrastructure financing and economic development. In J. Y. Abor, C. K. D. Adjasi, & R. Lensink (Eds.), *Contemporary issues in development finance*. Routledge.

OECD (Organisation for Economic Co-operation and Development). (2013, February). *The role of banks, equity markets and institutional investors in longterm financing for growth and development*. Report for G20 Leaders. http://www.oecd.org/finance/privatepensions/G20reportLTFinancingForGrowthRussianPresidency2013.pdf

OECD (Organisation for Economic Co-operation and Development). (2015a). *G20/OECD principles of corporate governance*. OECD Publishing. https://doi.org/10.1787/9789264236882-en

OECD (Organisation for Economic Co-operation and Development). (2015b). *Infrastructure financing instruments and incentives*. https://www.oecd.org/finance/private-pensions/Infrastructure-Financing-Instruments-and-Incentives.pdf

Simpson, R., & Zimmermann, M. (2012). *The economy of green cities: A world compendium on green urban economy*. Springer Science and Business Media.

Standard & Poors. (2015, January). Lessons learned from 20 years of rating global project finance debt. *S&P, Credit Week, 35*(3).

Studart, R., & Gallagher, K. (2016). *Infrastructure for sustainable development: The role of national development banks*. Boston University Global Economic Governance Initiative. https://www.bu.edu/pardeeschool/files/2016/08/Infrastructure.Sustainable.Final_pdf

Weber, B., & Alfen, H. W. (2010). *Infrastructure as an asset class: Investment strategies*. Wiley.

World Bank. (2018a). *2017 Survey of national development banks*. World Bank.

World Bank. (2018b, June). *Infrastructure in developing countries* (Report v2).

World Bank. (2018c). *Poverty and shared prosperity 2018: Piecing together the poverty puzzle*.

CHAPTER 7

National Development Banks and Sustainable Development

7.1 Introduction

The issue of sustainable development is a major concern to both policymakers and scholars. This is because it provides the kind of development that does not have negative consequences for the environment. This can take the form of a middle class that wants to contribute to poverty reduction and the supply of public goods, and thus values stability, as well as economic and political freedom (Wagner, 2020). Sustainable development can also take the form of creating jobs that absorb the age groups that enter the labour market each year (Wagner, 2020). In other words, sustainable development can be presented as social, environmental and economic (Riaño et al., 2022). To ensure the attainment of sustainable development, the United Nations (UN) set an agenda known as the Sustainable Development Goals (SDGs) which seek to achieve sustainable development by 2030. Although there are other sustainable development policies such as Africa Agenda 2063[1] and the European Union climate law and policy,[2] the SDGs remain a widely accepted benchmark for social,

[1] Agenda 2063 is Africa's development outline to accomplish inclusive and sustainable socio-economic development north of a 50-year time frame.

[2] EU environmental policies and legislation help to protect the environment, keep air and water clean, dispose of waste properly, raise awareness of toxic chemicals and move towards a sustainable business economy.

© The Author(s), under exclusive license to Springer Nature Switzerland AG 2023

J. Yindenaba Abor, *The Changing Role of National Development Banks in Africa*, https://doi.org/10.1007/978-3-031-38639-8_7

economic and environmental change to bring about the changes needed for social recovery and prosperity (Riaño et al., 2022). The programme is also unique in that governments have made clear commitments to involve countries in the path of change that will lead to greater social and economic stability. According to Hege et al. (2019), the SDGs have been presented as a paradigm shift which has been welcomed by numerous academics and Non-Governmental Organizations (NGOs) by identifying its premises, cons and pros. It also has the opportunity to make human and ecosystem well-being central to international relations.

Agenda 2030 seeks to achieve 17 goals and 169 targets by the end of 2030. When these goals are implemented efficiently, countries will be able to attain sustainable development. Notwithstanding that, there are challenges that countries face when implementing the SDGs, and chief among them are financial constraints and recent pandemics such as the coronavirus disease of 2019 (COVID-19). These challenges have exposed vulnerabilities and inequalities in most societies (Riaño et al., 2022). For instance, poverty in Africa was expected to worsen as 23 million people were expected to be extremely poor due to the outbreak of COVID-19 pandemic (ILO, 2020; World Bank, 2020). Also, there is a need to raise an estimated amount of US$ 140–175 billion by 2030, to address climate change in the developing economies[3] and US$5 trillion to US$7 trillion annually to cater for infrastructure. An estimated US$1 trillion to $1.4 trillion is needed annually by developing countries to finance infrastructure (Bhattacharya & Romani, 2013). In Africa, an estimated US$43–55 billion is needed annually from 2030 to 2040 in order to produce clean energy such as electricity, which is contrast to the reality that the continent is able to raise US$8–9.2 billion per annum.[4] It is therefore imperative for governments with low domestic capital to partner with the private sector and (or) development institutions to help finance the SDGs, since the policy allows for both private sector and (or) government to finance the goals and targets. However, most countries rely on either private sector or development institutions as a complement to their domestic capital to finance these goals while their sustainable development lags behind. In

[3] https://openknowledge.worldbank.org/bitstream/handle/10986/4387/9780821379875_overview.pdf.

[4] https://www.unep.org/resources/un-environment-annual-report-2017.

Africa, for example, economic growth is around 5% per year, but poverty, inequality and unemployment remain challenges (World Bank, 2020).

NDBs have a special role and focus compared to other players, such as international agencies or MDBs. Their specialized knowledge and long-term relationships with the local private sector have given them the advantage of access to local financial markets and an understanding of the barriers to investment (Smallridge et al., 2012). NDBs are generally less risk-averse than other financial intermediaries and provide long-term financing in the local currency market. As some countries treading at a slow pace to attain sustainable development, can NDBs really help them to attain the sustainable development? Is it possible for NDBs to curb the challenges of financing sustainable development? This chapter examines the role of NDBs in sustainable development.

The rest of the chapter is structured as follows: Sect. 7.2 provides an overview of sustainable development, while Section 7.3 discusses the challenges of financing sustainable development. Section 7.4 examines the role of NDBs in driving sustainable development and Sect. 7.5 makes concluding remarks.

7.2 Overview of Sustainable Development

Sustainable development has various definitions from different authors, but some issues stand out, including development, environment, equity and society. The scholars of sustainable development differ in emphasis on what is to be sustained or developed, how to link environment and development and for how long such development can be achieved. For instance, the popular definition by the World Commission on Environment and Development suggests that sustainable development is development that meets the needs of the present without compromising the ability of future generations to meet their own needs. The Commission of Sustainable Development (CSD) defines sustainable development as the ability to meet human needs for food, water and health, and provide opportunities for education, employment and participation.[5] CSD believes that equity, health, education, housing, security and stabilized populations must be developed. Ecological Footprint on the other

[5] https://sustainabledevelopment.un.org/csd.html.

hand expressed sustainable development as the area of biological productive land and water required to produce the resources consumed and to assimilate the waste produced by humanity.[6]

The idea of sustainable development emerged in the year 1713, when focus was laid on forestry sustainability realized by only cutting re-grown timber to maintain soil fertility (Lees, 2012). While the concept was still growing, Carson (1962) raised the concerns about the environment. The concept of sustainable development received its most memorable global recognition in 1972 at the United Nations Conference on Environment and Development (UNCED) in Stockholm. The term was not referred to explicitly, but in any case, the global community agreed with the idea that both development and the environment can be controlled in a way that is beneficial to the whole, which is currently the basis of sustainable development.[7] The term was popularized 15 years later in the report of the World Commission on Environment and Development (WCED), titled '*Our Common Future*'. This report viewed sustainable development as development that meets the needs of the present without compromising the ability of future generations to meet their needs as discussed above.

After this report, diverse ideas of sustainable development emerged and made the definition very comprehensive in order to capture other factors. There was an additional summit by UNCED in 1992 in Rio de Janerio in 1992. This summit, which was called the *Earth Summit,* created the Agenda 21 (i.e. a global programme of action on sustainable development), statement of principle for the Sustainable Management of Forests and the Rio Declaration on Environment and Development as agreed by more than 178 governments.[8] This summit was organized in order to cooperate internationally on post-Cold War development issues. There were some mechanisms established to follow up on the seminar and these included the Commission on Sustainable Development, the Inter-agency Committee on Sustainable Development and the High-level Advisory Board on Sustainable Development (Lees, 2012). Also, the Rio Declaration on Environment and Development outlined 27 principles countries needed to follow to attain sustainable development.

[6] http://sustainablefootprint.org/about-this-project/sustainable-footprint/#:~:text=The%20ecological%20footprint%20of%20a,is%20produced%20by%20these%20same.

[7] https://www.sd-commission.org.uk/pages/history_sd.html.

[8] https://sustainabledevelopment.un.org/index.php?page=view&nr=23&type=400&menu=35.

Two years later, there was an additional conference held in Barbados called the Global Conference on the Sustainable Development of Small Island and Developing States.[9] This resulted in the development of a policy popularly known as the Bardados Programme of Action (BPOA), which addresses issues on the environment and social developmental vulnerabilities facing Islands. Thereafter, the United Nations Millennium Declaration (UNMD), which was signed in 2000, committed world leaders to fighting poverty, hunger, disease, illiteracy, environmental degradation and discrimination against women.[10] The Millennium Development Goals (MDGs) were derived from the UNMD and comprised 8 goals, as the name implies. However, the MDGs were confronted with some limitations, which led to the formulation of the SDGs. Most importantly, the MDGs did not capture other commitments made in the Millennium Declaration on Governance, Transparency, Participation and Human Rights.[11] These limitations have been addressed in the SDGs, as they capture the complexity of sustainable development. Since, the SDGs incorporate the full dimension of sustainable development, we proceed to discuss them in detail in the next section.

7.2.1 UN Sustainable Development Goals

The United Nations (UN) Conference on Sustainable Development (SD) in Rio de Janeiro in 2012, twenty years after the 1992 'Earth Summit' at the same location, began discussions on a new agenda and the process of setting post-2015 goals. The SD declaration, 'The Future We Want,' was unanimously adopted, paving the way for the UN SD summit. The vision 'Transforming Our World: 2030 Agenda for Sustainable Development' was adopted in September 2015. In July 2015, the Addis Ababa Action Agenda of the Third International Conference on Financing for Development, one of the foundation stones of the 2030 Agenda, was adopted following negotiations and agreements on development finance

9 https://www.un.org/documents/ga/conf167/aconf167-9.htm.

10 https://www.who.int/news-room/fact-sheets/detail/millennium-development-goals-(mdgs)#:~:text=The%20United%20Nations%20Millennium%20Declaration,degradation%2C%20and%20discrimination%20against%20women.

11 https://www.un.org/en/chronicle/article/millennium-campaign-successes-and-challenges-mobilizing-support-mdgs#: :text=The%20MDGs%20have%20their%20limitations,the%20achievement%20of%20the%20Goals.

practices, partnerships and investments, as well as measures to achieve the new agenda (UN, 2015; Mohammed & Abor, 2023).

In September 2015, members-states of the UN met in New York to agree on the Sustainable Development Goals (SDGs), an agenda that addresses the limitation of Millennium Development Goals (MDGs) and also takes into consideration emerging development challenges. The MDGs dealt with challenges countries face (though not exclusively) on social outcomes while key development priorities, such as infrastructure and energy, were absent from the list. Therefore, the SDGs took on a comprehensive methodology, accepting challenges faced by all nations and advancing the participation between the private and public sectors in the execution of the goals. During the time of the MDGs, individual members of the UN assumed responsibility for individual targets and carried them out with restricted respect for different targets. The absence of clear direction on arrangement changes or how the goals should be accomplished were part of the often-detailed difficulties to the implementation of MDGs (Fukuda-Parr, 2006; Gil-González et al., 2009).

The SDGs are comprised of 17 goals (see Table 7.1) and 169 targets. They also include 232 indicators, which were selected to track global, regional and national progress, providing an evidence-based framework for monitoring progress over 15 years. SDGs' vision and action plans are proud to unite efforts to eradicate poverty and increase the development of helpless countries. These goals and targets reconcile the three dimensions of sustainable development namely economic, social and environmental. The SDGs pursue a more inclusive and diverse approach by gathering funds and developing partners for both advanced and emerging economies. However, reconciliation between larger goals and objectives must be the focus. While this may be necessary, it is important to compare the pursuit of an unbalanced distribution of goals and a coherent approach to implementation, as set out in Goal 17 (Jaiyesimi, 2016). A critical arrangement development with the SDGs is the making of the UN's High-Level Political Forum (HLPF), which is planned to meet yearly at the clerical level, and each fourth year at the heads of state level. The HLPF is entrusted with guaranteeing the joining of the three elements of sustainable development in an all-encompassing and cross-sectoral manner at all levels. It is intended to have a higher authority than comparable past institutions at the UN, to coordinate, secure inter-linkages, mobilize resources for implementation and monitor progress (Bernstein, 2017).

Progress on huge programmes like the SDGs requires huge financial investments. The cost of alleviating extreme poverty globally is estimated to be about US$66 billion a year, while the annual investment in further developmental projects (water, agriculture, transportation, energy) is likely to be up to US$7 trillion globally.[12] Nations or foundations alone cannot implement the vision for sustainable and inclusive development, which is at the centre of the SDGs. While huge government funding remains the foundation, the private sector must become an important partner in this endeavour. A closer look at the appropriate sources of funding for each goal shows that there should be a variety of commitments from the private sector. Institutions in high-income countries, while politically stable, are often reluctant to create business boundaries in low-income countries. To direct such long-term private investment from high-income countries to low-income countries requires 'patient capital' resources—the assumption that the activity pays off over many years or more, rather than quarterly or annually, is directed to low-income countries. In low-income countries, linkages between regions and nations are vital, especially in the early stages of market development, through the long-term interests of institutions and organizations that promote sustainable development. If SDGs are to be successful, they must enhance an inclusive approach to development, mobilize financial resources and eliminate the interest of unsustainable training in all nations (Jayesimi, 2016).

7.3 The COVID-19 Crisis and Sustainable Development

The COVID-19 crisis has impacted many aspects of daily life and has resulted in both economic and non-economic consequences. The coronavirus struck the whole world eight months after the first case of COVID-19 was discovered in Wuhan, China in November 2019 (named SARS-CoV-2). The WHO labelled the viral outbreak a public health emergency of global concern on the 30th of January 2020, and a

[12] https://sustainabledevelopment.un.org/intergovernmental/financecommittee.

Table 7.1 Millennium Development Goals (MDGs) and the Sustainable Development Goals (SDGs)

MDGs	*SDGs*
1: Eradicate extreme poverty and hunger	1: End poverty in all its forms everywhere
2: Achieve universal primary education	2: End hunger, achieve food security and improve nutrition and promote sustainable agriculture
3: Promote gender equality and empower women	3: Ensure healthy lives and promote well-being for all at all ages
4: Reduce child mortality	4: Ensure inclusive and equitable quality education and promote lifelong learning opportunities for all
5: Improve maternal mortality	5: Achieve gender equality and empower all women and girls
6: Combat HIV/AIDS, Malaria and other diseases	6: Ensure availability and sustainable management of water and sanitation for all
7: Ensure environmental Sustainability	7: Ensure access to affordable, reliable, sustainable and modern energy for all
8: Develop a global partnership for development	8: Promote sustained, inclusive and sustainable economic growth, full and productive employment and decent work for all
	9: Build resilient infrastructure, promote inclusive and sustainable industrialization and foster innovation
	10: Reduce inequality within and among countries

(continued)

Table 7.1 (continued)

MDGs	*SDGs*
	11: Make cities and human settlements inclusive, safe, resilient and sustainable
	12: Ensure sustainable consumption and production patterns
	13: Take urgent action to combat climate change and its impacts
	14: Conserve and sustainably use the oceans, seas and marine resources for sustainable development
	15: Protect, restore and promote sustainable use of terrestrial ecosystems, sustainably manage forest, combat desertification, and halt and reverse land degradation and halt biodiversity loss
	16: Promote peaceful and inclusive societies for sustainable development, provide access to justice for all and build effective, accountable and inclusive institutions at all levels
	17: Strengthen the means of implementation and revitalize the Global partnership for Sustainable Development

Source United Nations (2021)

pandemic on the 11th of March 2020 (Abor & Abor, 2021; Abor et al., 2022). While some of this impact enhanced sustainable development, others also hampered sustainable development. COVID-19 helped most countries to achieve UN's SDGs (i.e. climate action) as there was a reduction in carbon emission in some countries due to the shutdown of transportation. For instance, during social distancing in Los Angeles, there was a reduction in carbon emission of 1.1 million metric tons (Cicala et al., 2021). In Europe, nitrogen dioxide (NO_2) emission dropped in northern Italy, Spain and UK (Ficetola & Rubolini, 2021). Also, in China, there was a 25% reduction of carbon emission as people were asked to stay home (Saadat et al., 2020). Furthermore, COVID-19 helped most countries to achieve the UN's SDG 7 (i.e. affordable and clean energy) as most countries consumed clean energy and reduced the consumption of polluting fuels in power stations. Air quality in most countries changed since the usage of carbon-emitting machines was reduced. The pandemic resulted in cleaner beaches than ever, reduced marine pollution and also reduced environmental noise. By implication, COVID-19 helped most countries to maintain the environment, which is a key component of sustainable development, especially the attainment of a green earth.

Regardless of the unmistakable advantages of COVID-19, there were some negative consequences identified. COVID-19 limited the efforts of governments and their development partners to attain sustainable development. This happened when the pandemic threatened to exacerbate vulnerabilities in communities. The consequences of this increased social insecurity, suffering and inequality and indirectly affected social peace. This outcome of COVID-19 hindered the efforts of most countries to achieve the UN SDGs 1, 10, 8 and 16. In the period between 2015 and 2018, the rate of poverty reduced by 0.5%.[13] Nonetheless, due to the devastating impact of COVID-19, the poverty rate shot up for the first time since 1998 (Elavarasan et al., 2022). The outlook for income inequality in Africa has not been rosy after the coronavirus pandemic, which was expected to push nearly 23 million people into extreme poverty in 2021 (World Bank, 2020). Specifically, income inequality was expected to increase after the coronavirus pandemic due to slow economic growth and disrupted informal activity (IMF, 2020). COVID-19 as well affected most growth-enhancing sectors such as the travel and tourism sectors, small-scale industries and the manufacturing sector. For example, the estimates as of June 2020 suggested an overall drop in passengers ranging from 2.29 billion to 3.06 billion, which resulted in gross revenue losses between US$302 billion and US$400 billion.[14] Also, world trade was expected to fall by between 13 and 32% owing to the effects of the pandemic.[15] As most small-scale industries were affected, it will hinder the development efforts of most continents. In Africa, for example, small domestic firms account for the largest share of job creation, sales and employment growth, so if these firms collapse, there is the likelihood of high unemployment and low development. Manufacturing industries have a significant impact on the economies of underdeveloped countries because they provide overall economic growth, hence, COVID-19's effect on manufacturing sector will dampen economic growth.

In a nutshell, COVID-19 did have both negative and positive effects on sustainable development, but the negative effects outweigh the positives. This represents a challenge to the implementation of most SDGs.

[13] https://www.worldbank.org/en/topic/poverty/overview.

[14] https://unstats.un.org/sdgs/report/2020/goal-02/.

[15] https://www.wto.org/english/news_e/pres20_e/pr855_e.htm.

7.4 Challenges of Financing Sustainable Development

The challenge of sustainable development is centred on how a sustainable world must strive to meet the basic requirements of current generations ('intragenerational equity') without jeopardizing future generations' ability to meet their own needs ('intergenerational equity'). To surmount this challenge, strict procedures for financing sustainable development that meet the demands of present and future generations would be required. Sustainable development finance is a type of financing that uses a combination of clean and innovative sources to address the demands of current and future generations. The funding method could come from both local and foreign sources, including public and commercial funds like environmental finance, private sector finance and innovative finance for sustainable development (Abekah-Nkrumah et al., 2020).

Effective implementation of sustainable development, especially the SDGs, depends on how these goals are financed. However, most countries, especially those with developing economies, have difficulty financing these goals. Most countries have low domestic capital to finance these SDGs; hence they are encouraged to fall upon the private sector and development finance institutions. However, mobilizing funds from these sectors is associated with some challenges which affect the investment stream for sustainable development. These challenges include inadequate data, poor institutions and weak governance, corruption, high-risk perception and low level of technology.

Inadequate data is one of the barriers to financing sustainable development. While the signing of the SDGs set various targets and indicators to facilitate action, there was no definitive monitoring and evaluation scheme. Lack of data has made it difficult for countries to be accountable to donor partners, international society and civil society (Walker et al., 2019). For example, 77 out of 155 countries do not have adequate data on poverty (Serajuddin et al., 2015). This tends to limit the ability of investors to participate in the financing of the SDGs and limits the amount of capital required to finance such developments. Hence, to attract substantial funds to finance sustainable development, a data revolution is imperative. Funding investments can be valuable, but risk-averse investors are hard to convince without data. Without true and fair data, attracting private capital is difficult and may not allow such countries to achieve sustainable development (Espey, 2019).

In addition, poor institutions and weak governance within the recipient countries have been identified as major limitations to financing sustainable development. Poor institutions and weak governance discourage private sector participation in the investment of sustainable development. This is because when there are poor institutions and governance within country, investors lose confidence and are not ready to invest in it.

In addition, corruption is seen as a menacing factor to financing sustainable development. Corruption leads to the loss of financial resources from the public budget for private spending, including embezzlement of public funds. Globally, corruption activities such as embezzlement, money laundering and tax evasion amount to about US$ 800 billion to US$ 2 trillion annually.[16] Investments in electricity, sanitation and water are reduced by about 40% due to corruption (Walker et al., 2019). Controlling corruption could raise US$1 trillion in global income for developing countries (IMF, 2019). This means that if the income of developing countries is increased by US$1 trillion, there will be enough capital to finance sustainable development. Corruption in public procurement and state-owned enterprises has been found in most developing economies, resulting in less efficient public spending where less spending and investment is made in sustainable development indicators such as health, education and living standards.[17] For example, when embezzlement occurs in public institutions in developing countries, already scarce funds that could be used to plan and implement sustainable development projects are lost (Hope, 2020).

Risk perception of the investors also hinders the financing of sustainable development. Most developing countries receive a great deal of foreign capital. For example, in Asia and the Pacific region, which contains emerging economies, private finance can provide about US$10 trillion yearly.[18] Also, the Organization for Economic Co-operation and Development (OECD, 2016) indicates that despite the inflow of private capital to developing countries, most of the funds are not invested in sustainable development. This mostly occurs when investors perceive that there is high-risk associated with investment in sustainable development. Thus,

[16] https://www.adb.org/news/adb-president-calls-stronger-efforts-fight-corruption.

[17] https://www.pubpoli.com/posts/2021/1/26/7cpgb7sulm6vcq7l4r0j9g1flkslu4.

[18] https://www.adb.org/sites/default/files/publication/158432/making-money-work-overview.pdf.

they direct their capital to investment in other areas, other than sustainable development. This could limit the amount of funds needed to finance sustainable development.

Another major challenge of financing sustainable development is the low level of technology. Digitization can help reduce barriers to private financing and is a powerful tool for increasing investment in sustainable development. For example, technology minimizes asymmetric information in environmental sustainability by reducing information rents that are associated with CO_2 emissions (Asongu et al., 2018; Avom et al., 2020). However, developing economies are said to be characterized by low use of digitalization. For instance, while some developed countries use technology to extract renewable energy despite their limited renewable energy resources, Africa and other developing countries still lack the requisite technology to extract their renewable energy resources.

7.5 The Role of National Development Banks in Driving Sustainable Development

NDBs are any type of financial institution that is supported by the national government, partially (usually 30% owned) or owned by the government. These banks are able to coordinate between government and the private sector to undertake major projects. There is a need for a mechanism that can serve to bridge the gap in attaining sustainable development and NDBs play many important roles in promoting sustainable development. A discussion of some of the roles NDBs play in driving sustainable development follows.

NDBs have a critical functional role in sustainable development through the provision of development finance to support economic growth. This is apparent when they provide development finance to Small and Medium Enterprises (SMEs) and other important sectors of the economy such as agriculture and manufacturing. For example, Banco de Desenvolvimento de Minas Gerais (BDMG) allocated US$ 400 million to support SMEs in 2020. In most developing and African countries, SMEs contribute more to job creation, sales and employment, so allocating funds to support them will increase growth and development. They provide finance for the expansion of the manufacturing sector. For instance, the China Development Bank provided RMB 374.2 billion (US$ 53 billion) of loans to the manufacturing industry in 2015 to promote the sector. Development finance provided by NDBs is necessary for private sector growth and the eventual growth of the economy (see Box 7.1).

Box 7.1: Development Bank of Kenya Bolster Economic Growth in Kenya

Development Bank of Kenya (DBK), which is identified as development financial institution, was founded in 1963 and started operation in 1964. It concentrated its investment in a wide range of sectors such as agriculture, manufacturing, construction, communication and among others in Kenya. One of its current outstanding projects is how it provided €89 million to bolster economic recovery. The loan was approved by the bank in June 2021 and helped to provide funding for the second phase of the Competitiveness and Economic Recovery Support Programme (CERSP). This helped GDP growth to rebound strongly to 7.5% in 2021 from a contraction of 0.3% in 2020. The action of DBK has helped Kenya achieve SDG 8 through the attainment of economic growth. This activity also helps to achieve SDG 17 as they serve as developing partner to Kenya.

Source https://www.devbank.com/

NDBs initiate developmental projects and identify investors to finance such projects; therefore, they can be described as playing the role of lead developmental actors. For example, in China, the CDB helped develop policies to attract private investors to invest in renewable energy (solar energy) and provided significant seed funding. This has made China one of the world's biggest proponents of solar power.[19] In South Africa, the DBSA has identified a project such as Embedded Generation Investment Programme (EGIP), where it uses GCF and other stakeholders such as local people, commercial banks and other financial institutions to finance projects (see Box 7.2). The Infrastructure Development Bank of Zimbabwe is instrumental in providing long-term finance for major infrastructure development in South Africa.

[19] https://www.weforum.org/agenda/2019/05/why-the-world-needs-national-development-banks.

Box 7.2: Development Bank of Southern Africa (DBSA) promoting SDGs in Africa

The Development Bank of South Africa (DBSA) is a government-owned development finance institution founded in 1983 with the mission of promoting economic growth and regional integration for sustainable development. DBSA provides various kinds of projects that promote the welfare of South Africa. For example, in order to promote affordable houses in Africa, DBSA collaborated with Habitat for Humanity South Africa and participated in the Mandela Week building programme. This was accomplished when the bank sponsored the construction of five houses in Palm Ridge, near Katlehong, on the East Rand. Each house is expected to house a minimum of five family members. This project assists the government in meeting the housing challenge in South Africa and meeting the housing demands of South African citizens. This long-term project contributes to the achievement of SDG 10, which is to reduce inequality.

Furthermore, in order to promote hunger alleviation by 2030, the DBSA collaborated with Rise Against Hunger, an international hunger relief non-profit organization. This project was designed to help schoolchildren who are struggling by providing food to various development programmes such as the School Launch Programme and the Early Childhood Development Programme. The DBSA sponsorship extends beyond the provision of combined rice, soy, micronutrient flavoring mix, and dehydrated vegetables. The role of DBSA contributes to the achievement of SDG 2 (end hunger), SDG 3 (healthy living), and SDG 4 (quality education). This is because children who have access to food are more likely to focus on their studies. Furthermore, because the food is sourced from well-known food processing companies such as Kraft Heinz, whose products contain 20 essential vitamins and minerals, the students' health is improved. In 2019, DBSA sponsored 150, 000 meals which could feed 578 children in most schools.

Moreover, the bank has increased the Green Climate Fund by US$100 million to invest in solar photovoltaic (PV) and wind technologies. This investment contributed to the successful implementation of the Embedded Generation Investment Programme (EGIP). The goal of EGIP is to create an enabling environment and a new funding model for continuing renewable energy investments outside of the Renewable Energy Independent Power Producer Procurement Programme (REIPPPP). EGIP is a DBSA-initiated programme that promotes renewable energy production and consumption. The financial mechanism is expected to attract an additional $104 million in funding from local, commercial, and financial institutions.

The full implementation of EGIP will save 700,000 tonnes of CO_2 and add 330 megawatts (MW) of solar and wind generating capacity. The bank will provide approximately $84 million in financing to Black and/or Black-Employed (B-BBEE) beneficiaries to help engage local communities and small businesses in renewable energy projects under EGIP. This will assist in the attainment of SDG 7, SDG 10, SDG 8 (i.e., decent employment).

Source https://www.dbsa.org/

NDBs also facilitate coordination for developmental projects since they are able to access reliable information. This role allows them to gain access to long-term domestic and international financing as international partners, and also to work closely with international institutions. For example, the Inter-American Development Bank (IDB) partners with over 40 DFIs in the Latin American and Caribbean (LAC) region and has financed over US$2 billion in credit line programmes and leveraged more than US$6 billion in green private investments to date. The Development Bank of Ethiopia (DBE) and DBSA coordinate a project between the government and international development partner (see Box 7.2 and 7.3). For instance, DBE served as one of the implementing agencies and financial intermediaries for loans provided by the World Bank to finance Ethiopia's off-Grid Renewable Energy and Energy Efficient Programme (see Box 7.3). They used this opportunity to attract domestic and international investors to participate in investment for sustainable development.

Box 7.3: Development Bank of Ethiopia as the Implementing Agencies to Energy Programme

The Government of Ethiopia through the Development Bank of Ethiopia (DBE) developed an off-Grid Renewable Energy and Energy Efficient Programme. This promotes the use of off-grid energy by the private sector in Ethiopia. To ensure efficient implementation of this programme, the bank served as a financial intermediary and mobilised funds from World Bank to the government of Ethiopia. The programme had two phases; the first phase was achieved in 5 years (2012–2015) whilst the second phase was completed in 3 years (2016–2019)

Source Mugisha et al. (2021)

NDBs guarantee and serve as assurance components for investment and market creation. This means they create an investment portfolio for the private sector since they are better in managing and taking risk than commercial banks and other multinational banks. This important role builds confidence for investors to participate in financing sustainable development, especially financing climate change, thereby helping to scale up climate finance. This function of NDBs can help achieve goal number 13 of SDG, since they can mobilize sufficient funds to finance climate change. The role of NDBs in driving SDGs will require governments to focus on sustainable projects within the mandates of NDBs by creating a platform for blending instruments and co-financing phases in order to achieve sustainable development (Bhattacharya et al., 2016). This would be helpful in building, strengthening and scaling up sustainable businesses and connecting with the regional and global development finance community (Bhattacharya et al., 2016).

Finally, NDBs promote financial inclusion, which is a key factor in achieving the SDGs and is regarded as one of the important means of reducing poverty. NDBs are instrumental in providing financial access to SMEs and microenterprises including household agricultural activities on a long-term credit basis. NDBs are effective in improving financial access by pooling their customers' savings to support credit delivery to such customers at lower cost as opposed to the stringent conditions associated with commercial bank loans. One of the possible ways by which NDBs promote financial inclusion is through financing the portfolios of SMEs, which helps them to diversify idiosyncratic risk (Griffith-Jones et al., 2016). Such risk emerges when NDBs are in a dilemma in determining how an innovative project will be a success. Financial inclusion can also be promoted by NDBs through the provision of funds to other intermediaries such as credit unions and community banks that are closer to SMEs and local people in a community to support SMEs and such local people in the community (Griffith-Jones et al., 2018). The provision of financial assistance to other intermediaries by NDBs helps to promote financial inclusion in unreached communities. In Africa for instance, most communities are deprived of access to financial resources, which has caused the continent to be characterized by the lowest level of financial inclusion. Therefore, NDBs can extend financial resources to these SMEs and the poor in unreached communities.

7.6 Concluding Remarks

The pursuit of sustainable development is the desire of every world leader, but it is very difficult for developing countries or countries with limited domestic capital to achieve such development because of the level of investment involved. Also, the adverse impact of the COVID-19 pandemic has made most countries to lag behind as far as attaining sustainable development is concerned. This chapter has discussed NDBs and sustainable development. It was established that despite various attempts to address the issues confronting sustainable development, the SDGs are seen as the most comprehensive policy that could enable countries to attain sustainable development, if implemented effectively. The chapter has looked at the influence of the COVID-19 pandemic on sustainable development, and indicated that COVID-19 has helped most countries to achieve UN's SDGs (i.e. climate action) as there was a reduction in carbon emissions in some countries due to the shutdown of transportation. However, it hampered the progress of economies, economic agents and standards of living. We also identified the challenges in financing sustainable development, including inadequate data, poor institutions and weak governance, corruption, high-risk perception, and the low level of technology.

The chapter examined the important role that NDBs play in driving sustainable development. NDBs provide three major roles including the provision of development finance, initiating development projects, attaining information for facilitating coordination for developmental projects and serving as assurance components for investment and market creation. It is important for governments to support NDBs to perform the important role of financing sustainable development and minimizing financing challenges.

References

Abekah-Nkrumah, G., Assuming, P. O., Abor, P. A., & Mohammed, J. I. (2020). Financing sustainable development: New insights for the present and the future. In J. Y. Abor, C. K. D. Adjasi, & R. Lensink (Eds.), *Contemporary issues in development finance*. Routledge.

Abor, J. Y., Agbloyor, E. K., Donkor, G. N. A., & Alu, A. A. (2022). The COVID-19 pandemic and Africa's financial systems: How do we reform post-COVID-19 financial systems? In J. Y. Abor & C. K. D. Adjasi (Eds.), *The economics of banking and finance in Africa: Developments in Africa's financial systems* (pp. 1013–1037). Springer.

Abor, P. A., & Abor, J. Y. (2021). Implications of COVID-19 pandemic for health financing system in Ghana. *Journal of Health Management, 22*(4), 559–569.

Asongu, S. A., Le Roux, S., & Biekpe, N. (2018). Enhancing ICT for environmental sustainability in sub-Saharan Africa. *Technological Forecasting and Social Change, 127*, 209–216.

Avom, D., Nkengfack, H., Fotio, H. K., & Totouom, A. (2020). ICT and environmental quality in Sub-Saharan Africa: Effects and transmission channels. *Technological Forecasting and Social Change, 155*, 120028.

Bernstein, S. (2017). The United Nations and the governance of sustainable development goals. In *Governing through goals: Sustainable Development Goals as governance innovation* (pp. 213–239). MIT Press.

Bhattacharya, A., & Romani, M. (2013, March). *Meeting the infrastructure challenge: The case for a new development bank* (Vol. 21). G-24 Technical Group Meeting, Washington, DC.

Bhattacharya, A., Meltzer, J. P., Oppenheim, J., Qureshi, Z., & Stern, N. (2016). *Delivering on sustainable infrastructure for better development and better climate*. The Brookings Institution.

Carson, R. (1962). *Of man and the stream of time* (Vol. 36, No. 4). Scripps College.

Cicala, S., Holland, S. P., Mansur, E. T., Muller, N. Z., & Yates, A. J. (2021). Expected health effects of reduced air pollution from COVID-19 social distancing. *Atmosphere, 12*(8), 951.

Elavarasan, R. M., Pugazhendhi, R., Shafiullah, G. M., Kumar, N. M., Arif, M. T., Jamal, T., & Dyduch, J. (2022). Impacts of COVID-19 on Sustainable Development Goals and effective approaches to maneuver them in the post-pandemic environment. *Environmental Science and Pollution Research, 29*(23), 33957–33987.

Espey, J. (2019). Sustainable development will falter without data. *Nature, 571*(7765), 299–300.

Ficetola, G. F., & Rubolini, D. (2021). Containment measures limit environmental effects on COVID-19 early outbreak dynamics. *Science of the Total Environment, 761*, 144432.

Fukuda-Parr, S. (2006). Millennium development goal 8: Indicators for international human rights obligations? *Human Rights Quarterly, 28*, 966–997.

Gil-González, D., Ruiz-Cantero, M. T., & Álvarez-Dardet, C. (2009). How political epidemiology research can address why the millennium development goals have not been achieved: Developing a research agenda. *Journal of Epidemiology & Community Health, 63*(4), 278–280.

Griffith-Jones, S., Ocampo, J. A., Rezende, F., Schclarek, A., & Brei, M. (2018). The future of national development banks. In S. Griffith-Jones & J. A. Ocampo (Eds.), *The future of national development banks*. Oxford University Press.

Griffith-Jones, S., Xiaoyun, L., & Spratt, S. (2016). *The Asian Infrastructure Investment Bank: What can it learn from, and perhaps teach to, the multilateral development banks?* (IDS Evidence Report No. 179). IDS.

Hege, E., Brimont, L., & Pagnon, F. (2019). Sustainable development goals and indicators: Can they be tools to make national budgets more sustainable? *Public Sector Economics, 43*(4), 423–444.

Hope, K. R. (2020). Corruption reduction as a target of the sustainable development goals: Applying indicators and policy frameworks. In *The Emerald handbook of crime, justice and sustainable development* (pp. 105–130). Emerald.

IMF. (2019, April). *Curbing corruption* (pp. 39–66). IMF Fiscal Monitor.

IMF. (2020). *Assessment, E.B., IMF Executive Board Concludes 2020 Article IV Consultation with France.*

Jaiyesimi, R. (2016). The challenge of implementing the sustainable development goals in Africa: The way forward. *African Journal of Reproductive Health, 20*(3), 13–18.

Lees, F. (2012). *Lees' Loss prevention in the process industries: Hazard identification, assessment and control*. Butterworth-Heinemann.

Mohammed, A. S., & Abor, J. Y. (2023). The role of oil and gas in sustainable development in the global south. In J. Y. Abor & A. Karimu (Eds.), *Sustainability management in the oil and gas industry*. Routledge.

Mugisha, J., Ratemo, M. A., Keza, B. C. B., & Kahveci, H. (2021). Assessing the opportunities and challenges facing the development of off-grid solar systems in Eastern Africa: The cases of Kenya, Ethiopia, and Rwanda. *Energy Policy, 150*, 112131.

Riaño, M. A., Boutaybi, J., Barchiche, D., & Treyer, S. (2022). Scaling up public development banks' transformative alignment with the 2030 Agenda for Sustainable Development. *Review of Political Economy, 34*(2), 286–317.

Saadat, S., Rawtani, D., & Hussain, C. M. (2020). Environmental perspective of COVID-19. *Science of the Total Environment, 728*, 138870.

Serajuddin, U., Yoshida, N., & Eamatsu, H. (2015, April 30). *Much of the world is deprived of poverty data. Let's fix this*. Let's Talk Development: A Blog Hosted by the World Bank's Chief Economist.

Smallridge, D., Buchner, B., Trabacchi, C., Netto, M., Lorenzo, J. G., & Serra, L. (2012). *The role of national development banks in intermediating international climate finance to scale up private sector investments* (113 pp.). Inter-American Development Bank.

United Nations. (2015). *Addis Ababa Action Agenda of the third international conference on financing for development (Addis Ababa Action Agenda)*. United Nations.

United Nations. (2021). *The Sustainable Development Goals report 2021*. United Nations.

Wagner, L. (2020). *The allocation of resources of national development banks: Does it fit development goals?* (Working Paper).

Walker, J., Pekmezovic, A., & Walker, G. (2019). *Sustainable development goals: Harnessing business to achieve the SDGs through finance, technology and law reform*. Wiley.

World Bank. (2020). *Global economic prospects, June 2020*. https://doi.org/10.1596/978-1-4648-1553-9

CHAPTER 8

National Development Banks and Climate Finance

8.1 Introduction

Climate change poses the greatest threat to sustainable development, and its far-reaching and extraordinary consequences are severe for the most unfortunate and vulnerable groups. Climate change can be seen as changes in the weather pattern of a region due to frequent greenhouse gas emission (Ragavan et al., 2020; Werndl, 2016). In excess of 11,000 scientists affirm that the plant world is confronting outrageous climate conditions (Ripple et al., 2019). For instance, the sea level has risen between 25 and 30% due to glacier ice melt.[1] Most nations face challenges in combating climate changes (Bonnel & Swann, 2015). Due to the negative consequences of these climate changes, there have been diverse policies and conventions such as the United Nation Framework Convention on Climate Change (UNFCCC), Sustainable Development Goals (SDGs), European Union's (EU) policy to reduce high-carbon emission, Paris Agreement and African's Agenda 2063 that emphatically uphold the change to a low-carbon, more resource-proficient and sustainable economy.

The means through which climate change can be fought against is climate finance. Climate finance can be described as local, national or

[1] https://weather.com/science/environment/news/2021-04-16-earth-day-climate-trends-data-global-warming.

© The Author(s), under exclusive license to Springer Nature Switzerland AG 2023

J. Yindenaba Abor, *The Changing Role of National Development Banks in Africa*, https://doi.org/10.1007/978-3-031-38639-8_8

transnational financing that seeks to support the mitigation and adaptation of actions that will deal with climate, where funds are pooled from public, private and other sources of funds.[2] This funding is a global focus as most countries around the world work together to fund climate change. For example, the Copenhagen Accord agreed that the Annex 1 countries mobilize US$100 billion by the end of 2020 to finance climate change (OECD, 2015). However, some countries such as Mexico need US$5 billion each year from 2015 to 2029 for the clean energy project (PwC Mexico, 2015). Also, there is a need to raise an estimated amount of US$140–175 billion by 2030, to address climate change in developing economies.[3] In addition, an estimated US$43–55 billion is needed annually between 2030 and 2040 to produce clean energy, such as electricity, in Africa. This is against the reality that the continent is able to raise US$8–9.2 billion per annum (United Nations Environment Programme, 2017). The issue is that governments or world leaders alone cannot finance climate change. Therefore, it is necessary to rely on private capital because of the solidarity that will have a huge, innovative and long-lasting impact on all nations. However, there are few in the private sector engaged in financing climate change due to some challenges such as lack of transparency, high-risk levels and barriers, among others, due to economic inefficiency and underinvestment (Montero, 2017). Therefore, this creates an opportunity to involve NDBs to help overcome such challenges (Montero, 2017).

NDBs have been used because they play a unique role and are central to different players such as international agencies. For example, their specialized knowledge and long-term relationships with the local private sector give them the advantage of access to local financial markets and an understanding of the barriers to investment (Smallridge et al., 2012). One of the important roles played by NDBs is the promotion of environmental sustainability, particularly by combating climate change. Introducing measures of climate risk mitigation and adaptation and placing them at the core of NDB activities is necessary in maximizing their impact on sustainability. Hence, the overarching objective of this chapter is to examine the

[2] https://unfccc.int/topics/climate-finance/the-big-picture/introduction-to-climate-finance.

[3] https://openknowledge.worldbank.org/bitstream/handle/10986/4387/9780821379875_overview.pdf.

role NDBs can play in addressing the challenges in climate finance, scaling up climate finance as well as leveraging private finance.

The rest of the chapter is structured as follows: Sect. 8.2 provides an overview of climate finance. Section 8.3 discusses the challenges in climate finance and the role that NDBs can play. Section 8.4 identifies the sources, channels and mechanisms of climate finance, while Section 8.5 examines the roles of NDBs in scaling up climate finance. Section 8.6 looks at how NDBs leverage private finance and Section 8.7 concludes the chapter.

8.2 Overview of Climate Finance

The idea of climate finance started with UNFCCC, which took place in 1994. The idea behind the convention was to ensure that developed countries reduce greenhouse gas concentrations to levels that prevent adverse human-induced risks associated with climate systems. With this convention, industrialized nations were willing to provide financial support to less developed economies to fight against climate change. Grants and loans are currently being coordinated, overseen by the Global Environment Facility (GEF). Later, the Kyoto Protocol, which was adopted in 1997 but was operationalized in 2005, builds on the mission of UNFCCC.[4] Unlike, the convention, which only permits countries to adopt policies to mitigate climate change, the Kyoto Protocol commits its parties by setting internationally binding emission reduction targets. Currently, the Protocol has 192 parties and has an Adaptation Fund (AF) that helps in obtaining various means to help increase resilience to the impact of climate change. Among the various UNFCCC's summits, which are referred to as Conference of Parties (COP), COP 16, which was held in 2010, established the Green Climate Fund (GCF).[5] In 2011, the GCF was appointed as the financial mechanism operator. The COP sets the policy priorities and criteria for financing the financial mechanism, while the financial mechanism is accountable to the COP. The parties have also established two special funds, the Special Climate Change Fund (SCCF) and the Least Developed Countries Fund (LDCDF), but these funds are subject to the UNFCCC's GEF and the Kyoto Protocol's AF.

[4] https://unfccc.int/kyoto_protocol.

[5] https://unfccc.int/topics/climate-finance/the-big-picture/introduction-to-climate-finance.

Due to the persistent climate change and concerns raised by world leaders, the multilateral agencies also established another form of climate finance called Climate Investment Funds (CIF). CIF is one of the world's largest multilateral finance mechanisms for developing countries, which was created purposely to enhance low-carbon and climate-resilient development. CIF was launched in 2008 and it has joint funds provided by the partnership with government, the private sector, civil society, neighbourhood networks and six major MDBs, including the International Finance Corporation (IFC), African Development Bank (AfDB), Inter-American Development Bank Group (IDB), the World Bank, Asian Development Bank (ADB) and European Bank for Reconstruction and Development (EBRD).[6] Currently, CIF has a fund of US$62.8 billion with contributions from the private capital—US$19.5 billion, government—US$8 billion, bilateral and other agencies—US$15.4 billion, MDBs—US$17.9 billion, and the G7—US$2 billion.[7]

To strengthen global efforts to limit the global temperature rise, UNFCCC parties reached an agreement in 2015, known as the *Paris Agreement*, to fight against climate change through necessary actions and the required investment.[8] This agreement allowed all parties to have a common goal (i.e. to limit global warming to well below 2 or 1.5 degrees Celsius), and to make funds available to finance this goal (i.e. developed countries should take the lead to support developing economies, financially). To achieve this goal, the Parties were to submit their action, plan which is referred to as '*Nationally Determined Contributions (NDCs)*', by the end of 2020. Under this agreement, the operating entities (i.e. GEF and AF) of the financial mechanism and the special funding (such as SCCF and LDCF) would serve the Paris Agreement.

In addition, the 17 SDGs are based on decades of work by countries and the UN, where they allowed the involvement of private, public and charitable cooperation in financing the goals. For instance, the UN has created a finance scheme known as the Integrated National Financing Frameworks (INFF), which has been established in 80 countries to help shape the financing of the SDGs through reforms in budget, taxes,

[6] https://www.climateinvestmentfunds.org/about-cif.

[7] https://www.climateinvestmentfunds.org/finances.

[8] https://unfccc.int/process-and-meetings/the-paris-agreement/the-paris-agreement.

public–private partnership and access to finance and capital markets.[9] In 2021 alone, there was an investment of US$1.45 billion through 59 blended finance packages in 34 countries. At the regional level, Africa, which is one of the continents struggling with climate change consequences, has initiated a policy, which is Agenda 2063 (i.e. *The Africa We Want*). Goal seven of the Agenda 2063, seeks to promote environmentally sustainable and climate-resilient economies and communities.[10] Hence, Africa calls for partnership with various investors to finance this policy. For example, Africa welcomed a US$11.48 million grant from the African Development Fund, a portion of which was allocated financing climate change.[11]

However, important questions remain. How do you mobilize private investment in climate change action? How do you design risk and return arrangements to attract public and private investment? How do you provide incentives for public and private investment? In this sense, climate finance can act as a catalyst. The extant literature has no known or acceptable definition of climate finance. The UNFCCC sees climate finance as '*local, national or transnational financing-drawn from the public, private and alternative source of financing-that seeks to support mitigation and adaptation actions that will address climate change*'. Others also see it as '*climate-specific finance*', which means that there is a particular flow of funds that is aimed at low-carbon and climate-resilient development (Corfee-Morlet et al., 2009; Buchner et al., 2011). From the inception and various descriptions of climate finance, all these frameworks and policies call for investors to fund climate change.

Climate finance comes from a variety of sources, including the private sector, which provides US$37–72 billion in annual funding for climate finance, and US$21 billion annually from the government budget. Other sources of climate finance are US$2.2 billion a year from multilateral agencies, and voluntary/charitable donations of U$0.5 billion annually

[9] https://www.jointsdgfund.org/sdg-financing.

[10] https://au.int/agenda2063/goals.

[11] https://www.afdb.org/en/news-and-events/press-releases/african-union-welcomes-1148-million-grant-african-development-fund-strengthen-delivery-agenda-2063-49095#:~:text=of%20Agenda%202063-,African%20Union%20welcomes%20%2411.48%20million%20grant%20from%20the%20African%20Development,strengthen%20delivery%20of%20Agenda%202063&text-The%20African%20Union%20Commission%20(AUC,provide%20it%20with%20institutional%20support.

(Buchner et al., 2011). In 2020, MDBs' contribution to climate finance increased to US$ 38 billion, while US$28 billion was committed to high-income countries. Over the last five years, the World Bank has supported developing countries with over US$83 billion, with US$21.4 billion made in 2020 alone.[12] This has helped to reduce high levels of carbon and increased the consumption of renewable energy. Currently, the available climate finance financial mechanisms are GEF, AF, GCF and CIF.

8.3 Challenges in Climate Finance: What is the Role of National Development Banks?

As mentioned earlier, the finances required to prevent high greenhouse gas emissions are confronted with some challenges. The challenges identified in climate finance can be attributed to economic inefficiency and under-investment (Montero, 2017). Such challenges pave the way for the presence of NDBs to address such challenges. This chapter discusses these challenges and suggests how NDBs are needed to address them. These challenges include lack of transparency, lack of a common definition of climate finance, insufficient institutional arrangement, lack of expertise and potential risk.

8.3.1 Lack of Transparency

Lack of clear information on environmental information and project performance reduces the attractiveness of the project by creating information inequalities between investors and recipients (Pickering et al., 2017). Investors in climate finance are exposed to high-risk since there is information asymmetry. This results in mispricing of assets to accommodate the high-risk. In addition, in case of failure to act on the environment, society and governance (ESG) have no established rules, guidelines or green definitions, and there are low incentives and few serious consequences. NDBs can capitalize on this since they specialize in record-keeping. This means that NDBs must be climate ready with regard to planning, access and provision of climate finance. By implication, NDBs must be willing to accurately monitor and report on expenditures

[12] https://www.worldbank.org/en/news/press-release/2021/07/02/mdbs-climate-finance-for-developing-countries-rose-to-us-38-billion-joint-report-shows.

and returns. By doing so, they will attract investors, thus lessening their exposure to excess risk.

8.3.2 *Lack of Common Definition of Climate Finance*

Most recipients of climate finance are not able to distinguish them from Official Development Assistance (ODA). The difficulty in isolating such additional funds from ODA, makes their monitoring very difficult. For example, under the UNFCCC, developed countries include a commitment to provide funding that is new and additional to that already provided as ODA in their climate finance pledge. However, such funds are perceived as being inadequate (Tirpak et al., 2014). Since there is no clear definition of climate finance that shows disbursement and allocation of funds, NDBs can use this as an opportunity to partner with the government to ensure their efficient allocation. To achieve this, NDBs can help the recipient countries to distinguish between climate finance and ODA through enhancing the coordination of relevant national and international climate finance actors. This will help to allocate the funds to support the policy initiative and investment priorities.

8.3.3 *Insufficient Institutional Arrangement*

Inadequate institutional arrangements, including unclear roles and responsibilities, make it difficult for countries to determine where funds are flowing and whether they are being used as intended. Effective institutional arrangements, which are responsible for managing, monitoring and coordinating climate finance, help recipient countries to ensure efficient allocation of climate finance (Tirpak et al., 2014). Despite effective planning and implementation of climate related projects at the regional and local levels, measures put in place to monitor climate finance are limited. NDBs are recognized to play a major role in supporting programmatic or sectoral approaches. For example, since most participating countries have introduced multilateral and interagency committees, NDBs can work with such institutions to help monitor and coordinate climate finance.

8.3.4 *Lack of Technical Expertise*

Most developing economies have little understanding of low-carbon technology. Therefore, there is a need for developing a national technical knowledge and capacity that will explain the low-carbon technology to the stakeholders. A majority of climate-finance-receiving economies do not have the expertise in building portfolios of the investable projects (Montero, 2017). This is because national institutions do not have the capacity to design projects that ensure additionality of subsidies. NDBs are needed to provide the expertise to develop investment portfolios, since they are the only institutions that can issue external and internal financial instruments, and have the backing of the government of the host nations. In other words, NDBs are specialized in channeling long-term funds into the right instrument.

8.3.5 Potential Risk

Economic conditions differ across countries due to constant changes in financial markets, which present risk and challenge in attracting new sources of capital and potential investors (Griffith-Jones et al., 2020). Investors perceive high-risk to be associated with increased cost of funding and therefore demand higher returns on their investment. Also, any changes in the political system may influence the level of investment. In such situations, NDBs should guarantee and serve as assurance components for investment and market creation. This means that NDBs can create investment portfolios for the private sector since they are better placed in managing and assuming risk than commercial banks.

8.4 Sources, Channels and Mechanisms of Climate Finance

There are various sources of climate finance, but these sources can be classified broadly as public and private sources. The public sources deal with Development Finance Institutions (DFIs), climate funds, government budget and its agencies. Private sources, on the other hand, comprise commercial financial institutions, household, venture capital, private equity and infrastructure funds.[13] For more than a decade, global climate finance has been on the rise and despite its limited data on sources, channels and mechanism, Climate Policy Initiative has provided

[13] https://www.climatepolicyinitiative.org/publication/global-landscape-of-climate-finance-2019/.

some global data on climate finance which is presented in Fig. 8.1 and Table 8.2. According to Fig. 8.1, global climate finance has been increasing significantly. For instance, the least inflow of climate finance was US$342 billion in 2013 while the highest inflow was US$640 in 2020 (see Fig. 8.1). Also, from 2016, the inflow increased progressively.

As shown in Fig. 8.1, the private sector has been contributing more funds than the public sector. For example, in 2012 the private sector contributed US$224 billion whereas public actors contributed only US$136 billion. Additionally, Fig. 8.1 shows that climate finance increased from US$360 billion to US$383 billion in 2016. In 2015, climate finance reached a peak (US$437 billion) and fell by US$54 billion in 2016. Although the private sector contributes more to finance climate change, in 2019 public finance outweighed private finance (i.e. US$343 billion as against private finance of US$280 billion). Development finance organizations (DFIs), including multilateral, bilateral and national DFIs are the fundamental instruments that work with ODA streams including climate finance (see Table 8.1). In 2018, DFIs contributed about US$178 billion whereas they provided US$246 billion in 2019 to support the fight

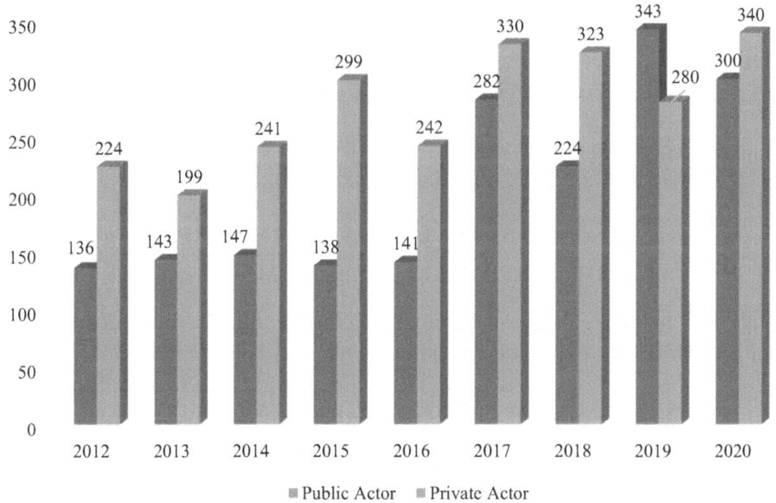

Fig. 8.1 Global Climate Finance by Sector, 2012–2020 (*Source* Climate Policy Initiative Report, 2021)

against climate change. In the period of the coronavirus pandemic, DFIs provided more funds (i.e. about US$193 billion in 2020) than any other source of climate finance. Among the DFIs, national DFIs, which are known as NDBs, provided more funds than the other DFIs. In addition, NDBs even provided more funds than the other public sources of climate finance. From 2012 to 2020, NDBs provided about 44% on average of the total public sources (see Table 8.2). In 2017, NDBs contributed 60% of overall public sources of climate finance.

Climate funds encompass both multilateral and national climate funds, which are basically made up of GCF, CIF and AP (see Table 8.1). However due to the adaptation needs of the world's least developed countries, UNFCCC established the LDCF. This fund is aimed at financing of the preparation and implementation of National Adaptation Programmed Action (NAPA). Climate funds attained only US$3 billion in 2020 after an increase in 2019 (such as US$3 billion). This fund is one of the least sources of public finance. The rest of the other sources are discussed in Table 8.2.

As mentioned earlier, NDBs have an important role in promoting environmental sustainability, in particular by combating climate change. NDBs intervene in financing climate change by scaling up or increasing their level of capital mostly provided by governments, as well as mobilizing and leveraging private finance **towards low-carbon and climate-resilient pathways** (Griffith Jones et al., 2018)**. NDBs' roles in** scaling up climate finance and leveraging private finance are discussed in Sections 8.5 and 8.6.

8.5 Scaling up Climate Finance: The Role of National Development Banks

There is a need to increase (scale up) climate finance altogether given that, by 2030, the expected investment needed to defeat climate change is assessed to be between US$140 billion and US$175 billion.[14] In addition, there is a need to increase the annual investment in mitigating projects to address the challenges of climate change in developing countries. Climate funds alone have not been effective in scaling up significantly and promoting programmatic approaches to influence private

[14] https://elibrary.worldbank.org/doi/abs/10.1596/978-0-8213-7987-5.

Table 8.1 Climate Finance Channels and Mechanisms

Types	*Mechanism*	*Description*	*Instrument*	*Uses*
Public Finance				
Government and Agencies	State of Connecticut (USA) Republic of Fiji, Tokyo Metropolitan Government (Japan), City of Gothenburg (Sweden), New York MTA (USA), Federal Government of Nigeria	Various government who raises fund to finance climate change	Green bond, grant, loan, government budget	Adaptation
Multilateral Development Financial Institutions (DFIs)	World Bank, ADB, EBRD, IFC, AfDB	Multilateral DFIs are issued by different countries and distribute finance and credit locally or globally	Grants, loans, soft loans, guarantees, bond issuance, carbon funds	Dual benefit, adaptation
Bilateral DFIs	CDC Group (United Kingdom), Swedfund (Sweden), International Development Finance Corporation (United States)	Bilateral DFIs, subnational DFIs, neighborhood, state/common or provincial venture banks, monetary corporations or development offices and multilateral DFIs all give finance to tasks and borrowers in different locales characterized by their legitimate status as banks inside characterized public and extraterritorial purviews	Grants, lending and concessional lending and carbon funds	Dual benefit, adaptation, mitigation

(continued)

Table 8.1 (continued)

Types	*Mechanism*	*Description*	*Instrument*	*Uses*
National DFIs	CDB, KfW Banking Group (Germany), Export–Import Bank of India, Lower Austria Guarantees and Investments, Buenos Aires Guarantee Fund, Rio de Janerio Development Agency	National DFIs are government-backed development banks or specialized Export–Import Banks, which are likewise authorized to get associations together with private sector to give value speculations and obligation-based finance, and will more often than not distribute or loan finance just to substances inside their locale	Donations, PPP, project-level market rate debt	Dual benefit, adaptation, mitigation
Climate Funds	UNFCCC's Adaptation Fund, GCF, Least-Developed Countries Fund, CIF, GEF, UNDP Low Emission Capacity Building Programme, UNEP Enlighten Energy Efficiency Initiatives, Indonesia Climate Change Trust Fund, UK International Climate Fund and the German IKI Initiative	The funds aim to support investment programmes for the implementation of countries' low-carbon development strategies, with the SCF providing three targeted programmes on renewable energy, forests and climate resilience	Project-level market rate debt, grant	Dual benefit, adaptation, mitigation
Private Finance				

Types	*Mechanism*	*Description*	*Instrument*	*Uses*
Commercial Financial institutions	BNP Paribas, Bank of America, Bank of China, Morgan Stanley	Financial institutions who invest in climate change	Balance sheet financing	Mitigation, dual uses
Corporations	Canadian Solar, Tesla Energy, Beijing Enterprises Water Group	Corporations that help to minimize carbon emission	Equity	Mitigation, dual uses, adaptation
Household/Individual	Bill Gate	Individual donors to mimic climate change	Project level equity	Mitigation, dual uses
Philanthropy	Rockefeller Foundation, Bloomberg Philanthropies, Energy Foundation, Ford Foundation	*Philanthropy* can *help* induce policy *change* through advocacy, communication campaigns or education	Project level equity, debts	Mitigation, dual uses, adaptation
Private equity, venture capital, infrastructure funds, institutional investors	Fannie Mae, Credit Agricole CIB, Toyota	They are interested in asset-based security	Project level equity	Mitigation, dual uses

Source Climate Policy Initiative (2021) and Bracking and Leffel (2021)

Table 8.2 Public Source of Climate Finance in USD Billion

Year	*NDBs (%)*	*Other Public Actors*	*Public Actors*
2012	60 (44.1)	76	136
2013	70 (49.0)	73	143
2014	64 (42.4)	87	151
2015	69 (50.0)	69	138
2016	56 (39.7)	85	141
2017	171 (60.6	111	282
2018	94 (42.0)	130	224
2019	137 (39.9)	206	343
2020	103 (34.3)	197	300
Total	824 (44.3)	1034	1858

Source Climate Policy Initiative 2021

predictions (Tirpak et al., 2014). NDBs play different important roles in scaling up climate finance as discussed below.

NDBs are part of the public sector or government-sponsored entities (Lundsgaard et al., 2018) and will be able to interact with government agencies, manage resources, influence policy and support the scaling up of climate finance. For instance, the China Development Bank (CDB) has close cooperation with the government; it educates the government on what policies to implement to attract more investment to partake in climate finance (Zhang, 2022). In addition, NDBs, as international partners, have access to long-term domestic and international funding and work closely with international organizations. Hence, they can use such an opportunity to attract both local and international investors to partake in climate finance. NDBs can apply techniques, for example, project incubators, innovation and impetus financial instruments, which will urge the private sector to partake in financing climate resilience projects. Ordinarily, the private sector would not support the financing climate resilience projects because of genuine or perceive barriers and risks associated with such projects. Another way to scale up climate finance is to limit the level of risk by combining small projects through a portfolio approach, and streamlining the application cycle to limit credit evaluation and transaction costs, thereby ensuring the participation of local private financial institutions in climate finance (Smallridge et al., 2012).

NDBs go past addressing market failures to making and moulding the market, which is vital for development (Mazzucato & Penna, 2016). For instance, NDBs represent the largest sources of public finance for climate change purpose. This important role provides investors with much confidence to engage in climate finance, thus help to scale up climate finance. Likewise, NDBs are seen as specialized banks that are actually magnificent and help in sensitizing commercial banks on the risk engaged with renewable energy investment (Geddes et al., 2018; Zhang, 2020). For example, CDB co-issued a financial support scheme to launch the programme and committed in creating innovative financial models to pilot and showcase fruitful financing structures, in this way boosting commercial banks to finance projects (Zhang, 2022). They can certainly capitalize on this opportunity to scale up climate finance.

Apart from multilateral and regional DFIs, national financial institutions such as NDBs are more and more considering climate change as an important factor in their operations, recognizing opportunities for investments that contribute to promoting climate change mitigation and adaptation. Box 8.1 shows the important role Uganda Development Bank Limited (UDBL) is expected to play in scaling up climate finance.

Box 8.1: Climate Change—Uganda Development Bank Limited
The Uganda Development Bank Limited (UDBL) is redirecting its investment towards carbon neutral projects to achieve the goals of the National Climate Change Policy, 2015 and Green Growth Development Strategy 2031. The bank is in the process of establishing a green finance strategy for carbon neutral, climate resilient investments. Such as initiative will place the Bank in a position to establish a green finance fund in order to consolidate and enlarge its investment portfolio with only carbon neutral investments by 2024.

8.5.1 The Conditions for Effectively Scaling Up Climate Finance

In order to scale up climate finance, there are two main conditions that need to be satisfied: a Pre-investment phase (or pre-construction phase) and an Investment (investment phase) (Griffith-Jones et al., 2020; Smallridge et al., 2012). The two conditions are discussed below.

8.5.1.1 Pre-Construction Phase

Pre-investment includes three main needs: regulatory development/enabling environment, national dialogue, demand generation and feasibility study (Griffith-Jones et al., 2020; Smallridge et al., 2012). Since, the private sector and other stakeholders to climate finance are more risk-averse as compared to NDBs, the latter should package the investment instrument to attract these investors. Therefore, they must create an enabling environment for these investors. For instance, NDBs must provide the necessary incentives and assurance to these investors to have trust in such investment. In addition, NDBs should educate stakeholders about the upcoming project in terms of its benefits, risk factor and duration of the project. Lastly, NDBs ought to foster feasibility studies for large ventures and investment plans for smaller tasks. For instance, the Development Bank of Southern Africa (DBSA) created a Project Preparation Fund, which is used to build an enabling environment for infrastructure project implementation, assist with costs to reach a financial close and help in conducting pre-feasibility and bankable feasibility studies (ABSA, 2013).

8.5.1.2 Construction Phase

After the pre-investment stage, NDBs should now prepare the instrument needed to source the fund for the project. In other words, NDBs will need to determine the financing structure—either source of debt on market terms, sources of equity on market terms and (or) both sources of capital (Griffith-Jones et al., 2020; Smallridge et al., 2012). NDBs often work with investors, governments, international organizations and/or donors to further develop their funding arrangements by combining their funding with government grants and international sources. As a result, they attract private investment. Because they are privileged, they can regulate various economic actors, from public administrations to private lenders and financiers. It is important that the instruments used are broad enough to match the level of development of the country and the depth of the stock market. It is useful to introduce new devices, but it is also useful to rely on proven and successful mechanisms.

8.6 How National Development Banks Leverage Private Finance

One way of dealing with climate change (greenhouse gas externality), is the raising and reliance on private sources of finance (Cudjoe et al., 2023). There is much more private sector finance than public finance; therefore, leveraging private finance in climate finance is expedient. This is because climate finance has not entirely mobilized adequate private funds for climate finance projects. The reason why private actors have not been fully engaged in climate finance is due to barriers, risk and low incentives among others, while NDBs can leverage it to attract the private sector to finance climate change. NDBs have a very knowledgeable and long-term relationship with the private sector, which helps them to better appreciate the local barriers to investment (Morgado et al., 2019) and allows them to provide large-scale financial services that meet the needs of the private sector. This role is necessary because most private sector players are risk-averse and are only willing to bear a limited level of risk (Smallridge et al., 2012).

In addition, information on activity-and-country-specific barriers is limited to areas that affect the return profile of private sector actors. Therefore, given the nature of NDBs, they can play an important job in facilitating climate investment, straightforwardly conveying climate finance or attracting private investment. For example, the NDB's green finance association with more than 40 DFIs in the Latin America and Caribbean (LAC) regions has financed more than US$2 billion in credit-line programmes and has mobilized more than US$6 billion in private green investments to date.[15] Furthermore, private actors cannot consider environmental externalities and integrate them into their investment decision, as they are not reflected in market costs (Griffith-Jones et al., 2020). Under such a circumstance, NDBs are in a better situation to leverage private finance since they are able to provide the assurance components for investment, thus accordingly offering extra motivations for the private actors to construct the investment. Consequently, they are more productive in taking risks that stimulate long-term investment than commercial banks and investment funds.

[15] https://blogs.iadb.org/sostenibilidad/en/the-future-of-ndbs-and-the-green-recovery/.

Additionally, since there are fewer incentives for private sector participation, the attraction of the private sector into climate finance is very minimal (Smallridge et al., 2012). This has caused only few private sector players to participate in climate finance. However, NDBs are able to create very attractive incentives for the private sector to participate in climate finance. This can be accomplished by giving financial instruments based on appropriate terms and conditions, helping private actors and domestic financial institutions to appreciate and address the particular investments, financial risks and barriers that keep private actors from engaging in green and climate-versatile projects. For example, the DBSA Climate Finance Facility (CFF) is the first climate finance fund in Africa to use the Green Bank model. It is targeted at de-risking and increasing the bankability of climate projects in order to crowd-in significant investments from commercial banks and projects sponsors as shown in Box 8.2.

Box 8.2: Development Bank of Southern Africa Climate Finance Facility

DBSA Climate Finance Facility (CFF) is the first climate finance institution in Africa to use the Green Bank model. This facility aims to de-risk and increase the bankability of climate projects to crow-in significant investments from commercial banks and ventures supports utilizing an initial capitalisation of about US$110 million from GCF (US$56 million) and DBSA's balance sheet (US$ 54 million). The facility is also interested in providing lines of credit such as subordinated debt and term extensions for business and infrastructure projects associated with climate change. For example, it provides funds to support off-grid power, mini-solar power, water conservation, distributed power, and urban solar farms. The facility is geared towards South Africa, Namibia, Lesotho and Eswatini.

In emerging markets like China, the CDB assisted in designing policies to attract private investors to invest in renewable energy (solar) and provided significant initial funding as shown in Box 8.3. This has made China one of the major global promoters of solar power.[16]

[16] https://www.weforum.org/agenda/2019/05/why-the-world-needs-national-development-banks.

Box 8.3: The Role of China Development Bank (CDB) in Climate Finance

The CDB has played a particularly important role in advancing climate finance by financing a wide range of clean energy infrastructure projects in all regions, using benchmarks to detail China's environmental strengths. Recently, CDB issued CNY 25 billion (US$3.7 billion) retail green bond to the public through commercial banks and break away from traditional method enhancing green financing involvement. CDB who is leading policymaker and financier of Belt and Road Initiative (BRI) mobilised substantial funds for BRI projects (such as transportation, water and renewable energy) from US$500 million and EUR 1 billion semi-sovereign green bonds in 2017. In same year, CDB sponsor BRI with US$17.1 billion. BRI bonds of US$350 million were issued in Hong Kong through Shin. CDB also engage with some developing partners such as China-Central and Eastern European Interbank Association, Shanghai Cooperation Organisations, China-ASEAN and China-BRICS Association.

CDB is also characterised with designing policies to attract private investors to participate in green financing. For instance, CDB was the lead underwriter of a CYN 1 billion (US$150 million) "panda" bond. Also, the bank engages in funding solar and also attracting private investors to partake in this financing. This has made China one of the world's biggest proponents of solar energy.

Sources https://www.cdb.com.cn/English/gykh_512/khjj/

Also in Mexico, the Nacional Financiera SNC (NAFIN) leveraged the local financial market along with several multilateral and international financial institutions, developed a financial scheme to finance the first wind farm in Mexico. It also engaged in the issuance of bonds attracting investors in financing eligible wind energy generation projects in Mexico (see Box 8.4).

Box 8.4: Nacional Financiera SNC Leverages Local Financial Markets

NAFIN's role in developing wind projects in Mexico. In 2010, wind energy was relatively new in Mexico. NAFIN filled the gap in the financing of construction of a wind farm in the country and created market to finance wind farming. In May 2010, recognising the need to move from petroleum products to clean wellsprings of power, NAFIN, alongside several multilateral and international financial organizations, developed a financial scheme to finance the principal wind farm in Mexico. Supported by the Mexican government (with its aim of fostering the breeze area in Mexico), NAFIN granted the principal financing for the construction and development of the largest breeze farm in Latin America: 'Eurus'. This is located in Juchitán de Zaragoza, in the State of Oaxaca and cost US$550 million to construct. Its 167 breeze turbines generate 250.5MW, adequate ability to supply about half 1,000,000 individuals and diminishing annual carbon dioxide discharges by 600,000 metric tons is estimated. Following this lead, NAFIN's Sustainable Projects Unit, has financed 13 breeze farms, one solar power installation and two hydroelectric plants across nine states in Mexico. These ventures address an investment of in excess of 4,000 MDD and 1.7GW of installed capacity, increasing NAFIN's portfolio by 700% from 2010 to the hour of composing.

In addition, NAFIN also participated in the issuance of bonds and was characterised as Mexico's financial institution that first issued green bond. The demand for financial support was high; the issue was oversubscribed five times, meaning that the investors were willing to buy a larger number of bonds than NAFIN had to sell. Proceeds from the $500 million five-year Green Bond are being used to finance qualified wind power generation projects in Mexico. In 2016, NAFIN issued the main peso-denominated green bond in the local market, selling seven-year bonds for 2 billion pesos (US$ 101 million). The proceeds was used to finance hydroelectric and wind projects in Mexico. These issuances paved the way for later green bonds. For example, in 2017 Mexico City became the main city in Latin America to give a green bond. The US$50 million issue, which was oversubscribed 2.5 times, will pay for energy efficient lighting, transit improvements and water infrastructure.

8.7 Concluding Remarks

Climate change has become an issue of concern which tends to affect economic performance and businesses. Therefore, there is a need to fight against climate change, and this requires the provision of appropriate financing. This chapter has examined the role of NDBs in climate finance and provided an overview of climate finance. It mentioned that climate finance started with UNFCCC where financial mechanism entity such as GEF was created to supervise the funds that are contributed by the parties of the UNFCCC. However, due to the limitation of

UNFCCC, which only permits countries to adopt policies to mitigate climate change, the UN also created another agency through the Kyoto Protocol that commits its parties by setting an internationally binding emission-reduction target. It was also noted that MDBs came in to also finance climate, hence set up an entity such as CIF to oversee the funds contributed by these MDBs. Despite all these efforts, the UN again realized that global warming keeps on increasing; hence the parties of the UNFCCC came to an agreement (i.e. Paris Agreement) to have a common goal of reducing global warming.

The chapter indicates that there are challenges associated with climate finance, including lack of transparency, lack of a common definition of climate finance, insufficient institutional arrangements, lack of expertise and potential risk. It has established that the presence of NDBs is necessary in addressing these challenges. The chapter looked at the broad sources of climate finance as public and private sources. The public sources include DFIs, climate funds, government budget and government agencies, while the private sources comprise commercial financial institution funds, household funds, venture capital funds, private equity and infrastructure funds. NDBs' intervention in climate finance involves scaling up or increasing the level of capital mostly provided by governments as well as mobilizing and leveraging private finance **towards low-carbon and climate-resilient pathways**. This is because NDBs are specialized in managing risk, are able to attract private capital, and to increase demand for investments and financing for climate-friendly projects. They are able to leverage private finance since they complement and catalyze the private sector.

References

Bonnel, A., & Swann, S. (2015). *Mainstreaming climate action within financial institutions* (Technical report). Emerging Practices.

Bracking, S., & Leffel, B. (2021). Climate finance governance: Fit for purpose? *Wiley Interdisciplinary Reviews: Climate Change, 12*(4), e709.

Buchner, B., Falconer, A., Hervé-Mignucci, M., Trabacchi, C., & Brinkman, M. (2011). The landscape of climate finance. *Climate Policy Initiative, Venice, 27.*

Corfee-Morlot, J., Kamal-Chaoui, L., Donovan, M. G., Cochran, I., Robert, A., & Teasdale, P. J. (2009). *Cities, climate change and multilevel governance.* OECD Publishing.

Cudjoe, M. A., Abor, J. Y., & Volschenk, J. (2023). Environmental and climate finance in developing countries. In J. Y. Abor (Ed.), *Sustainable and responsible investment in developing markets: A companion*. Edward Elgar.

Geddes, A., Schmidt, T. S., & Steffen, B. (2018). The multiple roles of state investment banks in low-carbon energy finance: An analysis of Australia, the UK and Germany. *Energy Policy, 115*, 158–170.

Griffith-Jones, S., Attridge, S., & Gouett, M. (2020). *Securing climate finance through national development banks* (ODI Report). ODI. www.odi.org/publications/16552-securing-climate-finance-through-national-development-banks

Griffith-Jones, S., Ocampo, J. A., Rezende, F., Schclarek, A., & Brei, M. (2018). The future of national development banks. In S. Griffith-Jones & J. A. Ocampo (Eds.), *The future of national development banks*. Oxford University Press.

Lundsgaarde, E., Dupuy, K., & Persson, Å. (2018). *Coordination challenges in climate finance* (No. 2018: 3). DIIS Working Paper.

Mazzucato, M., & Penna, C. C. (2016). Beyond market failures: The market creating and shaping roles of state investment banks. *Journal of Economic Policy Reform, 19*(4), 305–326.

Montero, E. G. P. (2017, March). *How can national development banks address key challenges associated with raising climate finance to increase investment flows for projects in their countries? Case study: The role of NAFIN in enabling climate finance flows into Mexico 'NAFIN Fellowship Programme'* (Working Paper No. 1).

Morgado, N., Taskin, O., Lasfargues, B., & Sedemund, J. (2019). *Scaling up climate-compatible infrastructure: Insights from national development banks in Brazil and South Africa*. OECD Publishing.

OECD. (2015). *Climate finance in 2013–14 and the USD 100 billion goal*. World Economic Forum.

Pickering, J., Betzold, C., & Skovgaard, J. (2017). Managing fragmentation and complexity in the emerging system of international climate finance. *International Environmental Agreements: Politics, Law and Economics, 17*(1), 1–16.

PwC Mexico. (2015). *Necessary investment for Mexico to fulfill the clean energy targets*.

Ragavan, M. I., Marcil, L. E., & Garg, A. (2020). Climate change as a social determinant of health. *Pediatrics, 145*(5), e20193169.

Ripple, W., Wolf, C., Newsome, T., Barnard, P., Moomaw, W., & Grandcolas, P. (2019). World scientists' warning of a climate emergency. *BioScience, 70*, 8–12.

Smallridge, D., Buchner, B., Trabacchi, C., Netto, M., Lorenzo, J. G., & Serra, L. (2012). *The role of national development banks in intermediating international climate finance to scale up private sector investments* (113 pp.). Inter-American Development Bank.

Tirpak, D., Brown, L., & Ronquillo-Ballesteros, A. (2014). *Monitoring climate finance in developing countries: Challenges and next steps*. World Resources Institute.

United Nations Environment Programme. (2017). *Atlas of Africa energy resources*. United Nations Environment Programme, Nairobi, Kenya.

Werndl, C. (2016). On defining climate and climate change. *The British Journal for the Philosophy of Science, 67*, 337–364.

Zhang, F. (2020). Leaders and followers in finance mobilization for renewable energy in Germany and China. *Environmental Innovation and Societal Transitions, 37*, 203–224.

Zhang, F. (2022). The policy coordinator role of national development banks in scaling climate finance: Evidence from the renewable energy sector. *Climate Policy, 22*, 754–769.

PART III

Business Models, Monitoring and Evaluation, and Impact Evaluation

CHAPTER 9

Business Models of National Development Banks

9.1 Introduction

National development banks (NDBs) are established by countries to bridge the financing gap by providing long-term financing. There has been renewed interest in the importance of NDBs, following the global financial crisis and the recent COVID-19 crisis, especially considering the important counter-cyclical role they play during a crisis. A number of countries have established new development banks, adding to the list of existing development banks. Some of the newly created NDBs in Africa are the Development Bank Ghana, and the Development Bank of Nigeria. Other countries like Kenya, merged some institutions to establish the Kenyan Development Corporation (i.e. a merger of Industrial and Commercial Development Corporation, Tourism Finance Corporation and Industrial Development Bank Capital Limited). Over the years, the role of NDBs has been evolving, reflecting the development dynamics of countries. As discussed in Chapter 4, NDBs perform a number of useful roles, including providing counter-cyclical financing; promoting innovation and structural transformation; enhancing inclusive finance; providing financing for infrastructure development; and financing the provision of public goods, especially combating climate change (see Griffith-Jones et al., 2018).

NDBs continue to constitute major players in the financial system of several economies, especially in EMDEs. Generally, state-owned financial

© The Author(s), under exclusive license to Springer Nature Switzerland AG 2023

J. Yindenaba Abor, *The Changing Role of National Development Banks in Africa*, https://doi.org/10.1007/978-3-031-38639-8_9

institutions represent a significant proportion of total assets in banking sectors across the globe (de Luna-Martinez & Vicente, 2012). Unlike other types of state-owned financial institutions, such as government-owned commercial banks or insurance companies, NDBs tend to have a specific mandate of delivering on public policy objectives in order to support the economic development of a country or region. Even though NDBs are concerned about making profit and remaining sustainable, their overall goal is to achieve development impact (Eurodad, 2017).

In spite of their relevance, not all NDBs are successful; and even those that are successful may experience major adverse development impacts with projects failing or causing damage to human rights or the environment. Though external shocks, such as economic crises can have major effects on NDBs, one key explanation for the differences in the performance of NDBs is the considerable variation in the institutions themselves with respect to their different mandates, functions and operational strategies (see Barone & Spratt, 2015; Bradlow & Humphrey, 2016; Marois, 2015; Povel, 2015). The business model employed by NDBs has implications for their performance. It is important to understand how they can improve their performance in terms of achieving the dual goals of development impact and financial sustainability. Another important issue is avoiding the challenges associated with poorly managed NDBs, given that financial resources tend to flow into well managed NDBs (Eurodad, 2017). In performing their roles, NDBs implement their business model in ways that enable them to achieve their objectives. The business model should be clear in terms of its target clients, its funding arrangement, the lending model, the financial instruments used in providing the finance, the financial products and services it offers as well as their pricing mechanism.

The chapter discusses the business model of NDBs. It is organized as follows: Sect. 9.2 explains the policy mandate of NDBs; Sect. 9.3 discusses sectors and clients served by NDBs; Sect. 9.4 identifies NDBs' funding sources and Sect. 9.5 examines their lending models; Sect. 9.6 identifies instruments used for providing finance; Sect. 9.7 discusses NDBs' financial products and services; Sect. 9.8 explains their pricing and subsidies; Sect. 9.9 discusses risks and costs of NDBs, while Sect. 9.10 concludes the chapter.

9.2 Policy Mandate of National Development Banks

NDBs are usually established with a particular policy mandate. As mentioned in Chapter 1, some NDBs have a narrow or specific mandate that clearly shows the sectors or activities that the NDB is supposed to support (e.g. MSMEs or agriculture). Others have a broad mandate, which is expressed in general terms without referring to any specific sector, activity or customer. Examples of NDBs with a specific mandate are the Tanzania Agricultural Development Bank and the Infrastructure Development Bank of Zimbabwe. For instance, the Tanzania Agricultural Development Bank has a specific mandate to facilitate development and support the transformation of the agricultural sector by providing short, medium and long-term financing for agricultural projects in Tanzania in order to promote economic growth, food security and a reduction of income poverty. The Infrastructure Development Bank of Zimbabwe also has a specific mandate to provide medium-and-long-term financing for key infrastructure projects, such as transportation, housing, energy, ICT, water and sanitation. The Development Bank Ghana, Uganda Development Bank and National Development Bank Botswana are examples of NDBs with a broad mandate.

9.3 Sectors and Clients Targeted

Generally, NDBs serve different types of customers, including MSMEs, exporters, large private firms, individuals, households, local governments and other financial institutions. The findings of the World Bank (2018) survey indicate a strong focus on serving local private sector enterprises by the NDBs. Most of NDBs indicated that they target MSMEs and large private sector corporations. Some NDBs mentioned that they focus on only larger enterprises, considering the nature of their policy mandate, with their entire private sector loans directed to large enterprises. In the World Bank study, a good number of NDBs tend to focus on supporting private financial intermediaries that obtain loans and guarantees from NDBs to on-lend to end customers. Others lend to state-owned enterprises, while some indicated that they support individuals and households mainly in agriculture. Examples of NDBs that serve smallholder farmers include Agro-bank (Malaysia) and Agriculture Bank of Sudan. NDBs in developing countries, such as those in Africa tend to focus more on serving the financing needs of individuals and households compared to those in developed countries.

In the case of export–import banks, their mandate and focus is mainly on firms involved in international trade. Borrowers from the development bank can include foreign enterprises and governments. For instance, the Ghana EXIM Bank focuses on providing financing and support for businesses that are involved in international trade.

9.4 Funding Sources of National Development Banks

NDBs obtain funding from various sources to finance their operations and activities. The main funding sources available to most NDBs include direct budget transfers from the government, mobilization of deposits, borrowing from other financial institutions, raising of capital from international capital markets, issuing of debt securities in domestic financial markets and acquisition of official development assistance (ODA) (see World Bank 2018).

- **Direct budget transfers from government**—Some NDBs receive direct budgetary support from government, which includes resources to cover interest rate subsidies under particular government programmes being executed by the NDBs (e.g. Uganda Development Bank; Development Bank of Nigeria). Usually, NDBs that are struggling and are unable to sustain their operations tend to rely on direct budget transfers to support their business operations.
- **Deposit mobilization**—Some retail NDBs may have the mandate to mobilize deposits from the general public (e.g. Rural Development Bank in Cambodia). Such retail NDBs tend to have specific mandates to provide financial services to unbanked households. Others are also permitted to take deposits from government institutions. A majority of NDBs are not deposit-taking since they mainly focus on long-term financing.
- **Borrowing from other financial institutions**—It is also common for NDBs to borrow from other financial institutions (such as commercial banks) through the local interbank market. Commercial banks and other financial institutions also lend to NDBs.

- **Raising capital from international capital markets**—This is a major source of financing for NDBs. It involves obtaining financing through the issue of bonds and placing them on the international capital markets. Most NDBs tend to rely on this source of funding.
- **Issuing debt securities in domestic financial markets**—NDBs also issue debt instruments such as bonds in the domestic bond market. This is also a major source of funding for NDBs.
- **Acquiring official development assistance (ODA)**—NDBs may obtain ODA through international financial institutions such as the World Bank Group and other regional development banks (RDBs). They are allowed to receive ODA from official agencies or multilateral institutions and such funding tends to be long-term in nature (typically more than 20 years) and are granted at concessional terms. NDBs have previously been part of the main recipients of loans and grants provided by multilateral development banks (MDBs). NDBs access loans from multilateral agencies and provide credit to customers, either directly or indirectly through other financial institutions. Considering that NDBs typically borrow internationally in foreign currency and provide lending to domestic market in local currency, they bear the currency risk in relation to the borrowing.

NDBs typically have an implicit or explicit sovereign guarantee on their debt that enables them to improve their risk profile for accessing capital markets or borrowing from other financial institutions on terms similar to their governments (see World Bank, 2018).

9.5 Lending Models of National Development Banks

The lending activity of development banks is a very important one. There are different types of lending models that development banks use, including the retail (tier 1) model, the wholesale (tier 2) model and a combination of the retail and the wholesale models (mixed model or hybrid model of lending).

9.5.1 Retail Lending Model

Under the tier 1 (or retail) lending model, the development banks engage directly with the target clients and that may require the development bank to have many branches to reach the target clients. This may require huge costs of operations for agriculture, housing and small and medium banks that typically have large clients spread across the country. Usually, the interest rate offered to the target clients may be lower with respect to the retail lending model because it does not involve channelling the funds through other financial institutions. Also, the development bank bears the credit risk under this lending model since it is responsible for providing the loans directly to the end customers (World Bank, 2018). African NDBs that use the retail model include Uganda Development Bank Limited, Development Bank of Ethiopia, Kenyan Development Corporation and National Development Bank of Botswana.

9.5.2 Wholesale Lending Model

With respect to the tier 2 (or wholesale) lending model, development banks tend to provide loans through private financial institutions or participating financial institutions, which then select and evaluate loan applications from the end clients. This lending model is associated with lower operating costs since the development bank is not directly involved in providing the loans to the target customers. One advantage with the wholesale model is that the NDBs, are able to reach many end clients and cover many locations without incurring huge operational costs. This model also fosters the growth of private financial intermediaries, which become arms of NDBs, reaching unserved and underserved sectors and customers (World Bank, 2018). Also, the private financial institutions that serve as intermediaries for the NDBs' funds bear the project's credit risk, while the NDBs assume the credit of the financial institution directly. Interest rates offered to the target customers tend to be higher with respect to the wholesale lending model because private financial institutions tend to pass on the intermediation cost plus their margins. In spite of this, wholesale NDBs tend to exhibit lower non-performing loan (NPLs) rates compared with retail NDBs. The Development Bank of Nigeria and the Development Bank Ghana are examples of African NDBs that employ the wholesale lending model.

9.5.3 Mixed Model

The third lending model is a hybrid approach, which combines both the retail and wholesale models. The findings of the World Bank study in 2017 showed that 10% of NDBs surveyed use only the wholesale lending model, 40% use only the retail model and 50% use the hybrid model (i.e. a combination of wholesale and retail models). The study also found that NDBs in developing countries focus mainly on the retail model (44% versus 29% for NDBs in developed economies). Conversely, most NDBs located in developed countries appear to employ the wholesale model (18% versus 12% for NDBs located in developing countries), and the mixed model (53% versus 44% for NDBs in developing countries) (see World Bank, 2018). The Development Bank of Rwanda (BRD) adopts both the wholesale and retail lending model.

Box 9.1 shows a graph on the use of the various lending models by NDBs.

Box 9.1: Lending Models used by NDBs

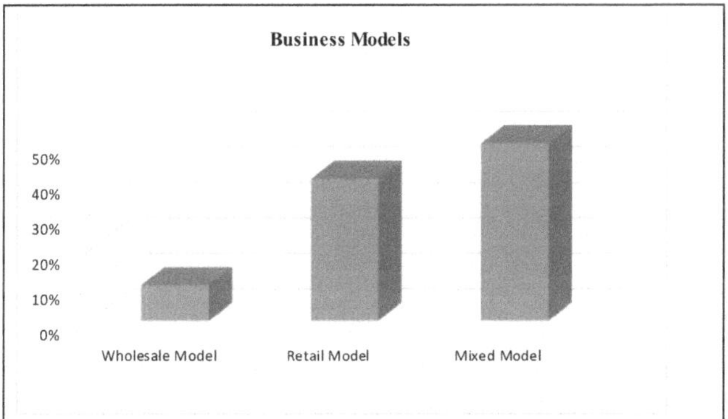

Source Author's construction based on World Bank (2018)

9.5.4 Summary of Business Models of Different NDBs

Table 9.1 provides a summary of the most relevant business model criteria that differentiates NDBs. The key criteria include Policy mandate, Sectors or Clients targeted, Funding sources, and Lending model. It is important to indicate that some NDBs have a mixture of the features indicated in Table 9.1. For instance, some NDBs like the Development Bank of Southern Africa target both public and private sector clients, and some also use a hybrid model, which is a mixture of both the retail and wholesale lending models. These include the Development Bank of Rwanda, Development Bank of Southern Africa, Development Bank of Namibia, Development Bank of Zambia and Eritrean Investment and Development Bank.

9.6 Instruments for Providing Finance

One instrument employed by NDBs in providing finance is *grants*. Other important instruments used by NDBs for providing finance in the origination process include *direct origination* and *indirect origination*. These are discussed below.

9.6.1 Offering Grants

NDBs provide grants, which are used for different activities during the pre-investment and the investment stages. During the pre-investment stage, grants can be used for technical assistance to assist the business or project to become investment-ready. Such grants may be used for training and capacity building at the firm level or preparing a business plan or carrying out a feasibility study. Grants are also relevant for promoting policy-relevant research, creating awareness and enhancing advocacy in order to improve the enabling environment. Moreover, grants may be useful during the pre-investment phase for building the capacity of local financial institutions for the work of the NDBs. During the investment phase, grants may be useful for reducing interest rates. They can be combined with commercial loans, used as a guarantee fund for losses in lieu of equity financing or extend repayment terms/periods for borrowers. These grants can be combined with loans from NDBs to support projects directly or channelled through other financial institutions (Smallridge et al., 2012).

Table 9.1 Summary of Business Models of Different National Development Banks

Criterion	*Features*	
Policy Mandate	*Narrow/Specific* Focus only on specific areas such as agriculture/SMEs/ export trade/housing/infrastructure, etc Example: Tanzania Agricultural Development Bank; Infrastructure Development Bank of Zimbabwe; Ghana Export–Import Bank	*Broad* Focus broadly on different sectors Example: Development Bank Ghana; Uganda Development Bank; National Development Bank of Botswana
Sectors or Clients Targeted	*Public* Target public sector clients Example: Iller Bank, Turkey	*Private* Target specific types of clients, such as financial institutions, public enterprises, large private corporations, SMEs and individuals Example: Development Bank Ghana; Uganda Development Bank; National Development Bank of Botswana; Development Bank of Rwanda
Funding Sources	*Deposit taking* Accept deposits from customers Example: the Rural Development Bank in Cambodia	*Non-deposit taking* Do not accept deposits from customers Examples: Uganda Development Bank; Development Bank Ghana; Development Bank of Nigeria
Lending Model	*Retail model (First tier)* Lend directly to end customers Example: Uganda Development Bank; Development Bank of Ethiopia; Tanzania Agricultural Development Bank; Development Bank of Mauritius; Development Bank of Seychelles; National Development Bank of Botswana; Infrastructure Development Bank of Zimbabwe; NIB and BPCI in Cote d'Ivoire and BFPME in Tunisia	*Wholesale model (Second tier)* Lend to banks and other financial institutions, which intend on-lend to end clients Example: Development Bank Ghana; Development Bank of Nigeria

Source Author's construction

9.6.2 Direct Origination

Direct origination is based on the NDBs' ability to independently originate debt or equity. It involves NDBs offering new credits based on terms and conditions (interest rate, maturity and guarantees) different from what pertains on the market. During the early stages of national development, NDBs were mainly used by government as tools for earmarking credit for capital expenditures in various sectors.

9.6.2.1 Providing Direct Loans (Tier 1 Loans)

These are also known as Tier 1 loans, which are provided directly by NDBs to finance businesses or projects. This instrument involves the development bank bearing the credit risk involved in the debt financing. Under this arrangement, the NDB provides the credit directly to a business or project and as mentioned earlier, this involves the retail lending model. NDBs' long-term debt finance may be senior debt (i.e. on equal footing with other debt finance providers), or subordinated debt (i.e. putting the NDB in a place of secondary creditor). Under these circumstances, the financing provided by NDBs can be combined with concessional funding (grant or low-interest loans) from international organizations (Smallridge et al., 2012).

9.6.2.2 Providing Equity Financing

Some NDBs provide equity financing to business, though it is an instrument that is not often used. They invest in technology firms and projects directly or through private equity and venture capital firms. In the World Bank study, 47% of NDBs provided private equity and venture capital financing (World Bank, 2018). NDBs can be in a first-loss position in relation to other investors, or they can invest together with other investors. For instance, Bancoldex Capital, a subsidiary of Bancoldex of Colombia, invest as Tier 2 investors. That is, they invest in venture capital funds managed privately, instead of investing directly in businesses or projects. In most cases, equity investment by NDBs in a fund is treated as leverage in attracting additional capital from the local and international capital markets (Smallridge et al., 2012).

9.6.3 Indirect Origination

The indirect origination is a mechanism by which NDBs create incentives for stimulating other financial institutions to provide credit in connection with government's targeted investment projects, businesses or sectors. Such incentives may include providing indirect loans; providing of guarantees; interest equalization; and, imposition of penalties (see Torres & Zeidan, 2016).

9.6.3.1 Providing Indirect Loans (Tier 2 Loans)

The provision of long-term funds by NDBs is very important for financing growth and development in the domestic economy, especially during the early stages of industrialization. Under this arrangement, NDBs provide loans to commercial banks and other financial institutions to on-lend to businesses and projects. As we discussed in Sect. 9.5, this involves the wholesale lending model, where the loans are provided through the financial institutions. For instance, in Brazil, BNDES uses this model in its operations with commercial banks. This mechanism strongly requires the use of fiscal or quasi-fiscal resources. It can be effective in situations where alternative sources of private funding are limited and expensive to obtain, thus giving governments the autonomy to determine such loan conditions (i.e. interest rates and maturity). Also, governments' incentives in the form of tax rebates or subsidies can motivate financial institutions to provide loans at lower interest rates or on better credit terms than they would usually offer to special clients, such as low-income farmers, MSMEs, exporters, etc.

9.6.3.2 Providing Guarantees

NDBs offer credit guarantees, which provide lenders and investors with comprehensive credit cover on the part of the loan or bond guaranteed by the NDBs. They also provide risk guarantees, which cover lenders against non-payment by the borrower caused by political risk events. The guarantees that development banks offer generally assist borrowers to obtain loans from third party lenders such as commercial banks. Guarantees also enable borrowers to obtain finance in their local currency where the development bank is unable to provide such financing directly from its own resources. Through this mechanism, the guarantor bears all or part of the risk of the loan. The guarantee reduces the cost of funding for the final borrower to a level closer to interest rates on public debt, which is normally the lowest in the domestic market. One important benefit with the use of a guarantees mechanism is the low demand for fiscal resources, but unlike provision of long-term finance, this does not generate or create, and therefore does not work when credit markets are shallow. This instrument is more useful during the later stages of NDBs' life cycle (Torres & Zeidan, 2016).

9.6.3.3 *Interest Equalization Scheme*

Interest equalization is another indirect mechanism, and it is a form of subsidy granted by NDBs or a government to the borrower by paying the lender's part of the cost of financing. It is a way of lowering the cost of financing or interest rate offered to the borrower. This scheme was widely used in the past by European export credit agencies (Torres & Zeidan, 2016) and it is still being used by countries like India to support MSMEs involved in exports. Equalization of interest rates enables exporters to access lower cost of capital and has provided some breathing space for a number of MSME exporters that experienced serious financial challenges in the wake of the COVID-19 crisis. From government's fiscal stance, the fiscal cost to government under this scheme may be higher than that of guarantees, though government does not hold the contingent liability and is not responsible for repaying the debt in the event of the borrowers defaulting. In developing countries, domestic financial markets may charge high discount rates for public guarantees and future flow of subsidies, thereby limiting their effectiveness. The local market may impose high rates for public credit or the risks associated with the payment under these indirect mechanisms may be considered too risky for private institutions, affecting the ability of a Treasury guarantee or subsidy to lower the cost of private loans (Torres & Zeidan, 2016).

9.6.3.4 *Imposition of Penalties*

Imposition of penalties is also used sometimes as an indirect mechanism of allocating credit. It involves providing funds to socially targeted sectors of the economy in order to create compulsory rules for allocating private funds. Under the mechanism, the government, instead of providing premiums to lenders, rather imposes penalties on lenders that fail to meet specific goals. This is not a very popular mechanism around the world. The Brazilian Central Bank's regulations have aspects of this mechanism, which expects commercial banks to provide a minimum percentage of credit to specific sectors of the economy, including, agriculture, housing or microcredit, lest significant fines are imposed on them (Torres & Zeidan, 2016).

9.7 Financial Products and Services

NDBs offer various types of lending and financial products and services to their clients. The following is a discussion of their lending products and services, as well as trade financing, infrastructure financing and other products and services NDBs offer.

9.7.1 Lending Products and Services

The lending products include long-term loans, loans for working capital, bridge or short-term loans, syndicated loans, business startup loans and loans for launching new products or bringing new products to the market.

- **Long-term loans**—These are a form of loan typically with repayment made over a period of three years or more. Long-term loans provided by NDBs provide enough space and time for borrowers to be able to repay the loans, since such loans are invested in long-term projects.
- **Loans for working capital**—NDBs also provide working capital loans to enable businesses to cover their daily recurring expenses. It is used for covering the borrowing firm's short-term operational needs.
- **Bridge or short-term loans**—These are short-term loans that the firm uses until it is able to secure permanent financing or remove an existing obligation. A bridge loan has a tenure of up to one year and enables the firm to meet its current obligations.
- **Syndicated loans**—These are loans offered by a group of lenders (known as a syndicate) who work together to provide the financing to a single borrower. Development banks sometimes work together with other lenders to provide financing to particular borrowers, which include companies, a large project or a sovereign government. Syndicated loans become necessary when a project requires huge funding that is too much for a single lender to provide or when a project needs a specialized lender with expertise in a specific asset class. Loan syndication reduces the credit risk for each

lender, allowing lenders to spread risk and participate in financial opportunities that may be too large for their individual capital base.
- **Business startup loans**—These are loans acquired for the purpose of starting a business. NDBs support entrepreneurship and innovation by providing funding for financing startups. Business startup loans are financing meant to help cover startup costs of new businesses. Such loans can be used for financing working capital, for purchasing supplies and inventory, for acquiring equipment, machinery and furniture and for the construction of real estate. NDBs also provide loans for launching new products.

9.7.2 Trade Financing

NDBs are very instrumental in providing trade finance for exporters. Trade finance is very critical in promoting international trade in both developed and developing countries. Trade finance includes the financial instruments and products that businesses use to facilitate international trade. It is an important tool for businesses to minimize the risk of non-payment and non-receipt of goods, improve cashflow and level of efficiency and boost export revenue. Some of the instruments used in trade finance include:

- **Lending lines of credit**—NDBs can provide lines of credit to assist both importers and exporters in a global trade.
- **Letters of credit**—These are letters that can be issued by NDBs guaranteeing that the importer's payment will be made on time and for the right amount. In case the importer is not able to make the payment, the NDB is required to effect the payment. Letters of credit help in reducing the risks connected with international trade since the NDB guarantees payment to the exporter for the goods shipped. Nonetheless, it also protects the importer since payment will not be made unless the exporter meets the terms in the letters of credit. Both the exporter and importer have to honour their part of the agreement for the transaction to be completed.
- **Factoring**—This involves a financial institution (known as the factor), which buys the receivables of an exporter and bears all administrative obligations and credit risks involved in collecting receivables. The factor usually pays the exporter based on a

percentage of the export's accounts receivables with the remainder collected from the debtor after costs are deducted.

- **Export credit**—This involves a form of working capital given to exporters. Governments through *Export Credit* Agencies (ECAs) or Investment Insurance Agencies provide *export credit* in support of national exporters seeking to sell their products and services on international markets. The financing may assume the form of credits (financial support) or credit insurance and guarantees or both.
- **Insurance**—This instrument can be used for shipping and the delivery of goods and can also protect the exporter from non-payment by the importer.

According to the World Bank (2018), many NDBs offer trade finance products such as export credits, guarantees and import credits (62%). The findings of the World Bank study showed that NDBs in developing countries are more focused than developed countries on guarantees (76% vs. 50%) and import credit (67% vs. 50%) and less focused on export credit (71% vs. 89%). Box 9.2 shows the role the Ghana EXIM Bank plays in trade financing in Ghana.

Box 9.2: Ghana Export-Import Bank

The Ghana Export-Import (EXIM) Bank was established in 2016 by Act 2016 (Act 911), with 29th March 2016 as the date of assent. It was launched to strengthen the Government's quest for a feasible and sustainable export-led economy. The Bank was formed by the unification of three government agencies namely, Export Trade, Agricultural and Industrial Development Fund (EDAIF), Export Finance Company (EFC), and Eximguaranty Company Limited. EDAIF was initially started in 2002 under Act 582 as Export Development and Investment Fund (EDIF) to provide financial resources for export oriented activities especially non-traditional products. This was changed to Act 823 as EDAIF in 2011 to make financial resources available for the expansion and advancement of Agriculture relating to agro-processing and agro-processing industry to provide additional attention and support to the sector. Furthermore, in 2013, Act 823 was replaced with Act 872 which added the provision of resources for industrial development to EDAIF's mandate. EFC was created in 1989 as a Special Purpose Vehicle (SPV) to provide financial and other related support to the non-traditional export sector (NTEs) in Ghanaian. The Eximguaranty Company Limited was also instituted in 1994 to provide credit guarantees and general financial risk management solutions SMEs. Once the merger was concluded, staff of the three institutions were incorporated into the Ghana EXIM Bank.

The Bank's mandate is to facilitate the transformation of Ghana's economy into an export driven one through providing support for and improving trade between Ghana and other countries, facilitating overseas investments by Ghanaian Companies and eliminating critical market failures in the Ghanaian economy to make the country stand out in the global economy. Its vision is to become a strong financial institution that will be a key engine in the development of Ghana's export trade, facilitate cross border trade and make Ghana a pillar in regional and continental trade. The bank supplies funding for exporters who have export orders and those who want to acquire raw materials to enable them produce for export. The Ghana EXIM Bank has five business units. These are Corporate Banking, Business Banking, Project and Business Development, Small-Medium Enterprises (SMEs), and Export Trade.

Source https://www.eximbankghana.com/vision-&-mission

9.7.3 Structured Trade Finance

One important form of trade finance, which has been identified as an important means of export financing is structured trade finance. It is an approach to trade financing that focuses on transaction-based lending. In structured trade finance, the focus shifts from the strength of the borrower to the underlying cash flow and structures that enhance safe financing. The technique originated from the Latin American financial crisis in the mid-1980s and has since been seen as an innovative means of financing international trade by not relying on balance sheet analysis, government guarantee and tangible assets as collateral, but rather by relying on the potential sale of the commodity for payment. Structured trade finance is particularly beneficial to developing countries, which may not be able to access straight commercial finance. While structured trade finance constitutes about 80% of loans to non-investment grade borrowers that of investment grade borrowers is 20–40% (Spratt, 2008). It also has been identified as a vital pathway to boosting international trade in Africa, and development banks, especially regional development banks have provided significant amounts through structured finance trade deals. African NDBs need to focus more on structured trade finance in order to facilitate international trade and enhance export revenue. There is a consideration of structured trade finance rather than the conventional method of balance sheet financing that excludes most enterprises with viable export trade transactions.

9.7.4 *Infrastructure Financing*

NDBs are central players in infrastructure investments. Many NDBs support infrastructure development by providing infrastructure finance mainly through the use of instruments such as long-term loans, guarantees and public-private partnerships. According to the World Bank (2018), about 59% of the NDBs provide infrastructure financing, using these instruments, demonstrating the commitment of many NDBs to financing infrastructure projects. Infrastructure development is critical for enterprise growth and for African countries to migrate from being consumer-based economies to investment-driven economies, infrastructure will be key. The private sector can thrive in an environment of solid infrastructure in the areas of transportation, water, ICT, energy and power. Project finance through a public–private partnership (PPP) helps in dealing with the issues of pricing, as well as risk sharing and rewards between the public and private partners in a manner that is mutually acceptable. The NDBs can be instrumental in achieving it. NDBs provide project finance loans to a sponsor of a project entity. They leverage the financing provided to crowd in private investment into the project in the form of a PPP arrangement. They also facilitate PPP deals between government and other private sector players.

Boxes 9.3 and 9.4 profile the Development Bank of Southern Africa (DBSA) and the Infrastructure Development Bank of Zimbabwe, which have been instrumental in providing financing for infrastructure development.

Box 9.3: Development Bank of Southern Africa and Infrastructure Development

The Development Bank of Southern Africa (DBSA) is a government-owned DFI, which was formed in 1983 with the aim of stimulating economic growth and regional integration for sustainable development projects and programmes in South Africa, SADC and the wider sub Saharan Africa. The purpose of DBSA is to build Africa's prosperity by driving inclusive growth and ensuring novel solutions that drive socio-economic development in emerging economies in sub-Saharan Africa. The Bank does this by mobilising funding resources which it channels into projects intended for erecting infrastructure that sustainable and contributes to development on the continent. Over the years, DBSA has added considerably to the economic growth of the SADC region through investment in economic & social infrastructure and supported regional integration.

In 2018, the South African government set up the Infrastructure Fund, which is presently domiciled within the DBSA, to meet the demand for blended finance for the efficient implementation of socio-economic infrastructure programmes and projects in South Africa. The Infrastructure Fund is meant to change the face of public infrastructure through bespoke blended financing solutions by sourcing and blending capital from the private sector, institutional investors, DFIs and MDBs. The Fund in collaboration with its key stakeholders, namely, the National Treasury, Infrastructure South Africa and the project owners, intends to lead the well-organized implementation of South Africa's infrastructure development programme in line with the principles of good governance and the use of fair, equitable, cost effective, competitive, and transparent procurement systems. The Infrastructure Fund has been supported with R100 billion (US$ 5.84 billion) in seed funds by the National Treasury for a ten-year period. The contribution is expected to be critical to the structuring of blended finance solutions. This seed funding is aimed at catalysing R1 trillion (US$ 58 billion) of infrastructure delivery within the country.

Source https://www.dbsa.org/

Box 9.4: Infrastructure Development Bank of Zimbabwe

The Infrastructure Development Bank of Zimbabwe is a NDB in Zimbabwe, established on the 31st of August 2005, assuming all the assets and liabilities of the former Zimbabwe Development Bank (ZDB). This NDB was mainly established as a vehicle to promote of economic development and growth, and improvement of the living standards of Zimbabweans through the development of infrastructure, such as energy, transport, water and sanitation, information communication technology (ICT) and housing. The Bank since its establishment has made significant contribution to infrastructure development in Zimbabwe.

Source https://www.idbz.co.zw/

9.7.5 *Other Products and Services*

In addition to offering lending products, trade financing and infrastructure financing, NDBs also provide other financial products and services as well as non-financial services. The other financial products include loan guarantees, private equity and venture capital, and deposit accounts. The non-financial products NDBs offer include, consulting and training, advisory and technical assistance and networking and business matching. NDBs can also be instrumental in assisting clients to structure complex deals, creating new channels to raise private sector financing, and building capacity of public and private sector organizations, undertaking policy and market-relevant research, creating and disseminating knowledge (World Bank, 2018).

Box 9.5 provides graphical illustrations on the key findings of the World Bank study with respect to lending products, while Box 9.6 illustrates financial products and services offered by NDBs.

Box 9.5: Lending Products

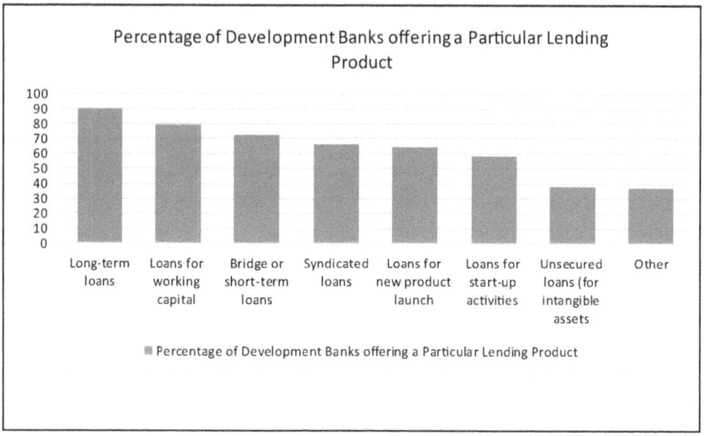

Source Author's construction based on World Bank Data (2018)

Box 9.6: Financial Products and Services

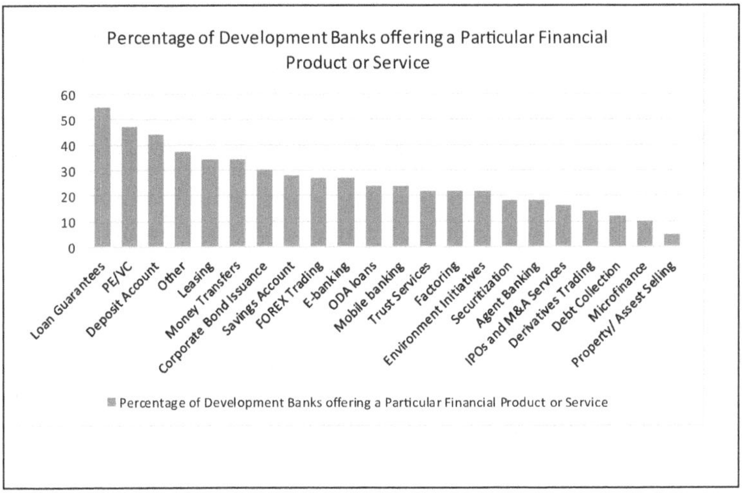

Source Author's construction based on World Bank Data (2018)

9.8 Pricing and Subsidies

One important issue development banks are confronted with is pricing of their financial products and services. For instance, they need to decide whether to price their loans based on prevailing market or commercial rates or they must subsidize their interest rates. There is always the confusion as to whether credit and guarantees offered by development banks should be based on subsidized interest rates or premiums. One school of thought believes that, subsidizing interest rates on credit will affect solvency and profitability positions of NDBs as well as distort the competitive environment. Another school of thought argues that subsidizing interest rates on credit is necessary to support promising businesses and startups, in as much as the subsidies are applied appropriately and for the intended purposes.

In the World Bank study, they found that 47% of the NDBs indicated they only provide loans priced at market interest rates, while 51% reported that they offer both market-based and subsidized credit products. With respect to NDBs which offer market-based and subsidized loan products, they mentioned that they fund their subsidized lending through a combination of concessional (interest free or subsidized) loans obtained from international donors or multilateral development banks like the World Bank Group; government funding; and other profitable business lines that enable them do this without incurring losses. NDBs that are not able to obtain such concessionary funding to support their subsidized lending tend to incur losses, leading failure. It is essential for NDBs not to underestimate the need for financial soundness in their bid to provide subsidized lending. Obtaining concessionary funding is a necessary determinant for offering credit at subsidized interest rates (World Bank, 2018).

In order to avoid the financial challenges associated with subsidized lending, some NDBs are able to distinguish between loans offered on a commercial basis and those offered to specific sector or borrowers at subsidized interest rates. The commercial loans are typically financed from the NDBs' internal resources or from loans they have also acquired on a commercial basis. On the other hand, the NDBs' subsidized lending is mainly financed from concessionary funding obtained from government and other sources. Usually, NDBs receive fees for underwriting, disbursing, supervising, monitoring and collecting such loans. However, the performance of the loans does not in any way impact their profitability since the loans are treated on the NDBs' balance sheet. The strategy adopted by some NDBs is to capture the loans offered at subsidized interest rates with the associated concessionary funding as off-balance items. This strategy enables the development banks to pass on any losses arising from borrowers' default to the funding source, without capturing this on their balance sheet. Clearly, this is a good approach, which allows the NDBs to separate the high-risk involved in offering such subsidized lending from lending based on their own internal resources.

9.9 Risks and Costs of National Development Banks

NDBs have the potential to be important players in their nations' economies and financial systems. Their whole existence is to respond to market failures in order to improve their respective countries' economies. NDBs must recognize and manage the risks and costs they encounter in order to fulfil their purpose. Considering their purpose/mandate and ownership, which are the two fundamental characteristics that separate NDBs from commercial banks, they are not immune against risks and their accompanying repercussions, and may suffer them more keenly than commercial banks. Because of their government ownership or support, NDBs are entrusted with delivering a specific public policy mandate. The main costs of NDBs are the opportunity costs in relation to government's funds used in subsidized lending, possibly directly or indirectly, as well as the general and administrative costs associated with managing the NDBs.

In terms of risks associated with managing NDBs, these can be general risks and those related to direct or indirect origination in providing finance. Further, NDBs may crowd out private markets and hamper the development of capital markets. General risks involve the likelihood of selecting losers (Robinson & Torvik, 2005); agency costs (Musacchio & Lazzarini, 2014); crony capitalism (Carvalho, 2014); lack of efficiency due to small scale; and crowding out effects (see Torres & Zeidan, 2016).

Despite the ability of experienced staff to mitigate agency difficulties, Lazzarini et al. (2015) suggest how agency issues can develop in public financial institutions. Considering the effect of government-driven resource allocation, agency costs increase the risk of selecting losers. Carvalho (2014) demonstrates that government ownership of financial institutions results in significant government clout over companies' real-world actions, with enterprises which are not in the financial space allocating funds based on political pressure rather than profitability and productivity. Corruption is a major worry for the efficient operation of NDBs, as it is for other public organizations, and that is why having generally stable institutions are a prerequisite for NDB development.

According to Griffith-Jones et al. (2020), real economy risk exists, i.e. risk associated with development benefits, such as borrowing or funding in initiatives that drive technology as well as other advances, often with significant positive externalities that assist development. In other words, there is a risk associated with the impact and benefits of development. One example of a positive effect is persuading corporate investors to participate in ventures having protracted yields that are in accordance with their long-term commitments. On the other hand, the use of such technologies opens the door to value extraction, such as through the redistribution of wealth from development banks to private financial institutions.

There are also global risks, which refer to the likelihood of crises or variability affecting multiple countries at the same time. These include macroeconomic shocks like price fluctuations and worldwide interest rate volatility, which are influenced by the world's growing economy and unexpected situations like policy actions in large advanced economies. Another example is the potential for a monetary crisis. They also include risks that are not economically connected, such as environmental hazards and epidemic diseases like the COVID-19 that have a global impact. NDBs' tendency to have extensive vulnerabilities to systematic risks, including on a worldwide economic level, makes it difficult for some of them to minimize these risks or provide insurance to individual investors, especially when conditions are constantly changing, as they are in many emerging economies. This is particularly true in developing nations still in the process of modernization.

External shocks that do not transcend borders are one example of a national risk. Other types of these risks include those that are highly associated with policies. An example could be political risk or risk that is linked with macroeconomic policies. These kinds of national shocks cause risk premiums to rise, which discourages investment in a country. Endogenous shocks are characterized by the fact that decisions regarding policy can influence these risks. Although the financial instruments that NDBs deploy are unable to mitigate these risks, they can encourage more risk-reduction-oriented legislation. For example, if the government provides credit to a utility service or insures a transaction that the company will make to an independent power producer (IPP), the state has a vested interest in the public utility's financial viability. This could be accomplished, for example, by addressing inefficiencies that are present within the utility.

The costs incurred by society as a whole and the inefficiency with which resources may be allocated to long-term financial markets are both increased as a direct result of the risks associated with certain processes. If market actors do not have confidence in the payments that the government will make in the event of a default, or if the actions that the government takes are inconsistent over time, then guarantees are useless.

If the basic interest rate is established at a high level or if the banking system is small and superficial, interest rate equalization will not work effectively. In addition, the probability of crowding out effects would grow significantly if NDBs established interest rates which fall below the fundamental rate of the private market. When it comes to efficiently allocating resources, penalties are especially problematic, and this leads to an increase in the average interest rate across all local markets (Torres & Zeidan, 2016).

9.10 Concluding Remarks

NDBs contribute to bridging the financing gap by providing long-term financing to support sectors of the economy. There has been renewed interest in the importance of NDBs, following the global financial crisis and the recent COVID-19 crisis, especially considering the important counter-cyclical role they play during a crisis. They continue to constitute major players in the financial sector of several economies, especially in EMDEs. In spite of their relevance, not all NDBs are successful, and even those that are successful can have major adverse developmental impacts due to project failure. The business model employed by NDBs has implications for their performance. It is important to understand how they can improve their performance in terms of achieving the dual goals of development impact and financial sustainability.

In this chapter, we have discussed the business model of NDBs. We specifically looked at issues around the policy mandate of NDBs; sectors and clients served by NDBs; NDBs' funding sources; the business/lending models of NDBs; instruments used for providing finance; financial products and services offered by NDBs; pricing and subsidies; and risks and costs of NDBs. It has been revealed that some NDBs have a narrow or specific mandate that clearly refers to the sectors or activities that an NDB is supposed to support such as MSMEs or agriculture. Others also have a broad mandate, which is expressed in general terms without referring to any specific sector, activity or customer. NDBs mainly serve different types of customers, including MSMEs, exporters, large private firms, individuals, households, local governments and other financial institutions. NDBs obtain funding from various sources to finance their operations and activities. The main funding sources available to most NDBs include direct budget transfers from the government, mobilizing of deposits, borrowing from other financial institutions, raising capital from international capital markets, issuing debt securities in domestic financial markets and acquiring official development assistance.

NDBs adopt different types of business or lending models, including the retail (tier 1) model, the wholesale (tier 2) model and a combination of the retail and the wholesale models. The retail lending model involves NDBs engaging directly with the target customers and may require the NDBs to have many branches to reach the target customers. In the wholesale lending model, NDBs provide loans through private financial institutions or participating financial institutions, which in turn on-lend to the end customers. The third lending model is a hybrid approach, which is a mixture of both the retail and the wholesale models. The instruments used by NDBs to provide finance include grants, direct loans, equity financing, indirect loans, guarantees and interest equalization schemes. NDBs also offer various types of lending and financial products and services to their clients. Some of the lending products are long-term loans, loans for working capital, bridge or short-term loans, syndicated loans, business startup loans and loans for launching new products or bringing new products to the market. In addition, some NDBs provide trade financing products and infrastructure financing. Apart from offering lending products, trade financing and infrastructure financing, NDBs also provide other financial products and services as well as non-financial services. The other financial products include loan guarantees, private equity and venture capital and deposit accounts. The non-financial products NDBs offer include, consulting and training, advisory and technical assistance and networking and business matching.

References

Barone, B., & Spratt, S. (2015). *Development banks from the BRICS* (Evidence Report No. 111). Institute of Development Studies (IDS).

Bradlow, D., & Humphrey, C. S. (2016). *Sustainability and infrastructure investment: National development banks in Africa* (GEGI Working Paper 002). Boston University. https://doi.org/10.2139/ssrn.2802713

Carvalho, D. (2014). The real effects of government-owned banks: Evidence from an emerging market. *The Journal of Finance, 69*(2), 577–609.

de Luna-Martínez, J., & Vicente, C. L. (2012). *Global survey of development banks* (World Bank Policy Research Working Paper, No. 5969). World Bank.

Eurodad. (2017, April). *Public development banks: Towards a better model.* European Network on Debt and Development.

Griffith-Jones, S., Ocampo, J. A., Rezende, F., Schclarek, A. and Brei, M. (2018). *The Future of National Development Banks in S. Griffith-Jones and J. A. Ocampo (Eds.)*, The Future of National Development Banks, London: Oxford University Press.

Griffith-Jones, S., Attridge, S., & Gouett, M. (2020). *Securing climate finance through national development banks* (ODI Report). ODI. www.odi.org/publications/16552-securing-climate-finance-through-national-development-banks

Lazzarini, S. G., Musacchio, A., Bandeira-de-Mello, R., & Marcon, R. (2015). What do state-owned development banks do? Evidence from BNDES, 2002–09. *World Development, 66*, 237–253.

Marois, T. (2015). Banking on alternatives to neoliberal development. In L. Pradella & T. Marois, (Eds.), *Polarizing development: Alternatives to neoliberalism and the crisis*. Pluto Press.

Musacchio, A., & Lazzarini, S. G. (2014). *Reinventing state capitalism: Leviathan in business*. Harvard University Press.

Povel, F. (2015, July). *The RAison d'Etre of public development banks and recommendations for successful development banking*. Paper presented at KfW FfD panel on Development Banks, Addis Ababa. Retrieved on 21 May 2022 from http://www.un.org/esa/ffd/ffd3/wp-content/uploads/sites/2/2015/07/Raison-detre-of-DBs-nonpaper-Addis.pdf

Robinson, J. A., & Torvik, R. (2005). White elephants. *Journal of Public Economics, 89*(2), 197–210.

Smallridge, D., Buchner, B., Trabacchi, C., Netto, M., Lorenzo, J. G., & Serra, L. (2012). *The role of national development banks in intermediating international climate finance to scale up private sector investments* (113 pp.). Inter-American Development Bank.

Spratt S. (2008). *Development finance: Debates, dogma and new direction*. Routledge Taylor and Francis.

Torres, E., & Zeidan, R. (2016). The life-cycle of national development banks: The experience of Brazil's BNDES. *The Quarterly Review of Economics and Finance, 62*, 97–104.

World Bank. (2018). *2017 Survey of national development banks*. World Bank.

CHAPTER 10

Monitoring and Evaluation, and Impact Evaluation

10.1 Introduction

It is obvious that Monitoring and Evaluation (M&E) as well as Impact Evaluation (IE) are important concepts that are key to inclusive economic development. They are programmes and systems designed to help institutions and corporations build an 'evidence-based policy'. They are critical in creating awareness and stirring up debate about the effectiveness and efficiency of the programmes and policies. The importance of the M&E role within development finance institutions has been reinforced by the growing voice of M&E practitioners and emerging development partners who have brought to the fore the issues of good governance and a more effective development impact. The global trend towards more accountable, responsive and sustainable development goals has fuelled the pursuit of M&E capacity development, which has been a key focus of efforts to advance development projects, programmes and policies in the context of a comprehensive development framework. This is becoming increasingly important for development banks, including National Development Banks (NDBs) in developing and emerging economies, to network among M&E practitioners and share knowledge on M&E and IE related to delivery and effective development outcomes.

National Development Banks (NDBs) are increasingly expected to systematically report on the impact of their operations, particularly their development mandates. For this reason, some NDBs have adopted

© The Author(s), under exclusive license to Springer Nature Switzerland AG 2023

J. Yindenaba Abor, *The Changing Role of National Development Banks in Africa*, https://doi.org/10.1007/978-3-031-38639-8_10

specific M&E systems to assess the impact of their activities on development to determine what works and what does not in policy formulation and implementation. The adoption of M&E systems also helps NDBs to make adjustments throughout the phases of the developmental project or programme cycle. Donor countries and development partners are increasingly calling for a greater role in development. NDBs are instrumental to this change of paradigm. NDBs are engaged in providing support to key sectors of the economy, both public and private. However, due to the need to demonstrate positive development impacts, NDBs have come under scrutiny in achieving the sustainable development goals. Thus, advocating for a stronger orientation and assessment of M&E and IE systems towards development results is important for identifying what has been done, what needs changes and benefits that have been achieved from development interventions.

Given the important and increasing role of NDBs in the development landscape, analysing these concepts is important to understand the current issues, strengths and weakness, and find out approaches in which they can be enhanced. In addressing M&E and the IE as well as development challenges among national development banks in Africa and other developing and emerging economies, selected issues may vary from the policy-focused evaluation challenges to key challenges of M&E and IE in different economies. This chapter offers a general overview of the concept of M&E and IE of National Development Banks. It proposes a framework for evaluating M&E and IE systems in the context of development impacts.

The rest of the chapter is structured as follows: Sect. 10.2 provides the definition and concepts of M&E; Sect. 10.3 provides the M&E framework of NDBs; Sect. 10.4 looks at concepts and techniques of impact evaluation; Sect. 10.5 provides the theoretical framework of impact evaluation of NDBs; Sect. 10.6 discusses the design and implementation of impact evaluation practices; Sect. 10.7 looks at the approaches to Ex Post impact evaluation of NDBs; Sect. 10.8 examines the methods for analysing the impact evaluation of NDBs; Sect. 10.10 looks at how to evaluate deliverables/outcomes of NDBs; Sect. 10.11 identifies the challenges of impact evaluation practices; Sect. 10.12 examines the recent developments in impact evaluation of NDBs; and finally Sect. 10.13 provides concluding remarks.

10.2 Monitoring and Evaluation: Definition and Concepts

Monitoring is an ongoing process of gathering and analysing information about a programme. It can also be defined as the systematic and routine collection of information from projects and programmes for the following purposes: (1) lessons learned to improve practices and activities in the future; (2) internal and external accountability for resources deployed and results achieved; (3) making informed decisions about the future of the initiative; and (4) promoting the empowerment of beneficiaries of the initiative. This is a task that periodically recurs in the beginning stage of a project or programme planning. Monitoring helps to check progress or compare the *actual* against what has been *planned* in order to judge how well the intervention is being implemented within the planned results. It helps the documentation of planned results, processes and experiences to be employed for decision-making and learning processes. The data collected from the programme itself is used in the monitoring process. The existence of a reliable monitoring system that is based on the information acquired or data collected in the monitoring processes is used for evaluation.

Evaluation is a process that entails the 'systematic and objective assessment of all elements of an ongoing or a completed project or progrmme, from design to the implementation to the achievement of the results', to determine its significant value. Evaluation allows the data and information from a project or a programme to be appraised in order to inform strategic decisions for the improvement of the project or programme. The primary objective of evaluation is to offer credible information for decision-makers to identify ways in which more of the desired results can be achieved. Generally, evaluation is grouped into two main types, namely *performance evaluation* and *impact evaluation*. While performance evaluation focuses on the quality of service delivery and the results achieved by a programme, impact evaluation, discussed later in this chapter, looks at changes in the results or outcomes of the project or programme being evaluated. In principle, evaluation helps to draw conclusions about the relevance, effectiveness, efficiency, impact and sustainability of interventions. The data and information collected in line with the process of monitoring offer the foundation for the analysis of evaluation.

Monitoring and Evaluation (often known as M&E) are aspects of the policy process and are seen as an embedded concept and constitutive part of any project or programme design. It involves a combination of data collection and analysis (monitoring) and assessment of the extent to which a programme, project, policy or intervention has, or has not, met its specified objectives (evaluation). M&E processes enable policymakers and managers of a project or programme to assess how an intervention is evolving over time (monitoring) and how effectively a project or programme has been implemented and whether there are gaps between conception and achievement of results (evaluation); and whether the changes in value or results are solely attributable to the project or programme (impact evaluation). M&E is not a control instrument imposed by the development partner or an optional concept of a project or programme, but an approach to dialogue about development and its progress between all those involved. Monitoring takes place when a project or programme is implemented and evaluation takes place at the end of a project or programme. M&E includes information about the costs of the monitored or evaluated project or programme and helps to compare the benefits with the costs of the project or programme.

10.3 Monitoring and Evaluation Framework of National Development Banks

The main goal of M&E is to improve current and future management of outputs, outcomes and impact. Many international organizations and government entities use the monitoring and evaluation processes to assess their programmes and interventions. Development banks also use monitoring and evaluation to assess the financing interventions they make in specific areas. M&E processes can be managed internally by the development bank or they can be outsourced to private firms. Some development banks may have a monitoring and evaluation department with dedicated officers responsible for this. The monitoring and evaluation team or evaluators must be independent and the credibility and objectivity of monitoring and evaluation reports will depend heavily on this. In all, their expertise and independence are crucial to the success of the process.

NDBs have a clear mandate to serve specific sectors of the economy that traditional financial institutions such as commercial banks are unwilling to serve given the high level of risk involved. Despite this, they are expected to be financially sustainable in order to achieve their economic goals, which poses a major challenge for NDBs. In addition, monitoring and evaluating NDBs provides a core set of tools that can be integrated into NDBs development project, programme or policy framework to review and improve the quality, efficiency and effectiveness of policies and programmes at different stages of implementation—or to focus on results. Many NDBs do not have effective monitoring and evaluation systems in place to help them to regularly assess their performance and take corrective action when necessary.

Therefore, designing and implementing an effective monitoring system will be critical for NDBs to be able to achieve the expected results based on their objectives. Without proper monitoring and evaluation, it will be difficult for NDBs to achieve their goals and they will not be able to judge which programmes and strategies work and in which context, and the reasons. What this means is that, NDBs may spend a considerable amount of time and resources only to realize later they could have achieved their goals more efficiently using a different approach. Effective rating evaluation systems are required to ensure NDBs are fulfilling their mandate. Knowing which programmes and financial instruments are producing results and which are not is important to ensure that NDBs are effective and efficient (Heider, 2017). For instance, in the case of Development Bank of Rwanda, a robust monitoring and evaluation system was rolled out, based on their 2018 annual report, to enhance evidence-based impact measurement. The system was put in place to monitor the impact of the project on the increase of access to basic infrastructure like electricity, the increase of access to affordable financing and on all aspects of the priority sectors of the economy.

A study by the World Bank indicates how monitoring and evaluation are conducted among NDBs, Fig. 10.1.

In Fig. 10.1, 56 percent of the NDBs surveyed have their own monitoring and evaluation unit. However, most of them do not have the tools to quantitatively or qualitatively evaluate their impact on development. Only 49 percent of NDBs indicated that they carry out economic impact evaluation of their products and services, while 37 percent indicated that they outsource their monitoring and evaluation function to third parties. Most NDBs use financial indicators to measure their development impact, similar to the assessment framework and tool used by private financial institutions to monitor their operations, financial strength and profitability. NDBs tend to use a limited set of indicators to measure the economic impact of their activities. For example, the World Bank (2018) report indicates that development banks that serve SMEs indicated that they carry out impact evaluation; 65 percent said they monitor new jobs created by the projects they fund; 49 percent monitor the productivity gains of their clients and 40 percent the survival rate of the SMEs they serve (see Fig. 10.2).

The tools NDBs use to monitor and evaluate their economic impact of their activities or operations vary from one institution to another. Some of the evaluation tools used by the NDBs include survey of customers (most commonly used tool), and randomized control trials.

Figure 10.3 shows the results based on the World Bank (2018) survey on how NDBs use the results of monitoring and evaluation frameworks.

In Fig. 10.3, 88 percent of NDBs reported that they share information with their boards, 76 percent use the results to expand well-performing programmes or adapt the design of programmes, and 64 percent share it with the ministry to which the institution belongs. Only 31 percent of institutions use the information and analysis they generate to weed out underperforming programmes, and only 28 percent are required to share it with the legislature.

Overall, the importance of establishing effective monitoring and evaluation systems for NDBs cannot be overstated. However, the use of vigorous and effective tools to monitor and evaluate the activities of NDBs is still in its infancy, in part because there are no international benchmarks that FIS can rely on. There is very little practical knowledge to guide efforts in existing NDBs. Furthermore, in order to have effective monitoring and evaluation systems, it is essential to adapt these structures to the specific characteristics and business activities of each NDBs.

Fig. 10.1 Monitoring and evaluation by NDBs (*Source* Author's construction based on World Bank 2018 Survey Report, 2022)

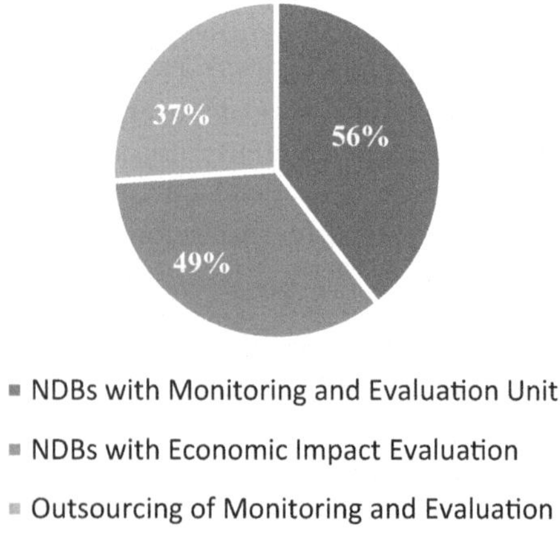

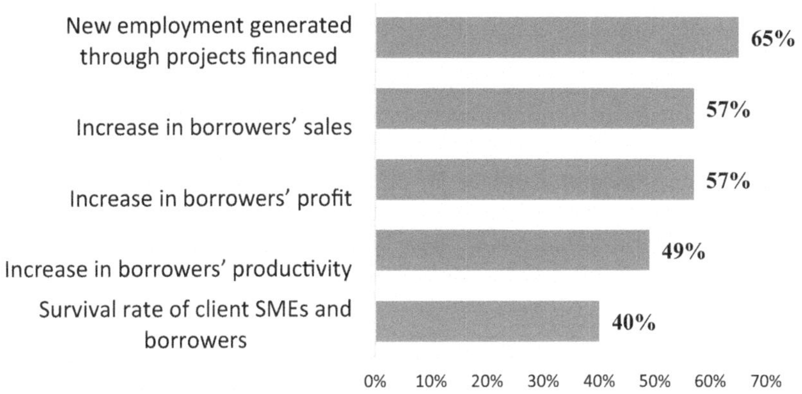

Fig. 10.2 Non-financial indicators used by development banks for monitoring economic impact of their activities (*Source* Author's construction based on World Bank 2018 Survey Report, 2022)

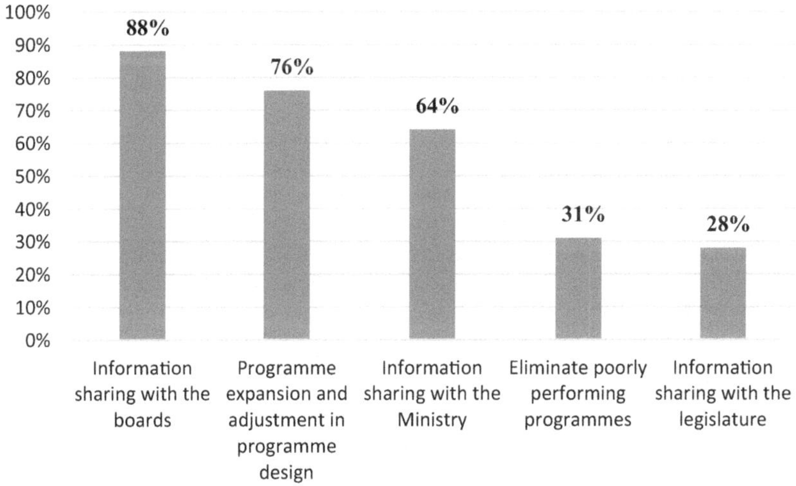

Fig. 10.3 How NDBs use the results of M&E frameworks (*Source* Author's construction based on World Bank 2018 Survey Report, 2022)

Since NDBs are generally publicly funded institutions, they must be accountable to various stakeholders for their performance and the resources made available to them. Evidence suggests that NDBs often face governance, development impact and result challenges. To support NDBs in playing their vital role as part of the broader financial system, there is a need to put in place an effective monitoring and evaluation system to monitor and evaluate their performance or development impact and results (World Bank, 2018). Box 10.1 contains recommendations on building sound rating systems for development banks.

Box 10.1: Recommendations for Building Sound Evaluation Systems for Development Banks

1. Understand market failures and mandate to design an effective evaluation system. When the development bank is not clear about the results it needs to achieve, it focuses on the services it wants to provide, regardless of whether these help overcome market failures.
2. Based on the mission, define specific results and meaningful measures and integrate financial performance indicators with indicators of social, economic and environmental results, as they can help or hinder the financial performance of the Development Bank.
3. Be selective with indicators. Many development banks are concerned about data costs. They don't have to collect all the indicators, but should identify other parties who are interested in the relevant indicators and possibly collect data that can be used. In some cases, this can serve as a basis for new partnerships.
4. The Institute's ability to collect and analyse data. Without systems that encourage the generation and interpretation of data in a way that is convenient for decision makers, data is collected haphazardly and therefore rendered useless.
5. Integration and use of data in decision-making. This is one of the most important and often overlooked steps. Improvement, course correction, and learning cannot happen unless evidence is used. Evidence is not the only driver of policy-making, but policy decisions must consider evidence and its implications.
6. Lead by example. Development banks have a significant benchmarking or role-modeling effect. Sharing data and showing how the Development Bank is acting on the data can send strong messages to other financial institutions.

Source Heider (2017) and World Bank (2018).

Though monitoring and evaluation is relevant for assessing the performance of NDBs, another important tool is impact evaluation.

10.4 Impact Evaluation: Concepts and Techniques

Impact is 'the long-term results produced by a project, programme or policy and they include intended and unintended results, positive and negative, direct and indirect impacts'. **Evaluation**, as discussed earlier is 'periodic, objective assessment of a planned, ongoing or completed project, programme or policy'. They answer specific questions that are in line with the design, implementation and results of the project, programme or policy. Evaluations address three questions relating to descriptive questions, normative questions and cause-and-effect questions. Descriptive questions aim to address what is happening and identify organizational processes, conditions and relationships and stakeholder views; normative questions compare what happens with what should happen; and cause-and-effect questions examine outcomes and attempt to assess what difference the intervention makes to outcomes.

Impact Evaluation (IE) is a method used at the results stage of projects or programmes to analyse differences in outcomes, with and without the project or programme. It describes a particular type of evaluation that seeks to answer a specific cause-and-effect of a programme on an outcome of interest. This relates to those changes that are attributable to a programme, its modality or design innovation. The governance structure of NDBs requires that impact evaluation practices are incorporated into the governance framework to produce strong and credible results. In addition, impact evaluations are needed to inform policymakers of NDBs on a range of decisions that curtail inefficient programmes, scale up workable or actionable interventions, adjust programmes that are beneficial and select alternative programmes that improve performance.

IE offers information about the impact of an intervention and allows for credible causal inference that changes occurred, at least in part, as a result of the project, programme or policy. Thus, it attempts to evaluate or assess the contributions generated from development interventions to any identified change. It seeks to assess the changes brought about by a project or programme, rather than focusing on activities and outcomes only. It assesses the extent to which a project or a programme has caused desired changes in the intended developmental impact. This informs decision-makers on whether an intervention should be continued, discontinued, repeated or expanded. It follows a rigorous and recognized research methodology to identify changes and contributions—and the results of IE can be applied to improve the delivery of a project or programme. It is mainly adopted when the intended use of the results can be clearly identified, taking into account the availability of resources and the timing of the intervention decisions under study. It estimates what would have happened if beneficiaries had not participated in the project or programme. The key significant feature of IE that distinguishes it from any other kind of assessment is the determination of causal effects of an intervention between the programme and its specific outcome.

In planning an IE of a project or a programme, the steps to consider are illustrated in Box 10.2.

Box 10.2: Steps Involved in Impact Evaluation

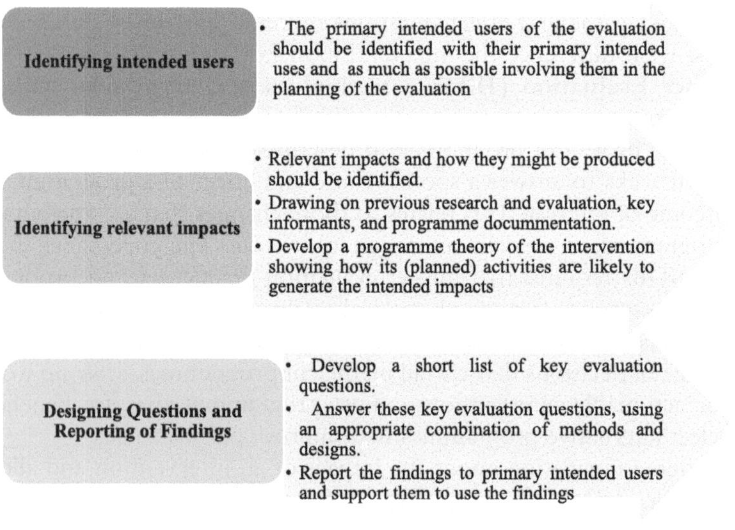

It is important to clarify impact evaluation terminologies due to their terminological differences and overall intended use. For instance, **causal attribution** is an appropriate term for causal inference when it is possible to confidently estimate what proportion of impacts has been caused by a particular project, programme or policy whereas **causal contribution** is an appropriate term when it is only possible to be confident about a project, programme or policy that has been one of the contributing factors generating the impacts. Therefore, IE focuses on causality and attribution, both characteristics of IEs. This helps to determine the methods that can be used. For example, to estimate the causal effect, or impact, of the results of a project, programme or policy, any method chosen must calculate the counterfactual—which describes and estimates what the outcome would have been for participants if they had not participated in the programme.

10.4.1 Types of Impact Evaluation

There are different types of impact evaluation that exist before, during and after project, programme or policy implementation.

- **Ex post impact evaluation** is a type of IE that gathers evidence about the actual impacts.
- **Ex ante impact evaluation** deals with the forecasts of likely impacts.
- **During implementation** collects information or evidence about whether the project, programme or policy is in order, or 'on track' to deliver the intended impacts.
- **Formative impact evaluation** is 'employed to inform improvements to a project, programme or policy, especially when there is an ongoing project, programme or policy commitment'.
- **Summative impact evaluation** is conducted to aid in making decisions about the beginning, continuity or expansion of a project, programme or policy.
- **Economic evaluation** joins evidence from an impact evaluation and the analysis of data about costs. Examples are cost–benefit analysis and cost-effectiveness. While cost–benefit analysis is usually used ex-ante, to estimate total benefit of a project, programme or policy compared to its total costs and to decide among different project, programme or policy options, cost-effectiveness analysis estimates a ratio between costs and a standardized unit of positive impacts and compares the costs of two or more projects, programmes or policies in yielding the same outcome.

10.4.2 Reasons for Impact Evaluation

In general, reasons for undertaking impact evaluation include:

- **Advocacy**—It is important to demonstrate the value investments of particular programmes.
- **Allocation**—It is important to make allocation of investments (funding, staff and other resources).
- **Analysis**—There should be analysis to inform continuous improvement including future programme design or plan.
- **Accountability**—Accountability is required and must follow legislation and best practices of performance management.

Although each reason stated above may require different evidence and different methods of gathering it, any given evaluation is more likely to have a combination of these reasons.

10.5 Theoretical Framework of Impact Evaluation of National Development Banks

Impact evaluation, as discussed earlier in this chapter, describes a specific type of evaluation that aims to respond to a specific cause and effect of a project, programme or policy on an outcome of interest. This refers to the changes attributed to a programme, its modality or design innovation. Impact assessment aims to find answers on what works and what does not and why resources are used most effectively. An impact assessment can be conducted with the aim of improving or refocusing a policy, or making decisions about whether to continue, discontinue, repeat or expand a policy. EI is a problem of missing data because you cannot observe the results of project, programme or policy participants unless they become beneficiaries.

Given the role of NDBs in development impacts, it is imperative to assess their IEs. The developmental project, programme or policy of NDBs require that impact evaluation practices are incorporated into their development impact framework to produce strong and credible results. The purpose is to raise awareness among managements and staff of NDBs on the value of IE as an instrument for enforcing development effectiveness, how it can be used to inform policy and if possible correct the intended design of interventions and to improve on the programme design. In addition, impact assessments are needed to inform FIS policymakers on a range of decisions that limit ineffective programmes and expand viable or actionable interventions, adjust projects, programmes or policies that are beneficial, and to select alternative programmes that improve performance.

The IE policy of NDBs sets out the framework for the conduct of IE and the goal is to improve the bank's development effectiveness and to further the achievement of the bank's mandate. The independent evaluation office is set out to oversee the independent evaluation of NDBs' strategies, policies, initiatives, processes and operations, with the aim of identifying lessons and offering recommendations for improving the efficiency and effectiveness of the bank. In providing the necessary support to achieve the effectiveness of NDBs' development mandate, the evaluation should cover a three core objective. These include: (1) promoting accountability for cost-effectiveness, development outcomes and impact that offer an evidence-based assessment for the achievements of the results through NDB's development financial support; (2) contributing to the improvement of learning and feedback, to enhance the quality of current and future projects, programmes, strategies, underlying processes, resources and skills/capacities required to achieve those results; and (3) providing independent feedback on the projects and programmes to the decision-makers to increase development impact and ensure compliance of the NDB's mandate. The core principles that govern IE of NDBs are driven by independence (providing legitimacy to evaluation to minimize conflict of interest), usefulness (must be relevant, reliable and credible), timelines (findings and recommendations of IE should be timely to inform decision-making) credibility and transparency (methodologies and expertise should be grounded on integrity, objectivity, rigorous approaches and testing to achieve its intended impact).

The IE of NDBs should serve both learning experience (lesson-learning) and accountability purposes. A well-designed IE can answer the question of whether the NDB's project, programme or policy is working or not, and hence provide an assistance to the decisions about scaling up. It can also provide answers to questions relating to project design (i.e. which aspects work and which aspects do not), and so offer policy-relevant information for redesign as well as for the future design projects, programmes or policies. In serving the bank's accountability objective, IE can provide answers to whether development assistance is working or not. Therefore, the IE helps NDBs align with results-based management and monitor the Bank's contribution to development finance assistance towards the SDGs. It is possible that not all interventions of NDBs can be assessed using IEs; rather there is a need to build a solid evidence base approach for the priority sectors from different perspectives in order to provide guidance for the policymakers. IEs are useful for interventions that relate to innovative schemes; pilot programmes graduating to a sustainable scaled up; interventions for which there may be scant solid evidence of impact within a specific context; and other interventions selected across an agency portfolio on an intermittent basis.

10.6 Design and Implementation of Impact Evaluation Practices

Impact Evaluation design is a planned project, programme or policy that measures 'the change in a development outcome that is attributable to a defined intervention'. In designing an IE, key elements that should be considered are: deciding whether to go ahead with the evaluation; key evaluation questions to be identified; design should be embedded in the project, programme or policy framework; comparison group should be a credible counterfactual; findings should be triangulated; and evaluation should be contextualized appropriately.

In the implementation of IE, the Terms of Reference (ToR) should be clearly defined; the intervention should be clearly understood and must be a prerequisite for the evaluation design. ToRs should emphasize the need for credible counterfactual analysis. Likewise, proposals or concept notes should clearly state how problems are addressed with an explicit assessment approach. From the perspective of management, project implementation requires an evaluation team that needs to be carefully chosen based on their unique expertise to ensure accurate reporting of data and results. The evaluation team must include personnel with the knowledge, skills and technical competence to implement it, the data sources, time and cost of the evaluation design and peer-review process. In the implementation process, transparency should not be omitted so that the data can be precisely interpreted.

There are several steps that need to be taken to ensure that there is evidence of effective and useful feedback. For instance, the significance and objectives of the evaluation during the project identification and preparation stage should be clearly stated. The structure of impact evaluation including the nature and timing evaluation should be outlined beforehand to guide the implementation of the intervention. To be able to assess the effects of the project, programme or policy, data availability and data quality should form an integral part. This heavily relies on the use of a quantitative, qualitative, mixed or triangulated method—and on whether the framework is ex ante, ex post or both.

For the collection of new data, concerns about the timing, sample design and selection, and survey instruments selection should be addressed and clearly stated. It is more appropriate to conduct a pilot survey on the field to understand the behaviour of the participants. This is useful for the purpose of validity and reliability testing. The team should make room for an ongoing data collection to keep the programme or project implementers current about its progress. Finally, the data must be carefully and accurately analysed and presented to policymakers, practitioners and other major stakeholders within the scope of the project, programme or policy—to enable potentially constructive and valuable feedback to be provided for correction and future policy design. Box 10.3 shows the roadmap for implementing an impact evaluation.

Box 10.3: Implementing an Impact Evaluation

Preparation

- Decide what to evaluate
- State objectives and questions
- Develop hypotheses

Organisation

- Choose evaluation design
- Confirm whether "design is ethical"
- Choose an evaluation team
- Provide evaluation time and budget

Sampling strategy

- Decide on the sample size
- Decide on the "sampling strategy"

Data Collection

- Decide the type of data to be collected
- Hire assistance and develop instruments
- Conduct a pilot test with instruments
- Conduct field work
- "Process and validate the data"

Reporting on findings

- Analyse the data
- Write the reporrt
- Discuss findings with policymarkers
- Disseminate findings

10.7 Approaches to Ex-Post Impact Evaluation of National Development Banks

In ensuring that the goals and activities of projects, programmes and policies are sound and that resources are adequately used to produce outputs, efforts are being made to assess policy choices ex ante, especially at the designing and monitoring stages. In addition, projects go through the stages of identification, preparation, evaluation, implementation and monitoring, as well as ex-post evaluation. However, significantly less effort is put into evaluating ex-post impact assessments. This section builds on previous evaluative work, including the experiences of other regulators. The ex-post impact evaluation measures the impact of specific NDBs interventions after the event (project, programme or policy). It addresses the key impacts that NDB interventions have had on stakeholders within their official mandate. This is done as strictly as possible to create a counterfactual and thus control the impact of other significant changes within the business model. The NDBs' assessment of whether the intended results were achieved, what worked and when something was not achieved, why not? are important questions which are applicable when using IE ex post. Ex-post IEs are important for NDBs because they help the bank identify what works and why, to inform policymakers on the choice of intervention methods and tools to use. It also provides a solid evidence base to ensure regulations are appropriate for development changes; it increases transparency about the effectiveness of deliveries; and it provides the ability to demonstrate and understand the bank's net impact. NDBs' efforts to achieve ex-post effects require them to commit their resources and make frequent ad hoc data requests from stakeholders. The criteria for selecting which interventions to evaluate include: the time since the intervention; the scale of the intervention; the novelty of the intervention; learning potential; likely reliability; and data availability.

Box 10.4 provides a case on impact evaluation of West African Development Bank (BOAD).

Box 10.4: West African Development Bank (BOAD)
The West African Development Bank (BOAD) introduced ex-post project evaluation in its cycle funding for projects like other multilateral development finance institutions. In 2012, the bank strengthened its position by setting up a department in charge of ex-post project evaluation. This involves a system of M&E and IE of project development outcomes including project performance evaluation, M&E, IE and socio-economic impact studies for projects funding by BOAD.

BOAD evaluated the performance of four projects, comprising of one (1) project in four (4) different countries (Burkina, Mali, Niger and Senegal). The Bank and some partners (African Development Bank, the Independent Evaluation Group (IEG) of the World Bank Group and the Islamic Development Bank) have taken the initiative (as of the sharing experiences in the area of evaluation) to evaluate a cross section of seven (7) projects, under socio-economic impact studies, in these four countries. The objectives of the evaluation of the project is: (1) 'to examine the extent to which the projects financed by the Bank were relevant and generally effective at sectoral level and in relation to national development objectives'; (2) 'to evaluate the impact of each of the projects on the lives of the beneficiary populations'; (3) 'to evaluate the success and failure factors which might have resulted in the impact noted for each project on its environment, with recommendations to be made into the bargain'.

Ex-post impact evaluations are one way in which the Bank assesses the impact of its interventions in the market. They focus on quantifying the impact (i.e. measuring the impact of discrete interventions), rules and guidance, remedies from market studies and market-wide recommendations that come from thematic reviews.

The Bank focuses on the quantitative and qualitative aspects, as is the best practice in evaluation across multilateral DFIs. The Bank measures the outcome of its interventions in the market against what would have happened without the intervention (or counterfactual). This is important as it allows the bank to understand its impact and learn lessons that will inform future interventions. The Bank seeks to value the benefits of the intervention and relate these to the cost of the intervention.

The ex-post IE attempts to evaluate the counterfactual (i.e. what would happen in the absence of an intervention). It measures the impact of an intervention on its outcome in a controlled manner for the effects of significant changes in the business environment. It can include qualitative discussions with stakeholders to understand why results are achieved as they are. It may also include studies that show that both are the case. The intermediate and final results changed the direction it was expected along an agreed causal pathway (from the policy implementation to the realization of benefits). Data analysis, coupled with stakeholder views, helps create a counterfactual.

These results enabled stakeholders and policymakers to draw lessons for the future and the Bank in particular, to enrich the implementation of its strategic plan.

A number of different approaches can be used in IE to address the fundamental question of the missing counterfactual. Although each approach has its own assumptions about how to resolve potential selection bias in the treatment effect of projects, programmes or policies, can be decomposed into the experimental methods (e.g. Randomization in practice in the development field experiments) and the quasi-experimental methods (e.g. applying propensity score matching, instrumental variables and regression discontinuity designs). This has been described in Box 10.5.

Box 10.5: Methods of Impact Evaluation

1. Randomized evaluations

It involves a randomly allocated initiative across a sample and has the advantage of avoiding selection bias at the level of randomization.

2. Matching methods (Propensity score matching)

It compares treatment effects across participant and matched nonparticipant units, with the matching conduct on a range of observed characteristics.

3. Double-difference (DD) methods

It assumes that unobserved selection is present and that it is time invariant - treating effect is determined by taking the difference in outcomes across treatment and control units before and after the programme intervention.

4. Instrumental variable (IV) methods

It can be used with cross-section or panel data and in the later case allow for selection bias on unobserved characteristics to vay with time.

5. Regression discontinuity (RD) & pipeline methods

These are extensions of IV and experimental methods; which construct a comparison group from subjects who are eligible for the program but have not yet received it.

6. Distributional impacts

This explores different econometric methods for evaluating policy interventions, including linear and nonlinear (quantile regression approaches.

7. Structural and other modelling approaches

This explores structural breaks econometric methods for evaluating policy interventions.

There are other unconstrained and constrained designs and methods that can be used in ex-post evaluation. Unconstrained designs include:

- **Quasi experimental designs**: These are used to compare group that is as good as random or obtained in a way that allows selection bias to be modelled.
- **Difference in difference method**: This is a method for analysing quasi-experimental data and compares how trends in outcomes change between treated and untreated groups over a time period that is relevant to the intervention.
- **Interrupted time series design**: This is used when the counterfactual is estimated from a forecast of the outcome measure before the intervention.

The constrained design includes:

- **Before and after studies**, where an outcome is measured before and after an intervention without a comparison group.
- **The use of process evaluation information** uses the qualitative methods and draws upon the findings of the studies' implementation and delivery of an intervention.

10.8 Methods for Analysing Impact Evaluation of NDBs: Qualitative vs Quantitative Methods

There are many types of evaluation methods. The methods for analysing IE are a type of data that is generated in the evaluation process. Drawing on qualitative and quantitative data, both can be used to answer the three types of questions above. While the qualitative are not expressed in numbers, but in text language or sometimes images, the quantitative are expressed in numerical measures. Qualitative data complement or complement quantitative IEs, and IEs that integrate qualitative and quantitative analyses are characterized as using the mixed method.

Many evaluations in practice are almost invariably mixed method evaluations. The qualitative analysis method includes focus groups and interviews with selected beneficiaries and other key informants. The use of qualitative information influences both the design and the interpretation of qualitative responses or data and supports a vital context. Thus, it is very useful during the three stages of an IE, including designing an IE, intermediate stage of an IE and the analysis stage of an IE. Qualitative information can also reinforce insights and deepen them. The quantitative method of analysis uses questionnaires as a survey instrument and then the sampling specialist must be able to perform power calculations to determine the appropriate sample size based on indicators derived from the evaluation questions.

While the qualitative method can help to explore, probe and explain relationships as well as explaining contextual differences, the quantitative method is able to analyse the relationships of the indicators established and can be used for testing theory deductively, conducting empirical analysis and statistical measurements of variables to establish the hypothesized relationship between independent and outcome variables. Where a rigorous approach has not been possible, triangulation is even more necessary to build a case based on a plausible association.

10.9 Management of Impact Evaluation

The management of IE encompasses decision-making at each step of the evaluation, from the design to the report and ensuring a well-implemented evaluation framework. For instance, within the process of planning and implementation of the IE, managers should revisit and make revision based on the choices they have made. In managing IE, managers and policymakers must be able to provide feedback on the implementation process or to evaluate the accessibility of the services regarding the project, programme or policy to vulnerable groups. They should ensure that the information required is clarified in terms of what purposes and this is a prerequisite to defining the evaluation type to be conducted. In the management process, the following tasks can be applied to guide the evaluative activities. Box 10.6 provides a framework for management tasks of impact evaluation.

Box 10.6: Management Tasks of Impact Evaluation

Stakeholder engagement

(1) Identify who has an interest in the IE in addition to the intended users.

(2) Identify whose interests need to be prioritized and why.

(3) Make sure they are involved throughout the IE process.

Decision-making process

(1) Specify how decisions will be made about the evaluation.

(2) Specify who will provide advice, who will make recommendations and who will make recommendations, and who will make the actual decisions.

(3) Clarify who will actually undertake the evaluation.

Resource determination and standards

(1) Identify what resources (time, money, expertise, equipment) will be needed and available for the evaluation. Consider both internal and external resources.

(2) Clarify appropriate quality and ethical standards and what will need to be done to ensure the evaluation standards are achieved.

Standards

(1) Clarify appropriate quality and ethical standards and what will need to be done to ensure the evaluation standards are achieved.

Management process

(1) Develop formal documents needed, example a brief and a Terms of Reference (ToR).

(2) Develop planning documents for the evaluation.

(3) Decide processes to review the evaluation process, findings and conclusions drawn.

Strengthen the IE capacity

(1) Build on and develop capacity for managing, undertaking and/or using evaluation.

(2) Consider involving human capital (knowledge and skills), organizational capital (technical and administrative infrastructure) and social capital (supportive networks).

10.10 Deliverables/Outcomes of National Development Banks

The deliverables or outcomes of impact evaluation measures programme or project effects or impacts in the target population by assessing the progress in the outcomes or deliverable objectives that the programme or project is to achieve. It provides the results of the programme or project effectiveness in achieving its ultimate goals. In most instances, data on earlier project findings are collected by placing the policy instrument or intervention that is evaluated in the perspective of other similar instruments and the intervention is described based on what makes it work and its deliverables or outcomes.

The use of IE based on key results is the cornerstone of any project, and the preparation of a result or deliverable is crucial during the design or proposal phase of a project, programme or policy. Interestingly, the NDBs integrate the broader goals of the DFIs with the goals of specific projects, so that the project-level goals become larger national priorities. The stages for IE design include inputs, activities, outputs, outcomes/ deliverables and impacts. In the early stage of project design, a set of indicators that measure the progress of the project are outlined and indicators are tracked at output and impact levels. Production-level indicators are measured continuously, while impact and outcome-level indicators are measured over time.

The impact evaluation deliverables include an inception report, a preliminary report, a draft report and a final evaluation report. These reports usually include a detailed account of the methodology used to answer the evaluation questions. It also includes a detailed description of the proposed information source and data collection process, as well as a detailed schedule of tasks to be performed, activities to be performed and deliverables to be delivered. It also clarifies the roles and responsibilities of each evaluation team member. The deliverables of each IE require planning and recording of all interim and final deliverables created by the IE and the project team throughout the project life cycle. This includes everything the team produced for the project, as well as any products or services the team provided to the client, customer or development partner. Deliverables also include any interim documents, plans, schedules, budgets, blueprints and project management documents that have been compiled. IE deliverables are tangible deliverables, measurable results or specific items that must be produced to consider the project or project phase completed.

In general, it is evident that the design and implementation of IE deliverables or outcomes have been well-developed among DFIs in advanced economies over the past decades but it is now attracting interest among policymakers in developing economies. The importance of IE deliverables or outcome in achieving a successful project, programme and policy and development impacts cannot be overemphasized, and hence, calls for development research into understanding the principles of IE deliverables or outcome. Given that NDBs in developing economies benchmark IE activities with the best practices of international DFIs, Box 10.7 provides the World Bank experiences in line with the activities of their IE deliverables.

Box 10.7: Impact Evaluation Deliverables

Financing for development through DFIs is provided in the form of projects, programmes, policies or interventions implemented by governments through DFIs. Each project is guided by a project manager through a cycle of preparation, approval, effectiveness, implementation and completion. A team designs operations with a government agency, including planned activities and disbursement schedules. During implementation, the recipient government sends disbursement or withdrawal requests to the development bank (i.e. NDB) after undertaking some activities. The bank's project team monitors the activities and ensures that disbursements are approved according to the bank's guidelines. Project funds disbursements are used as the main indicator for evaluating project success during implementation. Impact evaluations are conducted by the Bank's internal researchers, such as the Monitoring and Evaluation Unit, or the Unit/ Department for Impact Evaluation, etc., mostly in collaboration with external researchers. They use counterfactual analysis to evaluate policy interventions funded by the bank or the government. The IE team, project team or research team works with governments to influence project, programme or policy design, agree on research design and adjust strategy or implementation modalities, and employ data and evidence synthesized to review and effect changes in the implementation of projects or policy—thus influencing the decision to scale up or down.

IEs are often bundled with capacity building and monitoring activities. The project stakeholders, including government and project staff, attend workshops and training courses and are trained in the use of analytical tools for decision-making and international best practices based on international evidence and experiences. The IE research and field teams follow projects throughout their life cycle, overseeing IE implementation and data collection, and often assisting in the implementation of project activities. The role of the bank's IE team is to accurately document the project deliverables and then manage the project to produce them according to established and agreed criteria. Deliverables are the result of each development phase, and after the IE team has identified all deliverables, it documents all project requirements—which define the scope of the project plan, describe what a project must achieve and how the project must be built and implemented.

10.11 Challenges of Impact Evaluation Practices

The role of the NDBs in supporting national development, particularly, in ensuring sustainable development practices and mainstreaming impact evaluation in the projects, programmes or policies they fund as well as the decision to deploy resources to complement these efforts remain, therefore, crucial for achieving sustainable development goals. DFIs and development banks differ in the level of their IE systems. IE efforts are new in development banks and IEs are primarily conducted to complement project assessments. Unlike the regional DFIs, where IE is a corporate priority, development banks, in particular NDBs, have had limited resources to facilitate IE processes. The central challenge is to credibly assign observed changes in outcome variables to the intervention to be evaluated. The attribution difficulty arises because the intervention is not randomly assigned or people are not randomly enrolled in the programme. Simply comparing those 'treated' by the intervention and those not treated leads to bias in the assessment results and to misleading conclusions about the impact of the intervention.

The scope of an impact evaluation can vary greatly depending on the type of evaluator, the type of impact that may occur and the selection of aspects to be evaluated in detail. These decisions may be driven by decision-makers and/or researchers and may include the priorities of other stakeholders including the target groups. While much of the current debate on impact assessment focuses on arguments for and against Randomized Experiments (RE), in practice the validity of the results of any type of impact assessment, including REs, largely depends on the extent to which several key challenges of design and implementation are adequately addressed. The main challenges for impact evaluation are technical (example, framework flaws and design application problems) and managerial challenges (example, insufficient stakeholder engagement, problems in collaborating with partners, and mechanism and management transitions). These challenges can arise at different points in the planning and implementation of an IE, or after the project, programme or policy is completed.

When planning and implementing an IE, for more than half the planned duration of an NDB project, the team conducts a review to assess the progress of each NDB project. However, delays before the mid-term review are common. This means that projects may not be built or declared as planned. In addition, late projects may rush to make up for lost time as mid-term approaches and in the relatively short time between mid-term and project completion when the balance of the facility or loan has to be disbursed or is lost. Delays in project implementation as planned can result in rushed disbursements later in the project lifecycle, which can have a mitigating impact on project outcomes and damage the Bank's reputation. The main challenges of IE practices, based on their performance, are as follows: timing (when a performance should be performed); resources (how much money is available to develop the results); and quality (all the standards used to develop the results, development methods and many others).

10.12 Recent Developments in Impact Evaluation of National Development Banks

It must be emphasized that NDBs have huge potential to support their country's development strategies and fulfil their mandate. Yet these banks are insufficiently independent and tend to face political interference. The impact is strongest in situations where the operational and institutional environment is changing significantly and the original mandates have not been reviewed or adjusted for an extended period of time. However, positive interventions can be achieved by employing an impact evaluation framework to minimize possible risks and mitigate any negative influence from the government as well as other possible influential factors that may affect the outcomes of NDBs' projects, programmes and policies.

In our world today, it is not easy to change the course of events. Good intentions are a great start, but how do we know we are making a significant difference or impact in the society? How do we know if improvements on policies, projects and programmes and the efforts of NDBs, are making a real difference in people's lives? Over the past few decades, rigorous IEs have become increasingly common in DFIs and they are now an integral part of many projects of stakeholders working with international development partners. For instance, KfW Development Bank's Evaluation Unit increasingly provides institutional and methodological knowledge to support the implementation of rigorous IEs. This is evident in the bank's evaluation designs in the projects in Yemen, Liberia, Burkina Faso and Tanzania.

The impact evaluation practices of NDBs, which aim to show how an intended outcome follows from policy or programme activities, have been ignored by policymakers. NDBs that have built-in IEs focus on ensuring proper impact measurement and reporting on project-specific key development impact indicators. While certain types of projects or models of financing products, such as agriculture, energy, manufacturing, exports,and affordable housing, have mobilized significant resources, NDBs have only recently begun to conduct in-depth research into what really works and what really stems from their own interventions. For example, development banks such as BRD have included monitoring and evaluation in their funded projects to assess the achievement of specific goals (Oduor et al., 2022). This initiative is necessary to better understand the results and lessons learned from the Bank's policies, programmes and projects. For example, the bank has committed to increasing the use of evidence-based approaches to impact evaluation in project design. Raising awareness of BRD impact evaluation initiatives can increase resource mobilization and quality of development through transparency and accountability. BRD's role in supporting national development, particularly in incorporating impact evaluation into the projects it finances and in deciding to allocate resources to complement these efforts, remains crucial. To ensure that the bank's mandate is consistent with transparency, accountability and a legal framework for development, efforts for maintaining monitoring and evaluation practices should not be overlooked.

Various approaches to impact evaluation are advocated—many supported by DFI experts—which is the best way to decide what NDBs expect from an evaluation and how it relates to the types of policies or initiatives they are involved in. NDBs are under increasing pressure to report extensively on the development impact of their activities. Therefore, strong IE systems are needed to identify how NDB interventions contribute or have contributed to developments. IEs are needed to inform policymakers on a range of decisions, from mitigating ineffective projects, programmes or strategies, to scaling up effective interventions, adjusting programme benefits and choosing between different programme alternatives. IEs are most effective when applied selectively to answer important policy questions.

Since NDBs are usually publicly financed institutions, they are required to be accountable to different stakeholders for their development impacts as well as the resources provided to them. Evidence suggest that NDBs often experience challenges in their development mandates and results. In order to support NDBs to play their important role as part of the broader financial system, an effective monitoring and evaluation system need to be established. Box 10.8 provides a case on impact evaluation of Development Bank of Rwanda.

Box 10.8: Development Bank of Rwanda

Recently, the Development Bank of Rwanda (BRD) has embarked on a one (1) year project (i.e. in the period 2021–2022) with implementing partners (e.g. GIZ, Expertise France) focusing on DFI's M&E and IE. The main goals of the development support is to work on the accreditation of the Green Climate Fund (GCF) and the M&E and IE. The policies, procedures and products of BRD have been assessed to define and identify how well they reflect the requirements of accreditation to the GCF. The project provides a technical assistance and capacity building to help meet these requirements by the bank. The guideline of the M&E and IE cover: (1) the institutional performance tracking (through the building of framework and procedures); (2) investment impact evaluation (through the development of impact dashboard and capacity-building activities); and (3) creating an efficient and transparent development IE scoring model for the bank's business models such as direct lending and on-lending.

Results from the Development Support

The requirements for the documentation of the policies/procedures including policies on gender, environmental and social safeguards—were reviewed and updated based on the requirements of GCF. Currently, the BRD's accreditation application is undergoing a review process. On the M&E and IE front, the BRD's board of directors adopted has a revised policy including a new impact dimension in BRD's Balanced Scorecard. Also a parameter and dashboard have been developed to monitor the bank's institutional performance and development impact. Thus, an IE measurement tool has been developed to assess the impact of projects before investment and lending decisions are made—and this new development is now in use by BRD. In conclusion, BRD's reporting of M&E and IE on impact development have been improved.

10.13 Concluding Remarks

This chapter has examined M&E as well as impact evaluation practices of NDBs. The chapter reveals that interventions and developmental impacts of NDBs lead to the achievements of their development mandate. It also observes that without proper monitoring and evaluation and impact evaluation, NDBs will find it difficult to achieve their goals and will not be able to assess which projects, programmes or policies work in specific contexts and for what reasons. Thus, effective evaluation systems are necessary to ensure that NDBs fulfil their mandate. The tools NDBs use to monitor and evaluate the social and economic impact of their activities or operations include surveys and randomized control trials. Also, to have effective monitoring and evaluation systems, it is imperative to adapt these structures to the specific characteristics and activities of each individual NDB. In adopting impact evaluation, NDBs aim to find answers to *what works and what does not work and why the resources are used more effectively*. The core principles of IE lie in promoting accountability for cost-effectiveness, contributing to the improvement of learning and feedback, and providing independent feedback on the project and programme to the evaluators to increase development impact and ensure compliance with the mandate of the bank.

Impact evaluation methods examine whether NDB's projects, programmes or policy effects can be identified, and they seek to understand whether changes in such outcomes can be attributed to the projects, programmes or policies themselves—and not to some other cause. Impact evaluations are usually based on a combination of surveys, traditionally based on questionnaires and interviews, and other methods aimed at directly observing the results of interest. The main challenges for impact evaluations are technical (framework flaws and design application problems) and managerial challenges (insufficient stakeholder engagement, problems in collaborating with partners and mechanism and management transitions).

In conclusion, policymakers and practitioners should work towards promoting the M&E and IEs in development banks, particularly, with more emphasis on the NDBs. They need to formulate more consistent implementation policies and reconsider the urgency in implementing the joint framework of evaluation systems, combining both M&E and IE standard practices and interventions, to yield a desirable project, programme or policy outcome.

References

Heider, C. (2017). Rethinking evaluation. World Bank Group, Working paper series

Oduor J., Sarmento, E. M., & Lannes, L. (2022). *Impact evaluation in development institutions: A look at the African Development Bank.* A quarterly knowledge publication from Independent Development Evaluation at the African Development Bank Group. http://www.ifpri.org/book-744/node/8242

World Bank. (2018). *2017 Survey of national development banks*. World Bank.

PART IV

Corporate Governance, Risk Management, and Regulation

CHAPTER 11

Corporate Governance of National Development Banks

11.1 Introduction

Over the years, the subject of corporate governance has progressed and has become a topical issue of public interest. However, researchers and policymakers have ignored the concept of good corporate governance practices among NDBs. Good corporate governance is an important segment in the corporate decision-making process of NDBs, and yet are the least considered in corporate governance literature. In an effort to minimize the cost and value of NDBs, it is important to understand the internal controls applied by the bank in achieving its mandate. Corporate governance includes management and control systems in which the share of responsibilities and rights of different parties are clearly defined with rules and procedures to be followed when making decisions (Akdogan & Boyacioglu, 2014; Clarke, 2004). The role of each participant in the corporate governance structure is significant in determining the performance of the organization. Corporate governance stands at the core of decision-making and reflects the systems by which firms are managed, controlled and directed (Adika et al., 2018). In addition, it describes the framework in which a company's objectives are formulated and how these goals can be achieved. In corporate governance, the board constitutes the most important internal control mechanism in NDBs. Proper board composition improves the bank's decisions and potentially improves its performance (Attridge et al., 2021). Within the NDB, the CEO and the

© The Author(s), under exclusive license to Springer Nature Switzerland AG 2023

J. Yindenaba Abor, *The Changing Role of National Development Banks in Africa*, https://doi.org/10.1007/978-3-031-38639-8_11

executive management take charge in the running of the bank, while the governance ensures that management and the bank are running in the right direction. Hence the board of directors is generally responsible for the bank's decisions and its performance.

Given this background, this chapter explores the issues of corporate governance and how the practices of good governance support the initiatives of the NDBs. The NDB has a mandate to ensure that corporate governance is focused on development results and impacts. In view of that, it has become crucial for the bank to reinforce its commitment to improve the corporate governance structure and accountability of its operations. This initiative is needed to properly capture the results and lessons of the corporate governance framework of the bank.

On one hand, the role of the NDB in supporting national development, particularly, in mainstreaming a governance decision to deploy resources to complement these efforts is still critical. The experiences of development banks have shown that the governance policies that assist developmental projects and finance may be technically sound, but may fail to deliver expected results for reasons connected to poor governance systems. To ensure that the bank's mandate is consistent with transparency, accountability and the legal framework for development, efforts towards maintaining good corporate governance practices should not be overlooked. On the other hand, efforts aimed at creating the awareness of good corporate governance practices at the institutional level are important for increasing accountability and amplifying the impact of governance interventions with the primary aim of improving the corporate governance structure, operations and performance of the bank. Therefore, the chapter provides a rigorous and systematic research on the issues of corporate governance of the National Development Bank.

The rest of the chapter is organized as follows: Sect. 11.2 discusses the theoretical perspectives of corporate governance; Sect. 11.3 examines the corporate governance characteristics of NDBs; Sect. 11.4 looks at political influence and the corporate governance of NDBs; Sect. 11.5 also examines corporate governance and the performance of NDBs; and Sect. 11.6 concludes the chapter.

11.2 Theoretical Perspectives of Corporate Governance

In terms of theoretical positions, a number of theories have attempted to address the issue of corporate sustainability practices. Prominent among these theories have been the agency theory, stewardship theory, stakeholder theory, the resource dependency theory, the institutional theory and managerialism.

11.2.1 Agency Theory

Agency theory is explained as the conflicting behaviour between owners and managers (Jensen & Meckling, 1976). The agency theory, proposed by Jensen and Meckling (1976) states that agents (managers) are hired to run the business of corporate organizations for the benefit of their principals (owners). From the perspective of Milton Friedman (1970), it has been proven that the social responsibility of a business is to increase profit for its shareholders. The key focus in the agency theory is that managers of the bank have the incentive to function efficiently in order to fulfil the owner's interest. However, this theory has received much criticism from many theorists. Green (1993) attributed the criticism to the fact the theory focuses on the interest of shareholders as against the interest of all stakeholders in the business. Especially, they believed that the agency theory seems to have contributed to the corporate scandal of Enron and WorldCom, as managers were consistently under pressure to maximize shareholders' value through excessive risk-taking. From the point of view of the agency theory, Jensen and Meckling (1976) argued that managers are risk-averse so they hedge for their personal benefits. On the other hand, owners are risk lovers and they have the incentive to diversify their portfolios in order to take more risks. This is because a majority of shareholders have the incentive to monitor managers and they have the control or right to replace them when they act contrary to the business objectives (Franks & Mayer, 2001). The theory emphasizes that the agent is given powers to make decisions on behalf of the principal. However, entrenched managers tend to take prudent risk decisions by choosing projects that maximize their benefits at the expense of shareholders. This eventually induces a greater agency problem, leading to the emergence of the *stakeholder theory* (Cadbury, 2004).

11.2.2 Stewardship Theory

On the *stewardship theory* front, a higher value is placed on the convergence between the principal and the agent, than the personal interest of the agent. This implies that the interests between managers and shareholders may align over time, leading to the pursuance of greater risk-taking that may increase shareholders' value. Thus, the individual goals of the stewards are aligned with the goals of their leaders (Davis et al., 1997). The theory has been developed as an alternative to the management theory of organizations, which is a long-term contractual relationship based on trust, reputation and the collective participation and goals of principals and agents. In this respect, stewardship theory focuses on an unreliable relations and organizational behaviour, theory of economics, with emphasis on the collective, pro-organizational and contractual behaviour, where the objective of collective interest is given the utmost priority, compared to individual's interest.

11.2.3 Stakeholder Theory

The *stakeholder theory* primarily speaks of the role stakeholders play in ensuring that corporate sustainable practices are adhered to. It also describes the ethical concept that deals with the outcome of business decisions, trends, profits, etc., and its collective impact on all the stakeholders mentioned above. This makes the company more responsible by ensuring that all these stakeholders are satisfied, the needs of the community are met and its environment is protected. In recent decades, stakeholders have placed more demands on corporations, putting them under enormous pressure to engage in investments and practices that are sustainable. The demand for information on the various engagements of companies from a wide spectrum of stakeholders has increased significantly (Fernandez-Feijoo et al., 2014). The expectation from these stakeholders is based on information about how their activities are impacting the environment and the social setting positively (KPMG, 2012). In any case, the stakeholders form part of the broader society within which the corporate sustainable practices will take place, thus justifying the need for stakeholders to place more demand on these firms (Fernandez-Feijoo et al., 2014). This theory opines that the corporate sustainability report is the right avenue to exact corporate sustainable practices on a firm whose aim is to satisfy the demands of a broad array of stakeholders.

11.2.4 Resource Dependency Theory

This theory posits that, one way a firm can consistently develop, maintain and improve its competitiveness in the market is through efficient management of its resources, which are valuable, cannot be substituted and yet scarce (Kraaijenbrink et al., 2010; Lourenço et al., 2012). The *resource dependency theory* is one of the influential theories in corporate governance—proposed by Pfeffer and Salancik (1978, p. 350)—which states that 'to understand the behaviour of an organisation, you must understand the context of the behaviour'. The resource-based theory or dependency theory shows how the managers of an institution can be very influential and powerful in relation to corporate organizations with a competitive advantage. For instance, the board of directors is capable of using resources that are not available internally to the firm and at the same time favour shareholders' interests. This theory suggests how the firm's external resources impact its behaviour. It explains the 'ability of an organisation to operate under an environment of complexity associated with its wider interdependencies is directly related to the quality and effectiveness of the directors who make up the board (Boyd, 1990; Daily & Dalton, 1994; Gales & Kesner, 1994)'. Moreover, it is concerned about the organization having to manage uncertainties and risks from its environment, and how for example, a board composed of suitably selected board members can mitigate these uncertainties.

The theory also explains how scarce resources are not only tied to the firm directly but rather are managed and controlled by various groups of stakeholders. It is therefore imperative that the firm ensures it maintains a good relationship between it and its stakeholders by providing information on its corporate sustainable practices through sustainable reporting standards. This will also help to ensure that these firms have continuous access to the needed resources to operate effectively (Ruf et al., 2001).

11.2.5 Institutional Theory

The *institutional theory* is one of the theories in corporate governance that has been used to examine the activities of the firm in relation to society, environment, economy and governance, among others. It is a process by which structures involving schemes, rules, norms and routines are established as guidelines for social behaviour (Campbell, 2007; Doh & Guay, 2006). It is about the pressures that impact on organizations to adopt CG practices, irrespective of their actual functional impact due to a combination of coercive, mimetic and normative pressures. They do this in order to achieve legitimacy. On one hand, institutional theory speaks about external pressures to adopt (no choice), and distinctively, on other hand, companies have the agency to adopt (choice) to secure legitimacy. The social legitimacy principle is one principle that helps to give clarity to this theory. The state of a firm feeling accepted by society (considered as external stakeholders) and as a result, a firm which refuses to act in line with social demands and to go according to socially acceptable norms is at risk of being considered illegitimate and therefore hampering the firm's growth (Doh et al., 2010). Based on this principle, firms need to strategically incorporate social and environmental demands in their planning and activities so as to obtain the goodwill of society and maintain legitimacy. Overall, the actions of agents that conflict with the interests of shareholders may affect the corporate governance structure.

11.2.6 Managerialism

Managerialism is inherent in the bureaucratic form of organization. A relevant aspect of the new political economy of managerialism is that the management tendencies of the world of transnational consulting are important to how corporate organizations govern their policies and work practices. Meyer and Bromley (2013, p. 379) propose that the characteristics of contemporary forms of organization in world culture, including managerialism, are found in changes in the identity and 'means-end purposiveness' of organizations. These include aspects such as the way information is controlled, including the use of individual performance testing measures and increased monitoring and evaluation of directors and staff. This also includes the use of consultants for the implementation of core tasks, based on the belief that skills honed in the marketplace can compete with those associated with bureaucratic organizational identity. The increased reliance on external consultants or advisors is directly related to how managerialism is changing the way corporations govern. Of particular importance here is how consultants are encouraged to behave in a way that secures future business. The operational modalities of the consultants favour 'short-term' and 'work-to-contract' behaviours when performing work for the organization. They also aim to leverage the interoperability of solutions across different organizational platforms (Seabrooke & Sending, 2019).

11.3 Corporate Governance Characteristics of National Development Banks

Corporate governance influences NDB's performance through interactions of the characteristics of governance. Aspects of the board structure have been shown to encourage corporate decisions in the interest of shareholders. Corporate governance of NDBs entails putting in place the structure, process and mechanisms that ensure that the bank is directed and managed in a manner that improves the long-term value of shareholders through accountability, transparency of managers and the performance of the bank. Thus, the effectiveness of corporate governance depends on the corporate board characteristics, including board size, board composition, board leadership structure and duality, CEO and board tenure, board gender diversity, audit committee, internal audit, executive compensation, transparency and reporting and ownership structure.

Figure 11.1 shows the composite index of an aggregate measure of governance characteristics of NDBs over the period, 2014–2018. The index consists of an aggregate of dummy variables, which includes: bank ownership, ownership control, absence of CEO duality, board composition, audit independence and the presence of a small board size. The index ranges from 0 (weak governance) to 1 (strong governance), with higher values indicating good governance characteristics. It can be seen in Fig. 11.1 that 2018 recorded the highest governance index, indicating the year with the best practices of governance among a sample of 20 NDBs in Africa.

The ensuing discussion of the corporate governance characteristics of NDBs looks at board size, board composition, board leadership structure and duality, Chief Executive Officer (CEO) and board tenure, board gender diversity, board meetings, audit committee, internal audit, executive compensation, transparency and reporting and ownership structure.

11.3.1 Board Size

Board size is an important corporate governance characteristic. It is argued that, the ability of the board to monitor and make useful corporate decisions increases with its size. It is believed that a large board is able to subject the management of the firms to greater scrutiny and monitoring (Abor & Fiador, 2016; John & Senbet, 1998). Corporate governance

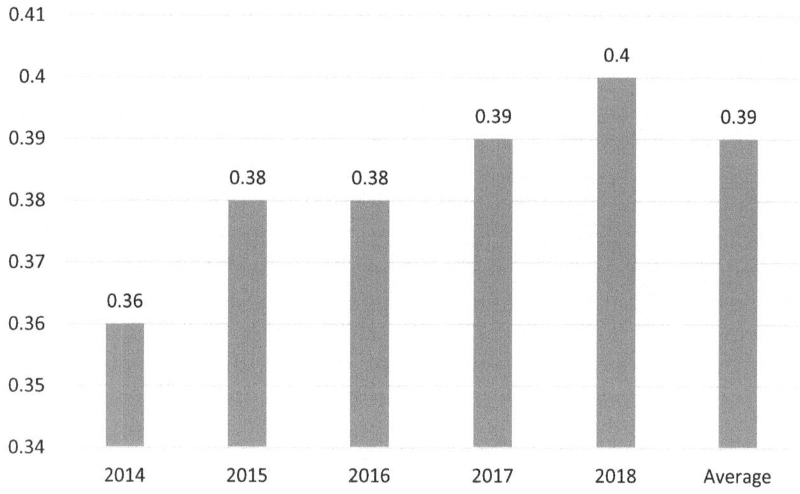

Fig. 11.1 Index of governance indicators of NDBs (*Source* Author's computation based on data from financial report of NDBs in Africa)

guidelines do not impose specific limits on the board size of NDBs in Africa, but imply that a board size between 8 and 16 members is considered ideal. However, Lipton and Lorsch (1992) suggest that an ideal board size should be between 7 and 9. Larger boards bring more information on board, due to their size, while board decision-making becomes difficult (Quayle & Gao, 2019). Organizational theory holds the idea that large groups take comparatively longer time to make decisions, and therefore, need more time to achieve a goal (Steiner, 1972; Wagner, 2011). There should therefore be an upper limit to board size to make it an effective corporate governance mechanism.

Figure 11.2 presents the board size of NDBs in Africa. It can be observed that size lies between 1 and 40 depending on the size of the bank (see Fig. 11.2). It is noted that many NDBs have 10 or fewer board members (see Fig. 11.2). This suggests that bank corporate boards are generally not very large. While increasing the size of the board is good for an NDB, a board that is too large becomes ineffective as decisions are not made or take a long time to make due to more extensive discussions among board members. Flexibility in decision-making, coordination and control are much more difficult to achieve as the board grows.

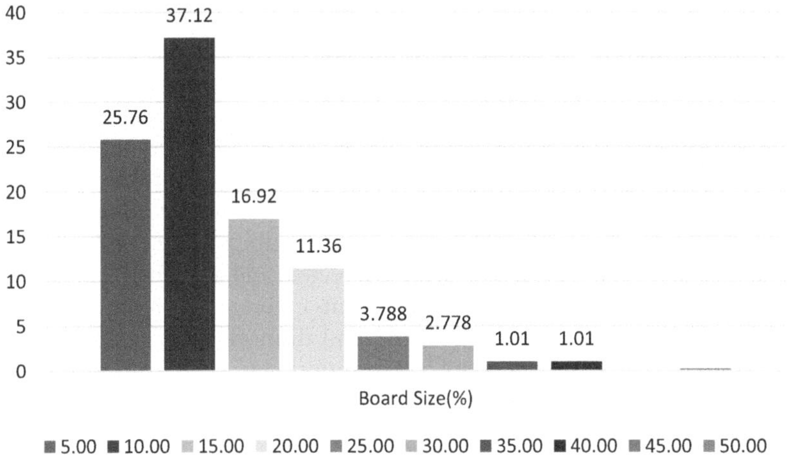

Fig. 11.2 Board size (*Source* Author's computation based on data from financial report of NDBs in Africa)

11.3.2 Board Composition

Board composition is essential for determining board effectiveness. Boards of most banks are composed of non-executive and executive directors. Non-executives are external directors, while executives are those involved in the daily management and operations of companies (Fuzi et al., 2016; La Porta et al., 2000). The role of the board is to represent the bank's shareholders, providing qualities and diverse expertise that enhance the board's effectiveness. Non-executive directors exercise an independent role, overseeing the activities of executive directors and management. A high proportion of non-executive directors enhances the independence of the board and therefore increases the quality of board monitoring. However, the presence of many executive directors reduces the level of board independence and limits the quality of board monitoring and effectiveness (Abor & Fiador, 2016; Yermack, 1996). A high proportion of non-executive or outside directors helps in better corporate decision-making, since the executive directors have less influence on them. It is also suggested that non-executive directors have the incentive of developing a reputation as experts in corporate decision-making, and this desire compels them to make quality decisions (Fama & Jensen,

1983; Jensen, 1993). The composition of the board should include an appropriate number of independent directors, typically one-third of the total size of the board (Quayle & Gao, 2019, Wooi & Ming 2009).

African NDBs are seen to follow the international corporate governance norms and standards (Nestor, 2018a, 2018b). The composition of the board varies from one NDB to the other. The bank conforms to good governance practice or norms in relation to the structure composed of varying boards of directors. The majority of members representing shareholders on the board are non-executive directors and a significant number of the banks in Africa has some government-appointed representation on the board. Appointment, restructuring and dismissals of the board and executive directors of NDBs are the responsibility of the government. The head of state takes the key decision in the nomination or approval processes of board appointments.

11.3.3 Board Leadership Structure and Duality

Another important aspect of the corporate governance system is the role of the CEO. It is suggested that the presence of the CEO on board committees has the tendency of improving board monitoring (Shivdasani & Yermack, 1999). The board of directors has the ability to help the CEO evaluate projects and select those that will increase the bank's value. The policy of this relationship is that the CEO generally prefers to have the board's loyalty, which allows him/her to gain its approval to invest in specific projects. The dual role of the CEO creates an overly powerful person who, in most cases, makes it difficult for the board as a whole to effectively fulfil its oversight responsibilities. The concept of CEO duality, as applied in central banks' governance system is where the CEO (or the governor) also serves as the chairman of the board. This situation allows for more focused leadership and quick decision-making for the bank. It has been shown in some cases that CEO duality improves decision-making and efficiency, and hence, eliminates disagreements on the board—leading to greater performance. However, boards that are prearranged to be more independent of the CEO are found to be more effective in monitoring the corporate decisions (Mallin, 2001). This implies that a bank that separates the functions of the board chair and that of the CEO is able to increase the value of the bank. When the roles of CEO and board chairman of the bank are exercised by the same person (i.e. no separation of CEO and chair), there is the likelihood that agency discord may occur and ultimately result in poor results (Nyamongo & Temesgen, 2013; Okoro et al., 2018). In the case of NDBs, CEOs are appointed by the government (Attridge et al., 2021). However, entrusting the appointment of CEOs to the board of directors rather than to political actors may be more instrumental in improving governance and performance simply by increasing institutional distance between ownership and management (Attridge et al., 2021).

11.3.4 CEO and Board Tenure

The tenure of independent directors affects the board structure. An independent director with externality may lose his/her independence or may become not so independent due to the rapport established with the internal directors and the managers. In the same vein, CEO tenure affects both company value and company decision-making. An extremely long tenure of independent directors or CEOs reflects a closeness of the relationship between them and management as well as lack of board renewal or absence of CEO end of tenure. It is therefore important to limit the tenure of a CEO or independent director to ensure effective board control. The board of directors and the CEO of NDBs are independently eligible to hold office up to five (5) consecutive years on the board and are eligible for reappointment for another term of up to five consecutive years on the passing of a special resolution by the bank. There is a mixed influence of CEO/board tenure on the performance of the bank. It has been shown that CEOs in longer terms of office may have the right frame of mind to understand the internal structures and risk-taking behaviours to monitor the bank, and hence influence decision-making and performance positively. However, a longer stay in office by independent directors or CEOs may lead to conflict of interest, complacencies and non-compliance issues, and eventually have a negative impact on the bank's performance (Murphy & Zimmerman, 1993; Weisbach, 1988).

11.3.5 Board Gender Diversity

Board gender diversity is also important in improving governance, performance and disclosure (Barako & Brown, 2008; Carter et al., 2003). It is argued in favour of women's involvement and participation in corporate leadership and governance, that women on the board or as

CEOs bring diverse opinions that positively affect corporate performance (Simionescu et al., 2021). The thinking here is that boards with a diverse gender background will enhance board independence and improve managerial monitoring as well as performance. Siciliano (1996) suggests that increased gender diversity on the board is associated with high levels of social agency mission achievement. Given the important role that gender diversity plays in corporate governance, many policymakers have developed certain principles to guide corporate governance practices. For example, in 2018, the governor of California signed legislation requiring state institutions to have at least one female director on their board. Similarly, some European countries have introduced gender quotas on company boards to support decision-making and serve the interests of shareholders. However, the inclusion and participation of women in corporate leadership and governance roles may not always promote, protect and maximize the performance of banks (see Adams & Ferreira, 2009; Dankwano & Hassan, 2018); and others report no significant effect of female involvement in corporate leadership and governance on firm performance (see Agyapong & Appiah, 2015; Noland et al., 2016).

In terms of the proportion of women on the boards of NDBs in Africa, it can be observed that women are in the minority on the boards of NDBs in Africa (see Fig. 11.3). It is evident that in a majority (i.e. 55.3%) of the NDBs in Africa, women represent 10% of the board members. However, less than 1% (i.e. 0.51%) of the NDBs in the sample have about 60–70% proportion of women on their board. Similarly, board gender independence is low among NDBs, representing about 10% of the proportion of gender independence on the board (see Fig. 11.3). This comes as no surprise. In Africa, and indeed in most parts of the world, women have only recently entered the workforce. Here, corporate culture and settings have been designed in such a way that women are disadvantaged in relation to men. As a result, few women will have the opportunity to sit on a bank's board. The inclusion of women on the board brings more diversity to the board. In addition, the approach taken by women is likely to be more conciliatory, leading to more consensus in boardroom discussions. Finally, it is noted that many NDBs have fewer than 10 board members (see Fig. 11.3). This suggests that bank corporate boards are generally not very large. While increasing the size of the board is good for NDBs, boards that are too large become ineffective in making decisions and arriving at consensus. This means flexibility in taking decision,

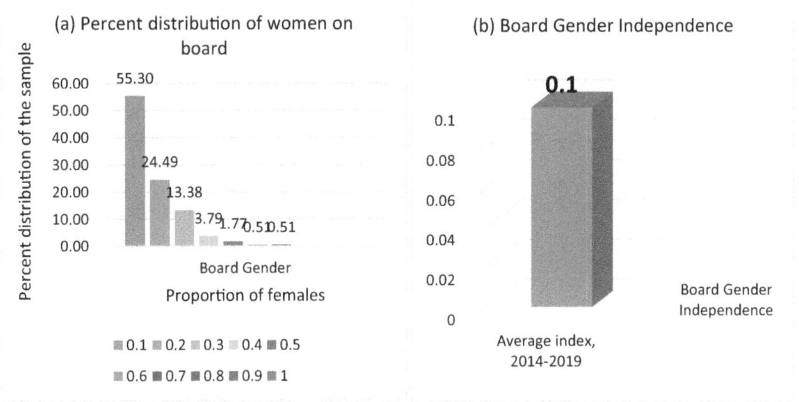

Fig. 11.3 Board gender diversity (*Source* Author's computation based on data from financial report of NDBs in Africa, 2022)

and ensuring coordination and control are difficult to achieve with an increase in board size .

Figure 11.3 shows the NDB distribution of the proportion of women on the board.

11.3.6 Board Meetings

Board meetings play a significant role in corporate governance, compliance and performance (Jensen, 1993; Lipton & Lorsch, 1992). The frequency of board meetings is an important measure of board effectiveness (Jensen, 1993; Lipton & Lorsch, 1992), although, the effectiveness of board meetings may differ, and consequently the effect of board meetings on other organizations may be expected to be different from what has been reported in Development Finance Institutions (DFIs). For instance, board meetings at DFIs are stated to occur at least 2–4 times a year, depending on the level of the action plan for the year and the board-planning calendar. Ntim (2009) notes that regular board meetings give board members ample time to deliberate, define strategy and evaluate management performance. This helps board members to stay informed and focused on important developments within the firm and thus better position them to address emerging critical issues in a timely manner (Mangena & Tauringana, 2008). Actually, Sonnenfeld (2002) points out that attendance at meetings is seen as a mark of a conscientious leader. Attridge et al. (2021) argue that the frequency of board meetings of NDBs signifies the intensity of the board's activities and the quality or effectiveness of its supervision, and hence affects the bank's performance. They provide evidence to support the fact that a higher frequency of board meetings among NDBs leads to a higher quality of the board's oversight with a positive impact on the bank's financial performance.

11.3.7 Audit Committee Independence

An audit committee is central to an effective corporate governance system. Financial crises and corporate scandals have led many countries to establish corporate governance guidelines, such as the Sarbanes–Oxley Act (2002) and the UK's Combined Code (FRC, 2003), which place much importance on Audit Committees (Rustam et al., 2013). The role of the Audit Committee is necessary in ensuring good corporate governance, as it helps in reviewing the firm's financial reports and also providing a communication channel between the board and auditors (internal and external auditors) so as to promote the interests of shareholders and stakeholders (Liao & Hsu, 2013; Song & Windram, 2004). Audit committee independence is an index capturing the degree of independence of audit committees. This ranges from 0 (low audit independent) to 1 (high audit independent) (see Fig. 11.4).

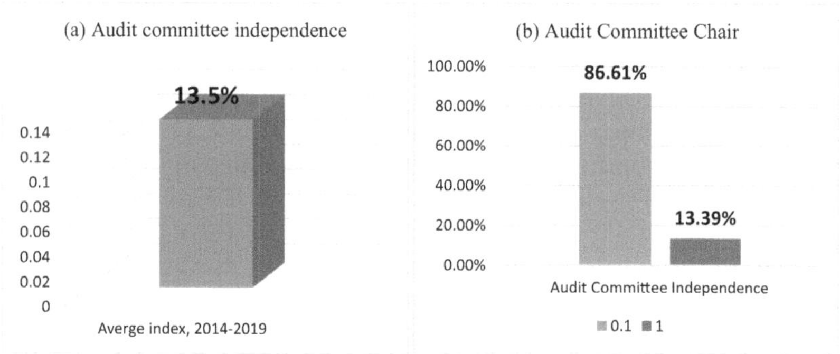

Fig. 11.4 Audit Committee Independence, 2014–2019 average (*Source* Author's computation based on data from financial report of NDBs in Africa)

Figure 11.4 clearly shows that most audit committees of the boards are not independent. Only 13.5% of boards have independent audit committees. This is because a large number of audit committees are headed by government-appointees and board independence is also dominated by men. In Fig. 11.4, about 13.39% of audit committees have a government-appointed audit committee chair, while 86.61% of audit committees adhere to the dictates of good governance by having a non-executive director chair of the audit committee.

11.3.8 Internal Audit

Internal audit is also an important corporate governance mechanism (Abbott et al., 2016; Tricker, 2015). Internal audit allows the board to 'provide independent assurance that risk management, governance and internal control processes operate effectively at all times'. The Institute of Internal Auding (IIA) (2017) has the framework that defines the primary purpose, nature, scope and practice of internal auditing. This framework states that:

> Internal auditing is an independent, objective assurance and consulting activity designed to add value and improve an organisation's operations. It helps an organisation accomplish its objectives by bringing a systematic, disciplined approach to evaluate and improve the effectiveness of risk management, control, and governance processes.

Like any corporate organization, including the banking sector, the NDBs have risk management policies that clearly describe the roles and accountabilities of the internal audit function. This may be done by the directors within the bank or by engaging any professional entity or expert outside the bank. The scope of the internal audit of NDBs is defined by the board of directors and they are required to submit their report to the board (which is the appointing authority) through the audit committee. The internal audit is responsible for creating an effective monitoring and control environment including risk assessment, control activities, information and communication and monitoring activities. The primary functions of the internal audit are: monitoring the choice of accounting policies and principles; oversight responsibities on the financial reporting and disclosure process; overseeing regulatory compliance, internal control processes and the hiring, performance and independence of the external auditors;

and the monitoring of risk management policies and practices (Alzebana & Sawan, 2015; Jones, 2013). Each function of the internal audit of NDBs cuts across and applies to the objective of selecting policies and procedures that help to ensure that the board's reports, actions and decisions are carried out effectively.

From a sample of 33 NDBs in Africa, Attridge et al. (2021) found that the banks employ an internal audit department as well as an independent auditor. In about half of the sample of NDBs in Africa, internal audit has a clear structure that reports to the board through audit committees while the remaining NDBs in the sample report through the line of executive management (Boolaky & Quick, 2016).

11.3.9 Executive Compensation

The numerous functions of a board of directors include monitoring and rewarding managers. In principle, an NDB's compensation structure should be aligned with sound risk management and promote the long-term health of the bank and appropriate risk-taking. Talented members on the board of directors tend to invest their energy and expertise in organizations with values and beliefs that match theirs. In order to achieve a good governance system, managers need to build culture, compensation and benefit packages, and target goals that reflect and raise certain shared values and beliefs. The board committee is designated to evaluate the performance and compensation of management. NDBs that tend to reward executive performance also tend to make prudent decisions and participate more regularly in earnings management. Moreover, executive compensation tied to shares fosters prudent decision-making and induces greater performance. Again allowing the board of directors to hold shareholder compensation attracts greater performance. Executive compensation paid to non-executive directors has to be fixed by the board of directors and approved by the shareholders in a general meeting. Oftentimes, there are limits imposed on the maximum number of stock options that can be granted to non-executive directors in any financial year.

11.3.10 Transparency and Reporting

Transparency and reporting are also seen as important corporate governance mechanisms as these ensure proper disclosure of information and mitigate asymmetric information. Solomon and Solomon (2004) suggest that increased corporate transparency is considered a key indicator of corporate governance reform. Attridge et al. (2021) indicated that the transparency and reporting standards of NDBs in Africa were relatively high but did not reflect most NDBs in their sample of NDBs. Thus, the vast majority of African development banks had poor transparency. Out of the 33 NDBs in the Africa sample, Attridge et al. (2021) identified three NDBs that employed international accounting standards in their financial statements, while the others used national accounting standards. Examples include the African Development Bank, Development Bank of Southern Africa, Botswana Development Corporation, etc. From the empirical findings of the work of Attridge et al. (2021), 13 NDBs in Africa focused on social and environmental impact frameworks, corporate social responsibility and sustainability and climate-oriented activities in their annual reporting. Examples of these banks are the Development Bank of Southern Africa (DBSA) and the Uganda Development Bank Limited.

11.3.11 Ownership Structure

From the perspective of ownership, a majority of NDBs are government-owned banks (see Attridge et al., 2021). The governments of African countries generally own, operate and oversee NDBs, provide strategic guidance and appoint senior management and board members, although the scope of governance may vary. In these NDBs, the government retains control over the bank and the private sector owns a portion of its capital. Some NDBs are partly owned by the state and international financial institutions. Shareholding is categorized into public and external bodies. Public shareholding dominates among NDBs in Africa and includes local governments, sovereign investment funds, pension funds or the central bank. The external shareholdings, which are privately, individually or internationally owned, are the least in the sample of NDBs in Africa. Examples of international shareholding NDBs in Africa include Bank for Development and Investment in Liberia and Nigeria Bank of Industry. A number of NDBs have undergone shareholding diversification over the last decade. For example, the government of Rwanda transferred its stake in the Development Bank of Rwanda to the Agaciro Development Fund.

Similarly, the Development Bank of Nigeria and Agricultural Development Bank in Ghana have reduced the level of shareholding by the central government.

11.4 Political Influence and Corporate Governance of National Development Banks

NDBs have enormous potential to support their countries' development strategies. They have a clear comparative advantage over multilateral or regional development banks, which include their close political embeddedness (Attridge et al., 2021). Opponents of state intervention often point to economic concerns. For example, Attridge et al. (2021) point to the need for a degree of independence from government influence to protect banks from undue pressure that could compromise their financial soundness or development purpose. Maintaining a balance between political engagement and independence will go a long way towards creating a virtuous cycle in which African NDBs can become effective delivery partners that integrate into national and international policy frameworks.

NDBs enjoy some autonomy in decision-making and they remain embedded in a favourable environment of political and economic institutions, depending on their public ownership (Thorne & du Toit, 2009). A bank that is not sufficiently independent may be subject to greater political interference. This interference may be due to a weak governance mechanism, where countries with weaker institutions can influence the allocation of resources to different sectors of the economy. The ownership and oversight structure of NDBs can be complex, involving many government institutions (such as the ministries of finance, agriculture, housing, trade and labour) and sometimes the legislature. This is because these entities have their own legitimate (and sometimes conflicting) expectations about the NDB's objectives. If the NDB's mandate is widely publicized, elected government officials and political officials will have a greater right to influence the bank's decisions, guidance and operations. The government remains the nominating authority for NDB boards. A key component maintained as standard is the board of directors, through which owners must exercise oversight, but without distorting the standards of good corporate governance. The representation of government officials on the board of NDBs can be a channel of political influence. However, the bank's internal structures, which are overseen by the central bank, are designed to minimize and mitigate adverse government influences. In addition, the inclusion of independent directors and the separation of the board and management are considered best practice.

The bank may become subject to political interference unless its institutional framework is strong enough to withstand political pressure. Likewise, the bank may be caught up with interest groups that influence the decision-making process. This, in combination with a sound monitoring and evaluation framework, may force the bank's boards and management to gradually become more tolerant of any deficiencies and poor performance that the bank may face. The root of problems affecting state-owned financial institutions is frequently ascribed to 'political interference' (Scott, 2007).[1] In the case of African NDBs, the problem of political influence is particularly pronounced. Banks with politically connected CEOs (CEOs) exhibit riskier lending behaviour and have higher default rates than government banks with less connected CEOs. Shen and Lin (2012) reiterated that banks where executive appointments coincide with election cycles are associated with poorer financial performance compared to non-politicized government banks or private sector banks. Again, given the potential of bank appointments to be used for political sponsorship, board and senior management appointments and removals are critical components in dealing with corporate governance and political influence. The governance structure must strike a balance between a bank's independence and political governance. Because there is a risk of principal-agent problems with the government due to an insufficiently 'integrated' bank. In addition, insufficient integration or cohesion between government agencies undermines a bank's effectiveness within national development structures.

11.5 Corporate Governance and Performance of National Development Banks

It is evident from the work of Attridge et al. (2021) that African NDBs are relatively small compared to those in other developing regions. Based on findings of Attridge et al. (2021), the total assets to country GDP ratio ranges between 1 and 23%. For instance, Caisse de Depots et de Gestion in Morrocco has an average asset to GDP ratio of 23% in the period, 2014–2019, while Small Enterprise Finance Agency of South Africa has an

[1] https://openknowledge.worldbank.org/handle/10986/7305.

average asset of 0.04% GDP. Again, they show that majority of NDBs in Africa have their total assets growing between 0.01 and 50% in the period 2014–2019, followed by those with their asset growing above 100% in the same period.

The study reveals that effective banking operations of NDBs led to an increase in the performance of the bank. Box 11.1 illustrates the performance of some NDBs in Africa.

Box 11.1 Performanceof BRD and ADB

Development Bank of Rwanda increased their average return of asset from 1.66% in 2020 to 2.05% in 2021. Similarly, Agricultural Development Bank (ADB) in Ghana recorded an average return of 1.14% of total asset in 2020, and then was increased to 1.26% in 2021. Thus, ADB was the best performing bank in the sample (Fig. 11.5).

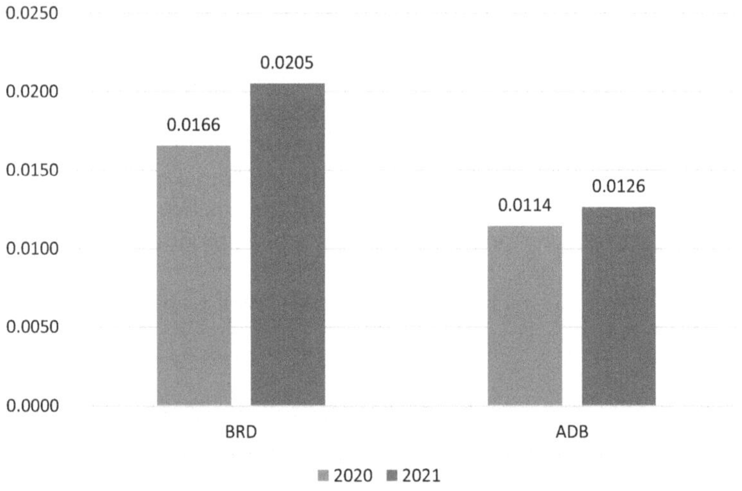

Fig. 11.5 Performance of BRD and ADB (*Source* Author's computation based on data from financial report of NDBs in Africa)

It was observed that the ADB posting 400% growth in profitability in 2020 was a significant leap in operational performance over past years. In terms of development banks in Tunisia, the latest trend in the loans to the economy by sector shows that total bank credits increased from

TND 65 billion (US$ 20.82 billion) in 2015 to TND 98 billion (US$ 31.4 billion) in 2020. The share of industry and agriculture and fisheries represent about 25% and 3% of GDP in 2020. In this balance, the private sector weighs more than 90% of total bank credits (see Attridge et al., 2021)

Good corporate governance helps maintain a stable or profitable banking system. Therefore, maintaining good governance is very important for NDBs. Many NDBs are trying to find different ways to integrate sustainability into their long-term plans. In order to achieve good governance, four main aspects need to be considered. These include; the social, environmental, cultural and financial aspects of governance. Social influence refers to how society influences banks and stakeholders. Environmental impacts refer to the Bank's impact on the geophysical environment. Organizational culture refers to the relationship between the bank, including managers, employees and internal stakeholders. Finally, the financial aspect refers to the impact of the bank's financial return in relation to the level of risk (Price, 2018). Good corporate governance is important so that banks can work even more effectively to improve access to capital, mitigate risk and protect partners (Tsoi, 2017). The greatest failure of corporate governance today is its notion of short-term performance (Subramanian, 2018). Employers or executives are under significant pressure to comply with quarterly reports and data, knowing that even a penny lost in earnings per share can be a deathblow to the stock price. Poor corporate governance can result in significant profit losses not only for the bank but also for society, which is why corporate governance makes banks increasingly accountable to their investors. According to Tsoi (2017), poor or weak corporate governance can make situations potentially irreversible and unfair for minority investors.

Given the earlier discussion on the governance characteristics, political influence and performance of NDBs, it can be deduced that the impact of a weak governance system and political interference by the government is stronger in situations where the operating environment changes substantially and the banks' initial mandates have not been reviewed or adjusted over a long period. However, there can be positive interventions through impact evaluation strategies to minimize possible risks and mitigate any negative influence that may affect the outcome of NDBs' projects, programmes and policies.

11.6 Concluding Remarks

The role of the national development bank in supporting national development, particularly in ensuring sustainable governance practices and mainstreaming governance decisions, and deploying resources to complement these efforts remain, is crucial for achieving sustainable development goals. In view of that, the chapter has explored the issues of corporate governance practices of NDBs. The chapter has emphasized the fact that it will be difficult for NDBs to achieve their goals without healthy governance practices. They will not be able to appreciate which governance policies work, and in which particular context, or for what reasons. Thus, effective governance systems are necessary to ensure that NDBs fulfil their mandate. Also, to have effective governance systems, it is imperative for NDBs to tailor well-structured governance frameworks to the specific features and business activities of the bank. The chapter reveals that good governance practices and effective banking operations of NDBs lead to an increase in the performance of the bank. It also emphasizes that NDBs have huge potential to support their country's development strategies and fulfil their mandate, yet they are insufficiently independent and face greater political interference. The government remains the appointing authority of the boards of NDBs and political appointees have the greater power to influence the decisions, directions, operations and performance of these banks. The impact is stronger in situations where the operating and institutional environment changes substantially and their initial mandates have not been reviewed or adjusted over a long period. However, there can be positive interventions by employing an impact evaluation governance framework to minimize possible risks and mitigate any negative influence from the government as well as other possible influential factors that may affect the outcome of NDBs' projects, programmes and policies.

In conclusion, policymakers and regulators should work towards promoting the corporate governance of NDBs. They need to formulate more consistent policies and reconsider the urgency in implementing the framework of strong corporate governance systems to yield desirable policies or programme outcomes.

References

Abor, J. Y., & Fiador, V. (2016). *Corporate governance and dividend payout policy: Evidence from selected African countries* (AERC Research Paper 314). African Economic Research Consortium.

Abbott, B. P., Abbott, R., Abbott, T. D., Abernathy, M. R., Acernese, F., Ackley, K., et al. (2016). Observation of gravitational waves from a binary black hole merger. *Physical Review Letters, 116*(6), 061102.

Adams, R. B., & Ferreira, D. (2009). Women in the boardroom and their impact on governance and performance. *Journal of Financial Economics, 94*(2), 291–309.

Adika, W., & Osly, P. J. (2018). Analisis Kinerja Operasional Kereta Api Jurusan Jakarta-Purwakarta (Studi Kasus Kereta Api Walahar Ekspres Dan Cilamaya Ekspres). *Indonesian Journal of Construction Engineering and Sustainable Development (CESD), 1*(1), 36–44.

Agyapong, D., & Appiah, S. O. (2015). Effect of gender diversity on the performance of non-financial listed firms in Ghana. *British Journal of Economics, Management & Trade, 8*(1), 55–67.

Akdogan, Y. E., & Boyacioglu, M. A. (2014). The effect of corporate governance on firm performance: A case of Turkey. *International Journal of Critical Accounting, 6*(2), 187–210.

Alzeban, A., & Sawan, N. (2015). The impact of audit committee characteristics on the implementation of internal audit recommendations. *Journal of International Accounting, Auditing and Taxation, 24*, 61–71.

Attridge, S., Chen, Y., & Mbate, M. (2021). *Financial performance and corporate governance: Evidence from national development banks in Africa* (ODI Report).

Barako, D. G., & Brown, A. M. (2008). Corporate social reporting and board representation: Evidence from the Kenyan banking sector. *Journal of Management and Governance, 12*(4), 309–324.

Boolaky, P. K., & Quick, R. (2016). Bank directors' perceptions of expanded auditor's reports. *International Journal of Auditing, 20*(2), 158–174.

Boyd, B. (1990). Corporate linkages and organizational environment: A test of the resource dependence model. *Strategic Management Journal, 11*(6), 419–430.

Cadbury, H. J. (2004). *The book of acts in history*. Wipf and Stock Publishers.

Campbell, J. L. (2007). Why would corporations behave in socially responsible ways? An institutional theory of corporate social responsibility. *Academy of Management Review, 32*(3), 946–967.

Carter, D. A., Simkins, B. J., & Simpson, W. G. (2003). Corporate governance, board diversity, and firm value. *Financial Review, 38*(1), 33–53.

Chen, Y., & Rezaee, Z. (2012). The role of corporate governance in convergence with IFRS: Evidence from China. *International Journal of Accounting & Information Management, 20*, 171–188.
Clarke, T. (2004). Theories of corporate governance. *The Philosophical Foundations of Corporate Governance, Oxon, 12*(4), 244–266.
Daily, C. M., & Dalton, D. R. (1994). Bankruptcy and corporate governance: The impact of board composition and structure. *Academy of Management Journal, 37*(6), 1603–1617.
Dankwano, R. N., & Hassan, Z. (2018). Impact of gender diversity on Indian firm's financial performance. *International Journal of Management, Accounting and Economics, 5*(5), 319–341.
Davis, J. A., Hampton, M. M., & Lansberg, I. (1997). *Generation to generation: Life cycles of the family business*. Harvard Business Press.
Doh, J. P., & Guay, T. R. (2006). Corporate social responsibility, public policy, and NGO activism in Europe and the United States: An institutional-stakeholder perspective. *Journal of Management Studies, 43*(1), 47–73.
Doh, J. P., Howton, S. D., Howton, S. W., & Siegel, D. S. (2010). Does the market respond to an endorsement of social responsibility? The role of institutions, information, and legitimacy. *Journal of Management, 36*(6), 1461–1485.
Fama, E. F., & Jensen, M. C. (1983). Agency problems and residual claims. *The Journal of Law and Economics, 26*(2), 327–349.
Fernandez-Feijoo, B., Romero, S., & Ruiz, S. (2014). Effect of stakeholders' pressure on transparency of sustainability reports within the GRI framework. *Journal of Business Ethics, 122*(1), 53–63.
Franks, J., & Mayer, C. (2001). Ownership and control of German corporations. *The Review of Financial Studies, 14*(4), 943–977.
Friedman, M. (1970). A theoretical framework for monetary analysis. *Journal of Political Economy, 78*(2), 193–238.
Fuzi, S. F. S., Halim, S. A. A., & Julizaerma, M. K. (2016). Board independence and firm performance. *Procedia Economics and Finance, 37*, 460–465.
Gales, L. M., & Kesner, I. F. (1994). An analysis of board of director size and composition in bankrupt organizations. *Journal of Business Research, 30*(3), 271–282.
Green, P. J., & Silverman, B. W. (1993). *Nonparametric regression and generalized linear models: A roughness penalty approach*. CRC Press.
Jensen, M. C. (1993). The modern industrial revolution, exit, and the failure of internal control systems. *The Journal of Finance, 48*(3), 831–880.
Jensen, M. C., & Meckling, W. F. (1976). Theory of the firm: Managerial behavior, agency costs, and ownership structure. *Journal of Financial Economics, 3*, 305–360.

John, K., & Senbet, L. W. (1998). Corporate governance and board effectiveness. *Journal of Banking & Finance, 22*(4), 371–403.

Jones, K. K. (2013). *The impact of legislation on the organization: Evaluating the impact of corporate governance regulation on the internal audit function* (PhD thesis). Georgia State University, Atlanta, GA.

KPMG. (2012). *Africa banking survey*. KPMG.

Kraaijenbrink, J., Spender, J. C., & Groen, A. J. (2010). The resource-based view: A review and assessment of its critiques. *Journal of Management, 36*(1), 349–372.

La Porta, R., Lopez-de-Silanes, F., Shleifer, A., & Vishny, R. (2000). Investor protection and corporate governance. *Journal of Financial Economics, 58*(1–2), 3–27.

Liao, C. H., & Hsu, A. W. H. (2013). Common membership and effective corporate governance: Evidence from audit and compensation committees. *Corporate Governance: An International Review, 21*(1), 79–92.

Lipton, M., & Lorsch, J. W. (1992). A modest proposal for improved corporate governance. *Business Lawyer, 48*, 59–77.

Lourenço, I. C., Branco, M. C., Curto, J. D., & Eugénio, T. (2012). How does the market value corporate sustainability performance? *Journal of Business Ethics, 108*(4), 417–428.

Mallin, C. (2001). Institutional investors and voting practices. An international comparison. *Corporate Governance: An International Review, 9*, 118–126.

Mangena, M., & Tauringana, V. (2008). Audit committees and voluntary external auditor involvement in UK interim reporting. *International Journal of Auditing, 12*(1), 45–63.

Meyer, J. W., & Bromley, P. (2013). The worldwide expansion of "organization." *Sociological Theory, 31*(4), 366–389.

Murphy, K. J., & Zimmerman, J. L. (1993). Financial performance surrounding CEO turnover. *Journal of Accounting and Economics, 16*(1–3), 273–315.

Nestor, S. (2018a). Board effectiveness in international financial institutions: A comparative perspective on the effectiveness drivers in constituency boards. In P. Quayle & X. Gao (Eds.), *Good governance and modern international financial institutions*. Brill (AIIB Yearbook of International Law 2018). https://doi.org/10.1163/j.ctvrxk459.4

Nestor, S. (2018b). *Corporate governance 2030: Thoughts on the future of corporate governance*. Harvard Law School Forum on Corporate Governance.

Noland, M., Moran, T., & Kotschwar, B. R. (2016). *Is gender diversity profitable? Evidence from a global survey* (Working Paper, 16-3). Peterson Institute for International Economics.

Ntim, C. G. (2009). *Internal corporate governance and firm financial performance: Evidence from South African listed firms* (PhD thesis). University of Glasgow.

Nyamongo, E. M., & Temesgen, K. (2013). The effect of governance on performance of commercial banks in Kenya: A panel study. *Corporate Governance: The International Journal of Business in Society, 13*(3), 452–454.

Okoro, C. B., Udoh, D., Ben, E., & Nwosu, M. O. (2018). Effect of Chief Executive Officer duality on the profitability of money deposit banks. *International Journal of Business Systems and Economics, 12*(1), 1–9.

Pfeffer, J., & Salancik, G. R. (1978). A resource dependence perspective. In *Intercorporate relations. The structural analysis of business*. Cambridge University Press.

Quayle, P., & Gao, X. (2019). Introduction: Good governance and modern international financial institutions. In P. Quayle & X. Gao (Eds.), *Good governance and modern international financial institutions*. Brill (AIIB Yearbook of International Law 2018). https://doi.org/10.1163/j.ctvrxk459.4

Ruf, B. M., Muralidhar, K., Brown, R. M., Janney, J. J., & Paul, K. (2001). An empirical investigation of the relationship between change in corporate social performance and financial performance: A stakeholder theory perspective. *Journal of Business Ethics, 32*(2), 143–156.

Rustam, S., Rashid, K., & Zaman, K. (2013, March). Retracted: The relationship between audit committees, compensation incentives and corporate audit fees in Pakistan. *Economic Modelling, 31*, 697–716.

Scott, D. H. (2007). *Strengthening the governance and performance of state-owned financial institutions*. World Bank Publications.

Seabrooke, L., & Sending, O. J. (2019). Contracting development: Managerialism and consultants in intergovernmental organizations. *Review of International Political Economy, 27*, 802–827.

Shen, C. H., & Lin, C. Y. (2012). Why government banks underperform: A political interference view. *Journal of Financial Intermediation, 21*(2), 181–202.

Shivdasani, A., & Yermack, D. (1999). CEO involvement in the selection of new board members: An empirical analysis. *The Journal of Finance, 54*(5), 1829–1853.

Siciliano, J. I. (1996). The relationship of board member diversity to organizational performance. *Journal of Business Ethics, 15*(12), 1313–1320.

Simionescu, L. N., Gherghina, Ş. C., Tawil, H., & Sheikha, Z. (2021). Does board gender diversity affect firm performance? Empirical evidence from Standard & Poor's 500 Information Technology Sector. *Financial Innovation, 7*(1), 1–45.

Solomon, A., Solomon, J., & Suto, M. (2004). Can the UK experience provide lessons for the evolution of SRI in Japan? *Corporate Governance: An International Review, 12*(4), 552–566.

Song, J., & Windram, B. (2004). Benchmarking audit committee effectiveness in financial reporting. *International Journal of Auditing, 8*(3), 195–205.

Sonnenfeld, J. A. (2002). What makes great boards great. *Harvard Business Review, 80*(9), 106–113.

Steiner, G. A. (1972). Social policies for business. *California Management Review, 15*(2), 17–24.

Subramanian, S. (2018). Stewardship theory of corporate governance and value system: The case of a family-owned business group in India. *Indian Journal of Corporate Governance, 11*(1), 88–102.

Thorne, J., & Du Toit, C. (2009). A macro-framework for successful development banks. *Development Southern Africa, 26*(5), 677–694.

Tricker, B., & Tricker, R. I. (2015). *Corporate governance: Principles, policies, and practices*. Oxford University Press.

Tsoi, P. (2017). *The importance of corporate governance.*

Wagner, A. (2011). *The origins of evolutionary innovations: A theory of transformative change in living systems*. Oxford University Press.

Weisbach, M. S. (1988). Outside directors and CEO turnover. *Journal of Financial Economics, 20*, 431–460.

Wooi, H. C., & Ming, T. C. (2009). *Directors' pay-performance: A study on Malaysian government linked companies* (pp. 1–19). Centre for Policy Research and International Studies.

Yermack, D. (1996). Higher market valuation of companies with a small board of directors. *Journal of Financial Economics, 40*(2), 185–211.

CHAPTER 12

Risk Management of National Development Banks

12.1 Introduction

There is certainly a clear difference in the treatment of risk between development banks and commercial banks. Commercial banks and other traditional financial institutions seek to maximize risk-adjusted expected returns, with a short-term view. They tend to focus on minimizing risks that could result in financial losses or lower profits. They typically do not have the objective of achieving development goals. Commercial banks are mostly committed to managing the complete range of economic, environmental and social risks, in as much as these risks affect financial returns. Development banks on the other hand tend to have a dual mandate and these are maximizing sustainable and inclusive development impact (which include economic, environmental and social impacts), and at the same time making profits or preventing financial losses (Griffith-Jones et al., 2020). As suggested by Griffith-Jones et al. (2020), development banks aim at maximizing a:

$$Dual\ Ratio = \frac{sustainable\ developmental\ impact}{risks\ to\ that\ impact\ or\ developmental\ risks\ evaluated}$$

$$subject\ to\ a\ minimum\ or\ positive\ risk\ adjusted\ financial\ return\ (RAFR)$$

© The Author(s), under exclusive license to Springer Nature Switzerland AG 2023

J. Yindenaba Abor, *The Changing Role of National Development Banks in Africa*, https://doi.org/10.1007/978-3-031-38639-8_12

One important issue is the fact that development banks' principal focus is achieving a high level of development impact, including making significant contributions to attaining the SDGs. As much as making good financial returns is important to development banks, this objective is somehow secondary to the main objective of development impact. Also, development banks tend to focus on long-term investments given the long-term nature of their liability structure, and considering that sustainable development outcomes tend to be evaluated over a longer time period in order to achieve sustainability. The extant literature and experiences show development banks evaluate their financial returns, but measuring this dual ratio can be difficult. Financial and economic crises have shown that this literature and experience do not ensure accuracy of future happenings, and it may even be very difficult to measure development impact and risk. A number of important studies are ongoing in this area, but there seems to be no agreement on how to measure sustainable development impact. There are financial instruments that can be used to manage some risks, but there are other risks that cannot be avoided. The financial instruments used by development banks may also influence some risks (mainly those related to financial engineering, or insufficient development impact). Identifying and categorizing the various types of risk may be helpful to NDBs in order to ascertain when and how to employ the different financial instruments appropriately (Griffith-Jones et al, 2020).

This chapter focuses on risk management in NDBs. It is organized as follows: Sect. 12.2 defines risk, risk exposures of NDBs and risk management; Sect. 12.3 provides the historical perspective of risk management; Sect. 12.4 discusses the financial instruments used by NDBs in normal times, while Sect. 12.5 discusses the instruments used by NDBs during pandemics. Section 12.6 explains how NDBs benefit from risk management; and Sect. 12.7 concludes the chapter.

12.2 What Is Risk?

It is important in the first place to distinguish between uncertainty and risk, based on the pioneering work carried out by Frank Knight (1921).

Uncertainty is a situation in which one is unable to predict what will happen in the future. Knight (1921) explains uncertainty as a situation in which probabilities cannot usefully be assigned (Knightian uncertainty).

It cannot be valued since it is unsusceptible to measurement. Uncertainty is the difficulty in predicting events and examples include difficulty in predicting the impact of digitalization on employment, unpredictable exogenous shocks or difficulty in predicting political risks. The impact of the COVID-19 pandemic is also considered a case of extreme uncertainty, in terms of its occurrence in the first instance, its progression in various countries; and its overall negative economic impact (Griffith-Jones et al., 2020). Taking the view of Griffith-Jones et al. (2020), the more the uncertainty, the more the difficulty in raising private financing, and the more it has to be well distributed. In theory, this explains the need for public action (see Arrow & Lind, 1970), which may include using instruments such as guarantees provided by NDBs, and other public interventions.

Risk is the circumstance in which the decision-maker is able to assign probabilities to the potential outcome of decision (Knight, 1921). Risk is also referred to as a condition in which there is a possibility of the undesirable occurrence of a particular result which is known or best quantifiable and therefore insurable (Periasamy, 2008). Risk can be valued, depending on the probability of an event and the potential losses/gains (or their expected values). The lessons learned from the events of the 2007/2008 global financial crisis as well as the COVID-19 crisis indicate that it is difficult to measure risk with accuracy, even if complex modelling techniques are used. Specifically, markets tend to underestimate or neglect incorporating 'tail risk' which is the risk of low probability events with severe outcomes. This is partly because of short-term investment horizons, uncertainty and relative difficulty to predict such events (Griffith-Jones et al., 2020).

It is also essential to note that certain types of risk can be positive and these include risks that may stimulate innovation and are central to investment decision-making, as investors seek to make returns for assuming such risks. There are obvious development impacts or benefits associated with certain types of investment risks, including providing lending or investing in projects that drive technological and other innovations, mostly with significant positive externalities. These have development benefits and the risk that produces investment, which creates value and development impact is known as 'real economy risk' (Griffith-Jones et al., 2020). There is a difference between real economy risk and other risks, including financial engineering risk, which is associated with the use of financial instruments. Financial engineering seeks to attract and leverage additional private finance. In principle, financial engineering must assist in distributing risks to economic agents who are in the best position of managing them. For instance, financial engineering enables various investors to meet their risk appetites by creating tranches, such as an investment grade, mezzanine, and equity—or high-risk—tranches. An example is attracting institutional investors to invest in long-term projects that match their long-term liabilities (Mazzucato, 2018).

12.2.1 Risk Exposure of National Development Banks

NDBs are exposed to different categories of risk and it is important to identify these categories of risk in order to appreciate the most appropriate financial instruments to manage, based on the different investment risks associated with them, and to mitigate new risks, which some instruments may generate. It is important to distinguish between exogenous risks and endogenous risks; and project level 'real economy' risks and financial engineering risks.

12.2.1.1 Exogenous and Endogenous Risks

Exogenous risks or global systemic risks are shocks or volatility that affect all countries across the globe at the same time. Examples are global macroeconomic shocks, including commodity price shocks, and global interest rate volatility, that are influenced by the evolution of the global economy and external events, including policy decisions by some developed countries. They also include non-economic risks, such as natural disasters and pandemics (e.g. COVID-19) that impact all countries. NDBs are exposed to systematic risks at both the global or national levels, and this makes it challenging to use hedging instruments such as derivatives to manage these risks, particularly in developing countries where capital markets are underdeveloped. Hedging instruments in developing countries tend to be short term in nature, thus making it difficult to hedge risks associated with long-term projects. Also, insurance companies in these markets do not have a strong capital base and are often unwilling to cover huge risks, and even when they do, this can be expensive. This situation creates difficulty for NDBs to appropriately mitigate the effects of such risks. A number of developing countries will require the support of international financial institutions, such as Multilateral DFIs or MDBs during systemic shocks, which tend to affect the liquidity position of NDBs. There is certainly the need to strengthen the system of development banks and ensure proper coordination between MDBs and NDBs. Broadening the support of MDBs for NDBs is very critical (Griffith-Jones et al., 2020).

Endogenous risks or national risks include policy-related risks, such as macroeconomic policy and political risk, as well as exogenous shocks that do not cross borders. Forest fires that affect particular economies are an example. Domestic endogenous risks introduce risk premiums and tend to discourage investment in a particular country. Such risks are mainly impacted by policymaking in a country. For instance, governments can minimize such risks by implementing sound macroeconomic policies, and strengthening enabling environments. Though financial instruments used by NDBs are not able to totally minimize such risks, they are useful in promoting enhanced policymaking targeted at reducing risk. While such national risks are systemic to the local economy, they may be considered idiosyncratic from a global perspective. This suggests that external players such MDBs can be involved in managing such risks through diversification. For instance, political risk insurance is diversifiable since it is mostly uncorrelated across countries. Currency risk is also an example of domestic endogenous risk, is uncorrelated with other currencies, and is therefore diversifiable. Clearly, diversification can be used to manage national risks that are not globally systematic and this provides the basis of insurance. Again, strengthening the system of development banks, in addition to enhanced global insurance markets, may be helpful for NDBs to be able to better manage such risks. For instance, MDBs need to consider creating portfolios of projects, which have relatively short-term maturities from different economies that could be securitized and sold to international investors as a way of diversifying risk, globally (see Griffith-Jones et al., 2020; Ketterer & Powell, 2018).

12.2.1.2 Real Economy Risks and Financial Market Risks

There are varied investment-specific real economy risks, based on the project and the timing in the investment cycle. For instance, the different phases of infrastructure projects, such as preparation, construction and operation introduce a variety of cost overruns and are exposed to other key commercial risks. The construction phase is also associated with technology and geological risks (see Griffith-Jones, 1993; Ketterer & Powell, 2018).

Financial engineering or intermediary risks are risks associated with counterparties and financial intermediaries, or are generated through investment structures. Risk management in the financial market suggests matching risks with economic agents who are best placed or prepared to assume such risks. It is important to note that financial products can themselves produce new risks for the guarantor (in this case where government guarantees for the development bank, government then is the funder, which implies the taxpayer bears the potential costs). This is because employing instruments leads to increased leverage and/or ensures risk transfers from private entities to NDBs. Also, using financial engineering products can have minimal sustainable development impact, as policy steer is mostly indirect, and can become diffused or nonexistent, particularly, when instruments are opaque (Griffith-Jones and Naqvi, op cit.) Additionally, public subsidies can involve the private sector in the investment process when it is not cost-efficient, and can lead to perverse incentives, including financial institutions engaging in excessive risk-taking (i.e. increasing a firm's debt level to a level where it adversely affects its long-term viability). It does not suggest that financial products are irrelevant. The point is that the use of such instruments should take into consideration the complete array of risks, both financial and developmental (Griffith-Jones et al., 2020).

12.2.2 Other Types of Specific Risks

NDBs are exposed to various types of specific or idiosyncratic risks. These risks are specific to a particular bank and can be diversified. Examples of such risks are: credit risk, market risk (interest rate risk, currency risk, and liquidity risk), strategic risk, operational risk, compliance risk and reputational risk.

Credit risk is the risk of default on obligations or the risk that the borrower will default in repaying the NDB's loan principal and interests, resulting in an interruption of cash flows and increased costs for collection. It is the likelihood of a loss due to failure on the part of the borrower to repay the loan or meet contractual obligations. It is also known as default risk.

Market risk is the risk that arises due to the fact that the cash flows of a financial instrument may change because of changes in market prices.

NDBs become more exposed if they invest in the capital market or portfolio trading. Market risk therefore reflects exposures such as interest rate risk, currency risk, liquidity risk and other price risks.

Interest rate risk is the potential for investment losses arising from a change in interest rates. If the NDB gives a fixed rate loan, an increase in interest rates affects its bottom line. Also, if interest rates increase, this will cause a decline in the value of the NDB's fixed-income investment.

Currency risk is the risk that arises from changes in value of a currency in relation to other currencies. It is risk associated with fluctuation in exchange rates. NDBs mostly provide loans in local currency but their funding from international capital markets and MDBs are in foreign currency. Thus, fluctuations in exchange rates affect their investments in loans and other assets.

Liquidity risk is the risk of incurring losses as a result of the NDB's inability to meet its payment obligations on time as and when they fall due or from being unable to do so at a sustainable cost. There are two types of liquidity risk. The first is **funding liquidity or cash flow risk**, which is the risk of inadequate capital/funding levels to sustain the NDB's business and execute its growth strategy. The second is **market liquidity risk** (also known as asset/product risk), which arises due to lack of marketability of an investment that cannot be bought or sold quickly enough to prevent or minimize a loss.

Strategic risk refers to the likelihood that unforeseen events may make the NDB's strategy ineffective or uncompetitive or that events or circumstances may occur which could limit the NDB's ability to implement its strategy and successfully deliver on its mandate. Strategic risk hinders the NDB's ability to achieve its objectives. It can have severe consequences that impact the NDB in the long term.

Operational risk is the risk of loss resulting from inadequate, ineffective or failed internal processes, people and systems or external events that has the tendency to disrupt the flow of the NDB's business operations.

Compliance risk is the risk NDBs are exposed to, such as legal penalties, financial forfeiture, material loss, loss of business opportunities and damaged reputation as a result of non-compliance to laws and regulations, internal policies or prescribed best practices.

Reputational risk is failure to prevent and respond to reputational risk events impacting on the NDB's goodwill and reputation. It is also concerned with the reputation of the NDB that will send bad signals of the bank to its stakeholders. It is the damage that may occur to the NDB when it fails to meet its stakeholders' expectations.

12.3 Risk Management

Risk management involves the process of formulating the benefit–cost trade-offs of risk reduction and deciding on the course of action to take. It involves a systematic attempt to analyse and deal with risk, and the process includes risk identification, risk assessment, selection of risk management techniques or instruments, implementation and review (Bodie et al., 2009). Williams and Heins (1989) suggest that the main objectives of risks management can be put into two categories: pre-loss objective ('several risk management objectives prior to the occurrence of loss') and post-loss objective (objective after a loss occurs). They identify five steps for risk management which include: *Identify risk, Analyse risk, Evaluate the risk, Institute risk response planning and Monitor and review the risk*. Türsoy (2018) defines risk management in banking as 'the logical development and execution of a plan to deal with potential losses'. It involves managing an institution's exposure to losses or risks and protecting the value of its assets. Türsoy (2018) summarizes the risk management process as three main steps, and these are: (1) Identifying and assessing the potential risks associated with the business of banking; (2) Developing and executing a plan of action in dealing with and managing these activities that result in potential losses; and (3) Reviewing and reporting on a continuous basis, the risk management practices after they have been implemented.

The Bank for International Settlement (2010) describes risk management as the 'function responsible for identifying, measuring, monitoring, controlling or mitigating, and reporting on risk exposures which should encompass all risks to the bank, on- and off-balance sheet and a group-wide, portfolio and business-line level, and should take into account the extent to which risks overlap'. The overall objective of the risk management process is evaluating the potential losses that may arise in the future and then taking the necessary precautions in dealing with them when they do occur.

12.3.1 Historical Perspective of Risk Management

Prior to the 1990s, the concept of risk management was limited to explaining the techniques and risks in connection with insurance. This was mainly related to buying an insurance policy appropriate for covering risks and providing protection against future mishaps. The notion of risk management in banking emerged sometime in the 1990s and in recent times, derivatives have been used in the financial market as risk management tools for hedging against risks. This approach to risk management is mostly referred to as financial risk management. The use of derivatives is important in managing risks associated with financial transactions and activities. Derivatives help banks to manage the mismatch in the maturity structure of their asset and liabilities. Apart from hedging against risk, derivatives are also used for the purpose of speculation and arbitrage (Abor, 2018; Türsoy, 2018).

Specifically, the concept of risk management in banking became necessary in 1997 following the publication by the Basel Committee on Banking Supervision (BCBS) on the 'core principles' for effective banking supervision. The Basel framework provides an important connection between capital and risks. Particularly, banks are expected to adopt risk measurement and risk management procedures and processes to ensure risk-adjusted return in their operations. Therefore, the main concept of risk management in banking is ensuring the profitability, soundness and the safety of the banking sector.

Such risk management procedures and processes can also be related to NDBs. The next section is discussion of the financial instruments that are used by NDBs in managing risks.

12.4 Financial Instruments Used by National Development Banks in Normal Times

In situations where there is adequate compensation of risk (i.e. high return to risk ratio), private investors may assume such risks without using public finance. However, if returns on the investment are uncompetitive in relation to other opportunities on a risk-adjusted basis, and there are obvious positive externalities (developmental impacts), then support or interventions by NDBs will be required. Similar to the instruments discussed in Chapter 9, Griffith-Jones et al. (2020) also identified five main instruments that NDBs use to support investment which are:

(i) loans (concessional and ordinary) and grant financing; (ii) guarantees; (iii) grants; (iv) equity investments (including venture capital and private equity); and (v) insurance type products, securitization and other diversified products.

12.4.1 Loans and Grants Financing

NDBs use loans as their top financial product. The loans are classified as 1st Tier (i.e. direct loans provided by development banks) and 2nd Tier (i.e. indirect loans transferred through the process of subsequent lending by other types of financial institutions including commercial banks, cooperative banks, sub-national development banks, and other types of institution). First-tier loans could be very helpful, especially for bigger and more important projects, because they give the development banks more control over policy. Due to differences in how much information is known, second-tier loans are good for smaller loans and situations where local knowledge may be crucial.

Loans supplied by NDBs are normally less expensive than what commercial banks provide, and because of the guarantee NDBs obtain, their funding costs are typically lower than those of commercial banks. Loans can be made concessional in two ways: by providing subsidies for either the principal or the interest payments. The former is preferable in many circumstances due to the reduced transaction costs involved. An investment with good social or environmental externalities but not enough return to attract individual investors can benefit from subsidized credit. For the most important development impact externalities, subsidized loans or partial grants are the most appropriate options during the project design stage (e.g. lowering carbon emissions). With adequate reporting and monitoring, subsidized loans and grants can be utilized for direct funding towards sustainable development benefits. Financial inclusion and new market investment can be encouraged by subsidies. The temporary aid is given to new markets or industries. When new activities, such as solar and wind energy, become competitive, they may be discontinued. MSMEs and other underrepresented markets might benefit from subsidized loans. These subsidies can be sustained for an extended time (such as in poverty) since they are directed at high-risk or low-return areas. Subsidies help microfinance companies to bridge the revenue and service cost gap.

Subsidies for loans and guarantees are meant to encourage private participation, but they should not compensate private investors excessively. The project could be awarded to the lowest bidder in an auction by the NDB. With respect to infrastructure, viability gap funding strategies have been developed to ensure projects are financially appealing without increasing user prices. The qualifying private sector bidder seeking the lowest subsidy is selected in these methods. Strong governance systems serve as a baseline for the concessionality of projects in related businesses and nations and are an additional tool for bolstering subsidy allocation

12.4.2 Guarantees

Guarantees are also a very important way for NDBs to obtain finance. The overall theoretical rationale regarding public guarantees (including those from NDBs) is based on Arrow and Lind (1970), a foundational conceptual model for understanding the state's role in carrying risk when risk aversion is present. Arrow and Lind (1970) indicate that capital can be valued at risk-neutral levels by distributing risk among many investors. As a result, the state has the potential to disperse risk across a wide selection of people because of its intertemporal tax and borrowing capabilities. Private investment or lending can be encouraged through development bank guarantees due to a fear of individual investors or lenders taking on too much risk (see Anginer et al., 2011). Extreme aversion to risk can be triggered by specific new ventures or industries or by national or international crises, such as the 2008/2009 financial crisis and the recent COVID-19 crisis.

However, in countries with less developed financial systems, guarantees may be used to temporarily boost private investment, though this is less common, as evidenced by the lower use of guarantees in developing countries. To deal with heavy tails of specific risks that markets do not tend to price on their own, they can be useful in more mature markets (Anginer et al., 2011).

In general, guarantees might be suitable when utilized to deal with: (i) specific risks when private investors or lenders are highly risk-averse, when financial systems are undeveloped, and when there are heavy tails in well-developed markets; (ii) substantial uncertainty, as evident after the 2008/2009 global financial crisis or the COVID-19 pandemic.

Although utilizing guarantees to assist in alleviating credit rationing may seem like a good idea at first glance, it is not apparent if the cost to taxpayers of such guarantees is taken into consideration, and if credit rationing is caused for example by adverse selection in connection with asymmetric information (see Stiglitz & Weiss, 1981). Hence, Greenwald and Stiglitz (1989), Lacker (1994) and Anginer et al. (op cit.) argue that public guarantees cannot contribute to promoting socially better outcomes since there is not an informational advantage and there is not the possibility to cross-subsidize.

Aside from these limitations, guarantees can be used in certain situations. If governments or development banks are ready to carry almost all of the risk, they may not be able to minimize the intensified risk aversion of bankers in downturns and particularly since there is considerable uncertainty. In fact, a guarantee of close to 100% may be required to stimulate private lending in high-uncertainty situations. A counter-cyclical instrument provided by guarantee programmes may therefore be ineffective. A first-tier development bank may be the only way to increase financing in these situations. To do this, however, development banks may need branches or the establishment of new development banks in regions to operate. A deep understanding of the local economy can assist in alleviating information disparities and enhancing regional benefits.

In addition to this difficulty, it is typically more challenging for the government to evaluate the effect that on-lending or guaranteeing will have on development. This highlights the need for comprehensive data on the intended recipients. This may involve policies that ensure that NDBs submit accurate reports. A compensation scheme could help mitigate the risks associated with lending money to initiatives with little influence on development. For instance, the African Development Bank's AFAWA project gives advantageous terms to organizations achieving pre-established goals for women's access to funding.

12.4.3 Equity Investment

Equity investment is an important financial tool used by NDBs. It is the most appropriate tool employed by NDBs. This type of financing can be provided directly to individual businesses, through portfolio diversification, or using the private equity or venture capital business model. Although it is possible that not all of the companies looking for investors will be successful in the end, the profits made by just a few of them should be enough to make up for the failures of the others and might result in considerable net profits.

Development banks can 'catch the upside' by using financial instruments with equity sweeteners, for example, warrants. The European Investment Bank (EIB) and other development banks are currently using venture finance to aid 'innovative firms'. A portion of a company's increased profit goes to the EIB as compensation for taking on more risk. An equity-linked instrument such as warrants or profit participation is typically used to accomplish this. Private equity and venture capital finance can also be used to fund a company's growth stages, such as the transition from pilot production to mass production, R&D expansion and worldwide expansion.

Many countries' capital markets remain undeveloped and largely unavailable to small firms, thus, making private equity or venture capital an important source of equity financing. Only US$2.5 billion in private equity and venture capital has been spent yearly in Africa during the past five years, a notably low amount. Market development may be aided by development banks in the absence of self-sustained markets by providing equity support for sustainable development initiatives. This kind of financing might be organized such that businesses would only utilize public funds if they truly needed them. Finding the right risk-reward sharing mechanism and the right level of public involvement may be challenging. In order to evaluate the outcomes of public assistance mechanisms, it is necessary to have openness and monitoring measures in place.

Additionally, private equity has come under scrutiny for its heavy reliance on debt to boost investment returns. Overly risky leveraging might make businesses less able to withstand economic downturns and have systemic consequences.

12.4.4 *Resource Financed Infrastructure Instrument*

Resource financed infrastructure (RFI) is a mechanism through which a government is able to obtain essential infrastructure without having to produce sufficient revenues to support the financing (Halland et al., 2014). It is a way for governments to integrate two distinct industries, economic development and the extraction of natural resources. The China Development Bank and the China EXIM Bank use RFI, and most of China's massive infrastructure finance come from the use of the RFI instrument.

RFI contributes to the funding of infrastructure, notably in poorly governed underdeveloped nations. Historically, governments of developing countries borrowed from foreign creditors to create public infrastructure and repaid their loans using tax revenues. Debtor governments, on the other hand, frequently fail to make credible undertakings to return their loans. Two new discoveries have been made in a recent study (Xu, Ru, et al., 2021). To begin with, RFI loans are substantially greater than traditional sovereign debts. Secondly, countries that have received RFI loans have worse governance than those that have not. RFI helps to mitigate it, although inadequate country-level governance frequently worsens credit rationing. There appear to be two mechanisms by which RFI defends itself for the duration of the project, while reducing lending rates in countries with weak governance and abundant natural resources. First, rather than borrowing from governments, Chinese development banks send funds to firms building the projects. Second, resource revenue is sent to a separate escrow account set up to cover infrastructure loan obligations. Through the employment of these two strategies, lenders may rest assured that their funds will be put to good use since infrastructure investments will be repaid in full with revenues generated from the resource extraction (Xu, Ru, et al., 2021).

In spite of the benefits associated with the use of the RFI instrument, it restricts the ability of debtor governments to implement their own policies. In addition to weak governance, many countries or businesses may encounter debt-service challenges to other factors such as commodity price shocks, the global financial crisis and, more recently, the COVID-19 pandemic. The debtor government cannot be blamed because these extreme events are external. The RFI mechanism is beneficial to creditors since it secures payback. It is somewhat beneficial to borrowers because it may be useful in facilitating more lending for borrowers. However, borrowers may lose the freedom to manage their foreign exchange resources, since a portion of their export earnings is automatically deposited in an escrow account for the repayment of infrastructure loans. In the event of an external shock, the country would be unable to suspend payments to creditors in order to utilize scarce foreign cash for important spending.

12.4.5 Insurance Products, Securitization and Other Diversified Products

Insurance: Insurance is based on risk diversification, but it is the least utilized financial tool. Investors may be hesitant about investing if they consider some risks to be excessive and cannot be adequately addressed. Insurance allows for the transfer of risk to parties better suited to bear it. Some risks are however impossible to handle at the national level. NDBs, for instance, lack the capability to protect customers against global undiversifiable risks and shocks. In such instances, foreign markets may supply some hedging products. However, these may be costly and, as previously noted, may become illiquid during global economic shocks.

Securitization: Securitization is one of the methods of spreading risks among investors by combining transactions and benefiting from diversity. A development bank might sell a portfolio of loans to investors by issuing a financial security in these designs. This permits the issuing banks to free up balance-sheet space, and improve their lending ability. Diversification is used in this bundle by combining diverse assets with idiosyncratic risks. Since the mid-1980s, securitization has been used to enhance lending in the housing market in the US. The markets for car, student and SME loans in the US were worth over US$1 trillion in 2019. China is considered the world's second-largest securitization market, with issuance totalling over US$300 billion in 2019. MDBs have also made significant inroads into this market.

However, as the 2008 financial crisis proved, securitization is not without risks. Many sub-prime mortgage-backed securities were issued with highly linked loans prior to the global financial crisis. This was such that in the case of a downturn (i.e. increased systemic risk), it was possible that most households would fail at the same time (which actually occurred). Banks' lending requirements have also been reduced. Securitizations can be organized to mitigate these risks, but governments must have the regulatory and supervisory competence in issuing such instruments properly.

12.4.6 Additional Factors that Impact Instrument Choice

One key finding from interactions with development banks is that in certain circumstances, the instruments that DBs use are directly related to the financing they receive. One development bank that operates under a strict code of capital preservation, for example, cannot engage in activities like first loss guarantees, which can potentially violate that code. When the only funding source for the DB comes from government subsidies (not reported as a financial expense because they come from the aid fund), only a limited number of financial instruments can be employed. NDBs that rely extensively on capital markets have also reported tying instrument selection (and the degree of risk assumed) to fund selection, particularly when ratings are in danger in scenarios such as COVID-19.

In order to meet the shifting requirements posed by the real economy at various phases of growth, development banks will need to modify the financial instruments at their disposal. New structural economic analysis, as argued by Lin et al. (2013), suggests that 'there is a good financial structure for the economy at its current level of development. As the economy grows, so does the right financial structure for it'. Furthermore, their business strategies and tools must be tailored to the country's current degree of development and general features. Even though development banks in different countries can learn from each other, 'one size does not fit all'. Different tools (such as innovation) may be needed to accomplish specific goals, as has already been mentioned. In the same way, different tools may be needed to fund different sectors, such as agriculture and infrastructure.

12.5 Instruments Used by National Development Banks During Pandemics

Pandemics such as COVID-19 are associated with systemic risk globally. A number of factors tend to impact many activities of NDBs, including the requirement for enterprises to have liquidity (to offer assistance for working capital, not generally a role of development banks) to pay employees and suppliers; the need for particular financial instruments, especially those with sectoral priority such as health; and a focus on preventing disruption to value chains, which are all common considerations. To deal with the rising complexity of risk management and identify their purpose and aims as financial institutions for growth or expansion, NDBs are progressively being forced to deal with more uncertainty. The issue is torn between the possibility of a decline in the credit quality of NDBs' loan portfolios as the financial conditions of firms undermine their capacity to repay their loans and the necessity of giving credit that might help in the survival of enterprises and the preservation of employment. In responding to the COVID-19 crisis, NDBs could use the tools developed during the financial crisis of 2007/2009. Development banks seem to be comfortable lending directly to firms with which they already have business dealings. This is simpler and more efficient since they already have a better understanding of them. Many global DFIs utilize NDBs as intermediaries for this purpose. For instance, the UK CDC provides loans in Africa through TDB, and BNDES lend through the sub-national/regional development bank (DBMG) in Minas Gerais (Griffith-Jones et al. (2020)).

Griffith-Jones et al. (2020) suggest that to deal with the COVID-19 pandemic, the response of NDBs does not follow a linear or pre-defined strategy, but is more like a learning-by-doing process in which the financial institutions are always evaluating whether the instruments in place assist in achieving the goals or need to be altered. During the first phase of the COVID-19 pandemic, however, both NDBs and MDBs took similar measures, including:

- **Using fast-track procedures** to speed up the authorization of transactions;
- **Providing working capital** for firms in the form of loans, grants and guarantees;
- **Adopting standstill approach** involving maintaining existing loans, while extending the grace period;
- **Providing additional support** for the health sector and governments, particularly at the municipal level;
- **Involving other regional development banks and municipal funding banks and agencies** to provide financial support.

12.5.1 Using Fast-Track Procedures

During the uncertainties of the COVID-19 pandemic, many NDBs used fast-track processes to expedite action on loan disbursement and reduce the time it took from the time of the loan application to the loan payment. The amount of time saved tended to vary from one institution to another. The procedures involved the use of digital services to speed up loan applications and disbursements, enabling the NDBs to disburse financial resources in a shorter period of time compared to the pre-COVID-19 era.

12.5.2 Providing Working Capital with Loans, Grants and Guarantees

The outbreak of the COVID-19 pandemic has led to businesses now requiring more short-term loans to cover working capital needs. Contrary to standard practice, NDBs have significantly boosted the amount of working capital they provide to businesses so they can cover operating activities such as paying their employees and suppliers. The instruments used in disbursing working capital and liquidity include loans, grants and guarantees, and these are similar to instruments used in normal times. Firms needing working capital are now required to meet standards like sustaining steady employment and salary.

- **Loans and grants**—Short-term loans are preferable because of the ease with which the instrument can be rolled over. However, using debt comes with its own drawbacks, which implies a high level of leverage for the borrowing firms.
- **Guarantees**—During the COVID-19 times, guarantees gained greater significance, and an increased focus was placed on portfolio guarantees in particular. Guarantees, like loans, have the same credit risk. Nonetheless, guarantees are gaining in popularity because of the prospect of greater leverage and reduced liquidity risk, which comes at the cost of a greater contingent liability risk for NDBs. Guarantees come with a greater overall level of systemic risk considering that the National Treasury or the Ministry of Finance serve as the lender of last resort for NDBs. Anginer et al. (2011) suggest that guarantees work differently depending on the times they are adopted. In normal times, guarantees offer insurance against idiosyncratic risks. In times of aggregate systemic risk, with strong association between defaults, guarantee schemes may also require government subsidies or financial resources.

12.5.3 Adopting Standstill Approach

NDBs have utilized a standstill strategy on existing loans with prolonged grace periods during the COVID-19 pandemic period. Considering the difficulties of restructuring the terms of the contract, which would raise NDBs' expenses, the standstill strategy is preferred as a speedier and more cost-effective option. Rating agencies, on the other hand, typically view this passive instrument as a red flag and penalize financial institutions that use it. Some researchers suggest that this instrument is comparable to what has been proposed for GDP-linked bonds (see Benford et al., 2018) in that it is aimed at improving the quality of credit, and hence raises the likelihood of repayment. It is useful for rating agencies to modify their methodologies by incorporating such insights from academics and policymakers.

12.5.4 *Providing Additional Support for Health Sector and Governments*

NDBs also have a critical role to play in the provision of support for governments and the health sector. Such support includes injection of liquidity or provision of country-specific lines of credit for the health system. For instance, the AfDB launched country-specific credit lines, providing a total amount of US$1.35 billion to support private sector operations in specific countries. It also launched country-specific credit lines, providing US$5.5 billion for sovereign operations, and an extra US$3.1 billion for sovereign and regional operations as part of the African Development Fund. Provision of additional lines of support for the health sector and governments also involved some development banks issuing contingent credit lines for national public health systems.

12.5.5 *Other Regional Development Banks and Municipal Funding Banks and Agencies*

During the COVID-19 crisis, local public financial institutions also played a very important role. Sub-national regional development banks and municipal funding banks are distinct from NDBs and MDBs in terms of their nature, size and method of raising finance. Differences are also noticed within local financial institutions given the differences in scope, nations' credit-worthiness and corporate regulations.

12.6 How National Development Banks Benefit from Risk Management

The global financial crisis which mainly surfaced due to the breakdown of good corporate governance practices, has prompted and encouraged financial institutions including NDBs, to take the issue of risk management more seriously than before. To a larger extent, the shortfalls of the larger banks' management of risks, especially credit risks, have been exposed by the financial crisis or global economic meltdown. NDBs could benefit from implementing an efficient risk management system. This section discusses the benefits of risk management to the NDBs.

Long-term financing is typically associated with higher credit risks. However, NDBs can better manage the credit risk associated with long-term loans since their sources of funding are also held in the longer term as the loans. In fact, there is more flexibility in the portfolio management that helps in channelling funds into productive ventures or investments, thereby minimizing the vulnerability of the financial system. It is important to note that NDBs are able to renegotiate credit (long-term funds raised) on better terms which in the long-run minimizes default losses, which does not negatively impact upon the financial system. In the same vein, the information flow between the NDBs and other institutions improves as a result of the existence of long credit relations between them, thereby growing the interdependence of the parties, which eventually reduces the tendencies of credit default and delinquency (de Castro, 2018).

Just like global financial institutions and other local banks, NDBs have the 'broader objective of maximizing their risk-adjusted rate of return on capital (RAROC), although avoiding failure is a principal reason for managing risk'. This suggests that NDBs and other banks do not only avoid 'excessive risk exposures' but take into consideration 'measuring and managing risks relative to returns and to capital' as well. NDBs de-emphasize devoting attention to investments with both high-risks and return when focusing on RAROC. This strategy made NDBs allocate resources (capital) strategically. Thus, NDBs made better management decisions relating to allocation of capital and other resources. NDBs have been able to meet the appropriate demand of RAROC by shareholders and creditors of which other banks which do not concentrate on 'risk-adjusted returns' were not fully rewarded by the market.

NDBs are exposed to less/smaller market risks in trading portfolios as compared to their private counterpart banks since trading portfolio is not the core business of NDBs. A higher percentage of the Basel requirements regarding market risks lies in the trading portfolio by using the VAR or maturity ladder. As been explained earlier, the core activity of NDBs is not the trading portfolio; hence their major market risks tend to be currency risks. NDBs experience these kind of risks if and only if they support exports or fundraising at the international markets. For this reason they will bear the consequences of interest rate risks and dividend flow fluctuations in their banking books if they act as buffer capital markets. This situation leaves NDBs at an advantageous position on the issue of risk management since assets have less duration than the duration of the liability (de Castro, 2018).

NDBs have the advantage of supporting exports to high-risk destinations/countries as they benefit from specific support mechanisms including public funds and guarantees. It is very easy for NDBs to recoup funds expended on supporting the exporting activities in other markets or countries by institutions or clients as compared to the private banks. This is due to the fact that sovereign payments are more easily enforceable within the government and its agencies and they benefit from specific support mechanisms including public funds and guarantees (de Castro, 2018).

NDBs, like other banks, benefit from risk management through changes in the organizational culture. The attention placed on risk management by the NDBs makes them more proactive than other banks that do not put more emphasis on risk management, by being reactive. Risk management ensures that NDBs have a serious look at each section of their operations, thereby being able to forecast probable issues. As a result, they face less business disruptions since those issues that would have created those disruptions are always taken care of at an early stage. This has helped NDBs to identify failed projects at an early stage and saved them from spending extra funds on such projects.

The operations of NDBs have been diversified but are still relevant and competitive in business as a result of proper risk management strategies that are put in place. The management of risks has helped NDBs to minimize losses at critical points in their operations. This cannot be said of other organizations with poor risk management strategies. The ability of the NDBs to strategize in minimizing or eliminating losses in their operations has made them competitive and able to remain in business. It has been established that, in times of economic meltdown or crisis like a recession, 'companies with better risk management practices continue to stay afloat' and have considerable financial resources as compared to those without proper risk management practices. The communication levels between departments and other stakeholders of the bank are improved by the risk management processes, thus enhancing the competitive nature NDBs.

Moreover, NDBs enjoy protection of resources and the improvement in credit ratings through their risk management practices. This helps in the promotion of their resources rather than being wasted illegally. NDBs are able to build numerous business features that have palpable benefits, and also build up greater confidence particularly with stakeholders. This is capable of translating into improvements in their credit rating, since they have no issues with capital adequacy and so on.

NDBs have lower liquidity risk considering their own funding structure. They have a range of tools for risk management, which helps them to renegotiate the terms of debt more easily. But this is not available to private banks. This enables them to operate even under economic crises and the investments made in projects do not affect the financial health of the NDBs. Thus, there exist 'crossed assets and liabilities between the treasury and the NDBs, which allow a range of tools for risk management' (de Castro, 2018).

NDBs have been able to survive 'black swan events' (Avoiding Catastrophic Events) without going bankrupt. Due to proper risk identification and management by NDBs, they have been able to foster watchfulness in times of discipline and tranquility in times of disaster. This actually made them stronger to withstand all manner of economic shocks in the past. This has been possible because risk managers of these banks have been able to foresee small shocks which affect the daily operations, and also focus on black swan events which are impossible to predict due to their rare nature but are very catastrophic events when they occur.

Through risk management processes, NDBs are able to minimize risks, thereby saving costs and time. They are able to handle risks within the given 'assessments plans' since these risks are predicted in the business operations. When that is done, the NDBs are able to alter or modify 'policies and contingencies' that are made successful within the mapped business operations. This enhances the prevention of waste of certain resources and time.

Though NDBs interact with high-risk sectors, this does not automatically imply more losses. These sectors include SMEs and innovations. The operations of SMEs can be on either first- or second-tier basis. The risk is assumed by the financial agent if the operations of the SMEs are performed on the second-tier basis, while on the first-tier operations, the losses are taken care of by the large portfolios. There is no risk associated with the funding of innovation through the use of non-reimbursable funds (de Castro, 2018). Again, the activity will take place since the sustainability of the fund will be checked by the capital requirement.

12.7 Concluding Remarks

This chapter has discussed the risk management NDBs. It has identified the various types of risks that confront NDBs, including exogenous shocks and endogenous risks, as well as real economy risks and financial engineering risks. Other types of specific risks NDBs are exposed include credit risk, market risk (interest rate risk, currency risk and liquidity risk), strategic risk, operational risk, compliance risk and reputational risk.

Risk management involves the process of formulating the benefit–cost trade-offs of risk reduction and deciding on the course of action to take. It involves a systematic attempt to analyse and deal with risk and the process include, risk identification, risk assessment, selection of risk management techniques or instruments, implementation and review. The overall objective of the risk management process is evaluating the potential losses that may arise in future and then taking the necessary precautions to deal with them when they occur.

An important step in the risk management process is fashioning out appropriate financial instruments to manage the risks. We identified five main instruments that NDBs use in this regard and these include: (i) financing of loans (concessional and ordinary) and grants; (ii) guarantees; (iii) grants; (iv) equity investments; and (v) insurance type products, securitization and other diversified products. However, during crisis situations, such as the COVID-19 pandemic, NDBs employ different types of instruments in managing their risks. Some of these are:

- Using fast-track procedures to speed up the authorization of transactions;
- Providing working capital for firms in the form of loans, grants and guarantees

- Adopting standstill approach involving maintaining existing loans, while extending the grace period;
- Providing additional support for the health sector and governments, particularly at the municipal level; and
- Involving other regional development banks and municipal funding banks and agencies to provide financial support.

Risk management is extremely critical and NDBs could benefit from implementing an efficient risk management system.

References

Abor, J. Y. (2018). *Financial markets and institutions: A frontier market perspective* (2nd ed.). Digibooks.

Anginer, D., De la Torre, A., & Ize, A. (2011). *Risk absorption by the state: When is it good public policy?* (World Bank Policy Research Working Paper, 5893).

Arrow, K. J., & Lind, R. C. (1970, June). Uncertainty and the evaluation of public investment decisions. *American Economic Review, 60*, 364–378.

Bank for International Settlements (BIS). (2010). *Principles for enhancing corporate governance*. Basel Committee on Banking Supervision. http://www.bis.org/publ/bcbs176.htm

Benford, J, Ostry, J. D., & Shiller, R. (2018). *Sovereign GDP-linked bonds: Rationale and design*. A VoxEU.org eBook. CEPR Press.

Bodie, Z., Merton, R., & Cleeton, D. (2009). *Financial economics* (2nd ed.). Pearson.

de Castro, L. B. (2018). Financial regulation and risk management in development banks. In S. Griffith-Jones & J. A. Ocampo (Eds.), *The future of national development banks*. Oxford University Press.

Griffith-Jones, S. (1993). *Loan guarantees for large infrastructure projects: The issues and possible lessons for a European facility*. Office for official publications of the European communities.

Griffith-Jones, S., & Naqvi, N. (2020). *Industrial policy and risk sharing in public development banks: Lessons for the post-COVID response from the EIB and EFSI* (Working Paper No. 143). GEG.

Griffith-Jones, S., Attridge, S., & Gouett, M. (2020a). *Securing climate finance through national development banks* (ODI Report). ODI. www.odi.org/publications/16552-securing-climate-finance-through-national-development-banks

Halland, H., Beardsworth, J., Land, B., & Schmidt, J. (2014). *Resource financed infrastructure: A discussion on a new form of infrastructure financing*. The World Bank.

Ketterer, J., & Powell A. (2018). *Financing infrastructure*. IADB.

Knight, F. H. (1921). Cost of production and price over long and short periods. *Journal of Political Economy, 29*(4), 304–335.

Mazzucato, M. (2018). *The value of everything: Making and taking in the global economy*. Hachette UK.

Periasamy, P. (2008). *Financial management*. Tata McGraw Hill Education.

Stiglitz, J. E., & Weiss, A. (1981). Credit rationing in markets with imperfect information. *The American Economic Review, 71*(3), 393–410.

Türsoy, T. (2018). *Risk management process in banking industry* (Munich Personal RePEc Archive). Near East University.

Williams, C., & Heins, R. (1989). *Risk management and insurance*. McGraw-Hill.

Xu, J., Ru, X., & Song, P. (2021). Can a new model of infrastructure financing mitigate credit rationing in poorly governed countries? *Economic Modelling, 95*, 111–120.

CHAPTER 13

Regulation and Supervision of National Development Banks

13.1 Introduction

Banking regulations are said to be a set of laws and norms that are applicable to the banking sector (Nyantakyi & Sy, 2015). Governments across the globe regulate and supervise their banking sector. Since the banking sector plays a significant role in fostering economic and financial growth, global economies are being impressed upon to do whatever is required to avoid hurting financial markets, especially the banking industry. Prior crises have brought to the fore the need to enhance banking regulation and the instruments available to regulators to provide oversight over banks and respond swiftly during emergency situations (BCBS, 2016). It is also true that the functions of banks have evolved in response to the changing dynamics of banking regulation.

The essence of banking regulation includes ensuring the soundness and stability of the banking system, protecting depositors, preventing excessive risk-taking by banks (which can harm depositors and creditors) in order to avoid systemic banking crises, controlling money supply, monitoring credit, avoiding financial power concentration in a few banks, maintaining public confidence in the banking system and ensuring healthy coexistence (see Abor, 2018; Nyantakyi & Sy, 2015). Banks, as financial intermediaries play a vital role in African economies. Regulators can employ various regulatory tools including restrictions on assets and operations, capital requirements, competition restraints, separation of conventional

© The Author(s), under exclusive license to Springer Nature Switzerland AG 2023

J. Yindenaba Abor, *The Changing Role of National Development Banks in Africa*, https://doi.org/10.1007/978-3-031-38639-8_13

banking from other financial service industries, risk-based deposit insurance premiums and transparency requirements, bank chartering and bank examination (Abugre et al., 2022; Mishkin, 2016).

Development banks operate differently given their objective of development impact. They exhibit different characteristics in terms of their mandates, funding sources, business and lending models, operations, etc. Development banks, and for that matter NDBs, tend to have a mandate to support specific sectors of the economy. They are established to provide long-term finance to such sectors to foster economic growth and development. The regulatory framework adopted would certainly have implications for the functioning, operations and activities of NDBs. There is no single dominant supervision model among NDBs in Africa since it varies from one NDB to another (Quintyn & Taylor, 2002). The regulatory authorities responsible for the regulation and supervision of NDBs are the central bank and the government ministries like the line ministry and the finance ministry. Regulation and supervision by the central bank also covers private sector banks and state-owned banks.

While discussion of regulation of mainstream banks is well-advanced in the literature, the issue of regulation of NDBs is a difficult matter to address, considering their institutional diversity. There is good coverage in the extant literature of the effect of Basel Capital on the role of development banks in providing development finance. However, the issue of the place of Basel Standards in the regulation of NDBs is still evolving. This chapter contributes to the existing literature (see de Castro, 2018; Gottschalk et al., 2021) by examining the regulation of NDBs. Issues regarding the rationale for financial regulation, the distinction between NDBs and other banks, and whether NDBs should be regulated are addressed in this chapter.

The rest of the chapter is organized as follows: Sect. 13.2 provides justification for regulating financial institutions; Sect. 13.3 discusses the evolution of the Basel agreements; Sect. 13.4 discusses NDBs and the Basel regulatory framework, and finally, Sect. 13.5 presents the conclusion.

13.2 Justification for Financial Regulation

Historically, financial regulation emerged in response to the 1929 financial crisis, where the absence of a lender of last resort had severe effects on income levels, employment and economic growth. It was realized that unlike other sectors of the economy, the failure of one bank could extend to other banks (or have a contagion effect), converting a local challenge into national economic downturn and eventually resulting in a global economic crisis. In the period between the 1930s and the 1970s with the US as the pioneer, prudential financial regulation was meant to serve as a form of protection for banks in order to avoid crises, applying nationwide supervisory rules and showing particular interest in liquidity risk (Carvalho, 2003; Gottschalk et al., 2021). This framework started changing in the 1970s, gaining momentum from the 1980s and beyond. These developments brought into being the so-called Basel Capital Accords in 1988. The key justification for the shift from national regulation to global regulation was on account of the lack of harmonized financial regulation across the different countries, and the fact that several internationally active banks were engaged in the practice of regulatory arbitrage in order to have a competitive edge over other banks. The essence of the Basel regulatory framework was to create an even playing field for all of these banks (Gottschalk et al., 2021; King & Tarbert, 2011).

There is ample justification for regulating financial institutions and the focus of prudential financial regulation was to deal with systemic risk, which is traditionally associated with three features of the banking system: (a) the existence of fractional reserves, (b) the existence of interconnections between banks, leading to the problem of contagion and (c) the fact that banks form part of the national payment system that can cause a financial crisis to impact on the entire economy. Nonetheless, the idea of systemic risk has evolved over time, in that, any event with a significant impact is now considered 'systemic'. An example is if loan defaults increase to at least 10% of total banking assets or if the cost of depository financial institutions rises to at least 2% of GDP (Carvalho, 2003; Gottschalk et al., 2021).

The justification for financial regulation can be explained from two main perspectives: the market failure approach and the Keynes-Schumpeter-Minsky approach. First, the market failure approach suggests that information on the solvency of financial institutions is a 'public good', and therefore, the government needs to ensure its provision, requiring financial institutions to comply with information disclosure. According to Stiglitz (1993), financial markets are particularly prone to outcomes that are sub-optimal due to asymmetric information. Therefore, the government is in a position to minimize the likelihood of insolvency of financial institutions by monitoring and demanding the transparency of these institutions. Aside from monitoring and requiring transparency, the government can impose more efficient risk management by banks, thus limiting their opportunistic behaviour. With respect to the Keynes-Schumpeter-Minsky approach, the main argument is that though there might be the presence of market failures, those may not be the most critical issue to focus on. The thinking here is that public intervention in the financial market is considered a rule and not an exception. The notion of efficient allocation, used to address the issue of market failure, is regarded as inadequate in addressing the problem of development finance and financial fragility. The Keynes-Schumpeter-Minsky approach suggests that government intervention in the financial market is critical, since there is a recognition of the structural problems of financial markets—and not only 'failures'. In summary, the objectives of government's intervention include: (i) containing systemic risk; (ii) acting in a counter-cyclical manner; and (iii) fostering growth and development (Gottschalk et al., 2021).

The objective to contain systemic risk requires prudential regulation of banks, though bank regulation does not automatically and completely address the systemic risk. This is because of the means of connecting financial institutions to other players in the financial system. The objective to act in a counter-cyclical fashion is in line with the traditional defence of Keynesian intervention that needs to be followed during crises by regulation, and not through central banks' monetary policies and governments' fiscal policies only. In terms of the objective to foster growth and development, this involves incentivizing banks to be able to provide long-term finance for development projects. In this regard, they can establish public financial institutions (or promote capital market development), considering that the financial markets do not naturally provide long-term finance because of the high-risk involved. Development finance also entails supporting projects that minimize inequalities and that promote social inclusion, innovation and sustainable development. This suggests that NDBs are regarded as the key financial institutions to achieve such developmental objectives and are fashioned to contribute to reducing financial system fragility.

It might appear as the first and third objectives of the Keynes-Schumpeter-Minsky approach conflict. This is due to the fact that the objective to contain systemic risk (prudential regulation) applies generally to both commercial banks and NDBs, therefore, potentially restricting

NDBs from performing their counter-cyclical role as expected. It is, however, argued in practice that adopting financial regulation for NDBs may be useful in protecting them from political intervention. Therefore, the issue is not just excluding them from the framework of financial regulation, considering that the third objective may be helpful to them to focus more on their core mandates. Instead, it should be recognized that NDBs are distinct and as such may need different regulatory arrangement (Gottschalk et al., 2021).

NDBs are not involved in the types of activities nor do they create the types of risks that Basel III is focused on addressing. It stands to reason that the unselective adoption of Basel III may have adverse effects on NDBs, particularly, the small ones, owing to the enhanced capital quality and new quantitative requirements. Actually, through the wide-ranging measures of Basel III, it can substantially impact on NDBs and the functions they usually perform, and these include: (a) providing large-scale and long-term lending; (b) offering counter-cyclical lending; (c) financing complex infrastructure projects; (d) supporting innovation; and (e) providing climate finance, all in their bid to fulfil their mandates. It is important to note that NDBs can promote projects and activities that take into consideration all these functions at the same time and that include substantial risks. They provide long-term financing mostly geared to large-scale infrastructure projects that require significant amounts of frontloaded finance. NDBs are active in project finance to support the financing of infrastructure and large projects (Gottschalk et al., 2021).

13.3 The Evolution of the Basel Agreements

The Basel framework is made up of the complete set of standards of the Basel Committee on Banking Supervision (BCBS), which is the body with the primary responsibility of setting global standards for the prudential regulation of banks. These standards have been agreed upon by members of the BCBS to ensure their full implementation and application to the internationally active banks in their jurisdictions. The first Basel Capital Accord (Basel I) was launched in 1988 with a focus on credit risk, which involved establishing a minimum level of owned capital proportional to the bank's exposure to credit risks (Sobreira, 2008). Subsequently, in 1996, the capital accord was amended to incorporate market risks. The second Basel agreement (Basel II) was released in 2004 (which was reviewed in 2005 and 2006), by including operational risk in the minimum capital requirement. Basel II, therefore, was aimed at fashioning financial market operations in a manner that banks hope to achieve based on their interests, in order to minimize their exposure to credit, market and operational risks. The BIS in 2009 introduced an amendment with the focus on trade portfolio improvements and how to treat market risk. Eventually, Basel III was launched in December 2010 and reviewed in January 2011. BIS came out with rules for addressing short-term liquidity risk (one month) in January 2013, and also for dealing with long-term liquidity requirements (one year) in 2014, apart from requirements for bank exposure to central counterparties (de Castro, 2018).

We now discuss how the Basel I, Basel II and Basel III have evolved over time.

13.3.1 Basel I Regulatory Framework

Members or countries of the BCBS saw the need to develop a common banking capitalization standard to ensure stability and proper supervision of banking activities. This move was in reaction to the banking crisis of the early 1980s, coupled with the fact that banks with internationally active branches were able to circumvent regulatory authorities by moving their operations to other countries with less stringent regulations (Brownbridge, 2014; Goodhart, 2011). The Basel Capital Accord (Basel I), which was established in 1988, was in response to the idea that the main threat to banking stability was from credit risks. The key objective of Basel I was to ensure international convergence of regulations which govern the capital adequacy of international banks by providing clear guidelines to banks to hold adequate capital reserves in order to manage risks. In pursuing this objective, two other objectives became apparent from this regulatory framework:

- to strengthen the soundness and stability of the international banking system,
- to reduce existing sources of competitive inequality among international banks (Balthazar, 2006; BIS, 1988; Brownbridge, 2014).

It is imperative to note, however, that the Basel I regulatory framework was not meant for protecting banks from external risks caused by fluctuations in exchange rates or interest rates or to protect banks from other macroeconomic shocks. The focus was to help banks to hold adequate capital reserves to manage their risks (Toniolo & Clement, 2005). The Basel I regulatory framework was developed to suit member countries, which are all considered as developed economies. It was not considered optimal for developing or emerging economies with their unique risks and regulatory challenges (Balthazar, 2006; Demirgüç-Kunt & Detragiache, 2011).

The Basel I regulatory framework was made up of four pillars and these include: (i) Pillar 1—minimum capital requirements, (ii) Pillar 2—risk weighting, (iii) Pillar 3—a target standard ratio and (iv) Pillar 4—transitional and implementation agreements (BIS, 1997).

Pillar 1 (minimum capital requirements) prescribed the sources of capital that banks need to include in their capital reserves and the amount of each source of capital that a bank would have to hold. These sources of capital were broken into Tier 1 and Tier 2. The Tier 1 capital, also known as core capital, included capital arising from equity capital (issued and fully paid-up ordinary shares/common shares and non-cumulative perpetual preference shares) and published reserves from post-tax retained earnings (disclosed reserves) made upheld by banks. The Tier 2 capital or supplementary capital included different sources of capital, including subordinated debt held, reserves held to take care of potential loan losses, hybrid debt or equity holdings and potential gains from the sale of assets in future (revaluation reserves) (Demirgüç-Kunt & Detragiache, 2011; Goodhart, 2011).

Pillar 2 (risk weighting) regulated the risk weighting of a bank's asset book or off-balance-sheet exposure. The risk weighting system is the assets classification system to ascertain the minimum capital that banks need to have as a reserve to minimize the risk or protect them against the risk of insolvency. Thus, the total value of all bank assets and off-balance-sheet exposures are weighted according to their particular level of risk (Brownbridge, 2014; Girling, 2014; Goodhart, 2011). Bank assets that have low risk were counted lower than their real value and consequently, required less capital holding. Bank assets with high-risk were counted at 100% of their real value and needed higher capital holding. The risk weighting system was consequently applied in order that assets weighted at 100% would require the maximum capital requirement of 8% of the real value of the asset, whereas assets weighted at 50% would require a capital ratio of 8% of 50% of the real value of the asset (Brownbridge, 2014; Girling, 2014).

Pillar 3 (a target standard ratio) defined the minimum requirements to protect banks from credit risk and combined the first and second pillars. Cognizant of previous consultations and preliminary testing of the Basel I regulatory framework, the BCBS decided that the minimum standards set needs to provide a reasonable time for international banks to comply (Wandhöfer, 2014). In addition, there was an agreement for this standard to be set to achieve capital ratios for all internationally active banks in a gradual, sound and consistent manner. Hence, the BCBS confirmed that the target standard ratio of capital to risk-weighted assets should be 8% (of which the core capital element would be at least 4%).

Pillar 4 (transitional and implementation agreements) defined the stages at which each member country's central bank was requested to develop strategies to ascertain whether the Basel regulatory framework's requirements on supervision and control were being met (Van Roy, 2005). The 42 BCBS member countries successfully implemented the framework during the four-year period that was planned, with the exception of Japan that was suffering from a financial recession in the late 1980s and was granted an additional four years to complete implementation. In 1996, all BCBS member countries had successfully adhered to the Basel I regulatory framework (Van Roy, 2005). The Basel I regulatory framework was internationally argued and accepted as a safety and soundness standard to protect international and local banks from insolvency. However, regulators soon questioned whether the Basel I regulatory framework adequately captured the risks posed by the increasingly complex and volatile financial markets that were frequently encountered by the banking system. Furthermore, it became clear that banks could manipulate the financial system by moving assets off their balance sheets and using their portfolios to minimize their required capital, while they were not necessarily minimizing their actual risk exposure (Benink & Wihlborg, 2002; Girling, 2014).

In spite of the benefits of the Basel I framework, it was criticized on these grounds: no recognition of diversification benefits, incomplete coverage of risk sources, no incentives for improved overall risk measurement and management, and that a 'one-size-fits-all' approach was an unrealistic and arbitrary measure.

13.3.2 Basel II Regulatory Framework

Responding to the criticisms of the Basel I regulatory framework, the BCBS in 1999 came up with a new, very comprehensive capital adequacy framework. This new (Basel II) framework was titled: A Revised Framework on International Convergence of Capital Measurement and Capital Standards. The Basel II regulatory framework maintained the 'pillar' framework of the Basel I regulatory framework. However, each one of the pillars was significantly extended to deal with new approaches to credit risk; adjusting to the securitization of bank assets; providing for the management of market risk, operational risk and interest rate risk; and incorporating market-based surveillance and regulation (Balin, 2008; Brownbridge, 2014). Basel II basically consisted of three pillars: (i) minimum capital requirements; (ii) a supervisory review process; and (iii) market discipline and all these are still in the Basel III.

Pillar 1 (minimum capital requirement) proved to be the most significant expansion since the Basel I regulatory framework. The Basel II regulatory framework established a more sensitive measurement of the risk-weighted assets of a bank and attempted to eradicate the inadequacies in the first framework that allowed banks to assume additional risk, while cosmetically easing the minimum capital adequacy requirements. The first mandate of this new framework was to expand the scope of regulation in order to include assets of the holding companies of internationally active banks. The objective of this expansion was to eliminate the risk of banks concealing these assets from their financial statements by transferring them to their subsidiaries. This would enable banks to incorporate the financial well-being of the entire banking institution when computing the capital requirements for the subsidiary banks (Balin, 2008; KPMG, 2012). Pillar 1, in addition, contained the procedures for determining the minimum capital requirements for credit, market and operational risks, which were not included in the Basel I regulatory framework (BIS, 2006; Brownbridge, 2014).

Pillar 2 (Supervisory review process) focused on outlining key principles for supervisors on reviewing banks' adherence to the Basel II regulatory framework. Also, it provided guidance on risk management practices and promoted supervisory transparency and accountability with respect to banking risks. It showed how regulators were required to enforce soundness standards and provided a mechanism for additional capital requirements in covering any material risks that had not been appropriately captured in Pillar 1 (Brownbridge, 2014; Girling, 2014).

Pillar 3 (Market discipline) provided banks with a means of disclosing risk management and capital computation practices to the general public. The objective of Pillar 3 was to increase the transparency of risk management practices in the sector and allowed investors and shareholders a better understanding of banks' inner risk management practices. Subsequently, banks were encouraged to disclose accurate, and transparent information with respect to their capital position, and therefore empower shareholders to enforce strict discipline in banks' risk-taking and methods of reserve capital holding (Balin, 2008; Brownbridge, 2014; Girling, 2014).

The launch of the Basel II framework came with some criticisms related to: its pro-cyclicality; its hampering of access to credit for firms with low ratings, including small businesses; its bias against long-term lending; its bias against smaller banks, since they are probably less capable of developing internal models for saving capital; the difficulty in measuring operational risk; its indiscriminate use of Value at Risk (VaR); the absence of liquidity risk management enforcement, etc. Particularly, Basel II was accused of focusing entirely on microprudential issues, ignoring the macroprudential view. Apart from that, the Basel Accords were applicable to only banks, thus making room for regulatory arbitrage (de Catsrol, 2018). The Basel II also came under criticism in that the prescriptions were said to be inappropriate for developing economies and the attempts to comply created several challenges for developing economies (Balin, 2008). Many of the challenges confronting developing economies in 1999 when Basel II was launched continue to pose challenges to these economies.

13.3.3 Basel III Regulatory Framework

The Basel III regulatory framework adopts a similar arrangement as the Basel II regulatory framework. However, this has been modified to increase the effectiveness and efficiency in the manner that allow banks manage the various risks they are exposed to. The Basel III regulatory framework imposes stricter regulations on the minimum capital and liquidity requirements for banks and addresses acceptable levels of leverage (BIS, 2011).

The first pillar (enlarged minimum capital and liquidity requirements) of the Basel III regulatory framework regulates banks' minimum capital requirements, which the regulatory authorities need to monitor. With the new regulatory framework, the additional focus on increased capital control measures is pertinent. The relevant changes in the minimum capital requirements with respect to the Basel III regulatory framework include the following:

- The common equity increases from 2% to 4.5% of the risk-weighted assets of banks.
- The total amount of Tier 1 capital increases from 4 to 6% of banks' risk-weighted assets.
- The total amount of Tier 1 plus Tier 2 capital is set at 8% of banks' risk-weighted assets (BIS, 2011; Hannoun, 2010).

Pillar 2 (supervisory review) of the Basel III regulatory framework is in line with the design of Pillar 2 in the Basel II regulatory framework, albeit with enhanced requirements with respect to the supervisory review of enterprise risk management (ERM) and capital planning. The objective of Pillar 2 of Basel III regulatory framework is to enhance banks' ability to manage their operations and to enhance their coverage of internal capital assessments (BIS, 2011). The main component in this pillar is the internal capital adequacy assessment process (ICAAP). This type of supervisory process is essential for banks in safeguarding against risk exposure similar to the harm caused during the 2007/2008 global financial crises. Pillar 2 further seeks to promote sound ERM. Effective ERM is achievable by having a sound-board and senior management with the ultimate responsibility for risk management. Thus, it is critical for the board and senior management to be conversant with the bank's operations and have the requisite qualifications and experience to promote responsible, accurate decision-making (BIS, 2009, 2011).

The third pillar (market discipline) of the Basel III regulatory framework is also in tandem with the requirements of the Basel II regulatory framework. Banks are obliged to provide accurate and thorough information to the market participants regarding their risk exposures and risk measurement procedures. Additionally, banks are encouraged to ensure accurate, honest and transparent disclosure of information regarding their capital position to all their shareholders and the general public (BIS, 2011; Brownbridge, 2014; Girling, 2014).

13.3.4 Proportionality in Financial Regulation and Supervision

Proportionality in financial regulation and supervision ensures that rules and supervision practices are applied in line with banks' systemic importance and risk profile, and are suitable for the characteristics of a financial system. Generally, financial systems are heterogeneous and thus exhibit different characteristics in terms of bank size, extent of internationalization, level of sophistication and predominance of domestically owned (including government-owned) versus foreign-owned banks. Proportionality is a key principle in the application of the Basel rules, especially for jurisdictions with banks that are not really interactively active of G-SIBs. The principle of proportionality indicates that jurisdictions are allowed to implement the Basel requirements in a proportionate approach. The Basel framework sets minimum requirements for internationally active banks in member countries and also permits for a degree of proportionality by providing options of implementing simpler standardized approaches. Though the simpler standardized approaches in the Basel framework may also be appropriate for banks that are not internationally active, in certain situations, regulation might require even further adaptation Apart from banks, supervisory authorities also vary across jurisdictions. For instance, supervisory authorities tend to have different legal powers, organizational arrangements, availability of resources and levels of independence. These differences in characteristics are important in influencing the design and implementation of proportionate regulation and supervision (BIS, 2022).

13.4 National Development Banks and the Basel Regulatory Framework

NDBs may be classified into four possible categories with respect to banking standards: (i) self-regulation, meaning the NDBs are not under the supervision of central banks or other banks regulatory authority; (ii) full compliance with Basel standards; (iii) compliance with Basel standards, but with some exemptions; and (iv) specialized regulatory framework for NDBs (see Torres Filho & Xu, 2020).

Generally, NDBs are subject to specific national regulation and may or may not be under the supervision of the central bank. Thus, when Basel I was launched, many NDBs such as KfW in Germany, JBIC in Japan and Kore-Exim were not covered by the framework. But, BNDES in Brazil was under the Basel regulations, immediately the framework was introduced in the country in 1994. However, NDBs' adhesion to Basel II was much higher, whether it was binding or voluntary. The KfW, the China Development Bank, the Korean Development Bank and the Latin American institutions voluntarily adopted the Basel II framework (de Castro, 2018; Zendron & Sobreira, 2007). A number of reasons have been advanced for this development (see de Castro, 2018).

In the first place, Basel prudential regulation was no longer addressing only the problem associated with systemic risk but concentrated more directly on financial institutions' individual risks. This approach is based on the reason that regularly preventing individual risks would be useful in eliminating the causes of systemic risk. Such risk management practices were applicable to other organizations, including development banks. For instance, in the Brazilian case, when the Basel regulation was imposed, the explanation was the size of banks and the relevance of NDBs in the economy. This means the country could be exposed to huge systemic risk, given the large size of banking assets and the important role of NDBs in the economy.

Another reason for adhering to Basel II was the increase in the risks development banks were assuming, which required proper management in order to ensure financial sustainability. The potential risks of development banks increased with respect to credit, market and operational risks in connection with long-term projects. In addition, the financial deregulation process witnessed in the 1990s opened opportunities for raising external funds. However, this also increased the risk of mismatches on currencies and terms, and on interest rates among financial institutions and reduced financial returns. Additionally, share acquisition increased the risk of price fluctuations in development banks' balances. For instance, when a development bank supports a firm it has already given loans to, by acquiring shares, the development bank assumes double exposure on behalf of the firm. Again, the challenges of development banks' concentration on certain areas such as innovation funding, MSMEs and large-scale projects in new sectors of the economy have heightened credit and legal risks.

The third reason for development banks' adherence to the Basel regulatory framework is the fact that in the context of financial globalization, not only is better risk management necessary, but there is also increased importance in certifying this management. Basel II, in many ways, was seen as a 'quality seal' that was used to attract market resources. It explains why a number of development banks have opted to comply with the Basel II framework, even in countries where it is not mandatory to observe these rules. It is reported that adherence to Basel II has resulted in some improvements in risk management (de Castro, 2018). Some of the benefits have been the establishment of integrated risk management systems and improvements in risk governance.

Lastly, the Basel II framework was a somewhat flexible framework that allowed for the use of internal models. Therefore, it was difficult to explain to the market the rationale for development banks not subscribing to the framework. Development banks identified potential opportunities in saving regulatory capital by developing internal models, specifically, credit risk models, considering the history of low default rates and high recovery rates (low Loss Given Default). This is due to the presence of good-quality guarantees (normally sovereign or banking). Adhering to Basel II voluntarily discloses an important issue. Development banks did not consider the Basel regulatory framework as a limitation to exercising their mandate, the reason being that they ensured good practice as a number of their measures indicate. Though development banks are active in the higher-risk credit segment, they rely on risk management instruments that are not accessible by the market. That means, in the presence of more risks, there are also available tools in managing them (de Castro, 2018).

13.4.1 Should National Development Banks Be Subject to Basel III?

This section examines on how the Basel III regulatory framework may affect NDBs. The section does not focus on Basel III standards that may not be relevant to NDBs, including those that arise from the trading books of banks or the use of financial derivatives.

13.4.1.1 Solvency and Liquidity Problems

Capital Requirements

Basel III required banks to maintain higher minimum capital requirements in order to minimize insolvency risk in times of stress. Basel II required minimum capital requirements at 8% of risk-weighted assets, but under Basel III, an additional requirement of 2.5% of risk-weighted assets has been included as capital conservation buffers, to cushion banks against financial distress. Any time there is capital drawn down, banks are required to rebuild capital buffers by lowering the discretionary distribution of earnings. Counter-cyclical capital buffers have been created under Basel III. It is also a requirement for large banks such as global systemically important banks (G-SIBs) and domestic systemically important banks (D-SIBs) to build additional capital buffers.[1] Such large banks can create systemic risk given their size and extent of interconnectedness with other financial institutions. Also, with respect to Basel III, capital needs to be of higher quality, emphasizing Common Equity Tier 1 capital. Lastly, a 3% leverage ratio has been adopted under Basel III (i.e. a minimum level of capital against unweighted assets of banks). This represents a non-risk backstop measure to minimize banks' excessive leverage and avoid the problem that happened during the financial crisis of 2007/2008, when capital was insufficient and also of low quality (Gottschalk et al., 2021).

In the case of NDBs that subscribe to Basel III regulation, this may also excessively affect credit availability to exposures such as large and long-term projects that need more capital. With the national regulator's permission, NDBs may attempt to mitigate their exposure by using internal risk assessment models. Such models allow banks in assigning their risk weights to their asset portfolio, therefore, helping them to save capital. However, to prevent banks from issuing small amount of capital owing to the risk assessment models they use, the Basel Committee has come up with measures that limit banks from saving capital in such manner. These measures include the leverage ratio, prohibition of the use of internal models for specific exposures and the adoption of an output floor. The essence of the output floor is to make sure banks that use internal models maintain a minimum of 72.5% of capital in relation to what they would, assuming they adopted the standardized approach to determining capital. These measures are necessary in preventing major banks from gambling with the system. Nonetheless, they removed the advantage of NDBs using their own likelihood of default (PD), which is more appropriate for their own portfolio peculiarities, and is mostly

[1] D-SIBs are identified as such by national jurisdictions while G-SIBs are so by the Financial Stability Board (FSB) in consultation with the Basel Committee on Banking Supervision (BCBS, 2012; BIS, 2018a).

lower than the market because of the long-term lending relationship with their clients. The entire system also became predisposed to pro-cyclical behaviour of market ratings (Gottschalk et al., 2021).

Liquidity and Funding Requirements

Liquidity and funding requirements include the Liquidity Coverage Ratio (LCR) and the Net Stable Funding Ratio (NSFR). The essence of the LCR is for banks to maintain sufficient high-quality liquid assets to be able to cover their net cash outflows over a 30-day time period in a stress scenario. The aim is to prevent banks from having serious liquidity difficulties as the world witnessed during the global financial crisis. The purpose of the NSFR is for banks to maintain sufficient funding levels with maturities matching the maturities of their on-balance sheet assets and off-balance sheet commitments, over a one-year time period. This helps to avoid maturity mismatches. Introducing internal models for credit risk under Basel II and Basel III has features requiring higher levels of capital for longer-term lending (Gottschalk et al., 2021).

The key issue here is the fact that liquidity and funding requirements and for that matter LCR and the NSFR may further restrain the provision of long-term credit. However, in the case of NDBs, their liability structure may explain the extent to which these ratios affect them. NDBs are less bound by liquidity and funding requirements, since they are mainly non-depository financial institutions that depend largely on funding sources, such as direct budget transfers from the government, borrowing from other financial institutions, raising capital from international capital markets, issuing debt securities in domestic financial markets and acquiring official development assistance.

13.4.1.2 Systemic Risks

The Large Exposures Framework

The Basel framework has already addressed the large exposure risk and clarified definition and measurement, setting upper limits. The threshold set under Basel III is for the single exposures of banks not to exceed 25% of Tier 1 capital. An exposure, from one G-SIB to another G-SIB, is set at the upper limit of 15%. A single large exposure is the total of exposures to inter-connected counterparties, suggesting that one counterparty's failure may result in the other counterparties failing. Inter-connected counterparties may be in the form of ownership and economic relations. National supervisory bodies tend to adopt some kind of limits on large exposure, and whenever there are breaches of these limits, they advise on corrective actions or ask for additional capital injection (BCBS, 2019).

With respect to NDBs, this regulation restricts their ability to fund large projects, such as industrial projects and infrastructure. The exposure limits also restrict NDBs from financing projects that have development impact. This new regulation may be unsuitable for smaller NDBs. The degree to which this regulation affects a bank is dependent on how much the regulator further tightens regulation in line with the new Basel standard. A few exposures are important to internationally active NDBs as well as NDBs operating in the domestic economy since, they are exempted from the single large exposure regulation. These include exposures to sovereign states, their central banks, as well as public sector entities (BCBS, 2014; BIS, 2018b). The point is that NDBs' large exposures to public entities or, particularly to single large projects, needs to have government guarantees provided such exposures are in the national interest. An example could be carrying out a large energy power project required to address the setbacks to economic growth.

The large exposure regulation deals with one type of concentration risk, and the other types including those of sectoral and geographical nature, are addressed in the next paragraph.

Other Concentration Risks

Pillar II of the Basel framework deals with concentration risk and is based on principles for guiding supervisors, unlike Pillar I, which is more prescriptive. This qualitative-based approach provides flexibility for countries in deciding on what strategies and procedures to follow in achieving the objectives of Pillar II (BCBS, 2019). Therefore, the effects of Basel III on NDBs are dependent on how specific countries treat concentration risks. With regard to the mandates of NDBs, they have the tendency to hold concentrated portfolios in growth-enhancing sectors and important locations. National regulators need to consider this issue in deciding to target such risks so that these banks do not experience major restrictions in performing their developmental roles (Gottschalk et al., 2021).

13.4.1.3 The Pro-Cyclical Nature of Bank Credit

Counter-Cyclical Lending

Basel recognizes the pro-cyclical nature of bank credit. In order to address this, the Basel Committee initiated very rigorous stress tests to assist in limiting excessive risk-taking in the upside of the cycle, and, particularly, capital buffers that need to range between 0 and 2.5% of risk-weighted assets. Such buffers are required to increase in good periods and decrease during economic slowdowns (BCBS, 2011). Though these counter-cyclical buffers are relevant to traditional banks, in the case of NDBs their importance may be questionable since NDB behaviour regarding cyclical lending is less obvious. If NDBs' credit extension is mostly long-term in nature, provision of loans tends to be relatively fixed over the business cycle, in relation to other banks. During an economic downturn, such buffers may be useful, as NDBs tend to focus on scaling up credit to assist in fighting the recession and unemployment. However, in times of economic expansion, they are not likely scale down lending or credit (Gottschalk et al., 2021).

13.4.1.4 Market and Operational Risks, and Risks Associated with Innovation

Market Risks

Basel deals with market risks under Pillar I, which focus on the risks in trading books. However, the types of market risks NDBs are mostly confronted with include interest rate and currency risks in their banking books. In terms of interest rate risks in the banking books, these are treated under Pillar II of the Basel framework. Whenever a bank's interest rate risks in the banking books exposure show excessive risk, this may require additional regulatory capital (BCBS, 2016). With respect to currency risks, these are addressed under Pillar I of the Basel framework, including trading and banking book exposures. Currency risk is important for NDBs that do external borrowing in foreign currency that may cause a mismatch in the currency if they provide loans in local currency in the domestic economy. This may require a very expensive hedge to be undertaken, given the long-term nature of the credit provided. Also, a number of internationally active NDBs, which serve as the financial arms of the development agencies of their respective countries, may have their operations involving loans in currencies different from their funding. Moreover, some NDBs also operate internationally by lending in foreign currency in supporting national corporates' expansion and other interests abroad (Gottschalk et al., 2021).

Operational Risks

Using internal models for operational risk under Basel III (the advanced measurement approach [AMA]) has been eliminated. The Basel

Committee acknowledges the inherent complications with the AMA and the lack of comparability of methodologies among banks. NDBs, which planned to use such models to make savings in capital, will be unable to do so now, even though they are able to use their information to fulfil new information requirements under Pillar III. It is difficult to measure operational risks as it may result in double counting with respect to other types of risks, like credit and market risks. More so, NDBs mostly have exposure to large, complex projects that may comprise legal risks, incorporated in the operational risk concept and this can be somewhat serious, if it materializes. Project finance, a financing model mostly used by NDBs in large, complex projects, and which Basel already penalizes owing to various risks, has extra regulatory/legal risks to deal with. Generally, government agencies may provide guarantees but these are meant to minimize losses associated with credit risk, but not legal and regulatory risks. The regulatory framework for NDBs may have to focus more attention in this area (Gottschalk et al., 2021).

Risks Associated with Innovation and Climate Finance

NDBs are committed to supporting innovation and this is done with the use of various instruments and engagement in different practices. Two Basel III standards in this regard are discussed here. These are those that affect equity finance (i.e. an instrument used by NDBs in supporting innovation) and climate finance (that mostly involves backing untested clean technologies). Equity exposures (shares) classified in the trading book need to be submitted to capital requirements for market risk, while those where there is no plan to regularly negotiate them (classified in the banking book) need to be submitted to capital requirements for credit risk. The rationale is that if the share price falls significantly, it is like a default event, without guarantees in offsetting the losses. In term of equity exposures that are not held in the trading book, investments are risk-weighted at 100% in the standardized approach for credit risk. In the Internal Ratings-Based (IRB) framework, depending on the method, the weights may range between a minimum of 100% and a maximum of 1250%. These risk weights tend to penalize NDBs that have a huge share of equities in their total asset portfolio. In particular, the very high-risk weights disincentivize NDBs' exposures to blue-sky projects that may be categorized as speculative unlisted equity. In addition, by classifying shares in the banking book, their counterparty is essentially done on net equity. Therefore, total capital can significantly decrease or increase in line with movements in the market, and the Basel Capital ratio may be seriously affected, at times without any significant credit event (Gottschalk et al., 2021).

With respect to climate finance, NDBs play an important role in climate finance to support countries to move to a low- or neutral-carbon growth model. NDBs engagement in climate finance can help in reducing their risks by shifting their portfolios away from high-emission sectors. Supervisory institutions are concerned about the vulnerability of banks to such sectors and are now including climate-related risks in their supervisory function. Banks are required to report their risk assessment and management practices in this respect. Supervisory institutions' climate risk assessment, according to BCBS (2019), does not yet require additional capital from banks. More work is required on this given the fact that as NDBs increase their engagement in low-carbon growth projects, they may be penalized once supervisors consider such projects as high-risk, given that they mostly include new (and therefore difficult to assess) green technologies. This is certainly a challenge confronting all banks, although promoting sustainable investment happens to form part of the policy mandates of a number of NDBs. Moreover, NDBs may feel compelled to develop new practices of lending and instruments to support low-carbon growth, which supervisory institutions may consider peculiar and therefore demand additional capital for. In practice, it seems difficult to identify which standards are more relevant or binding for NDBs. This may be dependent on the NDB under consideration, since NDBs are generally quite distinct from each other (Gottschalk et al., 2021). The role of NDBs in climate finance was discussed in greater detail in Chapter 8.

13.5 Concluding Remarks

The chapter has discussed the financial regulation of NDBs. It has examined the justification or rationale for regulating financial institutions, how NDBs are different from other banks, the evolution of Basel agreements, and whether NDBs need to be subjected to the Basel III regulatory framework. The chapter has explained that the justification for financial regulations is based on two main perspectives. These are the market failure approach and the Keynes-Schumpeter-Minsky approach. While the market failure argument supports the justification for regulating banks that mobilize deposits from the public, in the Keynes-Schumpeter-Minsky approach, the rationale for financial regulation is to prevent systemic risk.

The reckless behaviour of NDBs through excessive borrowing and poor risk management has the tendency to adversely impact on a governments' fiscal position, creating inflationary risk, risk of a credit crunch, loss of investment, a dampening of growth and increasing unemployment. The impact that the activities of NDBs can have on the economy may justify the need to bring them under the regulation and supervision of monetary authorities. The issue then becomes, should NDBs be regulated in the same manner as the prudential regulation that is applied to other banks?

NDBs exhibit certain features that distinguish them from other banks. Apart from the objective of making profit, NDBs have a dual mandate of pursuing development outcomes and ensuring sustainability. Commercial banks are mainly interested in maximizing profit. While NDBs generally have state support and therefore have access to secure long-term funding, commercial banks rely mostly on deposits. NDBs have gained expertise in large, complex projects and in risk assessment and monitoring that commercial banks are not involved in. Also, NDBs serve as the financing arm of the government in pursuing strategic developmental objectives and driving sustainable development. They are counter-cyclical in nature and seek to protect the national economy from shocks and downturns.

Basel I, which was launched in 1998, focused on credit risk, which involved establishing a minimum level of owned capital proportional to banks' exposure to credit risks. Later in 1996, market risk was included. Basel II, which was launched in 2001, included operational risk in the minimum capital requirement. Basel II aimed at fashioning financial market operations in a manner that banks pursue based on their own initiative and interest in order to minimize their exposure to credit, market and operational risks. The BIS in 2009 introduced an amendment with a focus on trade portfolio improvements and how to treat market risk. Basel II aimed at correcting many of the problems associated with Basel I, many of which were in relation to development finance. Ultimately, Basel III was launched in December 2010 and reviewed in January 2011. Considering the differences in the financial systems across jurisdictions, the implementation of the Basel requirements needs to be done in a proportionate approach.

Generally, NDBs are subject to specific national regulation and may or may not be under the supervision of the central bank. Thus, when Basel I was launched, many NDBs were not covered by the framework. However, NDBs' adoption of Basel II was much higher, whether it was binding or voluntary. Some NDBs voluntarily adopted the Basel II framework and a number of reasons have been advanced for this development. In terms of whether NDBs should be subjected to the Basel III framework, the issue is that the wholesale adoption of Basel III may have an adverse impact on NDBs, especially, the small ones, owing to the enhanced capital quality and new quantitative requirements. Basel III standards that are relevant to NDBs include the higher capital requirements for nationally active banks, increased requirements of core capital and Tier 1, treatment of long-term liquidity risk, large exposures framework, greater control over concentration risk, counter-cyclical lending, market risk, particularly, interest rate and currency risks, operational risks and then risks associated with innovation and climate finance.

References

Abor, J. Y. (2018). *Financial markets and institutions: A frontier market perspective* (2nd ed.). Digibooks.

Abugre, J., Misati, R., Salami, I., & Antwi, S. (2022). *Recent developments in banking regulation and supervision in Africa*. In J. Y. Abor & C. K. D. Adjasi (Eds.), *The economics of banking and finance in Africa: Developments in Africa's financial systems*. Palgrave Macmillan.

Balin, B. J. (2008). *Basel I, Basel II, and emerging markets: A nontechnical analysis*. SSRN 1477712.

Balthazar, L. (2006). *From Basel 1 to Basel 3: The integration of state-of-the-art risk modeling in banking regulation*. Palgrave Macmillan.

BCBS. (2011, June). *Basel III; A global regulatory framework for more resilient banks and banking systems. Basel Committee on Banking Supervision*. Bank for International Settlements. Revised version. ISBN 92-9131-859-0.

BCBS. (2012, October). *A framework for dealing with domestic systemically important banks. Basel Committee on Banking Supervision*. Bank for International Settlements. ISBN 92-9131-141-3.

BCBS. (2014, April). *Standards. Supervisory framework for measuring and controlling large exposures*. Basel Committee on Banking Supervision. Bank for International Settlements. ISBN 978-92-9197-987-5.

BCBS. (2016, April). *Standards. Interest rate risk in the banking book*. Basel Committee on Banking Supervision. Bank for International Settlements.

BCBS. (2019, June). *Overview of pillar 2 supervisory review practices and approaches*. Basel Committee on Banking Supervision Discussion Paper. Bank for International Settlements. ISBN 978-92-9259-279-0.

Benink, H., & Wihlborg, C. (2002). The new Basel Capital Accord: Making it effective with stronger market discipline. *European Financial Management, 8*(1), 103–115.

BIS. (1988). *International convergence of capital measurements and capital standards*. Bank of International Settlements.
BIS. (1997). *Core principles for effective banking supervision*. Bank for International Settlements.
BIS. (2006). *Basel II: International convergence of capital measurement and capital standards: A revised framework*. Comprehensive Version. Bank for International Settlements.
BIS. (2009). *Basel Committee on Banking Supervision: Enhancements to the Basel II framework*. Bank for International Settlements.
BIS. (2011). *Basel III: A global regulatory framework for more resilient banks and banking systems*. Bank for International Settlements.
BIS. (2018a). *The G-SIB framework: Executive Summary*. FSI, Bank for International Settlements. https://www.bis.org/fsi/fsisummaries/g-sib_framework.htm
BIS. (2018b). *The treatment of large exposures in the basel capital standards – Executive summary*. FSI. Bank for International Settlements. https://www.bis.org/fsi/fsisummaries/largeexpos
BIS. (2022). *High-level considerations on proportionality*. Bank for International Settlements.
Brownbridge, M. (2014). How relevant are the Basel capital reforms for sub-Saharan Africa? *Journal of Risk Management in Financial Institutions, 8*(2), 153–162.
Carvalho F. C. (2003). Inovação Financeira e Regulação Prudencial: da Regulação da Liquidez aos Acordos da Basileia. *UFRJ: Textopara Discussão*. Rio de Janeiro.
de Castro, L. B. (2018). Financial regulation and risk management in development banks. In S. Griffith-Jones & J. A. Ocampo (Eds.), *The future of national development banks*. Oxford University Press.
Demirgüç-Kunt, A., & Detragiache, E. (2011). Basel core principles and bank soundness: Does compliance matter? *Journal of Financial Stability, 7*(4), 179–190.
Girling, P. X. (2014). *Operational risk management: A complete guide to a successful operational risk framework*. Wiley.
Goodhart, C. (2011). *The Basel Committee on Banking Supervision: A history of the early years 1974–1997*. Cambridge University Press. https://doi.org/10.1017/CBO9780511996238
Gottschalk, R., Castro, L. B., & Xu, J. (2021). Should national development banks be subject to Basel III? *Review of Political Economy*. https://doi.org/10.1080/09538259.2021.1977541
Hannoun, H. (2010). *The Basel III capital framework: A decisive breakthrough*. Speech at Seminar on Financial Regulatory Reform, Hong Kong. Bank for International Settlements. https://www.bis.org/speeches/sp101125a.pdf

King, P., & Tarbert, H. (2011, May). Basel III: An overview. *Banking and Financial Services Policy Report, 30*(5), 1–18.

KPMG. (2012). *Africa banking survey*. KPMG.

Mishkin, F. S. (2016). *The Economics of Money, Banking, and Financial Markets*, New York: Addison Wesley.

Nyantakyi, E. B., & Sy, M. (2015). The banking system in Africa: Main facts and challenges. *African Economic Brief, 6*(5), 1–16.

Quintyn, M., & Taylor, M. (2002). *Regulatory and supervisory independence and financial stability* (IMF Working Paper WP/02/46). International Monetary Fund. www.imf.org/en/Publications/WP/Issues/2016/12/30/regulatory-and-Supervisory-Independenceand-Financial-Stability-15679

Sobreira, R. (2008). Development banks, risk, and Basel II: Some assessments. *Cadernos, EBAPE.BR, 6*(4), 1–8.

Stiglitz, J. (1993). The role of the state in financial markets. *Proceedings of the World Bank Conference on development economics*. World Bank.

Toniolo, G., & Clement, P. (2005). *Central bank cooperation at the Bank for International Settlements, 1930–1973*. Cambridge University Press.

Torres Filho, E. T., & Xu, J. (2020, December). *Regulating national development banks: The historical experiences of the Brazilian Development Bank (BNDES) since 1952* (Ford Foundation Visiting Fellowship Working Paper). Ford Foundation and Peking University (Institute of New Structural Economics).

Van Roy, P. (2005). *The impact of the 1988 Basel Accord on banks' capital ratios and credit risk-taking: An international study*. SSRN 497264.

Wandhöfer, R. (2014). The journey from Basel I to Basel III: History and fundamentals explained. In R. Wandhöfer (Ed.), *Transaction banking and the impact of regulatory change* (pp. 87–158). Palgrave Macmillan.

Zendron, P., & Sobreira, R. (2007). *Implications of Basel II for development banks in Quem Controla o Sistema Financeiro?* Ibase.

PART V

Case Studies on National Development Banks in Africa

CHAPTER 14

Ghana's System of National Development Banks: The Case of Ghana Export-Import Bank

14.1 Introduction and Overview of Ghana's Banking Sector

Prior to achieving formal independence in 1957, Ghana had very few banks and between the early twentieth century and the fifties, foreigner-owned banks, particularly, Barclays Banks and the Bank of the British West Africa dominated the banking sector. The Ghana Commercial Bank was created in 1953, prior to Ghana's independence, to improve local farmers' and businesses' access to financing.

After the country gained its independence, the central bank became known for inordinate government intervention due to the fact that all of the banks that were formed between the late 1950s and the 1980s were either wholly or primarily controlled by the state. The growth of the economy and the construction of the country's social infrastructure were prioritized, and the central bank was selected as the vehicle through which the newly elected government would exemplify its sovereignty and independence and revitalize the economy. The country's primary focus was on economic development. The acute and protracted economic downturn, along with the government's strict control over the financial markets, had a catastrophic impact on the financial system, which resulted in a steepening of the financial markets and problems for banks (Brownbridge & Gockel, 1996). Consequently, as the economy expanded, the banking industry suffered because of the economic concerns that led to the change

© The Author(s), under exclusive license to Springer Nature Switzerland AG 2023

J. Yindenaba Abor, *The Changing Role of National Development Banks in Africa*, https://doi.org/10.1007/978-3-031-38639-8_14

in government in 1966. These issues were the driving force behind the shift. The nation continued to struggle economically until 1983, when it initiated the Economic Recovery Programme with the assistance of the World Bank and the International Monetary Fund (IMF) for resolving the nation's economic problems.

As a part of their Economic Recovery Programme (ERP), the government initiated the Financial Sector Adjustment Programmes in 1986. This was a significant step in reforming the country's Financial Sector (FINSAP). During the first stage of the programme, efforts were made, among other things, to resolve the governmental deficiencies that existed in the financial system. More specifically, efforts were made to completely overhaul unsettled banks, create prudential legislation and make it easier for private sector financial institutions to enter the financial markets. The second stage focused on the privatization of public sector banks and the growth of non-bank financial firms in order to address the gaps in the financial markets that are not covered by conventional banks. This was done in order to address the fact that conventional banks do not cover these gaps. Subsequently, there was continuous expansion in the number of banks. As of the year 2001, there were 17 banks operating in the country (five years after the ERP). The number increased to 26 banks by the end of 2010 (with half owned by Ghanaians). It further increased to 29 banks as of January 2013 (Quartey & Afful-Mensah, 2014) and subsequently to 34 banks.

The Banks and Specialized Deposit Taking Institutions Act 2016 (Act 930) enabled the Bank of Ghana to deal with sector aberrations more forcefully. Between August 2017 and January 2020, the Bank of Ghana embarked on a banking sector clean-up with the aim of strengthening Ghana's banking sector. The clean-up exercise witnessed a reduction in the number of banks from 34 to 23. The 23 were those that successfully complied with the GHS 400 million (US$86.96 million) minimum capitalization criteria (Abor, 2018; Bank of Ghana MPC Reports, 2018).

Ghana has also had a long history of development banking with the establishment of four main NDBs, including Bank for Housing and Construction, Ghana Cooperative Bank, National Investment Bank and Agricultural Development Bank. However, these banks have had limited success in delivering on their mandates due to hurdles such as the universal licences they hold and operate under, internal weaknesses, political interference, poor corporate governance and extensive non-performing loans. The Bank for Housing and Construction, and Ghana

Cooperative Bank were collapsed in 2000 due to mismanagement. The Ghana Export-Import Bank and the Development Bank Ghana (DBG) are two new NDBs that have emerged in Ghana's development finance landscape. The chapter provides a brief historical account of the Ghana Export-Import Bank, which has been in existence since 2016. The DBG was only established in 2020.

The rest of the chapter is structured as follows: Sect. 14.2 provides an overview of Ghana's development finance landscape. Section 14.3 discusses the Ghana Export-Import (EXIM) Bank by briefly looking at its history. Section 14.4 discusses the political economy and institutional context; Sect. 14.5 examines the corporate governance arrangements of Ghana EXIM Bank; Sect. 14.6 examines the Risk Management Practices, while Sect. 14.7 looks at the issues of Regulation and Supervision. Section 14.8 examines the Monitoring and Evaluation, and Impact Evaluation Practices; Sect. 14.9 discusses the Business Model of Ghana EXIM Bank; Sect. 14.10 discusses the Main Achievements and Contributions; Sect. 14.11 identifies the Challenges confronting the Ghana EXIM Bank, and finally, Sect. 14.12 concludes the chapter.

14.2 Ghana's Development Finance Landscape

14.2.1 Overview of Development Finance Institutions and Programmes

Ghana's approach to development and development financing at the time of Independence in 1957 into the mid-1960s was initially state-led. This period was characterized by public corporations dominating all sectors of the economy. The Ghana Commercial Bank was established in 1957 (out of the former Bank of the Gold Coast), with the objective of serving Ghanaian traders, farmers and businesses that had no access to the foreign banks that dominated the market, including the likes of Standard Chartered Bank and Barclays Bank. Recognizing the need for long-term financing led to the creation of three major development banks in Ghana and these were the National Investment Bank (NIB) in 1963, the Agricultural Credit and Cooperative Bank in 1965, and the Bank for Housing and Construction (BHC) in 1975. The Agricultural Credit and Cooperative Bank became known as the Agricultural Development Bank (ADB) and BHC went through some reforms but it eventually ceased operation in 2000. Both ADB and NIB have gone through substantial restructuring, and in 2004, they became universal banks, when BoG removed distinctions between commercial, development and merchant banks. The state-owned Merchant Bank was also established in 1972 and in 1976, the Bank of Ghana (BoG) issued regulations that allowed for the establishment of community-owned Rural and Community Banks (RCBs) as local unit banks with relatively low minimum capital requirements (Nissanke & Aryeetey, 1998; World Bank, 2016).

The introduction of economic reforms in the mid-1980s led to increasing financial sector liberalization in the 1990s, with so much attention given to demand-driven approaches and DFIs with lines of credit targeting specific sectors of the economy. The era of liberalization saw the government's drive to channel more finance to priority sectors, particularly in exports and micro, small and medium-scale enterprises (MSMEs), leading to the creation of new DFIs and programmes. The National Board for Small Scale Industries (NBSSI) was established in 1985 to promote SME development in the country to institute an enterprise culture, provide business development services, advance credit and encourage SME associations. In 1989, the Export Finance Company (EFC) was established to provide asset financing for firms, provide guarantees for financing export trade and also provide other money market instruments. In 1994, the Eximguaranty Company Limited (ECL) was also established with public institutional stakeholders to help financial institutions to provide credit to borrowers who did not have adequate collateral. It was also aimed at providing refinancing facilities for public financial institutions, facilitating financing and marketing of agricultural products, managing trust funds and providing working capital as well as insurance for local exporters. The year 2000 witnessed the establishment of the Export Development and Investment Fund (EDIF) with the mandate to support MSMEs and agricultural value chains (ACET, 2022; World Bank, 2016).

The Social Investment Fund (SIF), which was established in 1998 (as a private company limited by guarantee) to manage projects for community development, increased funding for microfinance in 2003 and small-scale enterprises in 2008. The ARB Apex Bank was established in 2002 under RFSP as a 'mini central bank' for Rural and Community Banks (RCBs) that own the ARB Apex Bank. It has served to manage various lines of credit in World Bank, IFAD and other projects for on-lending through the RCBs (World Bank, 2016). The Venture Capital

Trust Fund (VCTF) was also created in 2004 to provide funding for the development and promotion of venture capital companies to finance SMEs in priority sectors. In the bid to provide credit at interest rates lower that the prevailing market rates, the government established new local DFIs to achieve this and these include the Export Trade, Agricultural and Investment Fund (EDAIF) and the Microfinance and Small Loans Centre (MASLOC). EDAIF was initially set up under the name Export Development and Investment Fund (EDIF) in 2000 to address the funding shortcomings of EFC. Its mandate was extended in 2011 to include promoting development of agro-processing, as well as exports, and in 2013 to include industrial development and equity financing. It was subsequently renamed as the Export Trade, Agricultural and Industrial Development Fund (EDAIF). The creation of MASLOC in 2006 was also aimed at holding in trust and managing donor funds for micro- and small-scale credit; coordinating and promoting a decentralized microfinance system; and collaborating with non-bank financial institutions (ACET, 2022; World Bank, 2016). The EDAIF, EFC and ECL were later merged to become Ghana Export-Import (EXIM) Bank in 2016.

Other development finance initiatives by government included the establishment of the Ghana Infrastructure Investment Fund (GIIF) in 2014, and the Savannah Accelerated Development Authority (SADA) Development in 2010. The GIIF which was established as a development finance agency aimed at mobilizing, managing, coordinating and providing financial resources for *investments* in a diversified portfolio of *infrastructure* assets and projects. The Savannah Accelerated Development Authority (SADA) was aimed at facilitating economic development in the northern Savannah ecological zone. Considering the limited funding from government, SADA proposed the setting up of a wholesale development bank with the aim of facilitating long-term funding for regional development (World Bank, 2016).

14.2.2 Challenges and Failures of Development Finance Institutions in Ghana

DFIs in Ghana have had numerous structural and operational difficulties, which have resulted in the failure of some of these institutions. A number of factors are responsible for the failure of DFIs.

Pressure from the political environment is one of the biggest problems facing DFIs in Ghana. First, the DFIs are typically partnerships between the government and other state entities and mostly rely on donors and the government for their funding. They are, therefore, typically public or semi-public institutions. As a result, they become vulnerable to political meddling in their management and investment choices. This has created a significant obstacle to the ability of these institutions to fulfil their mandate and accomplish their goals. Additionally, political manifestos have had a significant impact on the construction of these DFIs for economic development. Therefore, the government that set them up and oversaw their boards of directors and administration was responsible for ensuring their viability. Political allegiance has occasionally had a significant impact on who gets appointed to the boards to perform senior management roles and occasionally to occupy lower-level positions. The lack of independence on the part of the board and management of many Ghanaian DFIs has tended to undermine their effective operations or resulted in their collapse.

Another major challenge or cause of the failure of DFIs is their poor risk management practices. DFIs serve a diverse spectrum of clients, many of whom carry substantial risks, consistent with the nature of the organization. It is frequently noted that the policies, methods and risk management frameworks of DFIs are not proportionate to the risk being assumed, nor indicative of the complexity of operations (ACET, 2022). This is due to the inherent hazards and lack of proper monitoring. DFIs mostly target clients such as SMEs that have difficulty accessing long-term finance. These SMEs are generally risky borrowers and their poor credit risk management practices have accounted for the high level of non-performing loans exhibited by Ghanaian DFIs, resulting in their collapse.

Additionally, DFIs in Ghana operate with little financial sustainability criteria. Most DFIs were required to prioritize development outcomes over profitability. This often resulted in the desire to design products that facilitate credit flow to the target sectors without including a safety net to prevent the DFIs from suffering losses. For instance, the majority of DFIs in Ghana were established by the government and were funded directly through disbursements from the government for balance sheet rebalancing or recapitalization in order to offset losses. The DFIs may not be motivated to assure operational sustainability and the preservation of core capital as a result of this readily available source of investment, which could present an easy way out. Direct government involvement in the allocation of funding and setting of interest rates generally undermines sustainability, impact and beneficiaries' motivation to return particular funds, and disbursement may be seen as politically driven (World Bank, 2016).

The financial and operational performance of DFIs in Ghana is also frequently hampered by the lack of a clearly defined mandate and target borrowers for financing. The question of 'what services or target population can the DFI provide proficiently?' might be complicated by a variety of factors, such as the existence of many authorities, finances and governmental institutions with distinct developmental agendas. This increases complexity and, in certain situations, forces DFIs to take on projects for which they are not operationally prepared.

Lastly, a significant number of DFIs do not adopt a structured strategy for pursuing objectives through specific business objectives, and very few conduct impact assessments of their actions. Even when the mandate and targets are clearly specified, stakeholders still find it challenging to assess performance and target achievement, which unintentionally makes it more difficult to spot gaps and flaws and implement adjustments to close those gaps or shortcomings. Some of these DFI-sponsored programmes had overlapping mandates and ambiguous operational procedures (ACET, 2022).

14.2.3 Establishment of the New Development Bank in Ghana

Ghana took a decision to establish a new NDB as a key instrument in its goal of transforming the economy and creating employment under the national strategy of 'Ghana Beyond Aid'. It has been argued that the new development bank will reflect new thinking on development financing as well as lessons from past experiences and current international best practice of development banking, underpinned by good corporate governance and sound business operations—unlike a regular bank. The government is expected to not repeat previous mistakes in connection with other state-owned banks, such as NIB, ADB and BHC. The new NDB is to raise long-term finance from both the domestic and international capital markets, as well as international financial institutions, based on the strength of its own balance sheet. The government has also indicated that the establishment of the new bank would be important in its effort to recover from the impact of the COVID-19 crisis (ACET, 2022).

The new development bank was established under the Development Finance Institution Act, 2020 (Act 1032) with the mandate of providing innovative and long-term financing instruments for specific sectors of the economy, particularly the agricultural and industrial sectors. The development bank was set up with an initial capital of US$200 million out of an equity contribution of US$250 million, and additional funding from the German KfW with €46.5 million. In October 2020, the World Bank's Board of Executive Directors approved US$250 million from the International Development Association (IDA) to support the establishment of the new development bank to increase access to long-term finance. With the support of the European Investment Bank (EIB) and other international DFIs, the country also secured a seed amount of €170 million to support the establishment of the new development bank.

The Development Finance Institutions Act, 2020 (Act 1032), which was passed by Parliament, provides the legal framework for the licensing, regulation and supervision of DFIs. The definition of this instrument suggests that development finance business is meant to provide short-, medium-and-long-term funding, guarantees and other credit-enhancement facilities to key sectors of the economy in a financially sustainable manner. The instrument provides four classifications of licences to be issued:

- The Development Finance Institution Class-1 licence provides for wholesale development finance.
- Class-2 licence provides retail-development finance.
- Class-3 licence provides guarantee-development finance.
- Class-4 licence provides a combination of any of the three indicated.

The new development bank is set up as a non-deposit-taking wholesale development bank under the Class-1 licence of the Development Finance Institution Act. This licence type does not permit the Bank to provide direct lending, but the financing must be done through participating financial institutions, including commercial banks, to be able to on-lend to the target borrowers.

Box 14.1 provides a brief profile of the New Development Bank: Development Bank Ghana.

Box 14.1 The New Development Bank: Development Bank Ghana

The new development bank, known as the Development Bank Ghana (DBG), was established in 2020 as a wholesale development bank that lends to commercial banks and other financial institutions for on-lending to Ghanaian businesses. The DBG is owned by the government of Ghana and was created to provide long-term financing to the productive sectors of the economy. These include agribusiness, with a focus on off-farm value chains activities, as well as manufacturing, ICT, software, and allied services, business-process outsourcing, and tourism. Another goal is to boost home ownership through affordable and longer tenure mortgage finance. Its business model involves providing the financing through private sector financial institutions to drive economic growth and shared prosperity.

As of June 2022, DBG's total assets were valued at almost US$800 million with shareholders' equity, which stood a US$250 million. As of June 2022, four commercial banks had signed on to participate by accessing funds from DBG, for on-lending to eligible businesses and they include Calbank, Consolidated Bank Ghana (CBG), Ghana Commercial Bank and Fidelity Banks Ghana.

Source https://en.wikipedia.org/wiki/Development_Bank_of_Ghana#History

14.3 The Case of Ghana Export-Import (EXIM) Bank

The Ghana Export-Import (EXIM) Bank is a development bank which serves as the principal export finance institution of the government of Ghana. It was established by the Ghana Export-Import Bank Act 2016 (Act 911) to provide support for Ghana government's pursuit of a feasible and sustainable export-led economy. Ghana EXIM Bank's vision is to become a strong financial institution that will be a key engine in the development of Ghana's export trade, facilitate cross-border trade and make Ghana a pillar in regional and continental trade. The bank's mission includes facilitating the transformation of Ghana's economy to become export-oriented by supporting and developing trade between Ghana and other countries, overseas investments by Ghanaian companies, and eliminating critical market failures in the Ghanaian economy thereby making Ghana competitive in the global marketplace.

The Ghana EXIM Bank has evolved following the merger of three DFIs discussed earlier. These are:

- Export Trade, Agricultural and Industrial Development Fund (EDAIF),
- Export Finance Company (EFC) and
- Eximguaranty Company Limited (ECL).

The EDAIF was initially established as EDIF in 2002 under Act 582 to provide financial resources for export-oriented activities, especially of non-traditional products. This was amended in 2011 to Act 823 as EDAIF to provide financial resources for the development and promotion of agriculture relating to agro-processing and the agro-processing industry, to give the agricultural sector additional attention and support. In 2013, Act 823 was replaced with Act 872, which extended the mandate of EDAIF to include the provision of resources for industrial development. The EFC was set up in 1989 as a Special Purpose Vehicle (SPV) to provide financial and other related support to the non-traditional export sector (NTEs) of Ghana's economy. The ECL was also created in 1994 to provide credit guarantees and general financial risk management solutions to SMEs. Given the specialized operations of these three institutions, the government finally merged them to form the Ghana Export-Import Bank (i.e. Ghana EXIM Bank) through the Act 911 in 2016.

The bank, over the years, has learnt from the experiences of other EXIM banks in the region and around the world—to understand their corporate governance and institutional arrangements, how they operate, their development mandates, their risk management practices, their regulation and their supervision. The Ghana EXIM Bank, as one of Africa's EXIM Banks, aims to accelerate inclusive industrialization on the African continent by expanding access to development finance to promote exports and industrialization. It is worth noting that the bank's development position and strategies are aligned to the national development policy and vision.

The bank operates as a policy and a development finance institution with the objective of expanding the high-growth export industry and other sectors of the economy. It plays a complementary role to commercial banks, and unlike commercial banks, Ghana EXIM Bank does not accept customer deposits. The intermediary services of the bank are targeted at the export sector with major emphasis on non-traditional exports like horticultural products, fish and seafood, manufactured foods and beverages, and handicrafts, with special attention to the underserved market segments. The operational activities of the bank are equally tailored to the achievement of regional and global targets of the sustainable development goals (2030) and African Union's Agenda 2063. The mandate of the bank has not changed from a policy instrument of development finance to facilitate the development of exports.

Given this background, the bank considers three key benchmarks, which are derived from development objectives, including employment creation, value addition through production-efficiency and foreign exchange revenue potential. The bank has not experienced any significant changes in the history and focus areas since its inception as it tries to complete existing projects. The key drivers for the changes in the development mandate are anchored or hinged on government policies and national development agenda.

14.4 Political Economy and Institutional Context

In emerging markets, the cozy ties that exist between development banks, politicians and governments, as well as the state ownership of development banks, give rise to a great deal of political influence in the business models of development banks, including the extension of credit and allocation of capital. The recent global economic crises have demonstrated that even advanced financial systems are not immune against political intervention. From the perspective of political economy literature, the failure of a number of development banks in Africa has been attributed to an overabundance of deficiencies, poor corporate governance and political interference that results from non-payment of loans by politicians and by large corporations connected to the political system. The role of the government is to invest and maximize social welfare and to improve sustainable economic growth in order to counter market failures. However, political interference and institutional arrangements are likely to lead to inefficiencies in development banking. Thus, development banks may be inefficient because of governments' deliberate policies of transferring resources to support their interests via the banks. Advocates of government intervention often point to political economic concerns in relation to the extent of political involvement in the developmental roles of NDBs—although these result in poor performance, particularly government influence on the allocation of funds towards unviable sectors of the economy. However, in the case of Ghana EXIM Bank, pursuing industrial policies and ongoing development goals have been successful despite the challenges they face from the political and institutional settings.

The development mandate of the Ghana EXIM Bank, on the whole, is inherently influenced by policymaking and political trends. The bank has continually made important contributions to the growth of the Ghanaian economy, while navigating the shift in the political dynamics. Although the executives of the bank believe that they are adequately shielded with government support, the bank is affected by the dynamics of government interference and flows of politics in the country. The bank supports the development agenda of the government by providing funding to support strategic areas or sectors within its mandate. The bank is heavily dependent on the executive branch of the government, and the government of Ghana is its main funding source. In terms of the parliamentary system, the government of Ghana has more direct control and influence of the bank. Therefore, any policy change or shift and political risk on the part of the government may pose an amplifying or cascading effect on the bank and its developmental mandate.

From the perspective of the global economy and development agenda, the bank makes an effort to incorporate international market requirements and standards in the achievement of the global SDGs. The bank has the tendency to borrow from the international market, which gives it the urge to abide by the international policies or to meet the international standards that guide external borrowing agreements. In addition, the bank has policies and procedures in place to ensure that it abides by such international policies in its operations. Looking at the Africa's agenda to create development partnerships, the bank has established a partnership relationship with USEXIM, which allows its customers to import equipment under a facility arrangement from the USA. Again, these partnerships help the bank to expand its developmental impact so that the specific sectors within its mandate can benefit from the partnership arrangements. For instance, the partnership helps the customers of the bank to secure or import equipment for their operations to be effective and efficient.

It is obvious that the global economic and political dynamics have an impact on the operational activities of the bank. For instance, the COVID-19 pandemic and the recent Russia-Ukraine war have had a negative effect on the bank's planned programmes. The geopolitical consequences of the Russian-Ukraine war have led to a sharp rise in the cost of borrowing, which has affected the economic activities, operating costs and profitability of the key sectors within the bank's market base.

Within the institutional context, the decisions and activities of the Ministry of Finance directly affect the governance and operations of the bank. For instance, the Ministry of Finance took the decision to allocate 0.75% of non-oil imports, which the bank has no control over. Thus, any decision in terms of funding the time of resource allocation from the Ministry of Finance can impact on the operations of the bank positively or negatively. Further, although the bank is not regulated by the central bank, the activities and decisions of the central bank indirectly influence the governance and operations of the bank, since the former functions within the mandate of DFIs and is also a financial institution. For instance, the Ghana EXIM Bank benchmarks its operations based on the provisions and requirements of the Bank of Ghana for commercial banks. For example, changes in the central bank's policy rates also affect the bank's cost of borrowing and also affect the ease of doing business even though the bank offers its customers credits on concessionary interest rates. Thus, the Ministry of Finance and the Bank of Ghana have a regulatory and political impact on the bank through its formal engagements with these institutions. In addition, the decisions, undertaken by the Food and Drugs Authority and other regulatory institutions, have a direct or indirect effect on the bank. For instance, the bank's customers from the food and drugs sectors of the economy may have to meet certain standards of the Food and Drugs Authority.

14.5 Corporate Governance Arrangement of Ghana EXIM Bank

The critical role of NDBs with respect to contractual and legal enforcement, including corporate governance mechanisms, cannot be overemphasized. It is generally accepted that good corporate governance pays for NDBs as it comes with a lower cost of capital, higher returns on equity, greater efficiency and more favourable treatment of all stakeholders of the bank. Thus, a greater level of corporate governance practice consistently demonstrates the effectiveness of the activities of any development bank. However, resistance by entrenched owners and managers of the bank, mostly the representatives or appointees of government, and the political economy factors at the level of markets and countries explain why development banks do not benefit from a good corporate governance system.

The Ghana EXIM Bank is a 100% government-owned NDB. Although the bank has the government as a shareholder, it operates within the governance development framework adopted by DFIs. The corporate governance development framework is a common approach towards addressing the corporate governance risks and opportunities in the operations and investments of DFIs. The Ghana EXIM Bank has integrated the corporate governance framework in its development projects, investments and business operations by adopting the principles, tools and protocols in line with the framework. In the bank's daily practice, it strives to adhere to high standards of corporate governance and continually works on improving the corporate governance practices by considering, employing and benchmarking the best international experience.

The bank conducts corporate governance assessments of its development projects and investments of clients and ensures that action plans are developed appropriately.

Table 14.1 presents the current structure of the board of Ghana EXIM Bank. The bank currently has a board size of nine (9) directors, made up of one (1) executive director and eight (8) non-executive directors (representatives of the government). There is no independent or non-executive director on the board and a CEO duality is absent. Out of the nine (9) board members, four (4) representing 44.4% are females, while the remaining five (5) representing 55.6% are males.

The board has different committees that report on various issues to it and these committees include: the Audit Committee, Credit and Investment Committee, Risk Committee, Strategy and Governance Committee, Human Resource, Administration IT Committee, and Finance and Procurement Committee. The corporate governance arrangements on the committees states that 'a committee established under subsection (1) shall meet at the place and time determined by the Chairperson of the committee and shall observe such rules or procedure for the transaction of business at its meeting as may be prescribed'. The Audit Committee is composed of two (2) members from the board and three (3) other members outside the bank and the board. The chairperson of the Audit

Table 14.1 Board characteristics of Ghana EXIM Bank

Board characteristics	*Number (%)*
Board size	9
Executive directors	1 (11.1)
Non-executive directors	8 (88.9%)
Of which independence non-executive directors	0
CEO duality	No
Female directors	4 (44.4%)
Male directors	5 (55.6%)
Number of committees	6
Size of Audit Committee	5
Number of Independent Members on Audit Committee	3
Audit Committee chaired by Independent member	Yes

Source Author's construction

Committee is a non-executive board member in line with best practice, giving the implication that there is a strong level of audit independence for the bank. The Audit Committee chaired by an Independent Committee member has been very crucial in preventing insiders from influencing the work and oversight of the committee and the work of the external auditors. Internal Control and Internal Audit are two separate departments. The Head of the Internal Audit department reports functionally to the Audit Committee of the board with administrative reporting lines to the CEO. The functions of the Audit Committee are to: (1) provide oversight supervision of the financial reporting process, the audit process, the system of internal control and compliance with laws and regulations; (2) to recommend an audit charter that sets out the general purpose, authority, composition and responsibility of the Committee for the approval of the Board; and (3) to deal with any other matters related to the functions of the Committee. The Internal Control department reports directly to the office of the CEO secretariat.

In accordance with its charter, the board strives to maintain good corporate governance in line of international best practice. As stated in the Ghana Export-Import Bank Act, 2016, the governing body of the Bank is a Board of Directors consisting of a chairperson, one representative of the Ministry of Finance, Ministry of Trade and Industry, the Bank of Ghana and the Ghana Export Promotion Authority—not below the rank of a director. The Board is responsible for the supervision of the management and affairs of the Bank and for the performance of any other functions conferred on it by any other provision for this Act. The other government agencies comprise a representative of recognized major private industry associations who serves on rotational basis; two other persons from the private sector at least one of whom is a woman; and the Chief Executive Officer of the Bank. From a stakeholder perspective, these institutions are represented on the board.

The appointment process of the CEO is undertaken by the Office of the President of the Republic. The President also appoints the board chair. From the Executive Arrangement of the Government of Ghana, 'the President shall appoint the chairperson and the other members of the board in accordance with article 70 of the Constitution. The President shall have regard to the knowledge and expertise of members in matters relevant to the functions of the Bank in making appointments to the Board'.

14.6 Risk Management Practices

Risk management practice is a critical issue in NDBs because it has a substantial effect not only on the behaviour of the bank but also on the economy. Like other development banks, the Ghana EXIM Bank has established and executed various policies and procedures to reduce or limit exposures in providing development banking activities. In view of that, quantifying risk and finding an optimal mix between the risks and the returns through the creation of capital are crucial for the bank. The structure of the corporate governance practices in Ghana EXIM Bank is based on the principles of risk management, internal control and internal audit. It embarks on the financing of capital-intensive projects and maintains institutions that can anticipate new needs, overcome risks associated with development impacts and help to coordinate multiple investments that may take place simultaneously.

The Ghana EXIM Bank is confronted with several forms of risk in its operations, including credit risk, liquidity risk, operational risk, strategic risk, political, social and environmental risks, as well as market risks (interest rate risk and currency risk). These risks are monitored regularly. Among them, credit risk and market risk are the main risks faced by the bank. The bank has in place a risk management framework together with efficient monitoring strategies to ensure that impairment and non-performing loans are kept at minimal levels. In terms of market risk, the bank is exposed to foreign exchange rate risk since it borrows in foreign currency and the loans are granted in the local currency. The bank is confronted with high foreign exchange risk due to its exposures to revaluation losses resulting from the depreciation of the local currency.

Mitigation measures are frequently developed to ensure that the impact level of risks on the operations of the bank is minimal even if they do occur. During the COVID-19 pandemic, the bank took a number of important measures. For instance, its credit committee met frequently to approve loans. However, it minimized the credit lines to manage credit risk exposures. Given, the extent of credit risk exposures, the bank intensified its monitoring of the customers. The approach adopted for the monitoring of customers was on a case-by-case basis. The bank also restructured the repayment terms of existing loans in its portfolio by giving borrowers a grace period to repay their loans. It also made available more working capital for clients to acquire urgent materials for manufacturing.

The bank disbursed funds to the pharmaceutical companies and other sectors of the economy for the manufacturing of Personal Protective Equipment (PPE), hand sanitizers, nose masks and other health medical supplies to help curb and combat the risks associated with the pandemic. In total, the bank provided more than GHS 10 million to fight COVID-19.

The bank also deployed an IT system which enabled the staff to work from home in order to ensure that effective financial services were delivered to the clients. Board meetings were held via Zoom to ensure that every urgent facility that needed attention was approved and did not suffer any delay.

14.7 Regulation and Supervision

It is clear how globalization pressures from DFIs have created the path for NDBs to be highly dependent on international development policies, leading to policy-driven convergence over time. Ghana remains one of the few cases where major actors (government, regulators and banks) are offered strong incentives to converge on international regulatory standards to achieve sustainable development. This has led to a substantial compliance among financial institutions including the Ghana EXIM Bank. This has been possible because the bank has a mandate to traditionally pursue a market-based approach to credit allocation. Given that the government has an agenda to pursue a development strategy that prioritizes integration into the expansion of development finance, it has become imperative for the regulators that have substantial autonomy and are embedded in an international policy environment to enforce the adoption and implementation of international standards. The bank has, so far, since its establishment, not experienced a divergence in its compliance with international standards, especially in situations where politicians and the business elite extensively use banks for political ends—where the regulator is sceptical about the implementation and applicability of the Basel standards for their development objectives.

The Ghana EXIM Bank is regulated under its enabling Act—the Ghana Export-Import Bank Act, 2016 (Act 911) and it is expected to be independent in the performance of its functions. The Bank is not subject to the regulatory and supervisory control of the Bank of Ghana or to the Banking Act, 2004 (Act 673) in its establishment or in the performance of its functions. The Bank is accountable to the minister for the achievement of its objective and compliance with this Act and the guidelines of the Bank.

The minister in his role of advising the Board: (1) shall by legislative instrument make regulations on matters relating to the equity and debt operations of the Bank including the priority areas, eligibility rules and the terms and conditions for facilities to be operated by the Bank; and (2) may by legislative instrument make regulations in relation to other matters to give effect to the provisions of this Act.

The Bank has a development objective and not for a commercial one. Although the Bank is not regulated by the Central Bank as found in other EXIM banks in the region or the world, it tries to benchmark its activities to the Central Bank's requirements for commercial banks. The bank currently complies with all the BASELS of the world and as well benchmarks all their activities to the international standard or best practices. The risk management practices of the bank such as the operational risk, credit risk, liquidity and all the other markets are in line with the principles of the BASELS. The bank has a robust regulatory system that helps it to effectively implement the Basel framework.

14.8 Monitoring and Evaluation, and Impact Evaluation

The Ghana EXIM Bank has adopted specific monitoring and evaluation (M&E) systems for monitoring its interventions. It has also instituted an impact evaluation system for assessing the extent of the development impact of their projects, programmes, policies, interventions or activities and also for making some relevant adjustments throughout the developmental project cycle of what it finances. The increasing role of the bank in the development landscape of the economy of Ghana makes it crucial to identify its strengths and weaknesses and to find ways in which they can be improved. The strengths and weaknesses are critically evaluated on the basis of governance, development impact, effectiveness and financial performance. The bank is increasingly under scrutiny due to the need to demonstrate positive results from the perspective of governance, development impact, effectiveness and financial performance. In view of that the bank has focused on managing developmental projects that yield substantial results. It has also developed approaches to strengthen the orientation of monitoring and evaluation systems towards developmental results. Thus, M&E issues are addressed from the project inception phase and that the guidelines for M&E are incorporated throughout the project cycle.

The monitoring process may include project design and preparation, project planning, project implementation and project maintenance. The bank has a Monitoring Unit, which carries out monitoring and evaluation. It is a unit under the Risk Management Department and reports to the head of risk. They use the project objective, the result framework, the logical framework, the data collection indicator framework and baseline information from projects to monitor the project performance and evaluate its development impact. The number of staff is seven and the minimum qualification is a first degree and a number of them have post-graduate qualification.

With respect to impact evaluation, the bank has a limited scope since it focuses on three key sectors of the economy: the pharmaceutical sector, the agricultural sector and agro-processing sector. Traditionally, projects and programmes financed by the bank have included an M&E component of the bank, but the bank has recently started conducting rigorous IE research on what actually works and about what can be attributable to its own intervention. The monitoring unit measures the bank's developmental impacts and achievements and sometimes consultants are engaged to conduct impact assessment for specific projects sponsored by GEXIM. The bank has internal policies that guide the framework enshrined in its constitution or establishing/legislative instrument for measurement of development impact. The internal policy manual strongly advocates the measure of developmental impact and makes provision for a periodic review of the framework by the appointment committee. Developmental impacts measured by constantly tracking project objectives in line with the project implementation planning and results framework.

In an effort to consolidate its gains and provide sustainable development and impactful interventions, the bank undertakes impact assessment in a full project life cycle, from planning and preparation through financing, building and sustaining—to increase its developmental impact in the context of a difficult operating environment and also to respond adequately to the global dynamics. Both the monitoring and evaluation as well as the impact evaluation are done by the Monitoring and Evaluation Unit. Every project is monitored by the monitoring team of the bank, and there is a framework containing a monitoring schedule for the year. The schedule for the monitoring process contains a list of projects that are financed by the bank and the M&E is done every quarter in the year. The monitoring team goes to the field and monitors the customers on the basis of their individual schedules or timelines and planning. For every individual client, the team provides a comprehensive report based on the parameters and scope of the monitoring plan for each project type. Thus, every project is expected to follow the bank's criteria, for impact evaluation to be successful.

In achieving the global SDGs, the bank has recently undertaken the green financing project which is in connection with the Bank of Ghana's guidelines on the sustainable banking principles that deal with the global Environmental, Social and Governance (ESGs) Principles. Ghana EXIM Bank has its own policy on ESG which helps to guide the bank in providing developmental support for projects and policies that help in the achievement of sustainable ESGs.

14.9 Business Model of Ghana EXIM Bank

The Ghana EXIM Bank has a well-defined plan for identifying the business models for its development projects, programmes and policies. The bank also has a defined target market and expected expenses. The business models of the bank are important for both developing new and established businesses, attracting investment, recruiting talent and new entrants, and motivation management and staff.

14.9.1 Policy Mandate and Sectors Served

The Ghana EXIM Bank draws its policy mandate from the Act that established it, particularly the Ghana EXIM Bank Act 911 and the government's 10-point Agenda for Industrial Transformation. The national development agenda allows the bank to support the government in achieving a sustainable export-led economy that is anchored on thriving industrialization and socio-economic development. The bank has a broad mandate but its primary functions include providing finance, risk-bearing services as well as trade and market information and export advisory services to the Ghanaian export community.

The bank has a 5-year strategic goal for sustainable development, spanning 2017 to 2022, with a broad focus on:

- Increasing the non-traditional exports from its initial average of US$2.4 billion to about US$5 billion.
- Developing Ghana's major exports such as avocado, cashew, sweet potatoes, coconuts and thereby reducing the import bill for poultry by US$300 million; and complementing the effort of exporters to make the economy of Ghana a pillar or hub for regional and global manufacturing and export of pharmaceutical products.
- Becoming a key financing partner and an agent of government—for the effective implementation of Ghana's industrialization agenda and strategic initiative of the 'One District One Factory (1D1F)', as stipulated in Act 911, Function 25.
- Financing and developing strategic import substitution products like poultry and rice.
- Increasing the capacity of Ghanaian exporters through effective partnership with key stakeholders, such as the Ghana Export Promotion

Authority, the Ghana Food and Drugs Authority (GFDA) and the Ghana Standard Authority (GSA).
- Developing human capacity to support the transformation of the economy through the export-led initiative.

The above strategies are aligned to the government's 10-point Agenda for Industrial Transformation.

The establishment of the legislative instruments provides a framework for the selection of sectors. It gives broad areas to operate within, but the board of directors specify the areas for development based on prioritization of the sectors.

The Act provides about 23 sectors for transformation but the bank focuses on developing specific sectors such as poultry, cashew, shea butter, a raw material base development for avocado, pharmaceuticals, pineapple, mango oil palm, cassava, creative arts textile, garments and apparel manufacturing and cocoa butter. The bank is focused primarily on the development of a raw material base since it identifies this as the key to sustain agro-processing within the agribusiness value chain. To put it in greater perspective, the Ghana EXIM Bank seeks to support the private sector with the expectation of improving the fortunes of the Ghanaian economy. In doing so, the bank, in line with the Act 911, chooses the enterprises it may want to support. However, the bank focuses on three major sectors or areas for development including the pharmaceutical, agricultural and agro-processing.

In the bank's business model, the selection of each sector is based on the potential competitiveness not only in the West African sub-region but also in the broader regional context and international space. In terms of what has been enshrined in the act, the bank or the board does not have any mandate to review or change the sectors of operations, but it can only make adjustments based on sectors of priority.

14.9.2 Funding Sources

The Ghana EXIM Bank is not a deposit-taking DFI and does not receive any support from the central bank. Its main sources of finance include issuance of marketable instruments, borrowing from the domestic and international capital markets and from local and international institutions, and ploughed back earnings. Debt financing may come from bilateral organizations, external DFI support, commercial banks, etc. For instance, in 2019, the bank obtained US$300 million in lines of credit from US EXIM Bank, and US$150 million from Credit Suisse, specifically for the pharmaceutical, poultry and cocoa processing sectors. Also, the bank signed a Memorandum of Understanding (MoU) with the Indonesia EXIM Bank, China EXIM Bank, India EXIM Bank and Slovenia EXIM Bank for technology transfer and capacity building.

14.9.3 Lending Model

The bank employs direct or retail lending models and most of the loans are channelled into the agricultural and agribusiness sectors as well as the agro-processing, and pharmaceutical sectors. It provides loans directly to its clients, including private companies, small and medium-scale enterprises (SMEs), among others. It also provides grants to some state-owned enterprises intended for capacity building. The bank does not provide wholesale lending as other DFIs do to banks to on-lend to the target clients—but it deals directly with its customers. To qualify for a loan facility, the client must have majority Ghanaian ownership and the loan request must meet the bank's criteria for acceptance, including socio-economic impact taking into account the suitability of the purpose of the loan, customer capability in line with the safety of the loan and business sustainability or profitability of the business. While the bank does not directly provide loans to commercial banks, it does issue guarantees that enable customers to borrow from these commercial institutions.

An application for loan by a customer is addressed to the CEO with documentation of all pre-requisite requirements attached including a business plan, business registration documents, audited financial statements for existing businesses, and off-taker agreements. Loan approvals are based on the bank's credit acceptance criteria, which are divided into three categories:

- Socio-economic impact: This considers the suitability of the loan's purpose.
- Customer capability: This assesses the customer's ability to generate sufficient cash flow from their business to meet their debt obligations.
- Business sustainability: This evaluates the long-term viability of the business.

The bank transacts with all designated financial institutions like commercial banks and disburses facilities only in the local currency, or the cedi equivalent of the transaction even if it is in another foreign currency. During the COVID-19 pandemic, the bank supported existing customers who needed raw materials and equipment to produce in order to fight the pandemic.

14.9.4 Products and Services

The Ghana EXIM Bank offers a wide range of financial products and services to different clients with different objectives who business falls within bank's focus areas. The focus of the bank is primarily to provide long-term financing, although it also extends medium-term and short-term financing to its clients. The bank provides export development finance through medium-to-long-term finance to exporters to enable them to start up new export projects, revitalize, acquire and expand existing product lines, and acquire machinery and equipment. It also provides import finance for machinery, industrial plants and equipment, and raw materials that are not available locally. The financial products and services offered by the bank include loans, grants for capacity building, working capital, syndicated loans, business start-up loans, equity investment in SMEs, trade financing, pre-shipment credit, post-shipment credit, contingent liabilities, export development finance, cross-border investment, project export and technical support. These products also serve as important sources of revenue generation for the bank. The bank also provides non-financial services to its clients. It provides consulting, networking and training to support its clients.

14.9.5 Pricing and Subsidies

The pricing and subsidy policy of the bank's products and services is dependent on the extent to which the policy is aligned to the mandate of the government of Ghana. The bank provides loans to its clients mainly based on concessionary terms. The interest rates offered are generally below the Bank of Ghana's monetary policy rate.

The bank has a pricing model that provides guidelines and parameters to assess the risk profile of each client. The recommended prices are based on individual customers' creditworthiness.

14.10 Main Achievements and Contributions of Ghana EXIM Bank

In past years, since the establishment of the Ghana EXIM Bank, it has become a key lever for transforming the Ghanaian economy, and in particular, contributing immensely to export development. Since its establishment, the bank has been playing a critical and pivotal role in the economy's long-awaited transformation into an export-oriented, private sector-driven industrial economy, fuelled by the country's abundant natural resources. The bank has not failed in its mandate of supporting the government's quest for attaining a feasible, vibrant and sustainable export-led economy that is hinged on thriving industrialization and socio-economic development. The bank has ignited the creation of new industries and provided significant support to a more inclusive development strategy. Most importantly, it is the prime financial driver behind the government's industrialization initiative.

The bank has contributed to the development of some key sectors of the economy. One of the sectors of its primary focus is the pharmaceutical industry, which has received a huge boost from the bank as it supports the industry in implementing the Good Manufacturing Practices (GMPs) required by the World Health Organization. Ghanaian drug manufacturers already supplied 30% of the West African Coastal States market and have the potential to increase that figure to 50% through GMP certification, even as they increase their 30% market share in Ghana. Projects currently under urgent review for approval are shea butter, sorghum, soybeans, plastic recycling plants, cotton growing and processing, and creative arts in the three northern regions.

The role of the Ghana EXIM Bank in providing long-term financing has contributed to employment creation in various sectors of the economy. The provision of finance by the bank has empowered entrepreneurs, by providing them new entry and favourable access to the market—hence creating jobs. Overall, the bank has financed a number of projects and created over 50,000 jobs since its establishment. Table 14.2 shows the number of projects funded for each focus area of the economy.

Ghana EXIM Bank's policy initiative to ensure a clean environment is hinged on supporting investments in Clean Development Technology that is geared towards curbing the adverse effects of global warming. The bank has delivered on its mandate to handle environmental issues through the Carbon Credit/Certified Emission Reduction programme.

Table 14.2 Developmental impacts of Ghana EXIM Bank

Sector/Areas	*Number of projects funded*	*Funds (GHS million)*
Poultry	14	168
Pineapple	7	845.2
Sweet Potatoes	2	432
Cassava	18	509.6
Avocado	1	44
Cashew	5	170
Fertilizer manufacturing	1	47
Brick and tiles	1	55
Pharmaceutical	9	339

Source Ghana EXIM Bank, 2023

It ensured that all its targeted sectors (manufacturing, agro-processing, pharmaceuticals and many others) have obtained an Environmental Impact Assessment (EIA) Certificates from the Environmental Protection Agency. It has established a women empowerment programme which, for example, provides finance to women in Shea butter processing. Again, the bank has advocated for and on behalf of its clients and beneficiaries to carry out environmentally sustainable practices. An example is the Juaben Oil Mills Project (i.e. Oil Palm Production and Export in Ghana) and agro-processing projects at Ekumfi.

14.11 Challenges Confronting Ghana EXIM Bank

The bank is also confronted with a number of challenges. First is the challenge of implementing its risk management system. Although it has risk management policies and procedures in place, these are not effectively implemented. Achieving the right balance in risk management can be challenging. There is also the challenge of serving a wide range of customers that commercial banks and the private sector cannot reach due to high risks or operational costs. In addition, the Bank may have minimal access to relevant information about the market positions it serves. It may not have a full understanding of the risks their customers face. Price fluctuations, natural disasters, insufficient infrastructure to store export goods, cost and time to resolve trade disputes between exporters and foreign customers can pose challenges. Access to developmental financial instruments (loan guarantees, insurance products and financial derivative instruments) to mitigate credit or market risks can be difficult.

Also, the bank faces the challenge of not being able to tailor its financial instruments to suit its customers' business needs. For instance, credit facilities or business products of the banks differ in terms of their payment terms and maturities, and therefore may limit the extent to which funds may be available to meet the needs of customers. Further, the fluctuating interest rate environment makes long-term financial instruments less attractive and lucrative for the bank, which in turn affects the financing of short-term loans. This points to the need for further restructuring and adjustment of loan terms and disbursements, which come with a major challenge, and hence affect loan tenors, payments and amortization schedules. It is obvious that internal policies and tools that allow the bank to limit its credit and commercialization risk by type, region or client activity affect the success of achieving sustainable development in line with its mandate. The bank is confronted with the challenge of adopting effective analytical tools to monitor the performance of its loan portfolio and effective loan recovery tools.

Another challenge the bank is confronted with relates to monitoring and recoveries of loans, which, therefore, adversely affects the credit reporting lines. Further, the representation of collateral by customers who apply for loans is a major challenge for the bank. There are more than enough applications for loans which the bank has no resource base to finance. Some projects of customers are stagnant or deteriorating. This is because the loans or facilities disbursed for the developmental projects may not be enough to complete them, and therefore, projects may be suspended. In addition, the bank has not been deeply involved in its role in climate finance in line with the SDGs.

A major challenge confronting the bank is the impact of political influence on its corporate governance and credit management. There seems to be much political influence in the board appointment process and lending decisions of the bank. Political influence in its corporate governance limits the role of the independent non-executive directors. As it stands, apart from the board members representing various stakeholder groups, the rest are appointed by the government. This practice tends to weaken the effectiveness of the board in exercising its oversight responsibility. The current board structure has no independent non-executive director to chair the Audit Committee as prescribed by best international standards. Credit risk has also been identified as a major risk affecting the bank. Undue political interference in its lending decisions has the potential to create huge non-performing loans (NPLs) for the bank as lending is influenced by political connectedness as opposed to business or project viability.

Also, access to long-term financing remains a challenge for the Ghana EXIM Bank. It is imperative for the bank to access long-term finance at concessionary rates to be able to pass it on to customers through subsidized lending. However, the funding source(s) for the bank, especially from government, is always insufficient in its quest to deliver on the mandate as spelt out in Ghana Export-Import Bank, 2016 (Act 911).

The COVID-19 pandemic affected the bank's operations as some loans had to be restructured to create financial space for its customers to operate, and to offer them some flexibility in repaying their loans. This arrangement certainly had an impact on the financial and liquidity position of the bank. During the COVID-19 pandemic, the bank imported some equipment but it could not arrive on time due to the lockdown. In some situations, the equipment arrived on schedule but there were no experts to assemble it for the clients.

14.12 Conclusion and Implications

Ghana EXIM Bank, as a policy bank, has the ultimate goal of facilitating Ghana's international trade and also supporting the local manufacturing industry. It is a key lever for transforming the Ghanaian economy, and in particular, contributing to export development. Since its establishment, the bank's response has been to further deepen its support by providing financing resources for targeted sectors of the economy, particularly, agricultural, agro-processing, agribusiness and pharmaceutical products. The bank is heavily dependent on the executive branch of the government since it is a 100% government-owned NDB. The Ghana EXIM Bank's structure of corporate governance, risk management principles, regulation and supervision are based on the guidelines enshrined in the Ghana Export-Import Bank, 2016 (Act 911). Although the bank faces major risks such as credit risk and market risk (interest rates and currency rate), it has a risk management system controlling these exposures. Further, the bank currently complies with international development policies including the Basel framework. In addition, the bank has a guideline for monitoring and evaluation as well as impact evaluation that focuses on managing developmental impacts and interventions.

The bank has contributed to the development of some key sectors of the economy, including the provision of finance to women in oil palm plantations and exports. It has also advocated for beneficiaries to carry out environmentally sustainable practices, provided development support to sectors like agriculture, agribusiness, agro-processing, pharmaceuticals and development projects. The bank has been an important lever for the transformation of the Ghanaian industry, but its main challenge has to do with the impact of political influence on its corporate governance and operations. Further, the funding source(s) for the bank, which come from the government, remain a challenge since this is not enough to deliver on the mandate.

Given that the Ghana EXIM Bank's mandate aligns directly with the national government agenda, the bank is positioned to provide support to capital-intensive projects and the growing demand of key sectors of the economy. In this regard, alternative financing and partnerships with regional DFIs should be considered. Again, it is important for the bank to focus on projects for which it has pre-knowledge.

The bank has a monitoring unit established under the risk management department that provides monitoring and evaluation of development projects. Thus, the nature of developmental impact requires that the bank establishes a department fully equipped with the skills and knowledge to analyse and handle all monitoring and evaluation as well as impact evaluation processes of its development mandate. The impact evaluation of all implemented programmes and projects is vital to the bank's developmental legacy.

The bank is currently regulated by the Ministry of Finance, which restricts it from financing development projects that appear risky. For this reason, the government should design separate regulatory and supervisory policies that benchmark the principles and guidelines of international DFIs and regional and national EXIM banks. Further, the government and its related ministries and agencies continue to appoint board members and executive management staff. It is important to address issues of corporate governance in line with international standards. A key point will also be to bring the Ghana EXIM Bank under the Development Finance Institutions Acts, 2020 (Act, 1032) with some oversight supervision by the central bank.

References

Abor, J. Y. (2018). *Financial markets and institutions: A frontier market perspective* (2nd ed.). Digibooks.

Bank of Ghana (BoG). (2018). *Monetary Policy Committee (MPC) report*. Retrieved on 5 October 2022 from www.bog.gov.gh

Brownbridge, M., & Gockel, A. F. (1996). *The impact of financial sector policies on banking in Ghana*. YPFS Documents (Series 1).

Nissanke, M., & Aryeetey, E. (1998). *Financial integration and development: Liberalization and reform in Sub-Saharan Africa*. World Bank.

Quartey, P., & Afful-Mensah, G. (2014). Financial and monetary policies in Ghana: A review of recent trends. *Review of Development Finance, 4*(2), 115–125.

The African Center for Economic Transformation (ACET). (2022). *Challenges and changes: The political economy of national development banks in Africa*. Ghana case study Agricultural Development Bank and National Investment Bank.

World Bank. (2016). *Project appraisal document on a proposed loan in the amount of US$93 million to the Land and Agricultural Development Bank of South Africa with the guarantee of the Republic of South Africa for a land bank financial intermediation loan* (No. PAD1122). World Bank. http://documents1.worldbank.org/curated/fr/221771484075116214/pdf/SA-PAD12302016.pdf

CHAPTER 15

Uganda's Experience with National Development Banks: The Case of Uganda Development Bank Limited

15.1 Introduction

NDBs are considered as development actors of the economy and are, therefore, used as important instruments by governments to promote economic development. They remain an essential part of modern financial systems in both developed and developing countries, and their relevance has been revived in the context of the recent COVID-19 pandemic and economic crises. The crises have prompted recent debates on the role of development banks, and public banks in general, as tools for addressing various economic, social and environmental challenges faced by emerging economies in Africa, including Uganda. After obtaining independence, Uganda, like many countries in the world, saw the need for rapid development in the various sectors of the economy, leading to pragmatic measures, including a national development plan achieve the sustainable development goals. Uganda Development Bank (UDB) was established to serve various sectors of the economy. On its commencement, the UDB was charged with 'the promotion and provision of short-to-medium and long-term development finance and to render managerial, technical and administrative advice and services to projects in the agricultural (crop and livestock), commercial and industrial sectors of the economy' (UDB, 1980). Thus, UDB was established to provide the needed resources for the economy, which hitherto had been starved by the existing banks.

© The Author(s), under exclusive license to Springer Nature Switzerland AG 2023

J. Yindenaba Abor, *The Changing Role of National Development Banks in Africa*, https://doi.org/10.1007/978-3-031-38639-8_15

Notwithstanding the important functions of NDBs, the expected impacts of these banks are not met due to inadequate funding from their respective governments and development partners as well as perceived weaknesses in their institutional and governance frameworks, political interference and poor performance. Given that Uganda and developing countries in the world have undergone several changes in their structural reforms and financial sector reforms over the past decade, it is important to understand the experiences and contemporary issues of with respect to NDBs and their contributions to national development in developing countries like Uganda. This chapter covers how Uganda Development Bank Limited (UDBL) in Uganda has evolved in the governance structures and operations, the impact on its financial and developmental performance, its contributions and the challenges it faces within its environment.

The rest of the chapter is structured as follows: Sect. 15.2 provides an overview of DFIs in Uganda; Sect. 15.3 provides a profile and historical background of UDBL; Sect. 15.4 discusses the political economy and institutional context of UDBL; Sect. 15.5 discusses the corporate governance system of UDBL; Sect. 15.6 examines the risk management practices of UDBL; Sect. 15.7 discusses regulation and supervision of the bank; Sect. 15.8 examines the bank's system of monitoring and evaluation, and impact evaluation; Sect. 15.9 discusses the bank's business model; Sect. 15.10 evaluates the financial performance of UDBL over a seven-year period; Sect. 15.11 discusses the main achievements and contributions of UDBL; Sect. 15.12 discusses the challenges affecting UDBL; and then Sect. 15.13 provides the conclusion.

15.2 Development Finance Institutions in Uganda

The role of DFIs in the economies of the developed and the developing countries cannot be overstated. They play a central role in the economic transformation of many economies, including Uganda's. The days of colonial dependence in Uganda saw commercial banking contributing very little to the local economic development. There only that operated in Uganda were branches of foreign banks, which were only interested in the facilitation of exports of raw materials to the colonial master's economy. It was just a coincidence that the activities of these banks contributed to the development of the local economy. The operations of these banks centred on assistance in the form of 'short-term self-liquidating loans to exporters of raw materials and to importers of consumer goods'. Surplus funds or resources were only allowed to be invested in Amsterdam, London or Paris.

The financial sector of Uganda is not different from that of many other developing countries in that they are incomplete since they lack the requisite range of markets and institutions to provide the financing needs of the economy. Just as most countries after the attainment of independence, Uganda as a country saw the need to achieve some level of economic growth and development. Due to the imbalance in the provision of financing to the various sectors of the economy by the existing banks, there was the need for a development bank. Therefore, a decade after independence, the Uganda Development Bank (UDB) was established in October 1972. This was in line with the Third Five-Year Development Plan of the government. It was the first indigenous or state-owned development bank that was established to promote the development of ailing sectors (which encompasses all sectors) of the local economy. This bank was not sector-specific like the Ugandan Cooperative Development Bank or regionally focused like East African Development Bank. The key mandate of UDB was the promotion and financing of investment in several commercial sectors of the economy with greater emphasis on commerce, tourism, agriculture, housing and industry, and as a matter of urgency to give technical, managerial and administrative advice for projects in areas such as manufacturing industry and agriculture. The bank was mandated to raise funds from both local and foreign sources to finance projects with social benefits that would be commercially and economically viable and also technically feasible. UDB was backed by statute and permitted to acquire funds from external financiers such as the African Development Bank, International Development Association, European Investment Bank, European Economic Community, Kuwait Fund, Organization of Petroleum Exporting Countries (OPEC Fund) and Arab Bank of Economic Development in Africa (BADEA).

In the 1980s, a number of African economies launched the Comprehensive Economic Recovery Programme (ERP). In the case of Uganda, ERP was launched in 1987. The motive was to reduce drastically and stabilize the inflation rate as well as reduce the imbalances in the Ugandan economy (Bategeka, 1999; Nabudere, 1990; World Bank, 1990). This brought about the revision of its Central Bank Act (Bank of Uganda Act, Cap. 51) to the Bank of Uganda Act (Cap. 54) which this time around was for the operation of both the non-financial institutions and the banks. Under the programme, the government was prohibited from owning any financial institution. The policy objective became fully operational in 2002 when the last state-owned commercial bank (Uganda Commercial Bank-UCB) was privatized. This was done to create room for increased private sector participation in the financial sector, to liberalize interest and exchange rates as well as remove non-performing loans from the balance sheets of commercial banks by improving the asset quality of commercial banks. However, the government managed to cover UDB and in 1993, the bank was categorized as Class III under the Public Enterprise Reform and Divestiture Act Cap. 98. This exercise created banking sector distress where four private local banks were closed down in 1999 (Brownbridge, 2002). These banks together contributed about 12.1% of the total banking sector deposits in that period.

The contributions of DFIs to the Ugandan economy are enormous. The UDB (now Ugandan Development Bank Limited—UDBL) together with other multilateral and regional DFIs including Islamic Development Bank, East African Development Bank, African Development Bank, African Export–Import Bank, KFW and World Bank/IFC has been instrumental in supporting the government in its developmental project delivery over the years. They have supported the underserved sectors with funds in the forms of short-term, medium-and-long-term loans to businesses, the private sector and the public sector.

15.3 Profile and Brief History of the Uganda Development Bank Limited (UDBL)

In the latter part of 1972, the former President of Uganda, Gen. Idi Amin, issued a directive expelling Asians living in the country. This situation created a big vacuum in the economy since most businesses were in the hands of the Asians. The President saw the need to establish a local bank to provide support to the local industries. Essentially, the UDB was established under 'Decree No. 23 of 1972 (later the Uganda Development Bank Act Cap. 56 of 1972), which Act sought to establish the Uganda Development Bank and the Credit Guarantee Fund and for other matters connected therewith' (UDBL, 2021). The mandate of UDB was different from those of Uganda Cooperative Development Bank (UCDB) and the East African Development Bank (EADB), which were for promoting the development of specific sectors and providing incentives for regional development, respectively (UDB, October 29, 1980). UDB was intended to cater for all sectors of the economy. Upon its incorporation, it was charged with 'the promotion and provision of short-, medium-and-long-term development finance and to render managerial, technical and administrative advice and services to projects in the agricultural (crop and livestock), commercial and industrial sectors of the economy' (UDBL, 2021).

UDB was empowered to support entities with a form of loans, and through equity participation, to secure funds from both local and external sources in order to achieve its objectives. The decree that established the UDB required that it finances projects that have commercial, social and economic impact and are technically feasible. Therefore, the projects that were given priority included existing projects requiring small assistance to improve their operations, projects with a scope to maximize utilization of the country's resources and add value to local products, projects aiming to produce quality products at internationally competitive prices targeted for export, and projects creating new job opportunities. Twenty-five years into its operations, the bank had granted term loans to products, such as livestock, cement, processing of fish, tea, coffee and cotton for export, and the manufacturing of sugar, and various other industrial products in excess of US$170 million.

In the 1980s, the banking sector in most African countries encountered many challenges to which the UDB was not immune. The bank was not all that focused during its initial operations as compared to its current state and had challenges with corporate governance practices and management issues, especially loan and risks management. Appointments were not made on merit but along political lines. Due to the kind of economic situation in the country during that period, the operations of UDB were negatively affected. This was fomented by the coercive nature of the existing state apparatus that might have compelled the UDB to engage in certain activities such as the Mafuta Mingi exercise, which it would not have done otherwise (Oloka-Onyango, 1987). The lending decisions were strongly influenced by the political interference and pressures, which landed UDB in a high ratio of non-performing loans/assets, making financial restructuring inevitable.

The government of Uganda, like the governments of most African countries, underwent restructuring of their economies in the 1980s and the 1990s under the instrumentality of the IMF and other powerful nations or former colonial masters. Under such conditions, the government was tasked to privatize all state-owned companies or enterprises as enshrined in the Public Enterprise Reform and Divestiture Act Cap. 98 in 1993. Fortunately, the government placed UDB under a 3-member committee including a Ghanaian to review the structure of the bank. This exercise spanned the period 1997–2000. At the end of the review, efforts were made in recovering the outstanding loans, which were classified as portfolio of performing and non-performing loans, under the debt collection agency (Non-Performing Assets Recovery Trust—NPART) set up by the government through the Ministry of Finance. Apparently, a new breeze blew on the bank in 2001 when the government gave permission for the bank to resume operations in a form of limited lending for a maximum of two years with internally generated funds to only existing customers. However, over time, the loan durations were adjusted for specific cases to periods ranging from 2 to 5 years. With a new management and board in place, the government transferred the mandate of the bank to the realm of Uganda Development Bank Limited (i.e. UDB now UDBL). Thus, UDBL was then a limited liability company wholly owned by the government of Uganda (with equal shareholding of the Ministry of Finance and Ministry of State for Investment) on 31 May 2001. This was made operational in law under the Public Enterprise Reform & Divestiture (Vesting of undertaking of UDB) Instrument of 2002. UDBL has been operating under the Companies Act since 2001.

The Uganda Development Bank Limited (UDBL) is an NDB, wholly owned by the government of Uganda and has had a staff strength ranging between 80 and 100 over the past few years. The bank has been a strategic partner to the government's initiatives, especially in financing private investments in the key sectors of the economy. In line with the government's Third Five-Year Development Plan, UDBL selected six key sectors of the economy to focus on, including agriculture, industry, tourism and hospitality, infrastructure, human capital (health and education), minerals, oil and gas. Since 2001, UDBL has remained focused and improved on its operations and financial performance. The bank, since 2014, has put in place several measures including internal audit and risk management units as well as other benchmarking standards in carrying out its mandate.

15.4 Political Economy and Institutional Context

Considering the mandate and ownership structure of the UDBL, it seems to suggest it must at all times dance to the tune of the policies of the government. For instance, UDB was a key institution in the execution of the government policy of reconstruction and rehabilitation especially under the Economic Recovery Programme of 1982. In fact, it has become a norm for the bank to align its policies and strategies with the development plans of the government. Currently, as the government's primary development financier, UDBL has aligned its 2nd Five-Year Strategic Plan (2020–2024) to the country's National Development Plan III (NDP III) in reference to the country's Vision 2040 agenda. Accordingly, 'the Ugandan society is to be transformed from peasant population to a modern and prosperous country by the year 2040' (Kulabako, 2013). Vision 2040 is a step towards the attainment of middle-income status hence the NDPs have identified priority sectors of the economy and key public and private delivery partners to help achieve this objective.

UDBL has survived the pressures from the economic downturn through the continuous support it has received from the government and other multilateral DFIs over the years. For instance, the Ministry of Finance, Planning and Economic Development announced in May 2020 the government's resolve to increase its share capital in UDBL from USh500 billion (US$136 million) to USh2 trillion (US$545 million). This action was in line with the bank's Five-Year Strategic Plan 2020–2024 (Oketch, 2020). The bank is also active in helping the government to address the issues of job creation, fighting poverty, skills training and so on. Its strategic plans of 2020–2024 are part of its sustainability strategy, and its interventions are guided by three High Impact Goals, underpinned by its Purpose Statement: 'Improving the quality of life of Ugandans'. These three High Impact Goals are *Reducing Poverty in Uganda while Protecting the Natural Environment, Building a Sustainable Food System for Uganda* and *Promoting Sustainable Industrialization in Uganda*. Achieving these strategic goals is critical to increasing household incomes with a medium to long-term impact of improving the quality of life of Ugandans. These strategies will help put the Ugandan economy on its path to socio-economic transformation despite the ravaging effects of the COVID-19 pandemic on the global economy (UDBL, 2021). It has put in place systems that measure its outputs or success regarding these issues and report periodically to the government.

On the regional level, UDBL has committed itself to the agenda of the Association of African Development Financial Institutions (AADFI) in line with Africa's agenda to create development partnerships. Internationally, UDBL is also in partnership with the European Organisation for Sustainable Development (EOSD)[1] in developing and executing the Sustainability Standards and Certification Initiatives (SSCI) and Financing 4.0 (UDBL, 2021). Through these initiatives, the bank has revolutionized and implemented the country's national development priorities in line with its mandate for the socio-economic development of Uganda.

UDBL is one of the first DFIs in Africa to have obtained the highest level of certification, Level 5, under the SSCI programme and is on record to be the first DFI to implement the Financing 4.0 programme. UDBL is inculcating climate change in its investment decisions towards carbon neutral projects to achieve the goals of the National Climate Change Policy, 2015 and Green Growth Development Strategy 2031 (UDBL, 2020). This will put UDBL on track for the establishment of a green finance fund to consolidate and enlarge its investment portfolio with only carbon neutral investments by 2024 (UDBL, 2021). The bank is undertaking a greater contribution to gender opportunity and equity, and thereby implementing a specialized product proposition that aims to increase the participation of women and youth in the development agenda of Uganda.

The government has some level of political influence on the operations of the bank since it has a strong influence in the appointments of the directors and managing director of the bank. The government to some extent still exerts some political pressure on UDBL notwithstanding the bank's good corporate governance structure and its internal controls. For instance, the bank is supervised by the Ministry of Finance and not the Bank of Uganda, and appointments to the board are politically determined, and it has become the norm for the bank to craft strategies that fall within the government's development agenda. However, the bank is able to surmount these pressures through the implementation of some sound

[1] EOSD is an organisation that partners governments and institutions, especially financial institutions in supporting the respective economies and the global economy on the transition to a new economy.

policies. Also, through the political influence the bank is able to attract external support from multilateral DFIs. The operations of the bank are also influenced by other institutions, including the Ministry of Justice, the Parliament of Uganda and the business associations in Uganda.

15.5 UDBL's Corporate Governance Arrangements

The primary role of UDBL's corporate board is to protect shareholder value over the long-term (UDBL, 2021). To achieve this, the board must ensure that the bank's operations meet the ethical and recommended standards of corporate governance. Thus, the mechanism of corporate governance structure ensures that the issues of accountability, transparency and other good corporate practices are successfully achieved. '*The bank recognizes and agrees with the principles stated in the King IV Report on Corporate Governance, that there is always a link between good governance and compliance with the law, and good governance cannot exist separately from the law and it is entirely inappropriate to unhinge governance from the law*' (UDBL, 2021). The bank has a corporate governance culture designed to foster compliance and best practice within the organization in line with international corporate governance trends (including the Companies Act, 2012; the Financial Institutions Act, 2004 and Financial Institutions Corporate Governance Regulations Act 2005 & 2016 (Amended)).

Under the corporate governance systems, the board is supposed to provide the policy directions while the management sees to their implementation. The Board Charter sets out the board's authority, responsibility and membership, to facilitate its effective operations and its relationship with the management of the bank (UDBL, 2021). The board is mandated with the approval of the bank's strategic objectives, to ensure that the necessary resources are in place for the implementation of the strategy and to approve the budget. The board is also 'responsible for the appointment, removal, remuneration and performance review of senior executives, for maintaining a sound system of risk management and internal controls to provide reasonable assurance regarding the achievement of organizational objectives, ensures the bank is managed with integrity and complies with all relevant laws, regulations, codes of business practice and good corporate governance practices, approves all operational policies of the bank, sanctions any amendments or waivers thereof and approves the financial statements' (UDBL, 2021). The directors are, therefore, accountable to the shareholders for the performance and management of the bank.

UDBL's board size is determined by the Memorandum and Articles of Association, which currently permits seven (7) board members, composed on six (6) non-executive directors and one (1) executive director (UDBL, 2018). This composition ensures a balance of power on the board such that no individual director has unfettered powers of the decision-making process. The director's skills, knowledge, experience and competencies, etc. are thoroughly reviewed by the bank so as to meet current and future needs. The board is chaired by an independent non-executive member. The board is also made up of two (2) females and five (5) males. The board of UDBL has three committees with each made up of three (3) members headed by an independent non-executive directors. These committees are the Board Audit and Risk Committee, Strategic Planning Committee and Credit Risk Committee. As indicated, the Audit Committee is chaired by an independent non-executive director who reports directly to the board. The Audit Committee has three (3) members made up of three (3) non-executive directors who are all independent non-executive directors. Table 15.1 shows UDBL board characteristics.

The selection of the directors is based on experience and expertise in at least one of the areas not limited to finance and accounting, economics,

Table 15.1 Board characteristics of UDBL

Board characteristics	*Number (%)*
Board size	7
Executive directors	1 (14.3)
Non-executive directors	6 (85.7)
CEO duality	No
Female directors	2 (28.6)
Male directors	5 (71.4)
Executive committee members	9
Number of committees	3
Size of audit committee	3
Number of Independent Directors on Audit Committee	3 (100)
Audit committee chaired by independent director	Yes

Source Author's construction

human resource management, corporate law and governance, development project management, enterprise development, etc. Non-executive directors are required to serve the board for a term of three (3) years and re-election for one further term of three (3) years subject to the directors' performance. The appointment to the board is made by the minister of finance on the recommendation of the central bank of Uganda. The Ministry of Finance identifies certain personalities and refers them to the central bank for due diligence regarding their suitability to hold such position. When satisfied with the process, the central bank then recommends them to the minister of finance for final appointment. Regarding, the managing director, the board vets or interviews the proposed candidate and makes recommendations to the minister of finance for the appointment or other appropriate action.

It is interesting to note that the corporate governance structure of UDB was weak and the board was without committees before it was restructured in the early 2000s. However, the story has changed substantially over the past few years. Now, there is a fully constituted, broad-based and independent board of directors in place. This board provides the overall strategic direction of the bank, provides oversight to the bank's management team and exercises control over the bank. There are also various policies that define the role of the board and the managing director with regard to specific matters, including staff hiring and discipline. Thus, the board charter and the committee Terms of Reference (ToR) guide the operations of the board and the committees of the board. Best practice demands that the board should have committees to make its work more effective.

In addition to the roles played by the board and its committees, the secretary of the bank is charged with additional responsibility of monitoring international and local governance trends and developments to enable the bank positively review its existing culture accordingly. Furthermore, the bank provides and reviews periodically, for relevance, policies to guide its operations and the conduct of employees.

15.6 Risk Management Practices

The business operation of UDBL is exposed to some key risks, including credit risk, market risk, liquidity risk, compliance risk, operational risk, strategic risk and reputational risk. In view of the important role that risk management plays in the bank, UDBL has created a Board Audit and Risk Committee (BARC), a risk management unit, and has also appointed a Chief Internal Auditor. The board, through the BARC, effectively manages risk exposures by adopting an enterprise-wide risk management (ERM) framework and approach. Based on the corporate governance regulations of the bank, 'the risk management committee shall provide oversight of the senior management's activities in managing credit, market, liquidity, operational, legal and other risks of the institution'. The risk management unit has the mandate to proactively anticipate probable risks that may face UDB and ensures that appropriate mechanisms are in place to mitigate the occurrence and/or minimize the effects of these risks if they occur. This approach has helped the bank in taking a holistic view of the risks inherent in its strategy and operations, and the management of risks is embedded into the mainstream planning, business and decision-making processes. The board-appointed chief internal auditor provides the technical and independent assurances on the effectiveness of the internal control environment to the board and management. The bank reviews the risks associated with it, thus giving those in charge the best understanding of the situation and the necessary mitigating actions to be employed.

During the COVID-19 crisis period, the bank counteracted the distortions by continuously providing reliefs to such sectors as education and tourism that were badly affected. The risk management activities were more focused on strengthening the bank's ERM, adopted fast-track procedures to speed up the authorization of transactions, adopted different a approach to the collection of loans, waived the penalty for defaults and extended credit repayments durations (the standstill approach) and involved other regional and multilateral DFIs to provide financial support. The bank through its Environmental and Social Risks Management Policy (UDBL ESRMP, 2020) recognizes that its business decisions and those of its clients have the potential to impact communities (social well-being) and the environment. In that regard, the bank avoids or mitigates any adverse impact and risks to the community and the environment, arising from the implementation of its financing activities and operations.

The bank also adopted technology in its operations. For instance, staff were able to work from home, and most meetings were virtually held, etc. Again, the bank instituted social protection (an internal scheme) to support staff during the COVID-19 pandemic.

15.7 Regulation and Supervision

Regulation and *supervision* of financial institutions are very critical elements in ensuring the sustainability of the financial sector. The bank's position regarding compliance with the codes and regulations as captured in its 2021 report states:

> For us conducting business in accordance with relevant legislation, regulations, standards, and codes is integral to our culture.... Compliance provides assurance to our stakeholders that the existing systems and processes in place will secure sustainability of the business, protect the reputation of the Bank, and provide competitive advantage in the market.... The Bank is regulated and monitored under the Public Enterprise Reform and Divestiture Act, Uganda Development Bank Limited has reporting obligations to the Parastatal Monitoring Unit (PMU) and is committed to complying with all legislation, regulations, and codes of best practice.

The literature suggests that NDBs are either regulated by the central bank or are self-regulated. Currently, UDBL is self-regulated and is supervised by the Ministry of Finance, Planning and Economic Development. The supervision of the bank is benchmarked against international standards. Since the Basel framework is not compulsory for DFIs, UDBL has not entirely adopted a specific Basel but it has adopted other regulations and codes from some organizations such as the AADFI and African Asian Development Financial Institutions, which have some aspects of the Basel III imbedded.

In furtherance of these actions of the bank, there are both internal and external audits to enhance the compliance of the bank regarding regulations and supervision. The Internal Audit department has a functional reporting line to the committee chairperson and an administrative reporting line to the managing director. The internal audit unit provides quarterly reports to the Board Audit and Risk Committee (BARC) on, among other things, the status of compliance risk management in the bank and significant areas of noncompliance. BARC reviews the effectiveness of these reports and approves them (Internal Audit department's Audit Plan) when it is satisfied with them. The external auditor is the Auditor General as enshrined in the law. However, the Auditor General normally appoints or delegates that exercise to an international certified auditor. So in 2020 and 2021, external audit was carried out by KPMG.

15.8 Monitoring and Evaluation, and Impact Evaluation

Monitoring and evaluation, and impact evaluation are critical activities in development banking. UDBL has a separate department under the Research and Knowledge Management Directorate responsible for monitoring and evaluation. This unit has a staff strength of six and is headed by an economist. The bank uses a Monitoring and Evaluation Planning Framework, which provides measurement and reporting guidelines. The bank has also institutionalized Monitoring, Evaluation and Learning (MEL) in its operations. The MEL approach incorporates the regular data collection on project activities and involves analysing, measuring and reporting development impact from the inception phase of every project and throughout the project cycle. Central to the framework are 'environmental, social and governance (ESG) criteria, which help in measuring the sustainability and ethical impact of projects the bank invests in' (UDBL, 2021).

Monitoring and evaluation processes are carried out in two stages at UDBL for every funded project. The first stage is the supervision phase, which entails the bank following up on projects that have received approval and funding. This exercise is done to ensure that funds are used solely for the intended projects and that such projects are built according to the stipulated specifications and standards to produce the expected output (physical structure). The second phase is the monitoring and evaluation stage, which involves looking at the outcomes (products) of the projects and this is done yearly depending on the nature of the project. With respect to impact evaluation, this is carried out by the bank after some years of the project's implementation. The impact evaluation ascertains how the project has created changes in the livelihoods of people, its impact on employment creation, its impact on revenue generation and the overall societal changes observed. The bank has an appropriate framework for such development impact assessment based on its policies, procedures and mandate. Again, it has adopted some of the benchmarks of monitoring and evaluation, and impact evaluation from other relevant professional bodies.

Apart from evaluating the funded projects, UDBL also evaluates its board annually. The bank undertakes a comprehensive review of the effectiveness of the board, its committees and individual directors. This exercise is very helpful since the bank is able to establish whether the board has been effective in carrying out its mandate, whether individual directors continue to make quality contributions to the discussions at meetings and continue to demonstrate a commitment to their director role, and whether there is presence of sufficient teamwork at the board (UDBL, 2021). For instance, the board contracted an Independent Consultant in 2020 to undertake an external assessment of the board, and the recommendations were implemented in 2021 based on the generated action plan. In 2021, the evaluation of the board was facilitated by the bank's secretary and the recommendations proposed for improvement were duly implemented in 2022.

15.9 Business Model of UDBL

15.9.1 Policy Mandate and Sectors Served

UDBL has multiple mandates since it was created to serve many sectors of the Ugandan economy. The main mandate was 'to operate as Uganda's Development Finance Institution, particularly through interventions in priority sectors and in line with the Government of Uganda's development priorities' (UDBL, 2020). Upon its incorporation, it was charged with 'the promotion and provision of short-, medium-and-long-term development finance and to render managerial, technical and administrative advice and services for projects in the agricultural (crop and livestock), commercial and industrial sectors of the economy'. This was aimed at driving the economic development agenda of the country.

The bank currently supports almost all sectors of the Ugandan economy but has six major sectors that it has prioritized, which are agriculture, human capital development, tourism and hospitality, infrastructure, industry, minerals, oil and gas. The bank is also pursuing issues of ESG in all its development initiatives and is redirecting its investment towards low-carbon risk projects to achieve the goals of the National Climate Change Policy, 2015 and Green Growth Development Strategy, 2031. The bank has plans of establishing a green finance strategy for low-carbon, climate-resilient (LCR) investments. This will give the bank the green light in establishing a green finance fund to consolidate and enlarge its investment portfolio with only low-carbon risk investments (clean projects) by 2024 (UDBL, 2020).

The bank, with the approval of the board, can vary the sectors it intends to prioritize. The bank has set for itself three high impact goals, which are to: (i) reduce poverty in Uganda while protecting the natural environment; (ii) build a Sustainable Food System for Uganda; and (iii) promote sustainable industrialization in Uganda.

15.9.2 Funding Sources

UDBL is funded through four main sources, including government of Uganda capital contribution (equity), borrowing (loans) from development partners, grants and administered funds, and internally generated resources (e.g. retained earnings). The government of Uganda is the main source of finance for the bank, mostly through guarantees. The bank is able to finance some of its projects through capital growth and realization. Thus, the proceeds from its operations are used to repay debts, and to cover operational costs thereby growing its balance sheet to reinvest in future developments. Like other NDBs, the first paid-up capital of UDB was by the government of Uganda, creating a direct link between the bank and the government. The government continues to increase capitalization of UDBL. For instance, the government made an additional injection of capital to the tune of Ushs104 billion (US$29.01 million) and Ushs509 billion (US$136.92 million) to the capital of UDBL in 2021 and 2020, respectively. Secondly, UDBL has received significant support from external financiers (multilateral and regional development banks) like the African Development Bank, International Development Association, European Investment Bank, European Economic Community, Arab Bank of Economic Development in Africa (BADEA), India Exim Bank and Islamic Development Bank over the years.

UDBL has continually received funds from the UN Capital Development Fund (UNCDF) for Support to the Agricultural Revitalization and Transformation (START) facility. This comes in the form of concessional loans, including, inter alia, conditions pertaining to financial control, reporting and auditing arrangements. The maximum contribution of UNCDF to the START concessional loan is up to EUR 2,000,000 (two million Euros) for a period of four years. Also, a Trust Fund is created in UDBL from a grant of US Dollars 7 million from Kuwait to the government of Uganda. The purpose of the fund was to finance farming and lending to small and micro business activities for the production of food and provision of related support services, including food processing, storage and marketing (UDBL, 2021). Moreover, the bank received a soft loan with a grant component from the European Union to help stimulate businesses operating in the tourism sector, which has been heavily impacted by COVID-19. The facility was made up of a soft loan of Ushs40 billion (US$11.16 million) plus Ushs21.8 billion (US$6.08 million) grant for this intervention.

15.9.3 Lending Model

UDBL adopts the retail lending model as it lends directly to the target customers. The bank was created to help channel the needed financial resources to the underserved sectors of the Ugandan economy so as to spur economic development and drive the agenda of the government. Considering that UDBL is a development bank, it does not aim at making abnormal profit, as loans provided to end customers are not based on commercial rates. During the COVID-19 pandemic, the bank directed more credits to the agricultural, tourism and manufacturing sectors (pharmaceutical industry in the manufacturing of some drugs). Figure 15.1 provides the gross loans to customers by sector composition, during the period, 2015–2021.

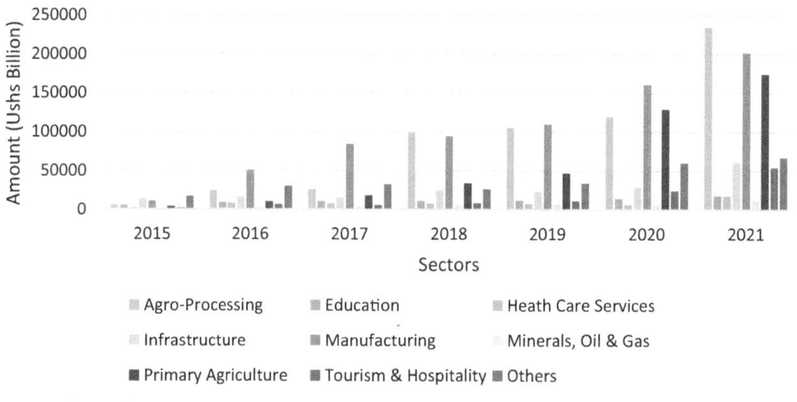

Fig. 15.1 Gross loans to customers by sector composition, 2015–2021 (*Source* UDBL and author's Construction based on UDBL's financials) (Color figure online)

15.9.4 *Products and Services*

UDBL supports a number of sectors of the economy with financial products and non-financial services. Regarding financial products, the bank gives short-term, medium-and-long-term loans to businesses, private and public sectors. The bank provides working capital and supports start-up projects or existing projects with short-term facilities when the projects face temporary cash flow deficits. This basically addresses key operational requirements in production such as the purchase of productive inputs or raw materials and has a tenure of 1–3 years. The bank gives medium-term loans to businesses undergoing expansion or diversification and the tenure for this facility is usually from 4 to 8 years. Also, some customers or projects receive long-term loans for financing long-term projects and the tenure of such facility is 9–15 years with a grace period of 3 years depending on the type of business. In addition, the bank provides other forms of financing including asset finance, trade finance and equity investments.

The bank also runs special programmes that create interventions for SMEs, women and the youth. It provides business advisory services and project preparation. In terms of business advisory services, the bank aims at promoting the growth and sustainability of SMEs in the priority sectors of the economy through improved business performance of these clients. The bank achieves this through tailored programmes in governance, management, project-related technical matters and financial management (UDBL, 2021). On the other hand, through the project preparation services, UDBL supports projects from identification through concept design, feasibility studies, financial and legal structuring in order to enable projects achieve financial close. The bank's objective is to bridge the gap between the project concept and bankability.

15.9.5 *Pricing and Subsidies*

As indicated earlier, UDBL provides loans to end customers at concessionary rates. On the average, the bank's current lending rate is 12% per annum with up to three years' grace period and a tenure up to 15 years, while the market rate is 18% and above. Occasionally, the government provides funds that are solely to be used for specific projects hence the bank's internal structures respond to the general standards laid down by the central bank (Bank of Uganda) and Ministry of Finance with regard to credit provision in relation to such funds. Funds the bank obtains from the government through the Ministry of Finance and those from the multilateral and regional DFIs are also offered to the target customers below the market rates. There are levels of approval of credit up to the maximum level by the board of directors.

15.10 Financial Performance

UDBL continued to sustain a balanced performance metrics such as operational performance, capital adequacy, asset quality, management efficiency, earnings and liquidity assets (see Table 15.2) have independently witnessed both changing and steady trends over the period.

15.10.1 Capital Adequacy

The bank has seen a steady improvement in its capital adequacy ratio over the period, 2016–2021, following a drop from 10.09% in 2015 to 5.48% in 2016 (see Fig. 15.2). The increasing levels of capital adequacy ratio over the period suggest that the bank has enough capital in its reserves to handle certain amounts of financial losses. This has been possible because of the continuous increase in the capital requirement of the bank over the same period.

15.10.2 Management Efficiency

Over the past few years, the bank's management efficiency has improved remarkably. The three ratios, cost-to-income, personnel expenses and non-interest expense ratios, have been declining from 2015 to 2018 but increased marginally in 2019 and declined again from 2020 onwards. The marginal increase in the ratios was attributed to the effects of the COVID-19 pandemic on banking sector operations. The bank's efficiency ratios generally remained healthy as shown in Fig. 15.3.

15.10.3 Asset Quality

The behaviour of the bank's credit risk is erratic in nature. In Fig. 15.4, the loan impairment ratio declined steadily from 7.9% in 2015 to 7.6% in 2017, but was unstable over the period, 2017–2021. This trend is partly

Table 15.2 Financial indicators

		2015	*2016*	*2017*	*2018*	*2019*	*2020*	*2021*	*Average*	*SD*
Capital adequacy	Regulatory CAR (%)	10.09	5.48	17.49	27.06	37.81	63.67	65.30	32.42	22.56
Asset quality	Loan impairment ratio (%)	7.90	8.00	7.60	10.60	10.60	6.23	6.60	8.22	1.62
Operational perfor-mance	Portfolio yield (%)	2.69	3.74	2.93	1.34	0.62	0.37	0.16	1.69	1.31
	Operating profit (%)	72.12	87.19	89.68	79.05	81.85	74.10	73.84	79.69	6.37
Earnings	Return on assets (%)	1.00	3.00	3.00	2.80	2.60	2.81	3.44	2.66	0.72
	Return on equity (%)	1.00	4.00	5.00	4.00	3.70	3.51	4.93	3.73	1.24
	Net interest income margin	99.00	98.00	95.00	94.00	92.61	94.22	96.76	95.66	2.15
	Net interest margin	7.95	7.84	7.70	9.58	8.64	6.61	9.24	8.22	0.94
	Interest margin to gross income (%)	80.43	72.66	74.17	84.87	88.28	91.82	95.72	83.99	8.07
Liquidity assets	Broad liquidity assets to total assets (%)	88.25	88.24	98.78	98.18	98.34	99.48	96.68	95.42	4.60
	Core liquidity asset to total assets (%)	83.25	85.11	87.64	88.72	91.84	96.34	96.67	89.94	4.85
Management Efficiency	Noninterest expenses to gross income (%)	58.33	49.40	49.41	44.35	46.95	31.28	23.42	43.30	11.05
	Personnel expenses to gross income (%)	30.00	30.23	25.87	23.41	25.80	18.22	15.10	24.09	5.27
	Cost-to-income ratio	25.0	33.0	55.20	45.0	48.0	47.0	45.0	42.60	9.42

Source UDBL Financial Statements, 2015–2021

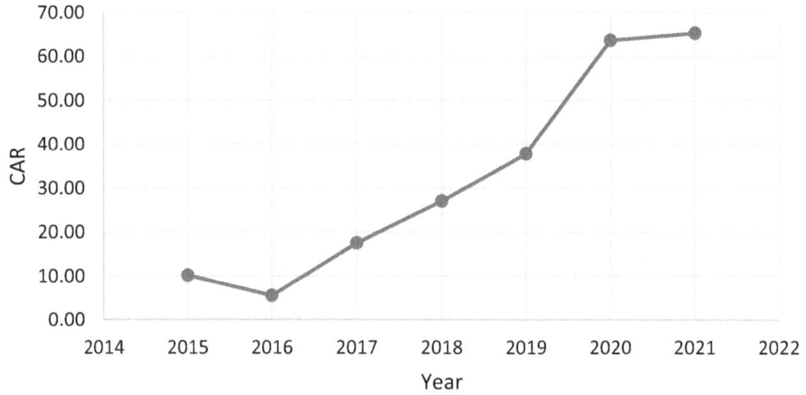

Fig. 15.2 Regulatory capital (*Source* Author's construction based on UDBL Financial Statements)

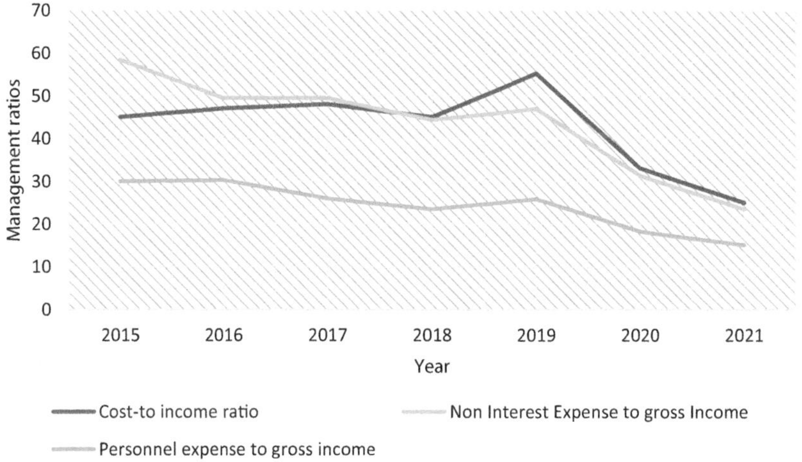

Fig. 15.3 Management efficiency (*Source* Author's construction based on UDBL Financial Statements) (Color figure online)

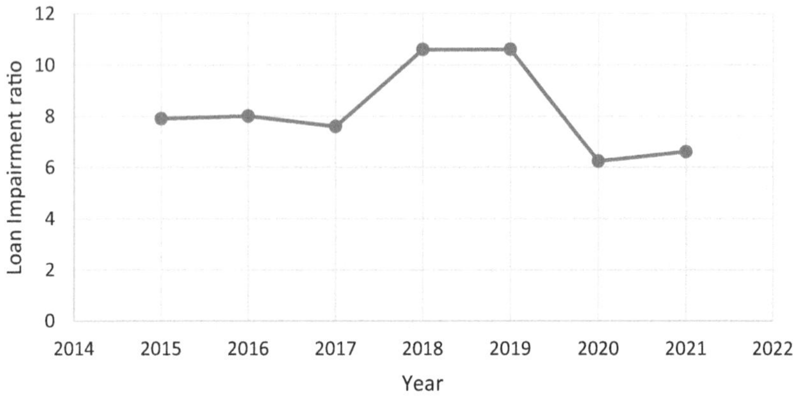

Fig. 15.4 Asset quality (*Source* Author's construction based on UDBL Financial Statements)

explained by the growth of the loans and advances and management overlays arising from a holistic assessment of NPL accounts for impairment (including the restructured and deferred client payments policy based on customer requests). This largely arises from the challenges attributed to the prolonged lockdown of the economy and low expected cash flows from the loan portfolios.

15.10.4 Operational Performance

The bank has demonstrated a reasonable commitment to developing tools that control operational risk and improve the risk culture of the bank. However, the portfolio yield, which shows the bank's ability to generate cash on the gross portfolio, has shown a declining trend over the period, 2016–2021. For instance, in Fig. 15.5, the bank's portfolio yield moved from 2.69% in 2015 to a maximum value of 3.74% in 2016. It started declining from 2017 till 2021 and the decline can partly be explained by the increasing average loan portfolio over the years. Moreover, this is expected because of the disparity between the bank's concessionary rate (12%) and the market rates (18%) over the same period.

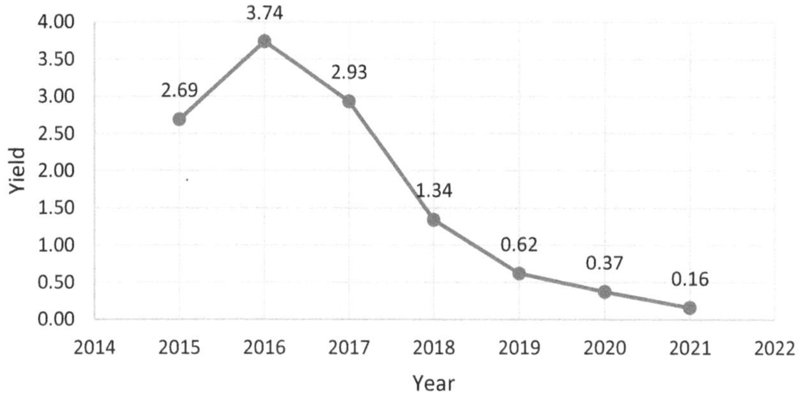

Fig. 15.5 Portfolio yield (*Source* Author's construction based on UDBL Financial Statements)

15.10.5 Earnings/Profitability

The bank enjoyed improvements in its earning/profitability ratios from 2015. Figure 15.6 shows that return on equity (ROE) was higher than return on assets (ROA) on a yearly basis from 2016 but the ratios recorded the same value in 2015. In 2021, ROE and ROA were 4.93% and 3.44%, respectively. It can be observed that both ratios saw a reduction in values in 2018 and 2019. On the other hand, the interest margin to gross income ratio increased steadily from 2018 and reached 95.72% in 2021.

15.10.6 Liquidity

The bank also exhibited positive liquidity ratios over the past few years with broad liquid assets to total asset ratio and core liquid asset ratio increasing marginally from 88.25% and 83.25% in 2015 to 96.68% and 96.67% in 2021 (see Fig. 15.7). The trends in the ratios suggest that the bank was liquid and solvent in the period under review.

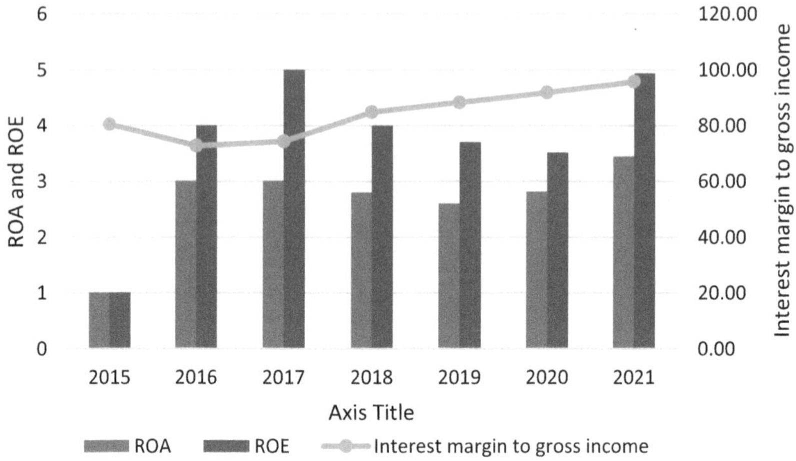

Fig. 15.6 Earnings/profitability ratios (*Source* Author's construction based on UDBL Financial Statements) (Color figure online)

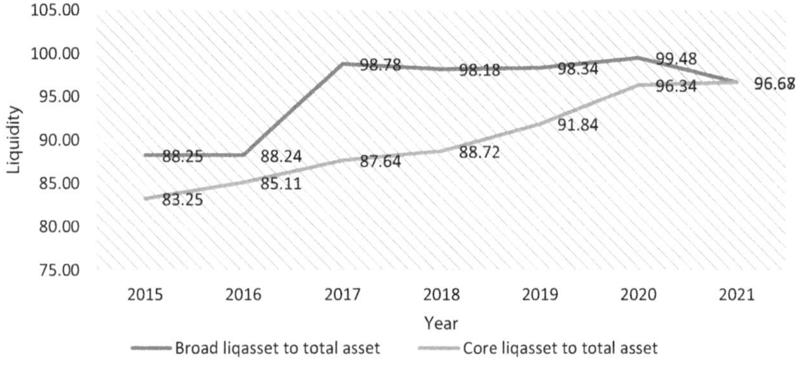

Fig. 15.7 Liquidity ratios (*Source* Author's construction based on UDBL Financial Statements) (Color figure online)

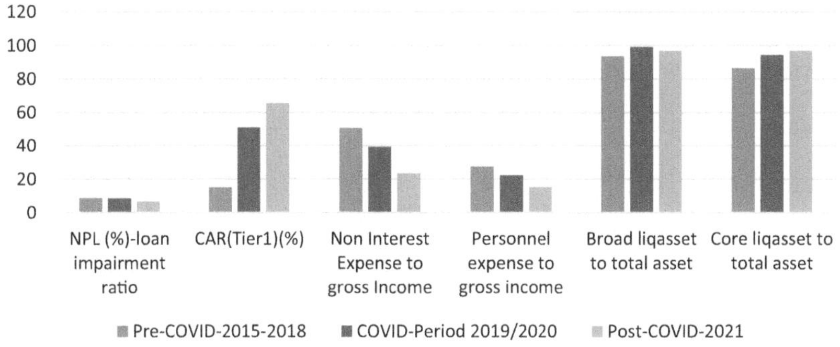

Fig. 15.8 Financial performance indicators—pre- and post-COVID-19 lockdowns (*Source* Author's construction based on UDBL Financial Statements) (Color figure online)

15.10.7 UDBL's Performance in the Pre-COVID-19, COVID-19 and Post-COVID-19 Lockdown Periods

The comparative analysis of the bank's performance Pre-COVID-19, COVID-19 and Post-COVID-19 lockdown periods indicates some positive trends for all the performance indicators suggesting that the good policies of the bank were working. For instance, NPL dropped from 8.535% in the pre-COVID-19 period to 6.6% post-COVID-19 lockdown. Again, personnel expenses also dropped from 27.38% in pre-COVID-19 to 15.10% post-COVID-19 lockdown period. Similarly, non-interest expense dipped from 50.37% to 23.42% (see Fig. 15.8).

The profitability ratios rather showed the same trend over the different periods where ROE is higher than ROA as shown in Fig. 15.9.

15.11 Main Achievements and Contributions of UDBL

UDBL has experienced some achievements because of the interventions undertaken since 2014. The bank has contributed to the socio-economic development of Uganda through the financing of several projects. It has channelled funds to expand the priority sectors of the economy including agriculture, infrastructure, industry, tourism and hospitality, and human capital development. This has resulted in improvements in the level of financial inclusion in the country. The bank has aligned its strategic plans

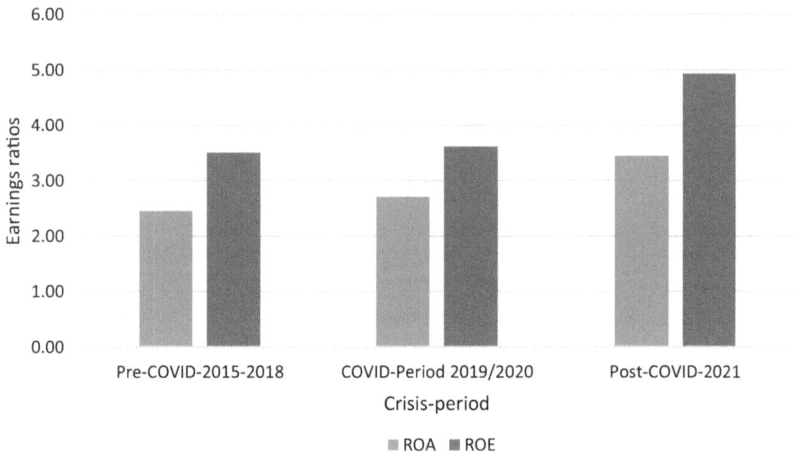

Fig. 15.9 Profitability indicators—pre- and post-COVID-19 lockdowns (*Source* Author's construction based on UDBL Financial Statements) (Color figure online)

to suit the national development plan of the country thereby generating revenue as well as creating numerous jobs for women and the youth in particular.

Since the inception of the bank, it has granted a great deal of support including loans at concessional rates to the various sectors, especially the prioritized areas, which has resulted in the generation of revenue, and creation of jobs for men, women and the youth. For instance, in 2021 alone 41,338 jobs were created and maintained, loans of Ushs1,160.9 billion (US$323.85 million) were granted, taxes worth Ushs570 billion (US$157.01 million) were paid and foreign exchange worth Ushs1,480 billion (US$412.87 million) was realized by UDBL (UDBL, 2021). These supports have helped in the establishment of factories and companies, which has resulted an expansion of the Ugandan economy as well as a reduction in the importation of some products, while enhancing the exportation of others. Despite the devastating nature of the COVID-19 pandemic on all sectors of the global economy, the bank was able to give more loans and created more jobs. Figure 15.10 shows the employment created/maintained by the bank over the period 2015–2021.

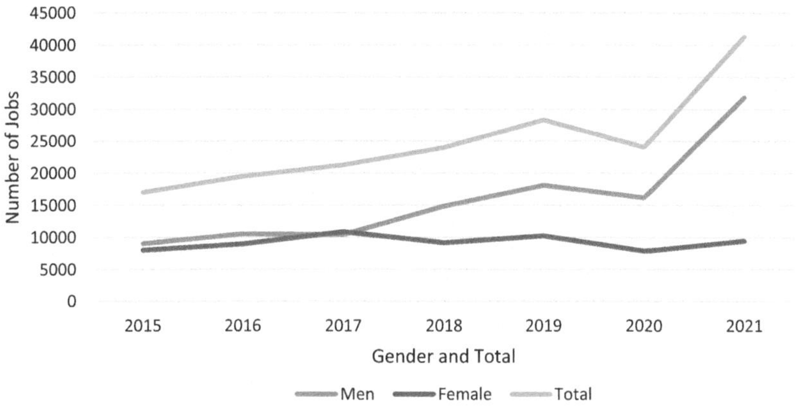

Fig. 15.10 Employment generated and maintained by the sectors supported by UDBL, 2015–2021 (*Source* UDBL and author's construction) (Color figure online)

In trying to address the issues of SDGs, climate change and others, the bank set three objectives to achieve: poverty reduction and protection of the natural environment; building a sustainable food system for Uganda; and promoting sustainable industrialization in Uganda. These assistances have resulted in helping the country to achieve some of the SDGs. For instance, there have been improvements in poverty reduction, a sustainable food system and sustainable industrialization in Uganda. Based on these objectives, the bank has been able to construct over 36 valley dams, developed 4 private irrigation schemes, supported 33 new Agri-SMEs, increased food production and yields in selected value chains, increased support for organic farming and adoption of climate-smart farming techniques by supporting 12 organic farming projects, supported 12 enterprises under the import substitution and export promotion strategy, supported 5 SMEs to adopt cleaner production technologies, supported 10 SMEs in industrial development, enabled improved post-harvest handling by financing 4 post-harvest handling facilities and supported financial inclusion for over 1000 smallholder farmers through FinTech (UDBL, 2021).

It is important to note that issues of SDGs, Climate Change, Green Finance and ESG are crucial in the operations of UDBL. Since 2014, the bank has aligned its Five-year strategic plan with the national development plan. The bank uses various benchmarks and international frameworks such as the Global Reporting Initiatives (GRI), G4 guidelines for reporting purposes; in addition to internal policies and procedures (UDBL, 2021). At the beginning of 2015, the UDBL re-branded itself with a view to re-positioning the bank in the credit market, increasing its brand visibility and raising its corporate profile. The bank's allocation of green finance to some sectors like agriculture and manufacturing has reduced GHG emissions, saved water and saved over 25,519 jobs in the country. Box 15.1 illustrates some selected projects supported by UDBL.

Box 15.1: Some Selected Projects Supported by UDBL

Gulu Agriculture Development Company, (GADC) was established in 2018 with support from UDBL which is engaged in primary production and processing of cotton in Acholi and west Nile districts. It has helped to boost cotton production in Uganda from around 55,000 bales to 200,000 bales and currently has a sizeable market share in Uganda which is over 20% of cotton export. The company has the potential to increase house hold income of the people through job creation especially for women and the youth in the sub-region.

Multi-tech Business School (MBS) was incorporated in May 2002. It began as a business college but has since grown to a fully fledged tertiary institution. It received a loan facility from UDB to complete civil works and procure furniture and equipment for its Kampala campus. It has over 1000 students in its three campuses providing much needed vocational skills to augment government efforts.

St. Joseph's Hospital Wakiso Ltd is a private health services provider registered under the Uganda Medical and dental practitioners' council. With the UDB funding, the facility will increase its bed capacity from 25 admission beds to 65 beds and 32 new private rooms for admissions. The project has created gainful and dignified employment for 41(33 females) Ugandans on a permanent basis and this is expected to increase to 58 upon completion.

Kinkiizi Development Company Ltd, (KDC) is an Agro-Processing company which started operations in January 2019 with tea production and processing in Kisoro and Kabale. The project or company receives its raw materials from over 50,000 small holder farmers. This project will help to increase house hold incomes of the population, increase the quantity and quality of the Uganda tea exports as well as creating more jobs for the population especially woman and youth in the sub-region.

Abu Baker Technical Services Ltd is a leading road contractor whose clientele include: government, government agencies and donor funded projects. It received massive support from UDBL in 2018 which enabled the company to procure a stone crushing and road traction equipment and UGX 4.5 billion to augment working capital for execution of its contracts. The company employed over 600 workers and paid UGX 100 million in taxes in 2018 which has been increasing over the years.

Steel and Tube Industries Ltd (STIL) is one of the leading manufacturers of various steel products in the country which was incorporated in 2002 with their marketing stretching around the whole of Uganda as well as within the entire East African region. UDBL has supported the company through provision of working capital facilities over the last three years which has made it possible for the company to create over 6000 jobs (with over 1068 permanent jobs) and making tax contribution of Ushs10.95 billion; foreign exchange savings of US$3.5 million through import substitution; foreign exchange revenues of Ushs14.2 billion equivalent to 35% of total sales have been earned from re-exportation, all these boosting the country's balance of payments.

Hotel Africana (Moroto) Ltd-Moroto Hotel (HAML) was incorporated on 8 April 2015 as a separate legal entity affiliated to Hotel Africana Kampala. The support from UDBL has enabled the company to set up an ultra-modern hotel. The company is expected to impact the economy of Uganda through job creation for over 40 workers, foreign exchange earnings and expected revenue of 30% in USD.

Bwendero Dairy Farm Ltd is an agro-industrial firm that began operations in the 1960s in Kitoba village Hoima District and was diversified into a distillery to produce extra neutral alcohol (ENA) for medical use in 2010 and further diversified into sugar production. With support from UDB, BDF has installed a 750TCD sugar mill complete with a 2 MW co-generation plant, creating 2,000 jobs. This project is expected to positively impact 35,000 people along the value chain creating jobs and generating income to boost the Ugandan economy.

Source UDBL (2020) and Author's Modification

To help the Ugandan economy to recover from the devasting effects of the COVID-19 pandemic, UDBL set out to enhance MSMEs access to affordable and patient credit through several initiatives. For instance, on 14 December 2021, UDB launched Special programmes to implement and manage interventions in the categories of SMEs, Women, Youth and Business Advisory Services from start-ups to existing businesses with appropriate financial and non-financial solutions.

UDBL was awarded the 'Sustainability Leader of the Year 2021 during the Karlsruhe Sustainable Awards ceremony held annually in Germany' (UDBL, 2021). The award was in recognition of the bank's continued exceptional leadership in creating social, economic and environmental values and globally advancing sustainable finance. The bank also received certification after developing and executing the Sustainability Standards and Certification Initiatives (SSCI) and Financing 4.0 in partnership with EOSD in September 2020. This granted UDBL the opportunity to be one of the first DFIs in Africa to implement the financing 4.0 programme. Other selected accolades for the bank include the outstanding achievement in financial reporting (FiRe) for 2014, 2015 and 2021. The bank also received an award for being the best performing development financial institution in Africa for 2014 and 2015. These awards were given by AADFI. The bank also received AADFI certificate rating index 'A' in 2021 for complying with the AADFI prudential standards and guidelines and on its development impact potential. On the other hand, Fitch rated UDBL B^+ in 2018 and 2019 with positive outlook.

15.12 Challenges Facing UDBL

The challenges of the UDB from its inception as DFI through to its current model have mainly been in the areas of corporate governance structure and prudential regulations, funding and credit risks. The political influence in appointments to the board and senior management positions like the CEO sometimes results in appointments which are not based on merit. This sometimes makes the management or the board inefficient, thereby making some uninformed decisions that eventually affect the operations of the bank negatively.

One main challenge facing the bank is inadequate funding. Though funding from government and other development partners to the bank has been increasing over the years, this is quite inadequate considering the broad mandate of the bank. The bank is a strategic partner to the government and has enormous responsibility in helping in the socio-economic transformation of the Ugandan economy.

Another issue concerns the interest rate. Though the bank's rate of 12% is below the market rate, there are calls for the bank to bring its rate to 10% and below. The UDBL has come under intense pressure to reduce its lending rates.

Like all financial institutions, UDBL has faced the issue of loan default (credit risks) over the years. For instance, the non-performing loan as a percentage of total loans as of June 2012 was 19%. The Bank's maximum exposure to credit risk ranged between Ushs446,670 million (US$120.59 million) in 2019, Ushs1,049,905 billion (US$282.42billion) in 2020 and Ushs11,181,365 billion (US$3119.2billion) in 2021. Borrowers perceive the UDBL as government's bank and therefore consider the loans from this bank as their share of the national cake. Retrieving such loans from some of these entities is problematic, especially from those with close ties to the government. The advent of the COVID-19 crisis has had a strong impact on the banking sector, constraining the ability of banks, including UDBL in recovering loans promptly.

15.13 Conclusion and Implications

UDBL, as a wholly state-owned DFI, has the mandate of accelerating socio-economic development through sustainable financial interventions in line with national development priorities. The bank, since its establishment, has aligned its strategic plans with the national development plans to intervene in SMEs and priority sectors such as agriculture, industry, human capital development, tourism and hospitality, infrastructure, and minerals, oil and gas. UDBL has a corporate governance culture designed to foster compliance and best practice within the bank in line with international corporate governance trends. The bank is self-regulated and is supervised by the Ministry of Finance, Planning and Economic Development. The supervision of the bank is benchmarked against international standards. Since the Basel framework is not compulsory for DFIs, UDBL has not entirely adopted a specific Basel but it has adopted other regulations and codes based on international standards. The business operation of UDBL is exposed to some key risks, including credit risk, market risk, liquidity risk, compliance risk, operational risk, strategic risk and reputational risk. However, these risks are controlled on the basis of the bank's risk management principles. The bank has also institutionalized Monitoring, Evaluation and Learning (MEL) in its operations including a framework for delivering development impact assessment based on its policies, procedures and mandate. Its main sources of finance include government capital contribution (equity), borrowings (loans) from development partners, grants and administered funds, and internally generated resources (e.g. retained earnings).

Over the years, the bank has made significant contributions to the development of some key sectors of the economy. For instance, UDBL has supported projects that are focused on SDGs, green finance, climate change, ESG, etc. In line with its development initiatives, the bank established three key goals including reducing poverty in Uganda, protecting the natural environment, building a sustainable food system for Uganda and promoting sustainable industrialization in Uganda. The implementation of these goals through policies and programmes has yielded some positive results including improvements in financial inclusion (for over 1000 smallholder farmers through Fintech) through access to financial services especially by women and the youth; youth empowerment and entrepreneurship development; financing for climate-smart agriculture and organic food production; construction and development of over 36 valley dams and 4 private irrigation schemes; support for 33 new Agri-SMEs; increasing food production in selected value chains by supporting at least 6 out grower schemes, small, medium and large size industries that aim to facilitate import and export as well as value-added exports in the areas of agro-industrialization, manufacturing and mineral-based value addition, etc. The bank has contributed to the improvement of the living standards of a good number of people especially, farmers, women and the youth. The government has directly or indirectly benefited from the activities of UDBL through job creation and revenue mobilization. Despite the sustainable achievements, the bank faces the challenge of inadequate capitalization and also credit risks. It is clear that the corporate governance structure of UDBL is influenced by political interference.

The important role played by UDBL in the Ugandan economy over the years cannot be overstated. However, issues of corporate governance arrangements, regulations, funding and credit risks are some challenges the bank faces in its endeavour to deliver on the mandate spelt out in the national agenda of Uganda. In this regard, it is important for the bank to engage stakeholders to enact laws that address governance and regulatory issues in line with the corporate governance and regulatory standards of international DFIs. On the funding of mega projects, a financing alternative that offers lower cost of capital should be considered, and it is important for the bank to focus on projects for which it has pre-knowledge. Again, with the right amount of funding and the adoption of the right technologies, the bank can deliver on its mandate. The risk management guidelines and impact assessment of all implemented projects that are in line with the Basel are vital to addressing credit risks and strengthening the bank's developmental legacy. Given that political interference remains a key challenge of the bank, it is important to advocate UDBL's independence with guidance from the government and international DFIs. The implementation of sound policies and programmes will help yield more significant results.

References

Bategeka, L. N. (1999). Uganda's achievements and challenges in the financial sector: Whose interests count? *Ugandan Banker, 7*(4), 6–10.

Brownbridge, M. (2002). Resolving bank failures in Uganda: Policy lessons from recent bank failures. *Development Policy Review, 20*(3), 279–291.

Kulabako, F. (2013, July 9). Uganda development bank to shift its market interest. *Daily Monitor*. Kampala. Retrieved 4 August 2016.

Nabudere, D. W. (1990). *The IMF-World Bank's economic stabilisation and structural adjustment policies and the Uganda economy, 1981–1989* (Research Report). African Studies Centre.

Oketch, M. L. (2020). UDB unveils 5-year plans. *Daily Monitor*. Kampala. Retrieved on 16 July 2020 from https://www.monitor.co.ug/uganda/business/finance/udb-unveils-5-year-plans-1892916

Uganda Development Bank (UDB). (1980, October 29). Speech given by the Managing Director of the UDB to the Executive Commiuce and members of the Kampala Chamber of Commerce. In Oloka-Onyango, J. (1987). Development financing: The case of the Uganda Development Bank. *Ufahamu: A Journal of African Studies, 15*(3).

Uganda Development Bank Limited (UDBL). (2018). "Financial Statement As of 31 December 2017" (PDF). *Uganda Development Bank*. Kampala, Uganda. Retrieved 11 August 2022.

Uganda Development Bank Limited (UDBL). (2020). "Financial Statement As of 31 December 2019" (PDF). *Uganda Development Bank*. Kampala, Uganda. Retrieved 11 August 2022.

Uganda Development Bank Limited (UDBL). (2021). "Financial Statement As of 31 December 2020" (PDF). *Uganda Development Bank*. Kampala, Uganda. Retrieved 11 August 2022.

Uganda Development Bank Limited (UDB ESRMP). (2020). Environmental and Social Management Systems.

World Bank. (1990). Uganda—Financial sector review: Summary and recommendations (English). http://documents.worldbank.org/curated/en/315901468318841229/Summary-and-recommendations

CHAPTER 16

The System of National Development Banks in South Africa: Development Bank of Southern Africa

16.1 Introduction

Development banks in recent times have been the antidote to the void in the funding mechanism of DFIs. In particular, the focus of development finance has been diverted to NDBs in attracting and mobilizing the needed capital to support their country's development efforts and structural transformation. NDBs can take risks that the private sector would not, and they support projects that have enormous social benefits but low financial returns. For instance, an increasing number of development banks in Africa are mainly owned by African governments, with the mandate to support various developmental sectors of their countries. Although several new African development banks have been created, there is a need for policymakers and practitioners to understand the development mandate of NDBs in Africa.

The Development Bank of Southern Africa (DBSA) is one of the leading African DFIs, wholly owned by the government of South Africa. In line with the unique role that NDBs play in the national development agenda, DBSA aims to deliver impactful development finance solutions that ignite transformative change in South Africa as well as the other economies on the African continent. The fundamental focus of the bank's development impact is to improve the quality of life of the people in Africa and to provide conservative financing to national priority projects with long-term repayment schedules. Like other NDBs, DBSA

© The Author(s), under exclusive license to Springer Nature Switzerland AG 2023

J. Yindenaba Abor, *The Changing Role of National Development Banks in Africa*, https://doi.org/10.1007/978-3-031-38639-8_16

provides counter-cyclical financing, promotes financial inclusion, supports infrastructure investment and financing, promotes innovation and structural transformation and provides public goods among others (le Pere, 2021). Given the important role that DBSA plays in Southern Africa, this chapter undertakes a case study of its operations and activities.

The rest of the chapter is specifically structured as follows: Sect. 16.2 provides an overview of DFIs in South Africa; Sect. 16.3 provides a profile and historical background of DBSA; Sect. 16.4 discusses the political economy and institutional context of DBSA; Sect. 16.5 examines DBSA's corporate governance arrangements; Sect. 16.6 examines the risk management practices; Sect. 16.7 discusses regulation and supervision; Sect. 16.8 examines monitoring and evaluation, and impact evaluation; Sect. 16.9 looks at the business model of DBSA; Sect. 16.10 evaluates the financial performance of DBSA over a seven-year period; Sect. 16.11 discusses the main achievements and contributions of DBSA; Sect. 16.12 identifies the challenges confronting DBSA, and Sect. 16.13 concludes the chapter.

16.2 Overview of Development Finance Institutions in South Africa

DFIs have played a significant role in the South Africa's economy in the pre- and post-apartheid eras. In the past, the country's state-led industrialization project was fundamentally dependent on DFIs. They participated in and contributed to shaping the private enterprise sector, but specifically with a view to reducing operational expenses, granting public funding and facilitating inexpensive access to network infrastructure. The successive apartheid administrations resorted to DFIs to increase the state's inclusion in the economy and, by extension, its ability to centrally manage the concentrated formalized private sector. This was particularly driven by the demands of growing global restrictions and the crippling effects of sanctions. DFIs were, therefore, essential parts of the state apparatus in creating a radicalized industrial sector, which later assisted in supplying the requisite shock-absorbing capability against the sanctions. DFIs in South Africa exist at the provincial and nationals levels.

Since 1994, DFIs in South Africa have been and are being repurposed as a component of the government's developmental programme, particularly in enhancing social safety nets and rectifying the ills of the apartheid era. The post-1994 order is characterized by two types of DFIs and these include those which incorporate equity and credit financing in corporate development activities and those which promote development through grants and other non-financial means. Although the investment philosophy of DFIs has changed to reflect the government's aims for development, they still have particular targets by sector and planning cycles. For example, national DFIs in South Africa are mainly arranged along industrial development, infrastructure development, agricultural development, small business support and empowerment support lines.

The mandates DFIs in South Africa are anchored on three main principles: (1) additionality principle, where DFIs only engage in activities and sectors that are challenging for the private sector capital to finance; (2) as a stimulus for rapid industrialization, employment generation, economic growth, and investment in human capital; and (3) as anchor points of sustainable growth to close investment shortfalls in the country. However, the goals of DFIs have been expanded to include addressing market failure occasioned by both external (as was the case in 2007/2008 global financial crisis and the COVID-19 pandemic) and internal shocks by aiding in the growth of private enterprise, encouraging employment and business opportunities, particularly through Black Economic Empowerment (BEE), strengthening the foundations of human capital and institutional capacity, aiding in local production and benefit, and funding infrastructure development.

There are close to forty DFIs operating in South Africa, mainly at the national and provincial levels. They adhere to the fundamental tenet of helping the economically marginalized and deprived segments of society by enhancing access to financial services, fostering the growth of small businesses, creating jobs and advancing infrastructure (le Pere, 2021). Table 16.1 provides a list of the main national DFIs that support South Africa's developmental agenda. These DFIs are differently structured in terms of their cost arrangements, cost-effectiveness, customer target, operational efficiency and governance structure. In terms of operational coverage, they invest across the Southern African Development Community (SADC) region and in the case of the DBSA, it focuses on the African continent. The government offers DFIs a variety of financial incentives, including low-cost guarantees, exemptions from reserve requirements and taxes, and partial or full government funding of its operational costs and capital transfers. DFIs often provide subsidized lending based on public funds entrusted to them. They are, therefore, crucial for providing strategic financing to industries, fields and areas of social and economic activity that are typically unattractive to private and commercial banks.

Table 16.1 List of the main national DFIs in South Africa, 2022

DFIs	*Mandate*
Industrial Development Corporation (IDC)	"The IDC is a self-financing, state-owned national DFI that provides financing to entrepreneurs and businesses engaged in competitive industries"
Development Bank of Southern Africa (DBSA)	"The purpose of the DBSA is to accelerate sustainable socio-economic development by funding physical, social and economic infrastructure. Its goal is to improve the quality of life of the people of the region. The bank plays a multiple role of financier, adviser, partner, implementer and integrator to mobilize finance and expertise for development projects"
National Housing Finance Corporation (NHFC)	"The NHFC was set up with a mandate to ensure that every South African with a regular source of income is able to gain access to finance, to acquire and improve a home of his or her own" Tel: 011 644 9800 Fax: 011 484 0204 https://www.resbank.co.za/
National Empowerment Fund (NEF)	"The NEF promotes and facilitates Black Economic Empowerment (BEE) and transformation Its mandate and mission is to be a catalyst of Broad-Based BEE through asset management, fund management and strategic projects"
Independent Development Trust (IDT)	"The IDT has a mandate to support government in meeting its social mandate of alleviating poverty in improving the quality of life of poor rural communities. It has created a reputation for being a development programme-implementing agency focusing on development planning, implementation, and the coordination of government programmes"

(continued)

Table 16.1 (continued)

DFIs	*Mandate*
Land and Agricultural Development Bank of South Africa	"The Land Bank is a specialist agricultural bank guided by a mandate to provide financial services to the commercial farming sector and to agribusiness and to make available new, appropriately designed financial products that would facilitate access to finance by new entrants to agriculture from historically disadvantaged backgrounds"
National Youth Development Agency (NYDA)	"The NYDA's mandate is to: advance youth development through guidance and support to initiatives across sectors of society and spheres of government embark on initiatives that seek to advance the economic development of young people develop and coordinate the implementation of the Integrated Youth Development Plan and Strategy for the country"
Micro Agriculture Finance Scheme of South Africa (Mafisa)	"Mafisa was developed as a micro and retail agricultural financial scheme for economically active poor people. Mafisa allows access to financial services through selected institutions on an affordable and sustainable basis. It assists with loans to target groups, individuals, farmersand other groups as well as savings and banking facilities at approved financial institutions"
Small Enterprise Finance Agency (SEFA)	"SEFA provides access to finance to survivalist businesses and small, medium and micro enterprises by delivering wholesale and direct lending; providing credit guarantees to SMMEs and supporting institutional development"

Source South African Reserve Bank: www.reservebank.co.za, 2022

Despite the critical role that DFIs play in providing the needed financial capital for socio-economic development in South Africa by disbursing R275 billion (US$16.19 billion) yearly, their financial performance has been characterized by growing losses, subpar loan recovery and a steadfast reliance on the government to meet operational costs. Much has not been done to improve efficiency and to lessen market failures; instead, resource utilization is highly ineffective and vulnerable to external shocks. Standard metrics, including non-performing loan ratios, return on equity and return on assets, show that most DFIs have underperformed in terms of achieving minimum requirements to make them liquid and efficient in order to achieve their social objectives of improving the lives of the people, especially the socially excluded through financial inclusion and social infrastructure development

16.3 Profile and Historical Background of Development Bank of Southern Africa (DBSA)

This section provides the profile and historical background of DBSA.

The DBSA is a DFI wholly owned by the government of South Africa. It has the mandate of promoting economic development and growth, the development of human resources and the building of institutional capacity by mobilizing financial and other resources from national and international private and public sectors for sustainable development projects and programmes in South Africa and the broader African continent. This would improve the quality of life for people in South Africa and throughout the continent by enhancing access to development finance and creating and implementing sustainable development solutions. The operations of DBSA cover the whole value chain of infrastructure development and involve active involvement in infrastructure solutions. Infrastructure-led economic growth, which responds to the socio-economic needs of the people as well as addressing the threat of climate change, serves as a vital tool for improving the lives of the growing African population.

The bank's development position and strategies are aligned to the national development policy vision of South Africa (NDP Vision 2030) and the integrated urban development framework as well as the SADC's Vision 2027. The operational activities of the bank are equally geared to achieving regional and global targets of the sustainable development goals, 2030 and African Union's Agenda 2063.

The bank has maintained a strong balance sheet, which is self-financing, and has very good domestic and international credit ratings.

In order to encourage the growth of capital accumulation for the Afrikaner people, an ethnic minority descended from Dutch immigrants, the apartheid administration in South Africa implemented a strategy of aggressive economic interventions through development banks, including the DBSA. The goal was to industrialize and diversify the country's economy by reducing its reliance on imports, and creating a robust financial safety net against escalating international sanctions. The DBSA was thus established in 1983 to support the development agenda of the apartheid government at the time and was initially intended to operate only in South Africa and the 'homelands' (South Africa and the current Republic of Namibia). The DBSA collaborated with business to develop a racially oriented industrial economy for the apartheid administration.

The DBSA extended the range of its operations to cover countries in the SADC region. After South Africa's independence in 1994, its new constitution changed the DBSA's mandate and purpose, transforming it from an economic development viewpoint into a NDB with a clear emphasis on Southern Africa's infrastructure development. Since 1994, it has primarily concentrated on funding and investing in physical, social and economic infrastructure. As a result of the expansion of its mandate to include the entire continent, it has assumed a variety of responsibilities, including project management and implementation, advisory services, joint venture and partnership options, and financial support. To address some of the numerous inefficiencies caused during the apartheid era, DBSA focused on financing development initiatives in South Africa after the apartheid regime. As part of efforts to sustain South Africa's post-apartheid economic growth as well as that of the SADC in general, the DBSA's strategy takes a cue from the government's development policy interventions. To align its strategic goal to that of the government, DBSA's current responsibilities include fostering 'socioeconomic development and growth within South Africa and in the Southern African region', with its main goal being to 'contribute towards sustainable economic development and growth, human resource development, and institutional capacity building by leveraging public- and private-sector resources'.

Since its establishment as a development bank, DBSA has considered itself more than merely a financial intermediary and supplier of funds to deficit economic units. The bank's mission statement is to 'mobilize and provide loan finance, technical assistance, and advice for sustainable development projects'. However, the bank has also become increasingly involved in economic reform issues pertinent to the environment in which it operates. DBSA is more focused on providing funding to develop social infrastructure, including the provision of basic services and economic infrastructure to eliminate capacity challenges and optimize economic growth potential. The 278 municipalities, public utilities, state-controlled organizations and other countries have been the primary targets of lending by the bank.

The mandate of the bank has since changed from a policy instrument of public finance to facilitate the development of infrastructure in the homeland pre-independence era to a sharper focus on need infrastructure investment in South Africa as enshrined in its Act from 1994 to 2000. Due to growing global financial and development complexities, DBSA expanded its mandate on impactful infrastructure provision to response to the social and economic needs of the people through a robust needs assessment analysis. This was intended to enhance its position as a DFI and improve its risk management capacity through an embedded robust governance structure from 2001 to 2006. In response to global development uncertainties from the 2007/2008 global financial crisis, the bank's strategy was transformed to include the delivery of infrastructure that addresses the gaps in social and economic infrastructure that can withstand the effects of any external shocks so as to reduce the vulnerability levels of the country within a fast-growing global economy. Recognizing the importance of regional and international integration in a globalized community, DBSA expanded its investment mandate to include a regional infrastructure development mandate from 2010 to 2016. In an effort to consolidate its gains and provide sustainable development and impactful interventions, the bank undertook a structural review in 2017 to shift focus from being a DFI concerned with traditional financing to a DFI involved in the full project life cycle, from planning and preparation through financing, building and sustaining, to increasing its developmental impact in the context of a difficult operating environment and also to respond adequately to the global dynamics occasioned by the global financial crisis.

16.4 Political Economy and Institutional Context

DFIs in South Africa have been categorized and mandated to perform specific developmental programmes to ensure a total transformation of the economy. Thus, access to infrastructure and participation have become a challenge in the country and have been identified as a development strategy in the national recovery programme of the government. Therefore, access to finance by both the private and public sectors to invest in the structural growth of the economy are vital to the recovery agenda of the South African national development policy strategy. Gaps that exist in terms of equitable access to various services of health, education, water and sanitation as well as ICT are addressed through interventions of the bank that are in line with the national development plans and strategies. This is done through the bank's infrastructure drive approach on planning, preparing and financing, executing, monitoring and maintaining development projects.

The bank is legally required to support sustainable development through its activities, and this is integrated into its strategy, as indicated in the DBSA's 2021 annual report. When designing its operational strategies in accordance with the national development strategy, DBSA collaborates with different parties but needs to align with the National Treasury as the shareholder in executing this responsibility. Additionally, the DBSA's stance on development is in line with South Africa's National Development Plan (NDP) Vision 2030, the African Union's Agenda 2063, the Sustainable Development Goals (SDGs) of the United Nations, and the Paris Agreement on Climate Change (DBSA Corporate Plan, 2019–2022).

In addition, other nations receiving DBSA funding have no influence on the bank's governance. The bank is wholly owned by the South African government, and all members of the board are South African nationals. Despite its makeup, the bank invests a significant amount of funds in its neighbouring nations through its partnership policy. It is required to invest 60% of its book in South Africa and 40% in the rest of Africa. In terms of the total number of loans as of 2021, Zambia had the highest portfolio, followed by Angola, Zimbabwe and Ghana (CCSI, 2021).

The DBSA has collaborative strategies to ensure a collective development, especially in the sub-region. The SADC, the Common Market for Eastern and Southern Africa (COMESA), the UN Economic Commission for Africa (UNECA), Association of African Development Finance Institutions (AADFIs) are all part of the DBSA's regional development and integration strategy, which aims to leverage infrastructure investments across the continent in order to improve connectivity and trade within Africa and foster the growth of local industries and markets within Africa.

Global economic and political dynamics have an impact on the operational activities of the bank. The global financial Crisis, the COVID-19 pandemic and the recent Russia-Ukraine war have had a negative effect on the bank's planned programmes. The bank's financing instruments include the issuance of bonds in the global and domestic capital markets or through bilateral partners. Hence, any external shocks that affect the cost of borrowing, limit capital flows, cause a liquidity crunch and uncertainty in the financial ecosystem globally, directly and indirectly affect the DBSA's ability to raise the needed capital to pursue its mandate.

The government of South Africa is the key stakeholder in the operations of the bank. The Stock Exchange Commission, Parliament, bilateral partners, institutional investors as well as the other DFIs and commercial banks constitute an important stakeholder group for the DBSA. The bank is partly regulated by the shareholder (i.e. the government) acting through the national treasury using its borrowing threshold policy. Rating agencies are also key partners in the bank's regulatory framework through regular engagements. The National Treasury gives approval to the bank's annual borrowing plan, which is subject to statutory capitalization requirements. The bank can leverage its equity position and borrow up to a maximum of two and half times shareholder equity.

16.5 DBSA's Corporate Governance Arrangements

The focal point of DBSA's corporate governance is the board of directors, which is governed by the DBSA Act and its regulations, as well as the relevant provisions in the Public Financial Management Act and the Companies Act. The DBSA board provides oversight on strategic direction and targets set within a robust strategic framework, while monitoring overall performance against targets. The board of directors is made up of thirteen (13) members, composed of ten (10) independent non-executive directors, one (1) person from the National Treasury representing the shareholder (non-executive director) and two (2) executive directors (i.e. the Chief Executive and the Chief Financial Officer). The board is chaired by an independent non-executive director. The board is made up of six (6) females and seven (7) males. Around 85% of directors are black (10 Africans and 1 Asian), two (2) whites and 46.2% are women (6 females). The race representation is in line with government policy that requires at least 75% black directorship. Though the bank has a 50–50 gender policy of representation at both the board and management levels, the board's composition could not achieve this noble objective of 50% female representation, falling short by 3.8%. The composition of the board is as presented in Table 16.2.

Table 16.2 Board characteristics of DBSA

Board characteristics	*Number (%)*
Board size	13
Executive directors	2 (15.4)
Non-executive directors	11 (84.6)
Of which independent non-executive directors	10 (76.9)
CEO duality	No
Female directors	6 (46.2)
Male directors	7 (53.8)
Number of board committees	6
Size of audit committee	8
Number of independent non-executive directors on audit committee	8 (100)
Audit committee chaired by independent non-executive director	Yes
Executive committee members	9

Source Author's construction

The Board Charter does not make a distinction between the fiduciary responsibilities of representatives of the shareholder and that of independent non-executive directors. The board is ultimately accountable and responsible for the performance, affairs and behaviour of the bank. The board of directors are appointed by the shareholder based on their expertise in relation to socio-economic development, finance, business, banking and/or administration. The appointment process of directors involves the Human Resource and Nominations Committees of the board considering nominations for appointments, and proposing a list to the board, after which recommendations are made to the Minister of Finance for approval. The board members are appointed on a performance contract for a period of three years and are eligible for reappointment, depending on satisfactory performance. The DBSA Act also allows the board to co-opt other persons with specific expertise to serve on committees of the bank. The appointment of the CEO involves the board appointing an independent assessor (a recruitment agency) to evaluate various applications, which makes recommendations to the board for appointment.

The board has various committees that work on specific areas of critical importance to the operations and sustainability of the bank and their functions are in line with international best corporate governance practices and in line with principles of the King IV Report. The committees of the board include the Audit and Risk Committee, Credit and Investment

Committee, Human Resources Committee, Nominations Committee, Social and Ethics Committee, as well as the Infrastructure Delivery and Knowledge Committee. These committees report to the board on various issues associated with operational efficiency and prudence, social and economic assessment, conflict of interest, project sustainability, internal control measures, human development and capacity, and financial stability of the bank among others. The board has a charter that guides its principal operations in line with the DBSA's act and outlines the fiduciary responsibilities of the directors, the relationship with executive management and the policy directions that both the board and the shareholder need to adopt to ensure the sustainability and efficiency of the bank. In addition, the board establishes and sets the charters of the board committees, which provide for the composition, roles, delegation of authority and responsibilities of each of the board committees.

The Audit and Risk Committee is made up of eight (8) members, chaired by an independent non-executive director with all the other members being independent non-executive directors. The Chief Executive Officer and Chief Finance Officer attend the committee's meetings. The committee can co-opt any person outside of the board with the needed expertise to aid in its work. The bank has a nine-member executive committee made up of the bank's senior management that oversees the direction and implementation of the board's decisions. Financial prudence, outcome deliverables and efficiency of the bank are critical components of the executive committee's overall objective.

16.6 Risk Management Practices

The Bank recognizes that in the current business climate, risk in terms of operations and reputation are pervasive and that all corporate organizations are vulnerable to risk from both the external and internal environments. The Audit and Risk Committee is responsible for overseeing and advising the board on risk management and internal control systems of the bank. Key among these are adherence to income, expenditure and capital budget requirements, treasury arrangements and fund mobilization strategies, transfer pricing policies, development loan impairments, management of assets and liabilities and the bank's overall financial health and sustainability.

While the corporate risk management approach and risk strategy are set by the Board to serve as the foundation for internal control, the

Bank's corporate governance codes on ethical behaviour, legal requirements and good accounting practice provide the basis for those processes. The responsibility for evaluating the effectiveness, scope and performance of control systems rests with the executive management.

The internal audit department periodically examines crucial procedures connected to the bank's important risks in order to give the board and management unbiased confidence regarding the efficiency of the internal control system. In order to guarantee that any serious audit problems that require the board's immediate attention are escalated, members of the Audit and Risk Committee monitor this function, and the chief audit executive has unrestricted access to both the committee's chairperson and the Board.

The internal audit department manages and coordinates a combined assurance function that the bank has put in place. 'Integrating and aligning assurance processes in a corporation to maximize risk and governance oversight and control efficiencies, and optimize overall assurance to the Audit and Risk Committee, considering the company's risk appetite', is how King III explains this concept. The model depicts the main threats to the DBSA together with the main procedures and safeguards in place to guarantee their reduction or elimination. The model also aims to identify the assurance providers for the primary risks identified, in addition to a five tiers of defence plan the DBSA has adopted. The assurance providers are listed in the Combined Assurance Policy, and through the combined assurance working committee, they submit the aggregate results of their assurance efforts to the Audit and Risk Committee.

Furthermore, the internal audit department provides written assurance on the total control environment to the Audit and Risk Finance Committee once a year, taking into account governance, cyber security, risk assessment and management, and operational and financial risk issues. Based on a risk-based audit strategy that is developed and approved, findings of audits and reviews conducted affirm this assurance or otherwise on the risk levels of the various operational areas of the bank.

The DBSA faces several forms of risk in its operations, including financial risk (credit and liquidity risks), strategic risk (political, reputation, sustainability and environmental risks), and business and operational risks (cyber security and technology, market volatility, development impact, infrastructure risks). These standard risks are monitored regularly. Mitigation measures must, therefore, be developed to ensure that their impact levels on the operations of the bank are minimal even if they do occur.

Portfolio diversification, monitoring of prudential limits, adoption of rigorous governance processes in the approval of deals with the bank among others are some of the mitigation measures that the bank has put in place to deal with the various forms of risk and prevent them from occurring.

The instruments DBSA uses in managing risk during normal times include loans (concessional and ordinary) and grants financing, equity investments and structured finance. The bank now wishes to move to the use of trade finance. When the COVID-19 pandemic struck, the DBSA resorted to giving more loans by increasing the intensity of credit. This meant the credit committee had to intensify its work by meeting very often to approve loans. The bank also reorganized existing loans by giving borrowers grace periods to repay their loans. Another area of intervention by the bank was providing humanitarian support.

16.7 Regulation and Supervision

The DBSA is regulated under the Development Bank of Southern Africa Act, No. 13 of 1997 (Amended Act No. 41 of 2014) (DBSA Act). The bank's operational activities are further guided by the King Code of Governance Principles for South Africa 2016 (King IV) and the protocol on Corporate Governance in the Public Sector of South Africa. The bank's sources of revenue, financial utilization, its mandate as well as sectors to be served are all outlined in the provisions of the Act. Further, the DBSA is regulated by the Companies Act of South Africa and the Public Financial Management Act. The Public Procurement Act of South Africa serves as the guiding document regarding the procurement processes and mechanisms that the DBSA adopts to source for the services of consultants and contractors in the discharge of providing infrastructure projects and technical services. It is worth mentioning that the DBSA is not regulated by the central bank. However, the sole shareholder through the National Treasury regulates the bank. This includes regulating the bank's borrowing from the capital market and capitalization requirements of a maximum two and half times shareholder equity and a minimum equity-to-loan ratio of 28.6% are approved and complied with. In terms of supervision, the Minister of Finance exercises supervisory powers over the activities of the bank.

Again, Parliament has the authority to vet and approve the corporate plan of the bank. Other state agencies such as the Stock Exchange

Commission also exercise oversight and supervisory roles over the bank. The issuance and floating of bonds in both the local and external capital markets are regulated by the provisions and guidelines of the Commission. The bank has, however, started engagements with the relevant stakeholders to streamline its regulated and supervisory mechanisms with the South African Reserve Bank (central bank) to ensure efficiency and robustness in the bank's finances and improve its credibility on the financial market as well as increase investor confidence in the activities of the bank. The bank applies the Basel III standard internally though this is not a regulatory requirement for the bank.

16.8 Monitoring and Evaluation, and Impact Evaluation

The investment of financial and human resources into infrastructure development and the enhancement of institutional and human capacity as is the case with the DBSA are as important as the monitoring and evaluation of the same. Checking, tracking and assessing the achievement of set targets and goals to examine the level of success or failure of a programme serves as the primary point of judicious and prudent use of scarce resources. The extent to which a project achieves its objective(s) depends on the deployment of various monitoring tools to assess it. This enables actors to determine the level of impact that the project is having on addressing the issue that needed the intervention. Periodic monitoring during the implementation of the project and conducting of an evaluation after a period of its completion to assess the impact of the project are very crucial.

The DBSA has a monitoring and evaluation unit, which operates under the financial operations department with about 10 staff members. The unit undertakes the monitoring of projects by tracking and checking the targets at the output level in line with the implementation of KPIs developed for particular projects. The unit does not conduct a comprehensive impact assessment of interventions executed and measures required to strengthen the impact evaluation of projects. The bank recognizes the importance of undertaking an impact evaluation and there is work in progress to strengthen the unit to include impact evaluation as part of its responsibilities.

16.9 Business Model of DBSA

16.9.1 Policy Mandate and Sectors Served

The DBSA draws its policy mandate from the Act that established it (Act No. 13) and the National Development plan, 2030. The bank has a broad mandate but its primary mandate as a DFI is to ensure infrastructure development and the accumulation of capital. Thus, the DBSA, among other things, undertakes the following:

- Promotes economic development and growth, human resource development and institutional capacity building.
- Enhances and protects the financial sustainability of the Bank.
- Monitors a robust governance framework and systems of controls.
- Mobilizes financial and other resources from the national and international private and public sectors for sustainable development projects and programmes.
- Appraises, plans and monitors the implementation of development projects and programmes.
- Provides technical assistance in the identification, preparation, evaluation, financing, implementation and management of development projects and programmes.
- Mobilizes funding for initiatives that minimize or mitigate the environmental impact of development projects or programmes.
- Encourages regional integration to achieve an integrated finance system for development.
- Addresses the developmental requirements of the SADC region and the rest of Africa.
- Promotes regional integration to support South Africa's commitments to bi-national co-operation and trade agreements with countries across the continent.

The sectors that the DBSA focuses on as part of its infrastructure development drive include local government support, energy, transport, water and sanitation, information and communication technology and social infrastructure including education and health. The bank, since its establishment, has invested heavily in these sectors and expanded the economic and social infrastructure base of South Africa. The provision of technical services and support to the local authorities in the form of grants and other forms of partnership has ensured a bottom-up approach in service delivery, which is crucial in the contemporary development agenda. Thus, the concept of participatory planning and development has been enhanced through the development approach of the DBSA in collaboration with the local government authorities in South Africa.

16.9.2 Funding Sources

The DBSA is not a deposit-taking DFI and does not receive any budgetary support from the central government. The main sources of funding for the bank's operations are debt and equity financing. Debt finance is obtained through the issuance of debt instruments in both the local and global capital market. For instance, the bank floated a green bond that yielded R4 billion in 2021 to finance its energy and climate-resilient infrastructure. Again, 68% of total liabilities in 2019 and 2020 represented debt finance raised from the local and external capital markets, with the remaining amounts coming from official credit lines (29%) and other sources (3%) (Annual Report, 2020). Further, SADC financing and domestic projects needing imports, credit lines from external DFIs at below-market rates and credit lines from commercial banks make up the greater percentage of the foreign currency funding. Other sources, such as private investments, bilateral organizations, external DFI support, commercial banks, have become reliable channels for raising capital for the bank. The policy of the bank to ensure sustainable and climate-resilient infrastructure development has led to the establishment of various funding mechanisms, which directly play a key role in raising capital for the bank. The DBSA also accessed the Green Climate Fund (GCF) and Green Infrastructure Fund (GIF) to on-lend.

16.9.3 Lending Model

The bank generates revenue through its lending activities to the public and private sectors and other countries on the continent. The bank employs both retail and wholesale lending models. It provides retail loans directly to its clients, including state-owned enterprises, private companies, commercial banks, small and medium-scale enterprises (SMEs), among others within South Africa and countries within SADC region as well as other African countries. The bank also provides wholesale lending to other DFIs to on-lend to their clients. The lending model of the

DBSA is 60–40. Thus, 60% of its lending funds is allocated to entities that operate in South Africa and 40% is allocated to the rest of the continent. Out of the 40%, half (50%) of the funds is allocated to the SADC region and the rest to other African countries.

16.9.4 Products and Services

The DBSA offers a wide range of financial products and services to different clients with different objectives and business orientations. State-owned enterprises, SMEs, other DFIs, local government authorities and countries are among the range of clients served by the DBSA through its tailored products and services. The financial products and services offered by the bank include loans, grants, equity investment in SMEs, and guarantees. These products also serve as important sources of revenue generation for the bank. The bank also provides non-lending financial support as well as technical and advisory services to its clients. Technical services may include project design and preparation, project planning, project implementation and maintenance. These services are available to both the public and private sectors who are into infrastructure delivery and capital formation for business development.

16.9.5 Pricing and Subsidies

The pricing of the bank is largely driven by the cost of funding in the capital market. The bank has a subsidy policy for its clients as a DFI whose objective is to promote capital accumulation and expand infrastructure. However, the extent to which subsidy is granted by the bank to its clients depends primarily on the cost of borrowing from the capital market and other economic variables affecting its bilateral partners that give loans to the bank. This is so because the structure of the bank's financing is based on debt instruments and equity financing and these financial instruments are sensitive to the externalities of the capital market. The bank offers subsidies to municipalities in the form of development funding since these municipalities are not well-established. The DBSA also grants partial recovery of loans to state institutions and private bodies that embark on infrastructure financing. In effect, the bank's pricing and subsidy policy is dependent on the extent to which the policy is aligned to its mandate.

16.10 Financial Performance

The DBSA has had improved performance in its financial indicators over the past decade. The bank had consistent financial performance for the period 2015–2021, despite the myriad of global shocks, such as the COVID-19 pandemic. Key performance metrics such as operational performance, capital adequacy, asset quality, operational performance, earnings, liquidity assets and management efficiency (see Table 16.3) witnessed steady improvements over the period.

16.10.1 Capital Adequacy

In Fig. 16.1, the regulatory capital ratio, which measures the total risk-weighted asset ratio (Tier 1 + Tier 2 capital ratio), increased steadily from 33.4% in 2015 to 41.5% in 2019 but saw a decline to 37.4% in 2020. It increased again to 39.1% in 2021. Thus, the capital ratio of the bank increased by an average of 37.67% over the period 2015–2021 for both tiers 1 and 2.

16.10.2 Asset Quality

The non-performing loans (NPLs) for DBSA saw an improvement from 5.1% in 2015 to 4.9% in 2019 as shown in Fig. 16.2. The performance of loan recoveries started to decline in 2020, falling to 7.2% in 2021, perhaps, due to the ramifications of the COVID-19 pandemic on the businesses of the bank's clients and their ability to fulfil their financial obligations, including loans contracted from the DBSA.

16.10.3 Operational Performance

Figure 16.3 shows the trends in the operational performance of DBSA over the period, 2015–2021. The portfolio yield of the DBSA, which shows the bank's ability to generate cash on the gross loan portfolio, increased from 0.66% in the 2015 to 1.47% in 2017. This performance, however, declined steadily to 0.30% in 2021.

Table 16.3 Financial performance indicators of the DBSA, 2015–2021

		2015	*2016*	*2017*	*2018*	*2019*	*2020*	*2021*	*Average*	*SD*
Capital adequacy	Regulatory CAR (%)	33.4	35.5	38.3	38.5	41.5	37.4	39.1	37.67	2.41
Asset quality	NPL to total gross loans (%)	5.1	3.7	3.3	4.5	4.9	7.2	7.7	5.20	1.54
Operational performance	Portfolio yield (%)	0.66	0.59	1.47	0.58	0.44	0.53	0.30	0.65	0.35
	Operating profit (%)	22.48	34.85	37.61	32.12	25.61	-6.38	26.22	24.64	13.62
Earnings	Return on assets (%)	1.8	3.4	3.4	2.6	3.5	0.5	1.7	2.41	1.05
	Return on equity (%)	5.7	9.7	9.2	6.9	8.7	1.3	3.7	6.46	2.88
	Net interest income margin	3.8	4.6	4.9	4.9	5.5	5.1	5.3	4.87	0.51
	Interest margin to gross income (%)	43.04	43.08	38.72	44.63	49.52	48.07	55.38	46.06	5.03
Liquidity assets	Broad liquidity assets to total assets (%)	101.00	100.86	99.40	99.45	99.42	98.70	89.79	98.37	3.59
	Core liquidity asset to total assets (%)	87.62	88.66	89.92	90.21	89.89	90.93	84.31	88.79	2.09
Management efficiency	Noninterest expenses to gross income (%)	16.40	13.19	8.83	10.52	10.03	10.68	10.48	11.45	2.35
	Personnel expenses to gross income (%)	11.24	9.89	6.37	8.16	8.28	8.16	9.46	8.79	1.44
	Cost-to-income ratio	34.4	28.7	18.8	21.7	22.9	28.4	25.4	25.76	4.83

Source DBSA Financial Statements, 2015–2021

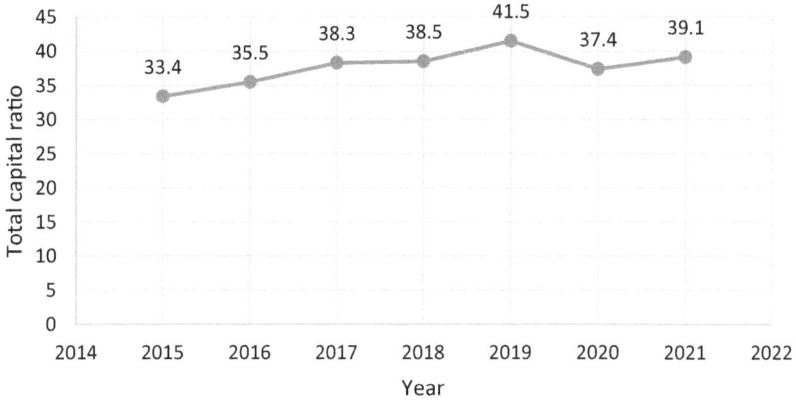

Fig. 16.1 Regulatory capital (*Source* Author's construction based on DBSA Financial Statements)

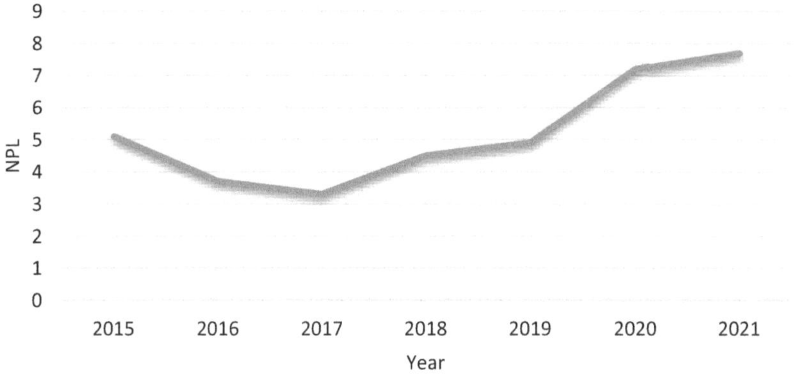

Fig. 16.2 Asset quality (*Source* Author's construction based on DBSA Financial Statements)

16.10.4 Earnings

DBSA's profitability measures (interest margin to gross income, return on asset (ROA) and return on equity (ROE)) show an interesting trend over the period 2015–2021. For instance, ROE increased from 5.7% in 2015 to 9.7% in 2016. This, however, was short-lived as it witnessed

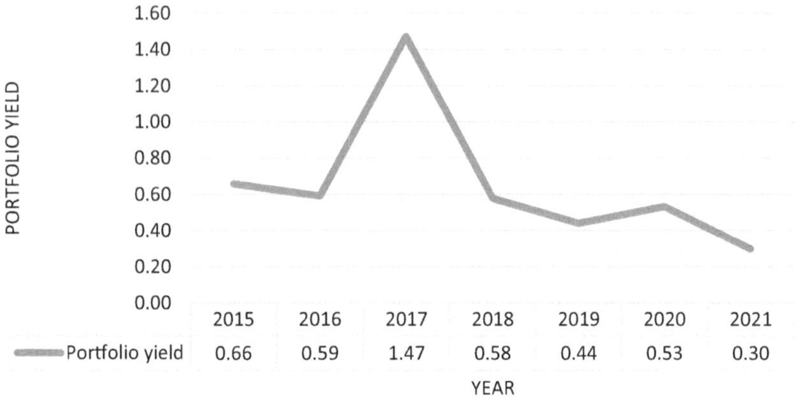

Fig. 16.3 Portfolio yield (*Source* Author's construction based on DBSA Financial Statements)

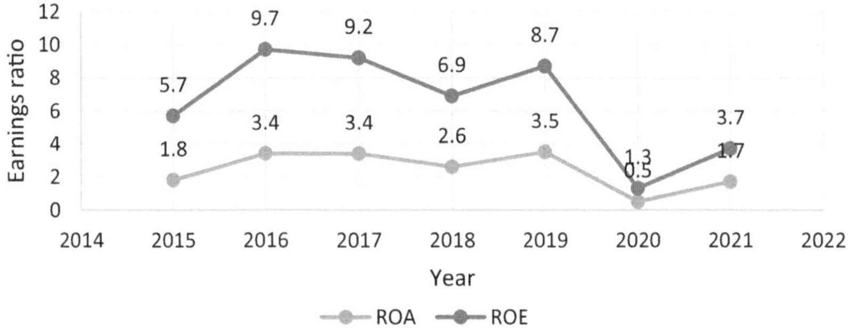

Fig. 16.4 Earnings/profitability (*Source* Author's construction based on DBSA Financial Statements) (Color figure online)

a sharp decline of 6.9% in 2018 but saw a rise to 8.7% in 2019. ROE saw a sharp decline of 1.3% in 2020. ROA, on the other hand, remained stable over the period 2016–2021, corresponding to a 3.4% in 2016 and 1.7% in 2021. Despite the bank's impressive performance over the period 2015–2016, it experienced a great shock in its profitability indicators in the period 2018–2020, and this is attributed to the global COVID-19 pandemic (see Fig. 16.4).

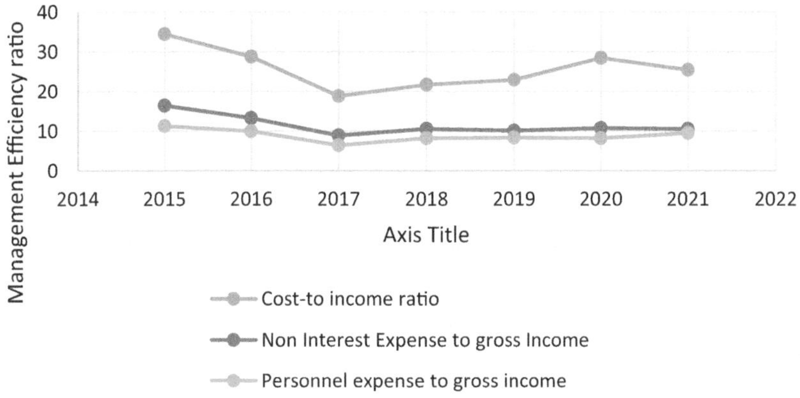

Fig. 16.5 Management efficiency (*Source* Author's construction based on DBSA Financial Statements) (Color figure online)

16.10.5 Management Efficiency

Figure 16.5 presents management efficiency ratios, which measure the non-interest expenses to gross income and personnel expense to gross income, have been marginally unstable over the entire period, 2015–2021. All the efficiency ratios saw a steady decrease from 2015 and remained marginally stable from 2016 to 2021. This implies that management are committed to staying within set limits on staff and management benefits as against the bank's income.

16.10.6 Liquidity Asset

DBSA depends largely on borrowings from the capital and returns from equity investments as sources of its liquidity. The bank's liquidity, based on its broad liquidity assets to total asset and core liquidity assets to total assets, remained largely stable over the period 2015–2019 but in the year 2021 it experienced a sharp decline from 98.70 and 89.79 in 2020 to 90.93 and 84.31, respectively (see Fig. 16.6).

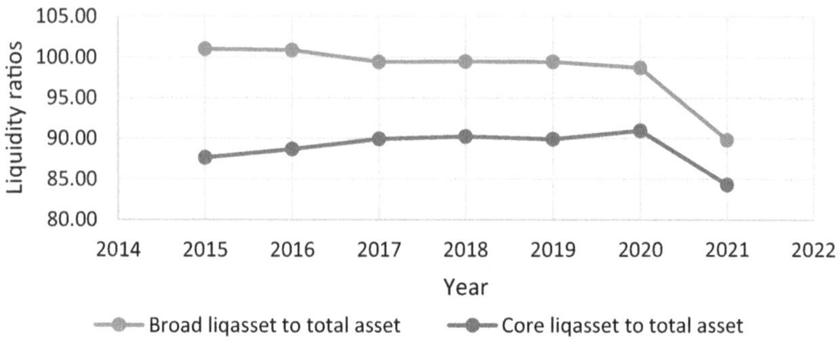

Fig. 16.6 Liquidity (*Source* Author's construction based on DBSA Financial Statements) (Color figure online)

16.10.7 Performance Indicators—Pre- and Post-COVID-19 Lockdown Era

Figure 16.7 shows that the average NPL was relatively higher during the COVID-19 period and post-COVID-19 lockdown era. The average regulatory capital ratio during the pre-COVID (2015–2018) was relatively lower than the COVID-19 and post-COVID-19 lockdown periods. This signifies the bank's ability to effectively utilize the amount of capital it has as reserves to maintain the amount of losses during the post-COVID-19 lockdown era (see Fig. 16.7). Again, the bank performed relatively better pre-COVID-19 on both non-interest expenses to gross income and personnel emoluments than COVID-19 periods (2019–2021). The liquidity position of the bank remained stable for the pre-COVID-19 and COVID-19 periods and began stumbling in the post-COVID-19 lockdown period.

The averages for ROA and ROE were substantially higher for pre and COVID-19 lockdown periods than for the post-COVID-19 lockdown period as shown in Fig. 16.8. It is clear from the figure that ROE fell steeply from the pre-COVID-19 era (2015–2018) to lower levels in both COVID-19 and post-COVID-19 lockdown periods (see Fig. 16.8). This implies that the bank was greatly hit as a result of the impact of the pandemic on its financial position and operations.

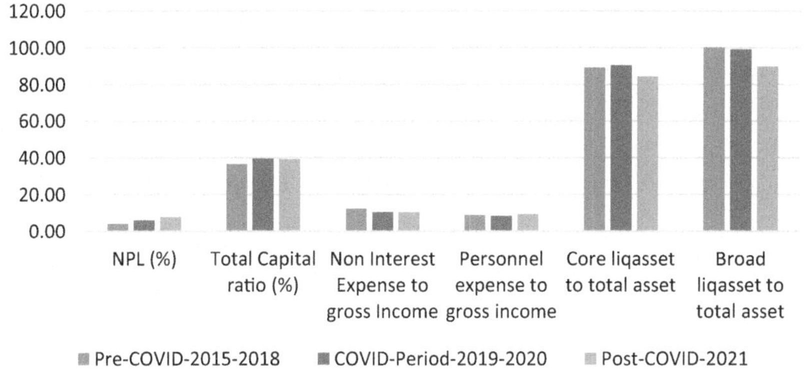

Fig. 16.7 Financial performance indicators—pre- and post-COVID-19 lockdown era (*Source* Author's construction based on DBSA Financial Statements) (Color figure online)

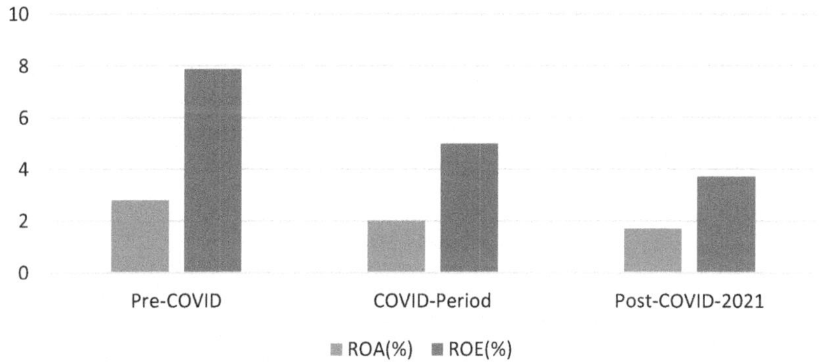

Fig. 16.8 Profitability indicators—pre- and post-COVID-19 lockdown era (*Source* Author's construction based on DBSA Financial Statements) (Color figure online)

16.11 Main Achievements of the DBSA

The DBSA over the years has made some major achievements with respect to infrastructure development and these are discussed below.

16.11.1 Project Planning and Preparation

The planning of projects has become one of the key interventions that the bank has invested in as part of its objective of improving infrastructure delivery, especially at the local level in South Africa. This is an important role the bank plays to help reduce delays in project implementation and the possible variations in project costs. The DBSA assists sponsors with planning and project preparation by creating a pipeline of projects that draws money from the public and private sectors for sustainable development in South Africa. For instance, in line with the support of project planning and preparation provided by the DBSA, the Ray Nkonyeni local municipality received infrastructure planning, spatial planning, project preparation, financing, embedded generation, asset care and income enhancement. The Ugu district municipality also received project preparation support and development. A revenue enhancement programme carried out by the DBSA and Ray Nkonyeni alliance has contributed to enhancing municipal revenue (DBSA SRP, 2021).

16.11.2 Infrastructure Financing

The DBSA has offered financing options to a variety of clients, including municipalities in South Africa, the private sector, state-owned companies, sovereigns and public–private partnerships around the continent. In addition to various financing products created by the Bank to address changing infrastructure requirements, the financing portfolio also comprises senior and mezzanine loans for balance sheet lending and project financing structures. For instance, the Student Housing Infrastructure Programme (SHIP), a joint initiative between the DHET and DBSA to minimize backlogs and subsequently improve student infrastructure and housing, received co-funding from the DBSA for 69.5% (i.e. R278 million (US$16.37 million)) of the project cost at the university of Fort Hare.

Municipalities and public utilities have traditionally been the primary recipients of DBSA credit facilities for the purpose of providing essential infrastructure services. Nearly two-thirds of the total outstanding portfolio in 2020 and close to 60% in 2021 were held by municipalities and public utilities, with the remainder going to private sector clients, educational institutions, provincial and national governments, and development financing organizations in SADC nations. Municipalities are given a lot of attention because there are not many long-term commercial financing options available to the majority of South Africa's 278 municipalities and local governments in SADC nations. Given the DBSA's emphasis on long-term financial stability, two-thirds of its loans have a duration of four years or more, which is suitable for infrastructure development (Bradlow & Humphrey, 2016). Thus, the bank set up an Infrastructure Fund in 2019 with a seed capital of R100 billion (US$5.89 billion) from the government over a 10-year period to provide long-term funding to both private and public institutions to provide infrastructures that are critical to the socio-economic transformation of the country.

16.11.3 Building and Maintenance of Infrastructure

DBSA offers implementation services, project management and capacity-building services to help its stakeholders construct and maintain infrastructure. The bank partially fulfils its duty by enhancing the state's ability to provide infrastructure, which also helps to improve service delivery and enable a greater standard of living. The bank's involvement in infrastructure delivery speeds up planned infrastructure development, promoting the green economy, and guaranteeing the delivery of infrastructure that is cost-effective. The DBSA enhances both the pace and quality of infrastructure delivery in collaboration with its stakeholders.

Through collaborations with the national, provincial and municipal governments, the DBSA developed new school infrastructure and renovated existing school infrastructure during the 2020–2021 year. It also supported broader infrastructure delivery within the social sector, among other activities. These accomplishments played a crucial role in the actions designed to combat the COVID-19 pandemic's rapid spread. By constructing portable prefabricated testing units and renovating existing facilities in five district municipalities in the Eastern Cape, Free State, Gauteng, KwaZulu-Natal, Limpopo, Mpumalanga and the North West, the bank actively contributed to enhancing the capacity of the health ecosystem (DBSA SRP, 2021). The bank also supplied and maintained personal protective equipment and ventilators worth 30.5 million rand and 6.9 million rand, respectively, to hospitals within South Africa and the SADC region during the pandemic.

16.11.4 Supporting Environmentally Focused Infrastructure Programmes

The DBSA recognizes the effect of climate change on its interventions. The bank has, therefore, taken steps to invest in climate change mitigation and adaptation programmes. The DBSA's climate finance initiatives involve managing facilities, funds and programmes that promote a greener economy, sustainable infrastructure delivery, and also support a 'Just transition' to a low-carbon economy with a net zero target by 2050. The bank invests in renewable energy, water and sanitation facilities and has signed on to several climate change treaties. DBSA signed on to the Green Climate Fund and finances most of its climate change programmes through it. For instance in 2010, the bank in collaboration with the Department of Minerals and Energy and the National Treasury funded the establishment of the Renewable Energy Independent Power Producer Programme to help manage and finance the activities and projects of the fund with emphasis on providing sustainable and clean energy to deprived municipalities across the country.

To actualize and give tangible effect to the targets of achieving low-carbon energy, the DBSA issued a fixed-rate green bonds worth 3 billion rand and 200 million euros in 2021 through private placements to fund climate mitigation and adaptation projects contained in the National Development plan in line with the SDGs. Currently, the DBSA is funding 8 capacity-development projects, 16 research development projects and 31 investment projects.

16.12 Challenges Confronting DBSA

This section identifies the challenges that confront DBSA, including competition from a liberalized financial market, inadequate technical expertise of stakeholders, and external shocks and unfavourable economic conditions.

16.12.1 Competition from a Liberalized Financial Market

The primary source of funding of the DBSA is through debt-raising from the open financial market. Therefore, global economic conditions determine the cost at which the bank accesses its capital. The bank also has to compete with other commercial banks in the market to raise its capital at the prevailing credit cost rates. These costs of raising capital by the bank whose motive is not to make profit could force it to transfer part of the cost to its clients. The relatively high cost of loans that DBSA may provide is a significant obstacle to its attempts to encourage sustainable infrastructure financing which it seeks to promote as part of its core mandate. DBSA has a somewhat high cost of funding based on its financing approach, which relies primarily on a fiercely competitive local capital market, which it must pass on to borrowers in order to maintain its financial viability. This is particularly troublesome because DBSA must fund itself in dollars when providing loans to nations outside of South Africa and competing with commercial banks that accept deposits. In South Africa, credit from the DBSA is cheaply priced compared with private sources. However, the requirements and procedural standards set by the bank are strict, as an important requirement to deal with credit risk.

16.12.2 Inadequate Technical Expertise of Stakeholders

Another major barrier is the lack of finance-ready projects, as it is for many other NDBs and MDBs, because of potential borrowers' lack of project design expertise (mainly municipal governments in South Africa and regional countries). The Infrastructure Investment Programme for South Africa (IIPSA), which is run by DBSA, was established in 2014 with € 100 million from the European Union to address this constraint. The IIPSA provides grant for the planning of infrastructure projects in South Africa and the SADC region. The fund has already shown to be effective in supporting sustainable projects, such as the Buffalo City solar project, from concept design to implementation even though it was not designated for sustainable infrastructure.

16.12.3 External Shocks and Unfavourable Economic Conditions

The DBSA operates in a globalized financial environment. Shocks within the global financial space have implications on the financial position of the bank and its ability to raise capital and discharge its core mandate. External factors such as the 2007–2008 Global Financial Crisis and the COVID-19 pandemic had serious repercussions on all financial institutions globally and the DBSA was not spared from the economic and financial ramifications of these shocks. The bank's ability to mobilize resources internally and externally is hampered during periods such as these. Again, due to external shocks, imbalances within the macro economy are occasioned, thereby, making borrowing within the country as well as funding of projects expensive. Hence, planned programmes and projects are affected unduly. Project cost variations could arise due to inflationary pressures and delayed executions.

16.13 Conclusion and Implications

The DBSA has the mandate of promoting economic development and growth. The bank, since its establishment, has invested heavily in providing support to the local government, support to energy, transport, water and sanitation, information and communication technology and social infrastructure including education and health. DBSA's corporate governance structure, regulations and supervision are based on the DBSA Act and its regulations, as well as the relevant provisions in the Public Financial Management Act and the Companies Act. Although the bank faces several forms of risks in its operations, these risks are monitored regularly. The bank applies the Basel III standard internally though this is not a regulatory requirement for the bank. In addition, the bank has a monitoring and evaluation unit, which operates under the financial operations department, and they are responsible for the monitoring of projects. However, the unit does not conduct comprehensive impact assessments of interventions executed. The bank has made significant contributions to the development of some key sectors of the economy. For instance, the bank has offered implementation services, project management and capacity-building services to help its stakeholders to construct and maintain infrastructure. The bank has taken steps to invest in renewable energy, water and sanitation facilities as well as climate change mitigation (Green Climate Fund Project) and adaptation programmes. The main challenges the bank faces are the costs associated with raising capital from the international market, inadequate technical expertise of stakeholders, external shocks and unfavourable economic conditions.

The role and impact of DBSA in the structural transformation of South Africa's and the African's economic and social sectors, especially infrastructure development, is evident. However, the funding source(s) for the bank which is/are through the capital market and equity financing remain a challenge in its endeavour to deliver on the mandate spelt out in the DBSA Act No 13. In this regard, an alternative financing source of the bank should be considered, and it is important for the bank to focus on projects for which it has pre-knowledge. Again, the support to both the private and public sectors in diverse forms ranging from credit support, technical and capacity provision and project financing should be strengthened through the prioritization of key infrastructure projects with needed finance, management, governance and implementation support to yield the needed dividends.

Given the complexities in the nature of developmental impacts, the establishment of a monitoring and evaluation unit, as well as an impact evaluation department within the bank is very necessary. The impact assessment of all implemented programmes and projects is vital to the bank's developmental legacy. This will promote a feedback mechanism for the bank to evaluate the impact of its interventions in the long-run.

The bank's development position and strategies are aligned to the national development policy vision of South Africa (NDP Vision 2030) and the integrated urban development framework as well as the SADC's vision 2027. In as much as the DBSA's act spells out the corporate governance and regulation guidelines for the bank, it is important for the bank, together with stakeholders, to advocate the independence of DBSA, with guidance from the government, and the enactment of laws that address governance and regulatory issues in line with the corporate governance and regulatory standards of international DFIs.

References

Bradlow, D., & Humphrey, C. S. (2016). *Sustainability and infrastructure investment: National development banks in Africa* (GEGI Working Paper 002). Boston University. https://doi.org/10.2139/ssrn.2802713

Columbia Center on Sustainable Investment. (2021). *Development banking in the global economy, state of play and future direction*. ccsi.columbia.edu

DBSA Sustainability Review Report, 2021.

le Pere, G. L. (2021). *Repositioning state-owned enterprises (SOEs) and development finance institutions*. Wits School of Governance, University of the Witwatersrand.

References

Abbott, B. P., Abbott, R., Abbott, T. D., Abernathy, M. R., Acernese, F., Ackley, K., et al. (2016). Observation of gravitational waves from a binary black hole merger. *Physical Review Letters, 116*(6), 061102.

Abdulghany, Y. (2022). *Agricultural Bank of Egypt*. https://egy-africa.com/en/2020/12/26/agricultural-bank-of-egypt/

Abekah-Nkrumah, G., Assuming, P. O., Abor, P. A., & Mohammed, J. I. (2020). Financing sustainable development: New insights for the present and the future. In J. Y. Abor, C. K. D. Adjasi, & R. Lensink (Eds.), *Contemporary issues in development finance*. Routledge.

Abor, J. (2007). Corporate governance and financing decisions of Ghanaian firms. *The International Journal of Business in Society, 7*(1), 83–92.

Abor, J., & Biekpe, N. (2007). Small business reliance on bank financing in Ghana. *Emerging Market Finance & Trade, 43*(4), 93–102.

Abor, J. Y. (2017). *Entrepreneurial finance for MSMEs*. Palgrave Macmillan.

Abor, J. Y. (2018). *Financial markets and institutions: A frontier market perspective* (2nd ed.). Digibooks.

Abor, J. Y., Adjasi, C. K. D., & Lensink, R. (2020a). Introduction to contemporary issues in development finance. In J. Y. Abor, C. K. D. Adjasi, & R. Lensink (Eds.), *Contemporary issues in development finance* (pp. 1–19). Routledge.

Abor, J. Y., Agbloyor, E. K., Donkor, G. N. A., & Alu, A. A. (2022). The COVID-19 pandemic and Africa's financial systems: How do we reform post-COVID-19 financial systems? In *The economics of banking and finance in Africa: Developments in Africa's financial systems* (pp. 1013–1037). Springer.

© The Editor(s) (if applicable) and The Author(s), under exclusive license to Springer Nature Switzerland AG 2023

J. Yindenaba Abor, *The Changing Role of National Development Banks in Africa*, https://doi.org/10.1007/978-3-031-38639-8

Abor, J. Y., Agbloyor, E. K., & Kuipo, R. (2014). Bank finance and export activities of small and medium enterprises. *Review of Development Finance, 4*(2), 97–103.

Abor, J. Y., Alu, A. A., Mathuva, D., & Nellis, J. (2020b). Global financial architecture: Emerging issues and agenda for reforms. In J. Y. Abor, C. K. D. Adjasi, & R. Lensink (Eds.), *Contemporary issues in development finance* (pp. 169–206). Routledge.

Abor, J. Y., & Fiador, V. (2016). *Corporate governance and dividend payout policy: Evidence from selected African countries* (AERC Research Paper 314). African Economic Research Consortium.

Abor, J. Y., Kusi, B. A., Amoah, L., & Agbloyor, E. K. (2023). Financial and other services sectors in Africa. In P. Carmody & J. Murphy (Eds.), *Handbook of African economic development*. Edward Elgar.

Abor, P. A., & Abor, J. Y. (2021). Implications of COVID-19 pandemic for health financing system in Ghana. *Journal of Health Management, 22*(4), 559–569.

Abugre, J., Misati, R., Salami, I., & Antwi, S. (2022). *Recent developments in banking regulation and supervision in Africa*. In J. Y. Abor & C. K. D. Adjasi (Eds.), *The economics of banking and finance in Africa: Developments in Africa's financial systems*. Palgrave Macmillan.

Adams, R. B., & Ferreira, D. (2004). *Gender diversity in the boardroom* (Finance Working paper 57, 30 pp.). European Corporate Governance Institute.

Adams, R. B., & Ferreira, D. (2009). Women in the boardroom and their impact on governance and performance. *Journal of Financial Economics, 94*(2), 291–309.

Adeabah, D., Gyeke-Dako, A., & Andoh, C. (2018). Board gender diversity, corporate governance and bank efficiency in Ghana: A two-stage data envelope analysis (DEA) approach. *Corporate Governance: The International Journal of Business in Society, 19*(2), 299–320.

Ades, A., & Di Tella, R. (1997). The new economics of corruption: A survey and some new results. *Political Studies, 45*(3), 496–515.

Adika, W., & Osly, P. J. (2018). Analisis Kinerja Operasional Kereta Api Jurusan Jakarta-Purwakarta (Studi Kasus Kereta Api Walahar Ekspres Dan Cilamaya Ekspres). *Indonesian Journal of Construction Engineering and Sustainable Development (CESD), 1*(1), 36–44.

Adzawla, W., Bindraban, P. S., Atakora, W. K., Camara, O., & Gouzaye, A. (2022). Economic viability of smallholder agriculture in the Savannah and transitional zones of Ghana: Implications of farm output commercialization and farm diversification. *Sustainability, 14*(18), 11548.

African Development Bank. (2018). *African Economic Outlook 2018*. https://www.afdb.org/fileadmin/uploads/afdb/Documents/Publications/African_Economic_Outlook_2018_-_EN.pdf

African Development Bank. (2022). *Tanzania—Tanzania agricultural development bank* (Project Completion Report). https://www.afdb.org/en/documents/tanzania-tanzania-agricultural-development-bank-project-completion-report-0

Agricultural Development Bank, Ghana. (2021). *Annual report and financial statements*. https://agricbank.com/wp-content/uploads/2022/08/Website_2021-ADB-Annual-Report.pdf

Agyapong, D., & Appiah, S. O. (2015). Effect of gender diversity on the performance of non-financial listed firms in Ghana. *British Journal of Economics, Management & Trade, 8*(1), 55–67.

Ahmad, R., & Matemilola, B. T. (2013). Determinants of bank profits and net interest margins. In *Emerging markets and financial resilience* (pp. 228–248). Palgrave Macmillan.

Akdogan, Y. E., & Boyacioglu, M. A. (2014). The effect of corporate governance on firm performance: A case of Turkey. *International Journal of Critical Accounting, 6*(2), 187–210.

Alzeban, A., & Sawan, N. (2015). The impact of audit committee characteristics on the implementation of internal audit recommendations. *Journal of International Accounting, Auditing and Taxation, 24*, 61–71.

Amoah, L., Adjasi, C., Soumare, I., Osei, K., Abor, J. Y., Anarfo, E., Amo-Yartey, C., & Otchere, I. (2020). Finance, economic growth, and development. In J. Y. Abor, C. K. D. Adjasi, & R. Lensink (Eds.), *Contemporary issues in development finance* (pp. 20–50). Routledge.

Anandajayasekeram, P. (2011). The role of agricultural R&D within the agricultural innovation systems framework. In *Innovation in small-farm agriculture* (pp. 75–87). CRC Press.

Anginer, D., De la Torre, A., & Ize, A. (2011). *Risk absorption by the state: When is it good public policy?* (World Bank Policy Research Working Paper, 5893).

Arestis, P., Chortareas, G., & Magkonis, G. (2015). The financial development and growth nexus: A meta-analysis. *Journal of Economic Surveys, 29*(3), 549–565.

Arrow, K. J., & Lind, R. C. (1970, June). Uncertainty and the evaluation of public investment decisions. *American Economic Review, 60*, 364–378.

Asongu, S. A., Le Roux, S., & Biekpe, N. (2018). Enhancing ICT for environmental sustainability in sub-Saharan Africa. *Technological Forecasting and Social Change, 127*, 209–216.

Atkinson, A. B., & Stiglitz, J. (1980). *Lectures on public economics*. McGraw-Hill.

Attridge, S., Chen, Y., & Mbate, M. (2021). *Financial performance and corporate governance: Evidence from national development banks in Africa* (ODI Report).

Attridge, S., te Velde, D. W., & Peter Andreasen, S. (2019). *Impact of development finance institutions on sustainable development: An essay series* (Overseas Development Institute [ODI] Report).

Avom, D., Nkengfack, H., Fotio, H. K., & Totouom, A. (2020). ICT and environmental quality in Sub-Saharan Africa: Effects and transmission channels. *Technological Forecasting and Social Change, 155*, 120028.

Balin, B. J. (2008). *Basel I, Basel II, and emerging markets: A nontechnical analysis*. SSRN 1477712.

Balthazar, L. (2006). *From Basel 1 to Basel 3: The integration of state-of-the-art risk modeling in banking regulation*. Palgrave Macmillan.

Bank for International Settlements (BIS). (2001). *The new Basel Capital Accord*. Basel Committee on Banking Supervision.

Bank for International Settlements (BIS). (2010). *Principles for enhancing corporate governance*. Basel Committee on Banking Supervision. http://www.bis.org/publ/bcbs176.htm

Bank of Ghana (BoG).. (2018). *Monetary Policy Committee (MPC) report*. Retrieved on 5 October 2022 from www.bog.gov.gh

Bank of Ghana (BoG). (2019). *Update on banking sector reforms*. Retrieved on 5 October 2022 from https://www.bog.gov.gh

Bank of Ghana (BoG). (2021). Bank of Ghana monetary policy report. *Banking Sector Developments, 5*(1). https://www.bog.gov.gh/monetary_policy_rpts/banking-sector-developments-report-january-2021/

Barako, D. G., & Brown, A. M. (2008). Corporate social reporting and board representation: Evidence from the Kenyan banking sector. *Journal of Management and Governance, 12*(4), 309–324.

Barone, B., & Spratt, S. (2015). *Development banks from the BRICS* (Evidence Report No. 111). Institute of Development Studies (IDS).

Barro, R. J., & Sala-i-Martin, X. (1998). *Economic growth*. MIT Press.

Bategeka, L. (1993). Sources of income as related to poverty in Karongo Village, Hoima District (Doctoral dissertation, MA Dissertation). Department of Economics, Makerere University, Kampala, Uganda.

Bategeka, L. N. (1999). Uganda's achievements and challenges in the financial sector: Whose interests count? *Ugandan Banker, 7*(4), 6–10.

BCBS. (2011, June). *Basel III; A global regulatory framework for more resilient banks and banking systems. Basel Committee on Banking Supervision*. Bank for International Settlements. Revised version. ISBN 92-9131-859-0.

BCBS. (2012, October). *A framework for dealing with domestic systemically important banks. Basel Committee on Banking Supervision*. Bank for International Settlements. ISBN 92-9131-141-3.

BCBS. (2014, April). *Standards. Supervisory framework for measuring and controlling large exposures*. Basel Committee on Banking Supervision. Bank for International Settlements. ISBN 978-92-9197-987-5.

BCBS. (2016, April). *Standards. Interest rate risk in the banking book.* Basel Committee on Banking Supervision. Bank for International Settlements.

BCBS. (2017a, December). *Basel III: Finalising post-crisis reforms.* Basel Committee on Banking Supervision. Bank for International Settlements.

BCBS. (2017b, December). *High-level summary of Basel III reforms.* Basel Committee on Banking Supervision. Bank for International Settlements.

BCBS. (2019, June). *Overview of pillar 2 supervisory review practices and approaches.* Basel Committee on Banking Supervision Discussion Paper. Bank for International Settlements. ISBN 978-92-9259-279-0

Behuria, P. (2020). *The political economy of central bank effectiveness: The case of National Bank of Rwanda* (ESID Working Paper No. 151). Effective States and Inclusive Development Research Centre, Manchester, UK.

Benford, J, Ostry, J. D., & Shiller, R. (2018). *Sovereign GDP-linked bonds: Rationale and design.* A VoxEU.org eBook. CEPR Press.

Benink, H., & Wihlborg, C. (2002). The new Basel Capital Accord: Making it effective with stronger market discipline. *European Financial Management, 8*(1), 103–115.

Bennett, D., & Sharpe, K. (1980). The state as banker and entrepreneur: The last-resort character of the mexican state's economic intervention, 1917–76. *Comparative Politics, 12*(2), 165–189.

Bernstein, S. (2017). The United Nations and the governance of sustainable development goals. In *Governing through goals: Sustainable Development Goals as governance innovation* (pp. 213–239). MIT Press.

Bhattacharya, A., & Holt, R. (2015). *Assessing the changing infrastructure needs in emerging markets and developing countries* (G-24/GGGI Paper Series).

Bhattacharya, A., Meltzer, J. P., Oppenheim, J., Qureshi, Z., & Stern, N. (2016). *Delivering on sustainable infrastructure for better development and better climate.* The Brookings Institution.

Bhattacharya, A., & Romani, M. (2013, March). *Meeting the infrastructure challenge: The case for a new development bank* (Vol. 21). G-24 Technical Group Meeting, Washington, DC.

BIS. (1988). *International convergence of capital measurements and capital standards.* Bank of International Settlements.

BIS. (1997). *Core principles for effective banking supervision.* Bank for International Settlements.

BIS. (2004). *International convergence of capital measurement and capital standards: A revised framework.* Bank for International Settlements.

BIS. (2006). *Basel II: International convergence of capital measurement and capital standards: A revised framework.* Comprehensive Version. Bank for International Settlements.

BIS. (2009). *Basel Committee on Banking Supervision: Enhancements to the Basel II framework.* Bank for International Settlements.

BIS. (2011). *Basel III: A global regulatory framework for more resilient banks and banking systems*. Bank for International Settlements.

BIS. (2018a). *The G-SIB framework: Executive Summary*. FSI, Bank for International Settlements. https://www.bis.org/fsi/fsisummaries/g-sib_framework.htm

BIS. (2018b). *The treatment of large exposures in the basel capital standards – Executive summary*. FSI. Bank for International Settlements. https://www.bis.org/fsi/fsisummaries/largeexpos

BIS. (2022). *High-level considerations on proportionality*. Bank for International Settlements.

Bitsch, F., Buchner, A., & Kaserer, C. (2010). Risk, return and cash flow characteristics of infrastructure fund investments. *EIB Papers, 15*, 1.

BNR (National Bank of Rwanda). (2021a, August). *Monetary policy and financial stability statement*. www.bnr.rw/news-publications/publications/monetary-policy-financial-stability-statement

BNR (National Bank of Rwanda). (2021b, August). *Directives and guidelines*. https://www.bnr.rw/financial-stability/bank-supervision/laws-and-regulations: Regulation No 04/2018 dated 24/01/2018 on business continuity management.

Bodie, Z., Merton, R., & Cleeton, D. (2009). *Financial economics* (2nd ed.). Pearson.

Bond, P. (2013). *The BRICS bank and shifts in multilateral finance: A view from South Africa*. Presented at the SouthGovNet conference panel: Institutions of South-South Cooperation. Fudan University Institute of International Relations, Shanghai, China.

Bonnel, A., & Swann, S. (2015). *Mainstreaming climate action within financial institutions* (Technical report). Emerging Practices.

Boolaky, P. K., & Quick, R. (2016). Bank directors' perceptions of expanded auditor's reports. *International Journal of Auditing, 20*(2), 158–174.

Boyd, B. (1990). Corporate linkages and organizational environment: A test of the resource dependence model. *Strategic Management Journal, 11*(6), 419–430.

Bracking, S., & Leffel, B. (2021). Climate finance governance: Fit for purpose? *Wiley Interdisciplinary Reviews: Climate Change, 12*(4), e709.

Bradlow, D., & Humphrey, C. S. (2016). *Sustainability and infrastructure investment: National development banks in Africa* (GEGI Working Paper 002). Boston University. https://doi.org/10.2139/ssrn.2802713

BRD (Development Bank of Rwanda). (2014). *BRD Strategic Plan 2015–2019*. Available on BRD website.

BRD (Development Bank of Rwanda). (2021). *Annual report 2021: Supporting Rwanda's economy amid the pandemic*. BRD, Kigali. https://www.brd.rw/brd/wp-content/uploads/2022/05/BRD_Annual_Report_2021.pdf

Brei, M. (2020). *The future of national development banks. The inside story from across the world* (Vol. 1). The World Bank.

Brei, M., & Schclarek, A. (2013). Public bank lending in times of crisis. *Journal of Financial Stability, 9*, 820–830.

Brei, M., & Schclarek, A. (2017). The countercyclical behaviour of national development banks in Latin America and the Caribbean. In *The future of national development banks*. Oxford University Press.

Brei, M., & Schclarek, A. (2018). The counter-cyclical behaviour of national development banks. In S. Griffith-Jones & J. A. Ocampo (Eds.), *The future of national development banks*. Oxford University Press.

Brownbridge, M. (2002). Resolving bank failures in Uganda: Policy lessons from recent bank failures. *Development Policy Review, 20*(3), 279–291.

Brownbridge, M. (2014). How relevant are the Basel capital reforms for sub-Saharan Africa? *Journal of Risk Management in Financial Institutions, 8*(2), 153–162.

Brownbridge, M., & Gockel, A. F. (1996). *The impact of financial sector policies on banking in Ghana*. YPFS Documents (Series 1).

Bruck, N. (1998). The role of development banks in the twenty-first century. *Journal of Emerging Markets, 3*, 39–68.

Buchner, B., Falconer, A., Hervé-Mignucci, M., Trabacchi, C., & Brinkman, M. (2011, October 27). *The landscape of climate finance*. Climate Policy Initiative, Venice.

Cadbury, H. J. (2004). *The book of acts in history*. Wipf and Stock Publishers.

Calderon, C., & Serven, L. (2004). *The effects of infrastructure development on growth and income distribution* (Policy Research Working Paper; No. 3400).

Campbell, J. L. (2007). Why would corporations behave in socially responsible ways? An institutional theory of corporate social responsibility. *Academy of Management Review, 32*(3), 946–967.

Carson, R. (1962). *Of man and the stream of time* (Vol. 36, No. 4). Scripps College.

Carter, D. A., Simkins, B. J., & Simpson, W. G. (2003). Corporate governance, board diversity, and firm value. *Financial Review, 38*(1), 33–53.

Carvalho F. C. (2003). Inovação Financeira e Regulação Prudencial: da Regulação da Liquidez aos Acordos da Basileia. *UFRJ: Textopara Discussão*. Rio de Janeiro.

Carvalho, D. (2014). The real effects of government-owned banks: Evidence from an emerging market. *The Journal of Finance, 69*(2), 577–609.

Chandrasekhar, C. (2016). National development banks in a comparative perspective. In A. Calcagno, S. Dullien, A. Marquez-Velasquez, N. Maystre, & J. Priewe (Eds.), *Rethinking development strategies after the financial crisis, Volume II—Country studies and international comparisons* (1st ed., pp. 21–30). UNCTAD.

Chen, Y., & Rezaee, Z. (2012). The role of corporate governance in convergence with IFRS: Evidence from China. *International Journal of Accounting & Information Management, 20*, 171–188.

Christiansen, J. (2021). *Development banking in the global economy.*

Cicala, S., Holland, S. P., Mansur, E. T., Muller, N. Z., & Yates, A. J. (2021). Expected health effects of reduced air pollution from COVID-19 social distancing. *Atmosphere, 12*(8), 951.

Claessens, S., Feijen, E., & Laeven, L. (2008). Political connections and preferential access to finance: The role of campaign contributions. *Journal of Financial Economics, 88*(3), 554–580.

Clarke, T. (2004). Theories of corporate governance. *The Philosophical Foundations of Corporate Governance, Oxon, 12*(4), 244–266.

Collier, P. (2009, May 1). Rethinking finance for Africa's small firms in "SME financing in SSA". *Proparco Magazine* on Private Sector and Development.

Columbia Center on Sustainable Investment. (2021). *Development banking in the global economy, state of play and future direction.* ccsi.columbia.edu

Corfee-Morlot, J., Kamal-Chaoui, L., Donovan, M. G., Cochran, I., Robert, A., & Teasdale, P. J. (2009). *Cities, climate change and multilevel governance.* OECD Publishing.

Cudjoe, M. A., Abor, J. Y., & Volschenk, J. (2023). Environmental and climate finance in developing countries. In J. Y. Abor (Ed.), *Sustainable and responsible investment in developing markets: A companion.* Edward Elgar.

Culpeper, R. (2012). Financial sector policy and development in the wake of the global crisis: The role of national development banks. *Third World Quarterly, 33*(3), 383–403.

Daily, C. M., & Dalton, D. R. (1994). Bankruptcy and corporate governance: The impact of board composition and structure. *Academy of Management Journal, 37*(6), 1603–1617.

Dalberg. (2009). *The growing role of the development finance institutions in international development policy.* https://www.findevgateway.org/sites/default/files/publications/files/mfg-en-paper-the-growing-role-of-the-development-finance-institutions-in-international-development-policy-2009.pdf

Dalberg and KfW. (2018). *Africa agricultural finance market landscape.*

Dankwano, R. N., & Hassan, Z. (2018). Impact of gender diversity on Indian firm's financial performance. *International Journal of Management, Accounting and Economics, 5*(5), 319–341.

Davis, J. A., Hampton, M. M., & Lansberg, I. (1997). *Generation to generation: Life cycles of the family business.* Harvard Business Press.

DBSA Integrated Annual Reports, 2015–2021.

DBSA Sustainability Review Report, 2021.

de Aghion, B. A. (1999). Development banking. *Journal of Development Economics, 58*(1), 83–100.

de Castro, L. B. (2007). Discutindo os Acordos da Basileia. *Revista do BNDES, 14*(28), 277–304.

de Castro, L. B. (2018). Financial regulation and risk management in development banks. In S. Griffith-Jones & J. A. Ocampo (Eds.), *The future of national development banks*. Oxford University Press.

Deloitte report on Project Bonds: An alternative source of Financing Infrastructure Projects. www2.deloitte.com/za/en/pages/finance/articles/project-bonds-an-alternative-to-financing-infrastructure-projects.html

de Luna-Martinez, J., & Vicente, C. L. (2012, February). *Global survey of development banks* (Policy Research, Working Paper; No. 5969). World Bank.

Demirgüç-Kunt, A., & Detragiache, E. (2011). Basel core principles and bank soundness: Does compliance matter? *Journal of Financial Stability, 7*(4), 179–190.

De Negri, J. A., Maffioli, A., Rodriguez, C. M., & Vázquez, G. (2011). *The impact of public credit programs on Brazilian firms* (No. IDB-WP-293). IDB Working Paper Series.

Development Bank of Southern Africa Corporate Plan, 2019–2022. www.dbsa.org

Dickinson, T. (2008). Development finance institutions: Profitability promoting development. In Organisation for Economic Co-operation and Development (OECD) (Ed.), *Turning African agriculture into a business—A reader*. OECD.

Dickinson, T. (n.d.). *Development finance institutions: Profitability promoting development*. http://www.oecd.org/dev/41302068.pdf

Dixit, A. K., & Pindyck, R. S. (1994). *Investment under uncertainty*. Princeton University Press.

Djankov, S., La Porta, R., Lopez-de-Silanes, F., & Shleifer, A. (2002). The regulation of entry. *The Quarterly Journal of Economics, 117*(1), 1–37. https://doi.org/10.1162/003355302753399436

Doh, J. P., & Guay, T. R. (2006). Corporate social responsibility, public policy, and NGO activism in Europe and the United States: An institutional-stakeholder perspective. *Journal of Management Studies, 43*(1), 47–73.

Doh, J. P., Howton, S. D., Howton, S. W., & Siegel, D. S. (2010). Does the market respond to an endorsement of social responsibility? The role of institutions, information, and legitimacy. *Journal of Management, 36*(6), 1461–1485.

Einhorn, C. S. (2013). Can you fight poverty with a five-star hotel? *Foreign Policy*.

Elavarasan, R. M., Pugazhendhi, R., Shafiullah, G. M., Kumar, N. M., Arif, M. T., Jamal, T., & Dyduch, J. (2022). Impacts of COVID-19 on Sustainable Development Goals and effective approaches to maneuver them in the post-pandemic environment. *Environmental Science and Pollution Research, 29*(23), 33957–33987.

Epstein, G., & Dutt, D. (2018). Public banks, public orientation and the great financial crisis of 2007–2008. In *Financial innovation and resilience* (pp. 327–343). Palgrave Macmillan.
Espey, J. (2019). Sustainable development will falter without data. *Nature, 571*(7765), 299–300.
Estrada, A., Garber, P. A., & Chaudhary, A. (2020). Current and future trends in socio-economic, demographic and governance factors affecting global primate conservation. *PeerJ, 8*, e9816.
Eurodad. (2017, April). *Public development banks: Towards a better model.* European Network on Debt and Development.
Fama, E. F., & Jensen, M. C. (1983a). Agency problems and residual claims. *The Journal of Law and Economics, 26*(2), 327–349.
Fama, E. F., & Jensen, M. C. (1983b). Separation of ownership and control. *The Journal of Law and Economics, 26*(2), 301–325.
FAO & World Bank. (2013). *Financing smallholder agricultural term investments.* http://www.ruralfinance.org/fileadmin/templates/rflc/documents/6_financing_smallholder_web.pdf
Fernandez-Feijoo, B., Romero, S., & Ruiz, S. (2014). Effect of stakeholders' pressure on transparency of sustainability reports within the GRI framework. *Journal of Business Ethics, 122*(1), 53–63.
Ferraz, J. C., & Coutinho, L. (2019). Investment policies, development finance and economic transformation: Lessons from BNDES. *Structural Change and Economic Dynamics, 48*, 86–102.
Ficetola, G. F., & Rubolini, D. (2021). Containment measures limit environmental effects on COVID-19 early outbreak dynamics. *Science of the Total Environment, 761*, 144432.
Finnerty, J. D. (2013). *Project financing asset-based financial engineering*. Wiley.
Food and Agriculture Organization. (2021). *FAOSTAT statistical database*. FAO. http://www.fao.org/faostat/en/#data/IC
Franks, J., & Mayer, C. (2001). Ownership and control of German corporations. *The Review of Financial Studies, 14*(4), 943–977.
Friedman, M. (1970). A theoretical framework for monetary analysis. *Journal of Political Economy, 78*(2), 193–238.
Fukuda-Parr, S. (2006). Millennium development goal 8: Indicators for international human rights obligations? *Human Rights Quarterly, 28*, 966–997.
Fuzi, S. F. S., Halim, S. A. A., & Julizaerma, M. K. (2016). Board independence and firm performance. *Procedia Economics and Finance, 37*, 460–465.
Gales, L. M., & Kesner, I. F. (1994). An analysis of board of director size and composition in bankrupt organizations. *Journal of Business Research, 30*(3), 271–282.
Gatti, S. (2013). *Project finance in theory and practice.* Elsevier.

Geddes, A., Schmidt, T. S., & Steffen, B. (2018). The multiple roles of state investment banks in low-carbon energy finance: An analysis of Australia, the UK and Germany. *Energy Policy, 115*, 158–170.

Gerschenkron, A. (1962). *Economic backwardness in historical perspective—A book of essays*. Harvard University Press.

Gil-González, D., Ruiz-Cantero, M. T., & Álvarez-Dardet, C. (2009). How political epidemiology research can address why the millennium development goals have not been achieved: Developing a research agenda. *Journal of Epidemiology & Community Health, 63*(4), 278–280.

Girling, P. X. (2014). *Operational risk management: A complete guide to a successful operational risk framework*. Wiley.

Glennerster, R., & Kudzai T. (2013). *Running randomized evaluations: A practical guide*. Princeton University Press.

Goldsmith, R. W. (1969). *Financial structure and development*. Yale University Press.

Goodhart, C. (2011). *The Basel Committee on Banking Supervision: A history of the early years 1974–1997*. Cambridge University Press. https://doi.org/10.1017/CBO9780511996238

Gottschalk, R., & Castro, L. B. (2020). *Financial regulation of national development banks-NDBs* (No. f83c9569-d73d-4295-a5eb-2675c8315417).

Gottschalk, R. Castro, L. B., & Xu, J. (2020, November). *Financial regulation of national development banks*.

Gottschalk, R., Castro, L. B., & Xu, J. (2021). Should national development banks be subject to Basel III? *Review of Political Economy*. https://doi.org/10.1080/09538259.2021.1977541

Green, P. J., & Silverman, B. W. (1993). *Nonparametric regression and generalized linear models: A roughness penalty approach*. CRC Press.

Griffith-Jones, S. (1993). *Loan guarantees for large infrastructure projects: The issues and possible lessons for a European facility*. Office for official publications of the European communities.

Griffith-Jones, S. (2015, July). *The positive role of development bank, financial for development*. 3rd International Conference, Addis Ababa, Ethiopia. https://www.un.org/esa/ffd/ffd3/blog/positive-role-development-banks.html

Griffith-Jones, S., Attridge, S., & Gouett, M. (2020a). *Securing climate finance through national development banks* (ODI Report). ODI. www.odi.org/publications/16552-securing-climate-finance-through-national-development-banks

Griffith-Jones, S., & Gottschalk, R. (2012). *Exogenous shocks—Dealing with the only certainty: Uncertainty*. Paper prepared for the Commonwealth Secretariat, London, p. 25.

Griffith-Jones, S., & Naqvi, N. (2020a). *Industrial policy and risk sharing in public development banks: Lessons for the post-COVID response from the EIB and EFSI* (Working Paper No. 143). GEG.

Griffith-Jones, S., & Naqvi, N. (2020b). *Leveraging policy steer? Industrial policy, risksharing and the European Investment Bank* (Working Paper 43). GEG.

Griffith-Jones, S., & Ocampo, J. A. (2008). A counter-cyclical framework for a development-friendly IFA. In J. Fanelli (Ed.), *Macroeconomic volatility, institutions and financial architectures: The developing world experience* (1st ed., pp. 25–44). Palgrave Macmillan.

Griffith-Jones, S., & Ocampo, J. A. (2014). Global governance for financial stability. In *Contributions to economic theory, policy, development and finance* (pp. 273–295). Palgrave Macmillan.

Griffith-Jones, S., Ocampo, J. A., Rezende, F., Schclarek, A., & Brei, M. (2018). The future of national development banks. In S. Griffith-Jones & J. A. Ocampo (Eds.), *The future of national development banks*. Oxford University Press.

Griffith-Jones, S., Spiegel, S., Jiajun, X., Carreras, M., & Naqv, N. (2020b). *Matching risks with instruments in development banks* (Working Paper No. 9). International Research Initiative on PDBs and DFIs Working Groups.

Griffith-Jones, S., Xiaoyun, L., & Spratt, S. (2016). *The Asian Infrastructure Investment Bank: What can it learn from, and perhaps teach to, the multilateral development banks?* (IDS Evidence Report No. 179). IDS.

Gu, J., & Carey, R. (2019). China's development finance and African infrastructure development. In *China-Africa and an economic transformation* (pp. 147–172). Oxford University Press.

Gurley, J. G., & Shaw, E. S. (1955). Financial aspects of economic development. *The American Economic Review, 45*(4), 515–538.

Gutierrez, E., Rudolph, H., Homa, T., & Beneit, E. B. (2011). *Development banks: Role and mechanisms to increase their efficiency* (World Bank Policy Research Working Paper Series 5729).

Halland, H., Beardsworth, J., Land, B., & Schmidt, J. (2014). *Resource financed infrastructure: A discussion on a new form of infrastructure financing*. The World Bank.

Hanieh, A. (2018). *Money, markets, and monarchies: The Gulf Cooperation Council and the political economy of the contemporary Middle East*. Cambridge University Press.

Hannoun, H. (2010). *The Basel III capital framework: A decisive breakthrough*. Speech at Seminar on Financial Regulatory Reform, Hong Kong. Bank for International Settlements. https://www.bis.org/speeches/sp101125a.pdf

Hausmann, R., & Rodrik, D. (2003). Economic development as self-discovery. *Journal of development Economics, 72*(2), 603–633. https://www.oecd.org/development/development-finance-institutions-private-sector-development.htm

Hege, E., Brimont, L., & Pagnon, F. (2019). Sustainable development goals and indicators: Can they be tools to make national budgets more sustainable? *Public Sector Economics, 43*(4), 423–444.

Heider, C. (2017). *Rethinking evaluation* (Working paper series). World Bank Group.

Helm, D., & Tindall, T. (2009). The evolution of infrastructure and utility ownership and its implications. *Oxford Review of Economic Policy, 25*(3), 411–434.

Ho, P. (2017). *Unmaking China's development: The function and credibility of institutions*. Cambridge University Press.

Ho, P. (2020, April). The credibility of (in)formality: Or, the irrelevance of institutional form in judging performance. *Cities, 99*, 102609. https://doi.org/10.1016/j.cities.2020.102609

Hope, K. R. (2020). Corruption reduction as a target of the sustainable development goals: Applying indicators and policy frameworks. In *The Emerald handbook of crime, justice and sustainable development* (pp. 105–130). Emerald.

Ho, S., & Marois, T. (2019). China's asset management companies as state spatial-temporal strategy. *The China Quarterly, 239*, 728–751.

Huang, B., Xi, T., & Xu, J. (2020). *Checks and balance, political leadership, and bureaucratic autonomy: Evidence from national development banks* (No. 6fb72d50-b8e9-40a3-9021-8b0348a55dd4).

IMF. (2019, April). *Curbing corruption* (pp. 39–66). IMF Fiscal Monitor.

IMF. (2020). *Assessment, E.B., IMF Executive Board Concludes 2020 Article IV Consultation with France.*

Ingabire, R. C. (2016). *The impact of financial inclusion on (econometric study: Quarterly data from 2006–2014)* (Doctoral dissertation). University of Rwanda.

Innovation Systems Framework. Conference Working Paper 6. http://www.ifpri.org/sites/default/files/publications/ananda.pdf

Intergovernmental Committee of Experts on Sustainable Development Financing. (2014). *UNCTAD*. https://www.ituc-csi.org/IMG/pdf/icesdf_report.pdf

International Finance Corporation. (2012). *Innovative agricultural SME finance models*. International Finance Corporation.

International Fund for Agricultural Development (IFAD). (2000). *Ghana: Rural financial services project, 2000.* http://www.ifad.org/gender/learning/sector/finance/41.htm

International Fund for Agricultural Development (IFAD). (2009). *Rural finance: Small amounts making a big difference*. http://www.ifad.org/events/microcredit/eng.pdf

International Labour Organization. (2021). *Key indicators of the labour market.* International Labour Organization.

Islam, M. M. (2020). Agricultural credit and agricultural productivity in Bangladesh: An econometric approach. *International Journal of Food and Agricultural Economics (IJFAEC), 8*(1128-2020-1530).

Issahaku, H., Asiedu, E., Nkegbe, P. K., & Osei, R. (2020). Financing agriculture for inclusive development. In J. Y. Abor, C. K. D. Adjasi, & R. Lensink (Eds.), *Contemporary issues in development finance* (pp. 287–317). Routledge.

Jaiyesimi, R. (2016). The challenge of implementing the sustainable development goals in Africa: The way forward. *African Journal of Reproductive Health, 20*(3), 13–18.

Jensen, M. C. (1993). The modern industrial revolution, exit, and the failure of internal control systems. *The Journal of Finance, 48*(3), 831–880.

Jensen, M. C., & Meckling, W. F. (1976). Theory of the firm: Managerial behavior, agency costs, and ownership structure. *Journal of Financial Economics, 3*, 305–360.

Jitpleecheep, P. (2012). *Mitsubishi to cut risk by making more parts.*

John, K., & Senbet, L. W. (1998). Corporate governance and board effectiveness. *Journal of Banking & Finance, 22*(4), 371–403.

Jones, E. (2020). *The political economy of bank regulation in developing countries: Risk and reputation* (p. 416). Oxford University Press.

Jones, K. K. (2013). *The impact of legislation on the organization: Evaluating the impact of corporate governance regulation on the internal audit function* (PhD thesis). Georgia State University, Atlanta, GA.

Joseph, A. (n.d.). *Development financial institutions in the Caribbean—The need for re-orientation.*

Ketterer, J., & Powell A. (2018). *Financing infrastructure.* IADB.

Kim, K. (2018). *Lean on me: Development financial struggles and national development banks.* Unpublished paper in Developing Economics, A Critical Perspective on Development Economics, Department of International Development at King's College, London.

Kim, L., & Nugent, J. B. (1999). *The Republic of Korea's small and medium-size enterprises and their support systems.* The World Bank.

Kindleberger, C. P., & Kindleberger, C. P. (1978). *Government and international trade* (No. 129). International Finance Section, Department of Economics, Princeton University.

King, P., & Tarbert, H. (2011, May). Basel III: An Overview. *Banking and Financial Services Policy Report, 30*(5), 1–18.

Knight, F. H. (1921). Cost of production and price over long and short periods. *Journal of Political Economy, 29*(4), 304–335.

Koloma, Y., & Kemeze, F. H. (2022). COVID-19 and perceived effects on agricultural financing in Africa: Evidence and policy implications. *African Development Review, 34*, S63–S79.

Kornai, J. (1979). Resource-constrained versus demand-constrained systems. *Econometrica: Journal of the Econometric Society, 47*, 801–819.

Körner, T., & Schnabel, I. (2011). Public ownership of banks and economic growth: The impact of country heterogeneity. *Economics of Transition, 19*(3), 407–441.

KPMG. (2012). *Africa banking survey*. KPMG.

Kraaijenbrink, J., Spender, J. C., & Groen, A. J. (2010). The resource-based view: A review and assessment of its critiques. *Journal of Management, 36*(1), 349–372.

Kukah, M. A., Amidu, M., & Abor, J. Y. (2016). Corporate governance mechanisms and accounting information quality of listed firms in Ghana. *African Journal of Accounting, Auditing and Finance, 5*(1), 38–58.

Kulabako, F. (2013, July 9). Uganda development bank to shift its market interest. *Daily Monitor*. Kampala. Retrieved 4 August 2016.

Kuttu, S., Fanta, A., Graham, M., & Abor, J. Y. (2020). Infrastructure financing and economic development. In J. Y. Abor, C. K. D. Adjasi, & R. Lensink (Eds.), *Contemporary issues in development finance*. Routledge.

La Porta, R., López-de-Silanes, F., & Shleifer, A. (2002). Government ownership of banks. *Journal of Finance, 57*(2), 265–301.

La Porta, R., Lopez-de-Silanes, F., Shleifer, A., & Vishny, R. (2000). Investor protection and corporate governance. *Journal of Financial Economics, 58*(1–2), 3–27.

Lazzarini, S. G., Musacchio, A., Bandeira-de-Mello, R., & Marcon, R. (2015). What do state-owned development banks do? Evidence from BNDES, 2002–09. *World Development, 66*, 237–253.

Lees, F. (2012). *Lees' Loss prevention in the process industries: Hazard identification, assessment and control*. Butterworth-Heinemann.

le Pere, G. L. (2021). *Repositioning state-owned enterprises (SOEs) and development finance institutions*. Wits School of Governance, University of the Witwatersrand.

Levine, R. (1997). Financial development and economic growth: Views and agenda. *Journal of Economic Literature, XXXV*, 688–726.

Liao, C. H., & Hsu, A. W. H. (2013). Common membership and effective corporate governance: Evidence from audit and compensation committees. *Corporate Governance: An International Review, 21*(1), 79–92.

Lipton, M., & Lorsch, J. W. (1992). A modest proposal for improved corporate governance. *Business Lawyer, 48*, 59–77.

Lourenço, I. C., Branco, M. C., Curto, J. D., & Eugénio, T. (2012). How does the market value corporate sustainability performance? *Journal of Business Ethics, 108*(4), 417–428.

Lucas, R. E., Jr. (1988). On the mechanics of economic development. *Journal of Monetary Economics, 22*(1), 3–42.

Luna-Martinez, D., Vicente, C. L., Arshad, A. B., Tatucu, R., & Song, J. (2018). *2017 survey of national development banks* (No. 125958, pp. 1–68). Disclosure. The World Bank.

Lundsgaarde, E., Dupuy, K., & Persson, Å. (2018). *Coordination challenges in climate finance* (No. 2018: 3). DIIS Working Paper.

Lynam, J., Beintema, N., & Annor-Frempong, I. (2012, June). *Agricultural R&D: Investing in Africa's future—Analyzing trends, challenges, and opportunities*. Reflections on the conference. http://www.ifpri.org/sites/default/files/publications/astifaraconfsynthesis.pdf

Mallin, C. (2001). Institutional investors and voting practices. An international comparison. *Corporate Governance: An International Review, 9*, 118–126.

Mallin, C. (2016). *Corporate governance*. Oxford University Press.

Mangena, M., & Tauringana, V. (2008). Audit committees and voluntary external auditor involvement in UK interim reporting. *International Journal of Auditing, 12*(1), 45–63.

Marcelin, I., & Mathur, I. (2015). Privatization, financial development, property rights and growth. *Journal of Banking & Finance, 50*, 528–546.

Marois, T. (2012). *States, banks, and crisis: Emerging finance capitalism in Mexico and Turkey*. Edward Elgar.

Marois, T. (2015). Banking on alternatives to neoliberal development. In L. Pradella & T. Marois, (Eds.), *Polarizing development: Alternatives to neoliberalism and the crisis*. Pluto Press.

Marois, T. (2021). *Public banks: Decarbonisation, definancialisation, and democratisation*. Cambridge University Press.

Marois, T. (2022). A dynamic theory of public banks (and why it matters). *Review of Political Economy, 34*(2), 356–371.

Marois, T., & Güngen, A. R. (2016). Credibility and class in the evolution of public banks: The case of Turkey. *Journal of Peasant Studies, 43*(6), 1285–1309.

Mazzucato, M. (2013). *Entreprenuerial state: Debunking public vs. private myths*. Anthem Press.

Mazzucato, M. (2018). *The value of everything: Making and taking in the global economy*. Hachette UK.

Mazzucato, M., & Penna, C. C. (2018). National development banks and mission-oriented finance for innovation. In S. Griffith-Jones & J. A. Ocampo (Eds.), *The future of national development banks*. Oxford University Press.

Mazzucato, M., & Penna, C. C. (2016). Beyond market failures: The market creating and shaping roles of state investment banks. *Journal of Economic Policy Reform, 19*(4), 305–326.

McDonald, D. A. (2016). To corporatize or not to corporatize (and if so how)? *Utilities Policy, 40*, 107–114.

McDonald, D. A., Marois, T., & Barrowclough, D. V. (Eds.). (2020*). Public banks and Covid-19: Combatting the pandemic with public finance.* Municipal Services Project (Kingston), UNCTAD (Geneva), and Eurodad (Brussels). https://publicbankscovid19.org/

McDonald, D. A., Marois, T., & Spronk, S. (2021). Public banks + public water = SDG 6? *Water Alternatives, 14*(1), 117–134.

McKinnon, R. I. (1973). *Money and capital in economic development* (1st ed.). Brookings Institution.

McKinnon, R. I. (1993). *The order of economic liberalization: Financial control in the transition to a market economy*. JHU Press.

Meggison, W. (2004). *The financial economics of privatization*. Oxford University Press.

Meyer, J. W., & Bromley, P. (2013). The worldwide expansion of "organization." *Sociological Theory, 31*(4), 366–389.

Miller, C., & Jones, L. (2010). *Agricultural value chain finance: Tools and lessons*. Practical Action Publishing.

Miller, M. H. (1988). The Modigliani-Miller propositions after thirty years. *Journal of Economic Perspectives, 2*(4), 99–120.

MINECOFIN (Ministry of Finance and Economic Planning, Rwanda). (2020). *Vision 2050*. Republic of Rwanda.

Mohammed, A. S., & Abor, J. Y. (2023). The role of oil and gas in sustainable development in the global south. In J. Y. Abor & A. Karimu (Eds.), *Sustainability management in the oil and gas industry*. Routledge.

Montero, E. G. P. (2017, March). *How can national development banks address key challenges associated with raising climate finance to increase investment flows for projects in their countries? Case study: The role of NAFIN in enabling climate finance flows into Mexico 'NAFIN Fellowship Programme'* (Working Paper No. 1).

Montiel, P. (2003). *Macroeconomics in emerging markets*. Cambridge University Press.

Morgado, N., Taskin, O., Lasfargues, B., & Sedemund, J. (2019). *Scaling up climate-compatible infrastructure: Insights from national development banks in Brazil and South Africa*. OECD Publishing.

Mudde, P. H. J. (2017). *The complementary role of official development finance: Some observations and recommendations*. Sustainable Finance & Insurance.

Mugisha, J., Ratemo, M. A., Keza, B. C. B., & Kahveci, H. (2021). Assessing the opportunities and challenges facing the development of off-grid solar systems in Eastern Africa: The cases of Kenya, Ethiopia, and Rwanda. *Energy Policy, 150*, 112131.

Muhammad, A. A., Muhammad, A., Ahmad, Z., Arif, M., Qasim, A., & Mahmood, R. (2013). Plant growth promoting rhizobacteria and sustainable agriculture: A review. *African Journal of Microbiology Research, 7*(9), 704–709.

Murphy, K. J., & Zimmerman, J. L. (1993). Financial performance surrounding CEO turnover. *Journal of Accounting and Economics, 16*(1–3), 273–315.

Musacchio, A., & Lazzarini, S. G. (2014). *Reinventing state capitalism: Leviathan in business*. Harvard University Press.

Nabudere, D. W. (1990). *The IMF-World Bank's economic stabilisation and structural adjustment policies and the Uganda economy, 1981–1989* (Research Report). African Studies Centre.

Ndikumana, L. (2006). *Revisiting development finance institutions for the purpose of accelerating African economic development*. African Development Bank.

Ndikumana, L. (2009). *Revisiting development finance institutions for the purpose of accelerating African economic development*. Proceedings of the 2006 African Economic Conference, African Development Bank, Tunisia.

Ndikumana, L. Naidoo, K., & Perez, F. (2021). *There a case for national development banks in Africa? Conceptual rationale and empirical evidence* (Working Paper Series). Political Economy Research Institute, University of Massachusetts Amherst.

Nestor, S. (2018a). Board effectiveness in international financial institutions: A comparative perspective on the effectiveness drivers in constituency boards. In P. Quayle & X. Gao (Eds.), *Good governance and modern international financial institutions*. Brill (AIIB Yearbook of International Law 2018). https://doi.org/10.1163/j.ctvrxk459.4

Nestor, S. (2018b). *Corporate governance 2030: Thoughts on the future of corporate governance*. Harvard Law School Forum on Corporate Governance.

Nissanke, M., & Aryeetey, E. (1998). *Financial integration and development: Liberalization and reform in Sub-Saharan Africa*. World Bank.

Noland, M., Moran, T., & Kotschwar, B. R. (2016). *Is gender diversity profitable? Evidence from a global survey* (Working Paper, 16-3). Peterson Institute for International Economics.

Ntim, C. G. (2009). *Internal corporate governance and firm financial performance: Evidence from South African listed firms* (PhD thesis). University of Glasgow.

Nyikos, G., & Kondor, Z. (2022). The involvement of national development banks promoting sustainable finance. *The Central European Journal of Regional Development and Tourism, 14*(1), 147–163.

Nyamongo, E. M., & Temesgen, K. (2013). The effect of governance on performance of commercial banks in Kenya: A panel study. *Corporate Governance: The International Journal of Business in Society, 13*(3), 452–454.

Nyantakyi, E. B., & Sy, M. (2015). The banking system in Africa: Main facts and challenges. *African Economic Brief, 6*(5), 1–16.

Nzobonimpa, O., Nkurunziza, J. D., & Ndikumana, L. (2006). *Promoting a development-oriented financial system in Burundi* (AERC research paper).

Ocran, M. K., Senadza, B., & Osei-Assibey, E. (2020). Foreign aid and economic development. In J. Y. Abor, C. K. D. Adjasi, & R. Lensink (Eds.), *Contemporary issues in development finance*. Routledge.

Oduor J., Sarmento, E. M., & Lannes, L. (2022). *Impact evaluation in development institutions: A look at the African Development Bank*. A quarterly knowledge publication from Independent Development Evaluation at the African Development Bank Group. http://www.ifpri.org/book-744/node/8242

OECD (Organisation for Economic Co-operation and Development). (2010). *Facilitating access to finance: Discussion paper on credit guarantee schemes*. http://www.ruralfinanceandinvestment.org/sites/default/files/45324327_pdf.pdf

OECD (Organisation for Economic Co-operation and Development). (2013, February). *The role of banks, equity markets and institutional investors in longterm financing for growth and development*. Report for G20 Leaders. http://www.oecd.org/finance/privatepensions/G20reportLTFinancingForGrowthRussianPresidency2013.pdf

OECD (Organisation for Economic Co-operation and Development). (2015a). *G20/OECD principles of corporate governance*. OECD Publishing. https://doi.org/10.1787/9789264236882-en

OECD (Organisation for Economic Co-operation and Development). (2015b). *Infrastructure financing instruments and incentives*. https://www.oecd.org/finance/private-pensions/Infrastructure-Financing-Instruments-and-Incentives.pdf

OECD (Organisation for Economic Co-operation and Development). (2015c). *Climate finance in 2013–14 and the USD 100 billion goal*. World Economic Forum.

OECD (Organisation for Economic Co-operation and Development). (n.d). *Development finance institutions and private sector development*.

Oketch, M. L. (2020). UDB unveils 5-year plans. *Daily Monitor*. Kampala. Retrieved on 16 July 2020 from https://www.monitor.co.ug/uganda/business/finance/udb-unveils-5-year-plans-1892916

Okoro, C. A., Hollis, N. D., Cyrus, A. C., & Griffin-Blake, S. (2018a). Prevalence of disabilities and health care access by disability status and type among adults—United States, 2016. *Morbidity and Mortality Weekly Report, 67*(32), 882.

Okoro, C. B., Udoh, D., Ben, E., & Nwosu, M. O. (2018b). Effect of Chief Executive Officer duality on the profitability of money deposit banks. *International Journal of Business Systems and Economics, 12*(1), 1–9.

Oliveira, F. N. D. (2019). Investment of firms in Brazil: Do financial restrictions, unexpected monetary shocks and bndes play important roles? *Revista Brasileira de Economia, 73*, 235–251.

Oloka-Onyango, J. (1987). Development financing: The case of the Uganda Development Bank. *Ufahamu: A Journal of African Studies, 15*(3).

Osakwe, J. O., & Ojo, M. O. (1986). An appraisal of public sector financing of agricultural development in Africa with particular reference to Nigeria. *Economic and Financial Review, 24*(2), 8.

Oxfam. (2015). *Billions in "out of control" IFC investments into third-parties causing human rights abuses around the world*. Oxfam International. https://www.oxfam.org/en/pressroom/pressreleases/2015-04-02/billions-out-control-ifc-investments-third-parties-causing-human-rights-abuses

Pagano, M. (1993). Financial markets and growth—An overview. *European Economic Review, 37*, 613–622.

Palermo, G. (2019). Power: A Marxist view: Coercion and exploitation in the capitalist mode of production. *Cambridge Journal of Economics, 43*(5), 1353–1375.

Pan, W. T., Zhuang, M. E., Zhou, Y. Y., & Yang, J. J. (2021). Research on sustainable development and efficiency of China's E-Agriculture based on a data envelopment analysis-Malmquist model. *Technological Forecasting and Social Change, 162*, 120298.

Periasamy, P. (2008). *Financial management*. Tata McGraw Hill Education.

Pfeffer, J., & Salancik, G. R. (1978). A resource dependence perspective. In *Intercorporate relations. The structural analysis of business*. Cambridge University Press.

Pickering, J., Betzold, C., & Skovgaard, J. (2017). Managing fragmentation and complexity in the emerging system of international climate finance. *International Environmental Agreements: Politics, Law and Economics, 17*(1), 1–16.

Povel, F. (2015, July). *The RAison d'Etre of public development banks and recommendations for successful development banking*. Paper presented at KfW FfD panel on Development Banks, Addis Ababa. Retrieved on 21 May 2022 from http://www.un.org/esa/ffd/ffd3/wp-content/uploads/sites/2/2015/07/Raison-detre-of-DBs-nonpaper-Addis.pdf

PwC Mexico. (2015). *Necessary investment for Mexico to fulfill the clean energy targets*.

Quartey, P., & Afful-Mensah, G. (2014). Financial and monetary policies in Ghana: A review of recent trends. *Review of Development Finance, 4*(2), 115–125.

Quartey, P., Turkson, E., & Abor, J. Y. (2017). Financing the growth of SMEs in Africa: What are the constraints to SME financing within ECOWAS? *Review of Development Finance, 7*(1), 18–28.

Quayle, P., & Gao, X. (2019). Introduction: Good governance and modern international financial institutions. In P. Quayle & X. Gao (Eds.), *Good governance and modern international financial institutions*. Brill (AIIB Yearbook of International Law 2018). https://doi.org/10.1163/j.ctvrxk459.4

Quintyn, M., & Taylor, M. (2002*). Regulatory and supervisory independence and financial stability* (IMF Working Paper WP/02/46). International Monetary Fund. www.imf.org/en/Publications/WP/Issues/2016/12/30/regulatory-and-Supervisory-Independenceand-Financial-Stability-15679

Ragavan, M. I., Marcil, L. E., & Garg, A. (2020). Climate change as a social determinant of health. *Pediatrics, 145*(5), e20193169.

Rezaee, Z. (2009). *Corporate governance and ethics*. Wiley.

Riaño, M. A., Boutaybi, J., Barchiche, D., & Treyer, S. (2022). Scaling up public development banks' transformative alignment with the 2030 Agenda for Sustainable Development. *Review of Political Economy, 34*(2), 286–317.

Riding, A. L., & Haines, G., Jr. (2001). Loan guarantees: Costs of default and benefits to small firms. *Journal of Business Venturing, 16*(6), 595–612.

Ripple, W., Wolf, C., Newsome, T., Barnard, P., Moomaw, W., & Grandcolas, P. (2019). World scientists' warning of a climate emergency. *BioScience, 70*, 8–12.

Robinson, J. A. (1952). The generalization of the general theory. In *The rate of interest and other essays*. Macmillan.

Robinson, J. A., & Torvik, R. (2005). White elephants. *Journal of Public Economics, 89*(2), 197–210.

Rodrik, D. (2004a). Industrial policy for the twenty-first century. *Harvard University*. https://doi.org/10.2139/ssrn.617544

Rodrik, D. (2004b, October, 8). *Rethinking growth policies in the developing world*. Draft of the Luca DÃ¡ gliano Lecture in development Economics.

Romer, P. M. (1989). Human capital and growth: Theory and evidence. *Carnegie-Rochester Conference Series on Public Policy, 32*, 251–286.

Rudolph, H. (2010). *Can they be relied on to kick-start lending? (Crisis response note* (No. 12, p. 7). The World Bank Group.

Ruete, M. (2015). *Financing for agriculture: How to boost opportunities in developing countries*. (Policy Brief, 3). Investment in Agriculture.

Ruf, B. M., Muralidhar, K., Brown, R. M., Janney, J. J., & Paul, K. (2001). An empirical investigation of the relationship between change in corporate social performance and financial performance: A stakeholder theory perspective. *Journal of Business Ethics, 32*(2), 143–156.

Ruiz, J. L. (2018). Financial development, institutional investors, and economic growth. *International Review of Economics & Finance, 54*, 218–224.

Rustam, S., Rashid, K., & Zaman, K. (2013, March). Retracted: The relationship between audit committees, compensation incentives and corporate audit fees in Pakistan. *Economic Modelling, 31*, 697–716.

Saadat, S., Rawtani, D., & Hussain, C. M. (2020). Environmental perspective of COVID-19. *Science of the Total Environment, 728*, 138870.

Saidi, M. D., & Wolf, C. (2011). *Recalibrating development co-operation: How can African countries benefit from emerging partners?* (Working Papers, No. 302). OECD Development Centre.

Sanderson, H., & Forsythe, M. (2013). *China's superbank: Debt, oil and influence—How China Development Bank is rewriting the rules of finance.* Wiley.

Savoy, C. M., Carter, P., & Lemma, A. (2016). *Development finance institutions come of age, policy engagement, impact, and new direction.* Center for Strategic and International Studies

Schclarek, A., & Navarrete J. (2016). *Industry diversification and financial development* (Working paper).

Schmidhuber, J., Bruinsma, J., & Boedeker, G. (2011). Capital requirements for agriculture. In *Looking Ahead in World Food and Agriculture: Perspectives to 2050* (p. 317). FAO.

Schumpeter, J. A. (1934). *The theory of economic development* (R. Opie, Trans.). Harvard University Press. (Original work published 1921).

Scott, D. H. (2007). *Strengthening the governance and performance of state-owned financial institutions.* World Bank Publications.

Seabrooke, L., & Sending, O. J. (2019). Contracting development: Managerialism and consultants in intergovernmental organizations. *Review of International Political Economy, 27*, 802–827.

Serajuddin, U., Yoshida, N., & Eamatsu, H. (2015, April 30). *Much of the world is deprived of poverty data. Let's fix this.* Let's Talk Development: A Blog Hosted by the World Bank's Chief Economist.

Shafiai, M. H. M., Moi, M. R., & Ahmad, R. (2015). The potential of Waqf in activating idle agricultural land. *Jurnal Pengurusan, 44*, 1–11.

Shapiro, C., & Willig, R. D. (1990). On the antitrust treatment of production joint ventures. *Journal of Economic Perspectives, 4*(3), 113–133.

Shaw, E. S. (1973). *Financial deepening in economic development.* Oxford University Press.

Shen, C. H., & Lin, C. Y. (2012). Why government banks underperform: A political interference view. *Journal of Financial Intermediation, 21*(2), 181–202.

Shirley, M. M. (1999). Bureaucrats in business: The roles of privatization versus corporatization in state-owned enterprise reform. *World Development, 27*(1), 115–136.

Shivdasani, A., & Yermack, D. (1999). CEO involvement in the selection of new board members: An empirical analysis. *The Journal of Finance, 54*(5), 1829–1853.

Shleifer, A., & Vishny, R. W. (1998). A survey of corporate governance. *Journal of Finance, 55*(2), 737–783.

Siciliano, J. I. (1996). The relationship of board member diversity to organizational performance. *Journal of Business Ethics, 15*(12), 1313–1320.

Simionescu, L. N., Gherghina, Ş. C., Tawil, H., & Sheikha, Z. (2021). Does board gender diversity affect firm performance? Empirical evidence from Standard & Poor's 500 Information Technology Sector. *Financial Innovation, 7*(1), 1–45.

Simpson, R., & Zimmermann, M. (2012). *The economy of green cities: A world compendium on green urban economy*. Springer Science and Business Media.

Skidelsky, R. (2011). The relevance of Keynes. *Cambridge Journal of Economics, 35*, 1–13.

Smallridge, D., Buchner, B., Trabacchi, C., Netto, M., Lorenzo, J. G., & Serra, L. (2012). *The role of national development banks in intermediating international climate finance to scale up private sector investments* (113 pp.). Inter-American Development Bank.

Sobreira, R. (2008). Development banks, risk, and Basel II: Some assessments. *Cadernos, EBAPE.BR, 6*(4), 1–8.

Solomon, A., Solomon, J., & Suto, M. (2004). Can the UK experience provide lessons for the evolution of SRI in Japan? *Corporate Governance: An International Review, 12*(4), 552–566.

Solomon, J., & Solomon, A. (2004). *Corporate governance and accountability*. Wiley.

Song, J., & Windram, B. (2004). Benchmarking audit committee effectiveness in financial reporting. *International Journal of Auditing, 8*(3), 195–205.

Sonnenfeld, J. A. (2002). What makes great boards great. *Harvard Business Review, 80*(9), 106–113.

Spratt S. (2008). *Development finance: Debates, dogma and new direction*. Routledge Taylor and Francis.

Standard & Poors. (2015, January). Lessons learned from 20 years of rating global project finance debt. *S&P, Credit Week, 35*(3).

Steensland, A. (2019). *2019 global agricultural productivity report: Productivity growth for sustainable diets and more*.

Stiglitz, J. (1993). The role of the state in financial markets. *Proceedings of the World Bank Conference on development economics*. World Bank.

Steiner, G. A. (1972). Social policies for business. *California Management Review, 15*(2), 17–24.
Stiglitz, J. E., & Greenwald, B. (2003). *Towards a new paradigm in monetary economics*. Cambridge University Press.
Stiglitz, J. E., & Uy, M. (1996). Financial markets, public policy, and the East Asian miracle. *The World Bank Research Observer, 11*(2), 249–276.
Stiglitz, J. E., & Weiss, A. (1981). Credit rationing in markets with imperfect information. *The American Economic Review, 71*(3), 393–410.
Studart, R., & Gallagher, K. (2016). *Infrastructure for sustainable development: The role of national development banks*. Boston University Global Economic Governance Initiative. https://www.bu.edu/pardeeschool/files/2016/08/Infrastructure.Sustainable.Final_pdf
Subramanian, S. (2018). Stewardship theory of corporate governance and value system: The case of a family-owned business group in India. *Indian Journal of Corporate Governance, 11*(1), 88–102.
te Velde, D. W. (2011). *The role of development finance in tackling global challenges*. Overseas Development Institute.
The African Center for Economic Transformation (ACET). (2022). *Challenges and changes: The political economy of national development banks in Africa*. Ghana case study Agricultural Development Bank and National Investment Bank.
The Economist. (2014, March 22). Infrastructure financing: A long and winding road. http://ww2.cfo.com/credit/2014/03/infrastructurefinancing-long-winding-road/
The One Love Campaign in South Africa: What has been achieved so far? http://www.comminit.com/hiv-aids/content/onelove-campaign-south-africa-what-has-been-achieved-so-far
Thorne, J., & Du Toit, C. (2009). A macro-framework for successful development banks. *Development Southern Africa, 26*(5), 677–694.
Tirpak, D., Brown, L., & Ronquillo-Ballesteros, A. (2014). *Monitoring climate finance in developing countries: Challenges and next steps*. World Resources Institute.
Toniolo, G., & Clement, P. (2005). *Central bank cooperation at the Bank for International Settlements, 1930–1973*. Cambridge University Press.
Torres, E., & Zeidan, R. (2016). The life-cycle of national development banks: The experience of Brazil's BNDES. *The Quarterly Review of Economics and Finance, 62*, 97–104.
Torres Filho, E. T., & Costa, F. N. D. (2012). BNDES e o financiamento do desenvolvimento. *economia e Sociedade, 21*, 975–1009.
Torres Filho, E. T., & Xu, J. (2020, December). *Regulating national development banks: The historical experiences of the Brazilian Development Bank (BNDES)*

since 1952 (Ford Foundation Visiting Fellowship Working Paper). Ford Foundation and Peking University (Institute of New Structural Economics).

Tricker, B., & Tricker, R. I. (2015). *Corporate governance: Principles, policies, and practices*. Oxford University Press.

Tsoi, P. (2017). *The importance of corporate governance*.

Türsoy, T. (2018). *Risk management process in banking industry* (Munich Personal RePEc Archive). Near East University.

Uganda Development Bank (UDB). (1980, October 29). Speech given by the Managing Director of the UDB to the Executive Commiuce and members of the Kampala Chamber of Commerce. In Oloka-Onyango, J. (1987). Development financing: The case of the Uganda Development Bank. *Ufahamu: A Journal of African Studies, 15*(3).

Uganda Development Bank (UDB), Uganda (2022). *Annual reports and financial statements*. https://www.udbl.co.ug/annual-reports/pdf

Uganda Development Bank Limited (UDBL). (2018). "Financial Statement As of 31 December 2017" (PDF). *Uganda Development Bank*. Kampala, Uganda. Retrieved 11 August 2022.

Uganda Development Bank Limited (UDBL). (2020). "Financial Statement As of 31 December 2019" (PDF). *Uganda Development Bank*. Kampala, Uganda. Retrieved 11 August 2022.

Uganda Development Bank Limited (UDBL). (2021). "Financial Statement As of 31 December 2020" (PDF). *Uganda Development Bank*. Kampala, Uganda. Retrieved 11 August 2022.

Uganda Development Bank Limited (UDB ESRMP). (2020). Environmental and Social Management Systems.

Uğurlu, E. N., & Epstein, G. (2021). *The public banking movement in the United States: Networks, Agenda, initiatives, and challenges*. Political Economy Research Institute.

UNICEF. (2011). *Inter-agency guide to the evaluation of psychosocial programming in emergencies*. United Nations Children's Fund. http://www.unicef.org/protection/files/Inter-AgencyGuidePSS.pdf

United Nations. (2015). *Addis Ababa Action Agenda of the third international conference on financing for development (Addis Ababa Action Agenda)*. United Nations.

United Nations. (2021). *The Sustainable Development Goals report 2021*. United Nations.

United Nations Children's Fund, Revised Evaluation Policy of UNICEF, UNICEF, New York, 2013, paragraph 54(c). See http://www.unicef.org/about/employ/files/2013-14-Final_approved_Revised_Evaluation_Policy.pdf

United Nations Environment Programme. (2017). *Atlas of Africa energy resources*. United Nations Environment Programme, Nairobi, Kenya.

Vahamaa, E. (2017). Female executives and corporate governance. *Managerial Finance, 43*(10), 1056–1072. https://doi.org/10.1108/MF-04-2016-0098
Van Roy, P. (2005). *The impact of the 1988 Basel Accord on banks' capital ratios and credit risk-taking: An international study*. SSRN 497264.
Wagner, A. (2011). *The origins of evolutionary innovations: A theory of transformative change in living systems*. Oxford University Press.
Wagner, L. (2020). *The allocation of resources of national development banks: Does it fit development goals?* (Working Paper).
Walker, J., Pekmezovic, A., & Walker, G. (2019). *Sustainable development goals: Harnessing business to achieve the SDGs through finance, technology and law reform*. Wiley.
Wandhöfer, R. (2014). The journey from Basel I to Basel III: History and fundamentals explained. In R. Wandhöfer (Ed.), *Transaction banking and the impact of regulatory change* (pp. 87–158). Palgrave Macmillan.
Wang, Y. (2016). *The sustainable infrastructure finance of China development bank: Composition, experience and policy implications* (Working Paper).
Weber, B., & Alfen, H. W. (2010). *Infrastructure as an asset class: Investment strategies*. Wiley.
Weisbach, M. S. (1988). Outside directors and CEO turnover. *Journal of Financial Economics, 20*, 431–460.
Werndl, C. (2016). On defining climate and climate change. *The British Journal for the Philosophy of Science, 67*, 337–364.
Williams, C., & Heins, R. (1989). *Risk management and insurance*. McGraw-Hill.
Woods, N. (1999). Good governance in international organizations. *Global Governance, 5*(1), 39–61. www.jstor.org/stable/27800219?seq=1
Wooi, H. C., & Ming, T. C. (2009). *Directors' pay-performance: A study on Malaysian government linked companies* (pp. 1–19). Centre for Policy Research and International Studies.
World Bank. (2011, June). *Supporting infrastructure in developing countries* (Report 65561 v2). Washington, DC.
World Bank. (2012). *Global financial development report 2013: Rethinking the role of the state in finance*. World Bank
World Bank. (2013a). *Rethinking the role of the State in finance* (Global Financial Development Report).
World Bank. (2013b). *History*. go.worldbank.org/65Y36GNQB0
World Bank. (2015). *Long-term finance report*. https://openknowledge.worldbank.org/handle/10986/22543
World Bank. (2016a). *Lessons from international experience in designing the Development Bank of Nigeria*. World Bank. https://openknowledge.worldbank.org/bitstream/handle/10986/30048/126401-WP-P146319-PUBLIC-Nigeria-Development-Finance-Study.pdf?sequence=1&isAllowed=y

World Bank. (2016b). *Project appraisal document on a proposed loan in the amount of US$93 million to the Land and Agricultural Development Bank of South Africa with the guarantee of the Republic of South Africa for a land bank financial intermediation loan* (No. PAD1122). World Bank. http://documents1.worldbank.org/curated/fr/221771484075116214/pdf/SA-PAD12302016.pdf

World Bank. (2018a). *2017 Survey of national development banks*. World Bank.

World Bank. (2018b). *Poverty and shared prosperity 2018: Piecing together the poverty puzzle*.

World Bank. (2020). *Global economic prospects, June 2020*. https://doi.org/10.1596/978-1-4648-1553-9

World Bank Group. (2013). *Global financial development report 2014: Financial inclusion* (Vol. 2). World Bank Publications.

World Bank Group. (2016). *Ghana's development finance institutions: Review of current status and principles for reform*. World Bank Group.

World Bank Group. (2017). *Report from the Executive Directors of the International Development Association to the Board of Governors*. Retrieved on 30 October 2018 from http://documents.worldbank.org/curated/en/348661486654455091/pdf/112728-correct-file-PUBLIC-Rpt-from-EDs-Additions-to-IDA-Resources-2-9-17-For-Disclosure.pdf

World Economic Forum. (2020). *COVID-19: What you need to know about the coronavirus pandemic*.

World Food Programme. (2020). *Risk of hunger pandemic as COVID-19 set to almost double acute hunger by end of 2020*. https://insight.wfp.org/covid-19-will-almost-double-people-in-acute-hunger-by-end-of-2020-59df0c4a8072

Xu, J., Marodon, R., & Ru, X. (2020). *Identifying and classifying public development banks and development finance institutions* (Agence Française de Développement Working Paper, 192).

Xu, J., Marodon, R., Ru, X., Ren, X., & Wu, X. (2021a). What are public development banks and development financing institutions?—Qualification criteria, stylized facts and development trends. *China Economic Quarterly International, 1*, 271–294.

Xu, J., Ru, X., & Song, P. (2021b). Can a new model of infrastructure financing mitigate credit rationing in poorly governed countries? *Economic Modelling, 95*, 111–120.

Yaron, J., Benjamin, M., & Charitenenko, S. (1998). Promoting efficient rural financial intermediation. *The World Bank Research Observer, 13*(2), 147–170.

Yermack, D. (1996). Higher market valuation of companies with a small board of directors. *Journal of Financial Economics, 40*(2), 185–211.

Yeyati, E. L., Micco, A., & Panizza, U. (2004). *Should the government be in the banking business? The role of state-owned and development banks*. Inter-American Development Bank.

Yüksel, S., Dinçer, H., & Karakuş, H. (2020). Determination of income and expense items that have a high impact on the profitability of Turkish banks. *Journal of Financial Economics and Banking, 1*(1), 1–9.

Zecchini, S., & Ventura, M. (2009). The impact of public guarantees on credit to SMEs. *Small Business Economics, 32*(2), 191–206.

Zendron, P., & Sobreira, R. (2007). *Implications of Basel II for development banks in Quem Controla o Sistema Financeiro?* Ibase.

Zhang, F. (2020). Leaders and followers in finance mobilization for renewable energy in Germany and China. *Environmental Innovation and Societal Transitions, 37*, 203–224.

Zhang, F. (2022). The policy coordinator role of national development banks in scaling climate finance: Evidence from the renewable energy sector. *Climate Policy, 22*, 754–769.

Index

© The Editor(s) (if applicable) and The Author(s), under exclusive license to Springer Nature Switzerland AG 2023
J. Yindenaba Abor, *The Changing Role of National Development Banks in Africa*, https://doi.org/10.1007/978-3-031-38639-8

S

W

The manufacturer's authorised representative in the EU is Springer Nature Customer Service Centre GmbH, Europaplatz 3, 69115 Heidelberg, Germany. If you have any concerns regarding our products, please contact ProductSafety@springernature.com

Printed and bound by CPI Group (UK) Ltd, Croydon, CR0 4YY

01/10/2026

02225854-0017